The Collected Works of Chögyam Trungpa

THE COLLECTED WORKS OF
CHÖGYAM TRUNGPA

VOLUME FOUR

Journey without Goal

The Lion's Roar

The Dawn of Tantra

An Interview with Chögyam Trungpa

EDITED BY
Carolyn Rose Gimian

SHAMBHALA · *Boston & London* · 2003

Shambhala Publications, Inc.
Horticultural Hall
300 Massachusetts Avenue
Boston, Massachusetts 02115
www.shambhala.com

9 8 7 6 5 4 3 2 1

First Edition

Printed in the United States of America

Distributed in the United States by Random House, Inc.,
and in Canada by Random House of Canada Ltd

Library of Congress Cataloging-in-Publication Data

Trungpa, Chögyam, 1939–
[Works. 2003]
The collected works of Chögyam Trungpa / edited by Carolyn Rose Gimian; forewords
by Diana J. Mukpo and Samuel Bercholz.—1st ed.
p.   cm.
Includes bibliographical references and index.
ISBN 1-59030-025-4 (v.1: alk. paper)—ISBN 1-59030-026-2 (v.2: alk. paper)—
ISBN 1-59030-027-0 (v.3: alk. paper)—ISBN 1-59030-028-9 (v.4: alk. paper)—
ISBN 1-59030-029-7 (v.5: alk. paper)—ISBN 1-59030-030-0 (v.6: alk. paper)—
ISBN 1-59030-031-9 (v.7: alk. paper)—ISBN 1-59030-032-7 (v.8: alk. paper)—
1. Spiritual life—Buddhism.   2. Buddhism—Doctrines.   I. Gimian, Carolyn Rose.   II. Title.

BQ4302.T7823   2003
294.3'420423—dc22   2003058963

CONTENTS

CONTENTS

THE LION'S ROAR:
AN INTRODUCTION TO TANTRA

THE DAWN OF TANTRA
By Herbert V. Guenther and Chögyam Trungpa

AN INTERVIEW WITH CHÖGYAM TRUNGPA

INTRODUCTION
TO VOLUME FOUR

VOLUME FOUR OF *The Collected Works of Chögyam Trungpa* is the first of three volumes that present the tantric, or vajrayana, teachings of Chögyam Trungpa Rinpoche. Volume Four is path-oriented, Volume Five is organized around the themes of lineage and devotion, and Volume Six deals with what one might call tantric states of mind or tantric experience. Not every item included in each volume conforms exactly to this structure, but I have attempted to group material with some affinity together.

From some point of view, Trungpa Rinpoche's approach was altogether tantric, or grounded in vajrayana, especially in the teachings that he gave after coming to North America. However, for the purposes of *The Collected Works,* the published material that was particularly focused on vajrayana teachings has been gathered together in Volumes Four to Six. Interestingly, the majority of these books have been published posthumously.

Even when presenting the most overtly tantric material, Trungpa Rinpoche guarded the integrity of the vajrayana teachings, being very careful not to introduce material prematurely to his students and not to cater to public fascination with tantra. There was certainly plenty of such fascination when he came to America in the early 1970s, which made him even more conservative in his approach. In many of his early talks, he focused on what tantra was *not*, dispelling preconceptions of wild behavior, indulgence in "tantric sex," and bizarre surges of energy. His teachings on the dangers of spiritual materialism were, in part, designed to cut through naive misinterpretations of tantra, which he saw as potentially very harmful to young American spiritual seekers.

He was also quite well aware that the misunderstanding of Buddhist tantra had a history in the West that was not particularly easy to overcome. There had long been misconceptions about Tibetan Buddhism, which went back to opinions primarily formed in the late nineteenth and early twentieth centuries, as well as in earlier times. Travelers to Tibet, including Christian missionaries, and scholars reading Tibetan Buddhist texts with minimal understanding of the language—and less of its meaning—often misinterpreted the symbolism. Tibetan Buddhism was sometimes referred to as "Lamaism," a generally disrespectful epithet that implied that Buddhism in Tibet was a distortion, some strange sort of primitive sect controlled by its priests, or lamas. Interestingly enough, the communist Chinese still use this term pejoratively to describe Tibetan Buddhism. It is as misguided now as it was historically.

There were notable exceptions to the closed-mindedness of Western scholars. W. Y. Evans-Wentz, Herbert Guenther, Marco Pallis, and David Snellgrove, among others, all had a very positive view of Tibetan Buddhism and had made considerable contributions to opening up the understanding of vajrayana, through their translations of major Tibetan tantric texts into English and their explication of the history of Tibet and Tibetan Buddhism. Nevertheless, in the popular arena, there remained many misconceptions. In addition to the negativity about vajrayana, there was an equally problematic romanticism and a view of tantra as wild abandonment to sense pleasures. Chögyam Trungpa was well aware of both extremes, and in his characteristic way, he charted a course that addressed both concerns while pandering to neither.

In *Cutting Through Spiritual Materialism* and *The Myth of Freedom*, his most popular books published in the 1970s (which appear in Volume Three of *The Collected Works*), he included material on the vajrayana, but only after properly laying the ground and only after many dire warnings about the dangers of trying to practice tantra without a grounding in the hinayana and mahayana teachings. He talked extensively about the teacher-student relationship, particularly in *Cutting Through*. There were other aspects of the tantric view, such as the five buddha families that describe five styles of human perception and experience, which he talked about quite freely. In addition to introducing the five buddha families in *Cutting Through*, he presented them in seminars on dharma art as well as in developing an approach to Buddhist psychology, which he called Maitri Space Awareness. He seemed to feel that it was a helpful way for students to understand the varieties of human experience and to develop their creativity. There is no doubt that a vajrayana sensibility affected much of what he taught.

In 1975 he made a particularly bold move, in terms of presenting tantra, with the publication of the translation of and commentary on *The Tibetan Book of the Dead*. This was a joint effort with Francesca Fremantle, an English scholar and a student of Rinpoche's. She produced the groundbreaking translation with his input, and she also put together the commentary—which was eye-opening for most readers—based on Rinpoche's teachings, mainly those given during a seminar on the *Tibetan Book of the Dead* in 1971. The style and language of the translation were a significant departure from earlier renditions. The English was evocative, elegant, and direct, and the book was very well received. The commentary from *The Tibetan Book of the Dead* appears in Volume Six of *The Collected Works*. Remarks by Francesca Fremantle on her work with Trungpa Rinpoche are also included there.

The first book that appears in Volume Four is *Journey without Goal: The Tantric Wisdom of the Buddha*. It was published in 1981 by Prajñā Press, a scholarly press with limited distribution established by Shambhala Publications in the late 1970s. When Prajña ceased publication, the book became a title under the Shambhala imprint.

Journey without Goal is based on a seminar given in 1974, during the first summer session at the Naropa Institute. The talks on which the book is based were recorded on video, along with all the other events at Naropa that year, so it's possible to see, outwardly at least, exactly to whom Rinpoche was talking. It was a large and varied audience of perhaps five or six hundred people, a young audience, the majority in their twenties, most of whom look like hippies, although some audience members distinguished themselves with more conservative hairdos and attire.

In his introduction to *Journey without Goal*, Rinpoche focused not on appearance but on the motivation and background of the students: "The audience was a very interesting mixture. There were many people whom we might call 'spiritual shoppers,' people sampling tantra as one more interesting spiritual 'trip.' There were also a number of people who were innocent and open. They happened onto this class by various coincidences and had very little idea of what tantra, or spirituality at all, might be. As well, there were a number of committed students who had been practicing meditation for some time."[1] He then points out the advice and the warnings he gave to everyone: "For all of these people, it was necessary to stress again and again the importance of meditation as the foundation of all Buddhist practice and the danger of ignoring this prescription."[2] The book itself is filled with warnings: "Working with the energy of vajrayana is like dealing with a live electric wire." "Tantric discipline does not cooperate with any deception at all." "Every book written on tantra . . . begins with that warning: 'Be careful; think twice; pay respect; don't just take this carelessly.'" It might seem amazing that anyone stayed through the whole course! In fact, the membership grew rather than decreasing over the weeks.

Rinpoche lectured several times a week during the second summer session. (During the first summer session, he presented a course on meditation and a fourteen-talk overview of the Tibetan Buddhist path.) In the material that makes up *Journey without Goal,* he shows an extraordinary ability to speak on a number of levels at the same time, so that he is illuminating things for one group of listeners or readers while obscuring the material for another component of the audience. If you connect with what Chögyam Trungpa is talking about, *Journey without Goal* is an amazing book. Even if you stumble upon this book with no previous background, you can pick up on the energy and the enthusiasm of the material, although many of the details remain somewhat fuzzy. Although you might not understand everything, the book might still make you feel that you'd really *like* to know more about what the author is talking about. Rinpoche had a way of drawing people in without giving the goods away, even when he was giving away secrets. He wasn't interested in creating some secretive tantric society that excluded people in what he would have termed a "self-snug" style. (That was a phrase he coined, which combined smugness with being snug as a bug in a rug.) He was also not interested in selling tantric secrets, the heart secrets of his lineage, on the street corner or in the lecture halls of Naropa. So he gave one talk that spoke very differently to different people in the audience.

Some of those attending his lectures were students who had graduated from the first Vajradhatu Seminary in the fall of 1973, where they

---

1. *Journey without Goal,* p. 9.
2. Ibid.

had received "transmission" to enter the vajrayana path and to begin their ngöndro, the foundation practices that eventually lead to full initiation into vajrayana sadhana practice.[3] Outside of the Naropa environment, these students held weekly meetings, called tantra groups, where they talked about the teachings they had received, the practice of prostrations they were embarking on, and how vajrayana was affecting their lives. From time to time, Rinpoche met with them, answering questions or giving them new food for thought. Ask any one of those people, and they would probably tell you that Rinpoche's talks were mind-blowing and that he spoke directly to them in the tantra seminar at Naropa that summer, addressing core issues in their vajrayana practice.

At the same time, these talks were not easy, for anyone. For some, especially his committed and more mature students, they were a challenge and an invitation. For others, they were intriguing but confusing; for a few, they were a closed door, a turn-off. Rinpoche would have had it no other way. He was happy to invite those with commitment, happy to intrigue those with an open mind, and delighted to shut the door on spiritual shoppers.

Journey without Goal begins with a number of chapters that describe different principles or components of the tantric path. The first chapter is on the nature of tantra and the tantric practitioner. It is about both continuity and egolessness. There are several excellent chapters on the nature of transmission in the vajrayana and on the relationship between student and teacher, who at this level is a vajra master. The extraordinary demands placed on both in the vajrayana are detailed here, as well as some idea of the extraordinary rewards that are possible. *Reward* is perhaps an odd word to use, since what is discussed here is complete surrender and letting go. Beyond that, through a combination of devotion, discipline, and supreme effort, it is possible that one will gain entry into the vajra world, in which the continued demands become the exercise of delight. Chapters toward the end of *Journey without Goal* discuss the different yanas, or stages, on the path. The final chapter, entitled "Maha Ati," is beautiful and surprising, as well as profoundly simple. I don't think you can read this book without being moved. If it's not for you, you simply won't make it to the end!

---

3. For more on the practice and the significance of ngöndro, see Trungpa Rinpoche's interview in *The Torch of Certainty*, which is included in Volume Five of *The Collected Works*.

Judith L. Lief began the editing of the book while she was editor in chief of Vajradhatu Publications. When she left to become the dean of the Naropa Institute in 1980, in spite of a great deal of work on her part, the book remained unfinished. I took over the last stages of preparing the book for publication, assisted by Sarah Coleman, as well as by Helen Berliner and Barbara Blouin. Although the book had a number of editors, it has a unified voice, I think, and quite a penetrating voice. Trungpa Rinpoche wrote the introduction when the manuscript was completed and ready to go to the publisher.

The next book that appears in Volume Four, *The Lion's Roar: An Introduction to Tantra*, edited by Sherab Chödzin Kohn, is based on two seminars given by Chögyam Trungpa in 1973. The book itself was published in 1992 in the Dharma Ocean Series. This series grew out of a meeting that Samuel Bercholz had with Chögyam Trungpa in 1985, about two years before Rinpoche's death. They decided to inaugurate a series that would eventually consist of 108 volumes of Rinpoche's teachings. The intent of the Dharma Ocean Series was "to allow readers to encounter this rich array of teachings simply and directly rather than in an overly systematized or condensed form." At its completion, it was meant to "serve as the literary archive of the major works of this renowned Tibetan Buddhist teacher." Judith L. Lief was asked to serve as the series editor. Since 1987, she and Sherab Chödzin Kohn have been the two editors for the series. All together, eight volumes in the Dharma Ocean Series have been published, which leaves only 102 more to come! This seems like an enormous number of books, but given Chögyam Trungpa's prolific activity as a dharma teacher, it is not at all out of the question. He gave several thousand talks that were recorded and archived during his seventeen years in North America, no two of which are the same. There is more than enough material in this collection to complete the volumes in the Dharma Ocean Series.

Although it was subtitled "An Introduction to Tantra," *The Lion's Roar* is quite a difficult book. It would be very slow-going for anyone not already acquainted with vajrayana Buddhism and unfamiliar with Trungpa Rinpoche's general approach and some of his other writings. That said, it is a valuable book, which provides an overview and quite a lot of detail—from the tantric perspective—of the nine yanas. It contains material that will not be found in any of his other writings. The two seminars on which *The Lion's Roar* is based took place in San Francisco in May of

1973 and in Boulder, Colorado, in December of the same year. As the editor tells us in his foreword, "Here, the complete teachings of bud-dhadharma are presented fresh and raw. . . . They are the mighty roaring of a great lion of dharma."

In *The Lion's Roar*, Sherab Chödzin Kohn has reversed the order of the original presentations, starting with the shorter Boulder seminar. The San Francisco talks were given a few months before the first Vajra-dhatu Seminary, the Boulder talks just after the completion of that event. At the Seminary, Rinpoche introduced the formal study of tantra to one hundred of his most senior students, who would begin their vajrayana practice within a few months of completing the Seminary. It's not purely coincidental that these two public seminars sandwich the presentation of vajrayana at the Seminary. Indeed, many of the themes and the view that he presented in that advanced program are previewed and echoed in *The Lion's Roar*. Larry Mermelstein, director of the Nālandā Translation Committee, recalls Trungpa Rinpoche's own comments on the signifi-cance of the first seminar in San Francisco: "I remember vividly the Vidyadhara Chögyam Trungpa Rinpoche returning home to Boulder after this seminar. He commented, quite excitedly, 'We finally did it—presented vajrayana for the first time in America!' He regarded this as a landmark event."[4]

The third book included in Volume Four is *The Dawn of Tantra*, a slim text, by Herbert V. Guenther and Chögyam Trungpa. This book was also edited by Sherab Chödzin Kohn, who at that time went by his West-ern name, Michael H. Kohn. Dr. Guenther is a Buddhist scholar and translator whose many important translations include *The Jewel Orna-ment of Liberation, The Life and Teaching of Naropa,* and *Kindly Bent to Ease Us*—works from both the Kagyü and Nyingma lineages of Tibetan Bud-dhism. As Sherab Chödzin Kohn said of him in the introduction to *The Dawn of Tantra*, "He has become one of the few Westerners to penetrate to a deeper understanding of Tibetan tantric texts. His books . . . bring us nearly the only accurate translations and commentaries from the Tibetan Buddhist tradition." Dr. Guenther has been criticized for using abstruse English philosophical terminology in his translations. Currently, there are simpler and perhaps more direct translations available, to be sure, but nevertheless his early renditions of Tibetan texts into English were,

---

4. E-mail communication from Larry Mermelstein to Carolyn Rose Gimian, May 2002.

if not easy to understand, yet faithful to the original, and his attitude toward the tradition was deeply respectful, based on genuine feeling for the material and a thorough and penetrating scholarship. Trungpa Rinpoche had the greatest admiration for Dr. Guenther. These two gentlemen were brought together by Shambhala Publications, who published works by both authors. Together, they conducted a weekend seminar on the basic principles and practice of tantra, alternating talks, and this book is the outcome of that meeting.

Dawn of Tantra reflects both Dr. Guenther's scholarly approach and the more immediate, popular approach that was Trungpa Rinpoche's hallmark. It would seem that each man came closer to the other in this situation: Dr. Guenther's presentations are more accessible and personal; Chögyam Trungpa's contributions are more scholastic. In addition to the talks from the weekend seminar, *Dawn of Tantra* includes a chapter titled "Visualization" that was based on a talk by Trungpa Rinpoche at the 1973 seminar that became part of *The Lion's Roar*. The chapter "Empowerment and Initiation" was edited from a talk by Dr. Guenther in Boulder in 1973. There is a great deal of detailed material on the philosophy and practice of tantra in this little book. Its inclusion in *The Collected Works* as well as its recent reissue in Shambhala Dragon Editions make it available to a new generation of readers.

Volume Four closes with "Things Get Very Clear When You're Cornered," an interview with Chögyam Trungpa that appeared in *The Laughing Man* magazine in 1976. In addition to personal and penetrating comments by Trungpa Rinpoche on the significance of his accident in England in 1969, the interview focused on the challenge of bringing the vajrayana teachings to America. It's a very candid exchange. Trungpa Rinpoche talks about creating a language "specifically to translate Buddhist ideas into English in a way that makes sense to people." He also expresses his conviction that the vajrayana will take root and be fully transmitted in America. He ends the interview with this prediction: "Not only that. Eventually Americans can go back to Tibet and teach Buddhism in that country. . . . anything is possible!" On that cheerful note, we conclude Volume Four.

CAROLYN ROSE GIMIAN
April 18, 2002
Trident Mountain House
Tatamagouche Mountain, Nova Scotia

JOURNEY WITHOUT GOAL

The Tantric Wisdom of the Buddha

Acknowledgments

J*OURNEY WITHOUT GOAL* is based on a series of fifteen lectures presented by Vajracharya the Venerable Chögyam Trungpa Rinpoche at Naropa Institute during the summer of 1974. Under his guidance, Mrs. Judith Lief, then the editor-in-chief at Vajradhatu, began editing the lectures for publication in 1975. Working with the author and other members of the editorial department, she completed the major part of the manuscript before leaving to become the dean of Naropa Institute in 1980.

The preparation of the final draft of the manuscript has been a collaborative effort by members of the editorial department: Mrs. Sarah Levy, Mrs. Barbara Blouin, Mrs. Helen Berliner, and myself. We have tried to maintain Mrs. Lief's approach to the material, which always respected the language of the original and showed an acute sensitivity to meaning and tone.

We are deeply indebted to the Vajracharya for the original presentation of this material and for allowing us the opportunity to deepen our own understanding through working with him on the manuscript.

We would like to thank the Nālandā Translation Committee for the translation from the Tibetan of the two poems that appear in the book. The first, "Intensifying Devotion in One's Heart," is by Jamgön Kongtrül the Great, whose contributions to the Practice Lineage of Tibetan Buddhism are discussed in chapter 10, "Abhisheka." The second, "Lord Marpa's Praise to the Gurus," is by Marpa the Translator, the first Tibetan holder of the Kagyü lineage. It is taken from a larger work, *The Life of Marpa*. Particular thanks go to Miss Christine Keyser of the translation committee, who completed the initial draft of the translation of Jamgön

Kongtrül's poem; and to Mr. Larry Mermelstein, the executive director of the committee, for editorial contributions to the entire manuscript.

We would also like to express our thanks to the Vajra Regent Ösel Tendzin and to Dr. Reginald Ray, Chairman of the Buddhist Studies Department at Naropa Institute, for their careful reading of the final typescript. As well, we would like to acknowledge the efforts of the many volunteers—typists, transcribers, and others—who worked on this book. Finally, we would like to thank the publisher, Mr. Samuel Bercholz, and the staff of Prajñā Press for their support of this book.

The reader may note that the language in this book is often poetic and evocative. These qualities have been treated as essential rather than incidental aspects of the original lectures, since they express most vividly the awake and brilliant experience of the vajra world.

The vajrayana wisdom that is presented here is powerful and authentic. We hope that this book will lead to a greater appreciation and understanding of tantric Buddhism, and we share in the author's wish that this book may benefit sentient beings and bring them to the path of dharma.

CAROLYN ROSE GIMIAN
Vajradhatu Editorial Department

Padma Tri-me, Jamgöm Kongtrül of Sechen (1901?–1960). The root guru of Chögyam Trungpa and an incarnation of Lodrö Thaye, Jamgön Kongtrül I.

Introduction

THE TEACHINGS OF the Buddha are a treasury of wisdom that has been passed down from teacher to student for over twenty-five hundred years. Many styles of teaching have developed, but all of the schools of Buddhism present the means to realize the awakened state of mind, and all of them emulate the example of the Buddha, the Awakened One. This is a very important point to realize, particularly in the context of this book, which presents tantra, or the vajrayana teachings of Buddhism. Many people in America have heard about tantra as the "sudden path"—the quick way to enlightenment. Or they may have heard that tantra is a form of free expression or sexual liberation or some kind of full-blown emotionalism. But it is important to realize that tantra is not separate from the rest of the Buddhist path. Exotic ideas about tantra are not just misconceptions; they could be quite destructive. It is both dangerous and fruitless to attempt to practice tantra without first establishing a firm ground in the basic Buddhist teachings.

The Buddhist path is traditionally divided into three major yanas or vehicles: the hinayana, the mahayana, and the vajrayana. Hinayana literally means the "small or lesser vehicle," but it would be more accurate to call it the "narrow way." The hinayana is small or narrow in the sense that the strict discipline of meditation narrows down, or tames, the speed and confusion of mind, allowing the mind to rest in its own place. The hinayana is also called the "immediate yana" because hinayana practice allows simple and direct experience of our own minds and of the world. We begin to realize that whatever we experience—whether good or bad, positive or negative—is workable, tamable.

As well as the discipline of meditation, the hinayana also stresses the importance of postmeditation discipline. Discipline in Sanskrit is *shila,* and in Tibetan it is *tsültrim (tshul khrims). Tsül* means "proper" or "appropriate"; *trim* means "regulation," "law," or "norm." So tsültrim is practicing "proper conduct" or "proper discipline," according to the example of the Buddha.

During his lifetime, the Buddha established disciplinary rules of conduct that are strictly applied in monastic life. These are called the *vinaya* in Sanskrit, or *dülwa ('dul ba)* in Tibetan. Both *vinaya* and *dülwa* literally mean "taming." So in general, vinaya can be understood as any discipline that we practice in order to tame our being.

In the hinayana, the only way to conduct ourselves is according to the message of vinaya, the message of discipline. Through practicing the proper conduct of tsültrim, our body, speech, and mind are thoroughly tamed, and we are able to quell, or cool off, the heat of neurosis. Because of that, we are able to practice the greater hinayana discipline of not causing harm to ourselves and others. And finally, based on practicing such total discipline, we are able to achieve what is called "individual liberation" (Skt. *pratimoksha;* Tib. *so sor tharpa.*) Individual liberation is a tremendous accomplishment, which enables us to express our basic goodness as human beings.

The mahayana, or the "great vehicle," is like a wide, open highway in contrast to the narrow path of hinayana discipline. The mahayana goes beyond the hinayana ideal of individual liberation alone. Its aim is the liberation of all sentient beings, which means that everyone, everything, is included in the vast vision of mahayana. All the chaos and confusion and suffering of ourselves and others is part of the path.

The primary discipline of the mahayana is helping others, putting others before ourselves. The training of the mahayana practitioner is to exchange himself for others. As a well-known mahayana slogan puts it: "Gain and victory to others; loss and defeat to oneself." However, it should be clear that this attitude is not based on self-denial or martyrdom, but rather springs from the development of genuine warmth and compassion. Thus, the mahayana is expansive and embracing.

The third yana, the vajrayana, literally means the "diamond or indestructible vehicle." The idea of indestructibility here is the discovery of indestructible wakefulness, the discovery of our own innate awakened state of mind, or vajra nature. Since this book deals with the vajrayana teachings, it seems unnecessary to explain too much about them here.

However, it is extremely important to understand at the outset that the vajrayana is a continuation of the previous two yanas and that without proper training in the hinayana and mahayana disciplines, it is impossible to step onto the tantric path.

Tantra literally means "continuity" or "thread." Hinayana, mahayana, and vajrayana are a continuous thread of sympathy and sanity, which is never broken. Vajrayana is further and greater expansion. It is the expression of greater sanity and greater sympathy, arising from the practice of hinayana and mahayana.

Throughout this book the reader will find numerous warnings about the dangers of vajrayana and the importance of beginning at the beginning—with the practice of meditation. When I presented this material at Naropa Institute in the summer of 1974, I felt that it was my duty to warn people about the dangers of vajrayana and also to proclaim the sacredness of these teachings—which go hand in hand.

The audience was a very interesting mixture. There were many people whom we might call "spiritual shoppers," people sampling tantra as one more interesting spiritual "trip." There were also a number of people who were quite innocent and open. They happened onto this class by various coincidences and had very little idea of what tantra, or spirituality at all, might be. As well, there were a number of committed students who had been practicing meditation for some time. It was quite a challenge to present tantra to such a mixed group. But for all of these people, it was necessary to stress again and again the importance of meditation as the foundation of all Buddhist practice and the danger of ignoring this prescription.

The entire Buddhist path is based on the discovery of egolessness and the maturing of insight or knowledge that comes from egolessness. In the hinayana, we discover the nonexistence of self through the practice of meditation. Assuming a dignified sitting posture, identifying with the breath, and simply noting thoughts and feelings—basic discursiveness—we begin to make friends with ourselves in a fundamental sense.

By applying mindfulness, or bare attention, to whatever arises during meditation, we begin to see that there is no permanence or solidity to our thought process, and at some point, we begin to realize that there is no permanence or solidity to us. In Sanskrit, the meditative practice of mindfulness is called *shamatha* and in Tibetan it is *shi-ne (zhi gnas)*. *Shi-ne* literally means the development of "peace." The meaning of peace here is precisely this sense of taming the wildness of mind so that we are alert and able to experience ourselves directly. We are not talking about peace as some kind of trance state: shamatha is the first step in waking up.

Mindfulness naturally leads to the development of awareness, which is a sense of expansion, being aware of the environment or space in which we are being mindful. Awareness brings tremendous interest in things, people, and the world altogether. We begin to develop sympathy and caring for others. The practice of awareness in Sanskrit is called *vipashyana* and in Tibetan, *lhakthong (lhag mthong),* which literally means "clear seeing." Vipashyana is traditionally connected both with the practice of meditation and with the formal study of the teachings and post-meditation activities in general. Vipashyana provides a link between the insight that is developed in meditation practice and our everyday experience. It allows us to carry that meditative insight or awareness into our daily lives.

Through the insight that comes from vipashyana, we begin to make a further discovery of egolessness. We begin to develop a precise understanding of how mind functions and how confusion is generated. We are able to see how the belief in ego causes tremendous pain and suffering to ourselves and others.

From this comes the desire to renounce samsara, the wheel of confused existence—the world of ego. Renunciation is expressed as the desire to refrain from harming ourselves and others. As well, we begin to long for the path that will liberate us from confusion. We begin to develop confidence in the Buddha as the enlightened example; in the dharma, or teachings of Buddhism, which are the path; and in the sangha, the community of practitioners who follow this path. Renunciation is utterly and absolutely necessary if we wish to practice the teachings of the Buddha. This theme runs through the entire path, from beginning to end. At the vajrayana level, renunciation is connected with devotion to the teacher, the vajra master. Devotion to the teacher in the vajrayana demands the total surrender of ego, the complete renunciation of all clinging to self.

Because of the discovery of egolessness in shamatha and the development of interest and sympathy in vipashyana, we naturally begin to expand our sense of warmth and friendliness to others. We are less interested in "this," "I," "me," and more interested in "that." The mahayana path is based on this discovery that others are more important than ourselves. Because we have discovered egolessness, because we have discovered that *me* does not exist, we find that there is lots of room, lots of space, in which to help others. That is the basis of compassion, karuna. Compassion in the Buddhist tradition is not based on guilt; it is based on having greater vision, because we can afford to do so.

The mahayana teachings are profound and vast, and what I am presenting here is like a drop in the ocean of the mahayana dharma. Nevertheless, helping others is absolutely essential. This is true, not only in mahayana practice, but in vajrayana as well. Trying to practice vajrayana without compassion is like swimming in molten lead—it is deadly. All of the power and the magic of vajrayana is based on working for the benefit of others and surrendering ourselves—absolutely.

The vajrayana teachings are very precious; they are very close to my heart and they are my inheritance, so I do not pass them on lightly. Still, I am delighted that we can present tantra in the American world. What is presented here is like a map; it is an entirely different experience to actually make the journey. It requires a guide to make this journey, and as well, we must make the proper preparations: Our minds must be tamed and trained through the practice of meditation. Only then can we see the vajra world.

As I have said, presenting these talks originally was quite demanding, but it was equally worthwhile. For those who connected with what was being transmitted, the experience of hearing these lectures was one of discovering devotion and beginning to surrender ego. It is my hope that, in a similar fashion, this book will inspire others to step onto the path of dharma.

VAJRACHARYA THE VENERABLE
Chögyam Trungpa Rinpoche
July 10, 1981
Boulder, Colorado

Intensifying Devotion in One's Heart

THE SUPPLICATION "CRYING TO THE GURUS FROM AFAR"

by JAMGÖN KONGTRÜL LODRÖ THAYE

NAMO GURAVE

THE PRACTICE OF crying to the gurus from afar is well known to everyone. The key to invoking blessings is devotion, which is aroused by sadness and renunciation. This is not a mere platitude, but is born in the center of one's heart and in the depths of one's bones. With decisive conviction that there is no other buddha who is greater than the guru, recite this melodic tune.

> Guru, think of me.
> Kind root guru, think of me.
>
> Essence of the buddha of the three times,
> Source of the holy dharma—what has been told and what
>   has been experienced—
> Master of the sangha, the noble assembly,
> Root guru, think of me.
>
> Great treasure of blessings and compassion,
> Source of the two siddhis,
> Buddha activity that bestows whatever is desired,
> Root guru, think of me.

Guru Amitābha, think of me.
Look upon me from the realm of dharmakāya, simplicity.
Lead us of evil karma who wander in saṃsāra
To the pure land of great bliss.

Guru Avalokiteśvara, think of me.
Look upon me from the realm of sambhogakāya,
    luminosity.
Pacify completely the suffering of the six realms.
Shake us from the depths of the three realms of saṃsāra.

Guru Padmākara, think of me.
Look upon me from the lotus light of Cāmara.[1]
The wretched Tibetan people who are without refuge in
    this dark age,
Quickly protect with your compassion.

Guru Yeshe Tsogyal,[2] think of me.
Look upon me from the celestial realm, the city of great
    bliss.
Help us who commit evil deeds to cross the ocean of
    saṃsāra
To the great city of liberation.

Gurus of the kama and terma lineages,[3] think of me.
Look upon me from the wisdom realm of unity.
Break through the dark dungeon of my confused mind.
Make the sun of realization arise.

Omniscient Trime Öser,[4] think of me.
Look upon me from the realm of the five spontaneous
    wisdom lights.
Help me to strengthen my primordially pure mind
And master the four stages of ati yoga.[5]

Incomparable Lord Atīśa, father and son,[6] think of me.
Look upon me from amidst one hundred devas in Tuṣita.
Arouse in me bodhicitta,
The essence of emptiness and compassion.

Three supreme siddhas—Marpa, Mila, and
    Gampopa—think of me.
Look upon me from the vajra realm of great bliss.
May I attain the surpreme siddhi of mahāmudrā, bliss and
    emptiness,
And awaken dharmakāya in my heart.

Karmapa, lord of the world, think of me.
Look upon me from the space which tames all beings
    everywhere.
Help me to realize that all dharmas are insubstantial and
    illusory.
Make appearance and mind dawn as the three kāyas.

Kagyüs of the four great and eight lesser lineages, think of
    me.
Look upon me from the land of sacred outlook.
Help me to clear away my confusion in the fourth moment
And perfect my experience and realization.

Five Sakaya forefathers,[7] jetsüns, think of me.
Look upon me from the realm of inseparable saṃsāra and
    nirvāṇa.
Help me to unite the completely pure view, meditation, and
    action
And walk upon the supreme secret path.

Incomparable Shangpa Kagyü,[8] think of me.
Look upon me from the completely pure buddha land.
Help me to learn properly the practice that liberates
    through skillful means
And attain the unity of nonlearning.

Great siddha, Thangtong Gyalpo,[9] think of me.
Look upon me from the realm of effortless compassion.
Help me to practice the yogic action of realizing
    insubstantiality.
Help me to master prāṇa and mind.

Only father, Phadampa Sanggye,[10] think of me.
Look upon me from the realm of accomplishing the highest
   action.
May the blessings of your lineage enter my heart
And may auspicious coincidence arise in all directions.

Only mother, Machik Lapkyi Drönma, think of me.
Look upon me from the realm of prajñāpāramitā.
Help me to uproot ego-fixation, the cause of pride.
And realize the truth of egolessness beyond conception.

Omniscient enlightened one of Tölpo,[11] think of me.
Look upon me from the realm endowed with all the
   supreme aspects.
Help me to still the shifting breaths in the central channel
And attain the immovable vajra body.

Jetsün Tāranātha,[12] think of me.
Look upon me from the realm of the three mudrās.
May I tread the secret vajra path unhindered.
And attain the rainbow body in the celestial realm.

Jamyang Khyentse Wangpo,[13] think of me.
Look upon me from the wisdom realm of the two kinds of
   knowing.
Help me to remove the obscurations of my ignorance
And expand the vision of supreme knowledge.

Ösel Trülpe Dorje, think of me.
Look upon me from the realm of the five rainbow light rays.
Help me to cleanse the impurities of bindu, prāṇa, and mind
And attain enlightenment of this youthful kāya in the vase.[14]

Padma Do Ngak Lingpa, think of me.
Look upon me from the unchanging realm of bliss and
   emptiness.
Enable me to completely fulfill
All the intentions of the victorious ones and their sons.

Ngakwang Yönten Gyatso,[15] think of me.
Look upon me from the realm of the union of space and
    wisdom.
May the habit of solidifying reality fall apart
And may I bring whatever occurs to the path.

Son of the victorious ones, Lodrö Thaye, think of me.
Look upon me from your nature of maitrī and compassion.
Enable me to realize that all beings are my kind parents
And wholeheartedly accomplish the benefit of others.

Padma Kargyi Wangchuk, think of me.
Look upon me from the realm of great bliss and luminosity.
Help me to liberate the five poisons into the five wisdoms.
And destroy my clinging to loss and gain.

Tennyi Yungtrung Lingpa, think of me.
Look upon me from the realm in which saṃsāra and
    nirvāṇa are equal.
May natural devotion be born in my being.
May realization and liberation simultaneously increase.

Kind root guru, think of me.
Look upon me from the top of my head, the place of great
    bliss.
May I meet my own mind, the face of dharmakāya
And attain buddhahood in one lifetime.

Alas!
Sentient beings like myself, evildoers with bad karma,
Have wandered in saṃsāra from beginningless time.
Even now we experience endless suffering,
And yet not even an instant of remorse has occurred.
Guru, think of me; look upon me quickly with compassion.
Grant your blessings so that I give rise to renunciation from
    my depths.

Although I have obtained a free and well-favored human
     birth,
I have wasted it in vain.
I am constantly distracted by the activities of this futile life.
Unable to accomplish the great objective of liberation and
     overcome by laziness,
I return empty-handed from a land of jewels.
Guru, think of me; look upon me quickly with compassion.
Grant your blessings so that I fulfill the purpose of human
     birth.

There is no one on earth who will not die.
Even now, one after another they pass away.
I also will die very soon,
And yet like an idiot, I prepare to live for a long time.
Guru, think of me; look upon me quickly with compassion.
Grant your blessings so that I curtail my worthless schemes.

I will become separated from my lovers and friends.
The wealth and food which I hoarded in miserliness will be
     enjoyed by others.
Even this body I hold so dear will be left behind.

My consciousness will wander in the unknown pardos of
     saṃsāra.
Guru, think of me; look upon me quickly with compassion.
Grant your blessings so that I realize the futility of life.

The black darkness of fear escorts me along.
The fierce red wind of karma chases after me.
Yama's hideous messengers beat and hack me.
Thus, I experience the unbearable suffering of the lower
     realms.
Guru, think of me; look upon me quickly with compassion.
Grant your blessings so that I free myself from the chasms
     of the lower realms.

My faults are as large as a mountain, but I conceal them
    within me.
Others' faults are as minute as a sesame seed, but I proclaim
    and condemn them.
I boast about my virtues, though I don't even have a few.
I call myself a dharma practitioner and practice only
    nondharma.
Guru, think of me; look upon me quickly with compassion.
Grant your blessings so that I subdue my selfishness and
    pride.

I hide the demon of ego-fixation within, which will ruin me
    permanently.
All of my thoughts are the cause of perpetuating kleśas.
All of my actions have unvirtuous results.
I have not even gone toward the path of liberation.
Guru, think of me; look upon me quickly with compassion.
Grant your blessings so that I uproot my selfishness.

Just a little praise or blame makes me happy or sad.
A mere harsh word causes me to lose my armor of patience.
Even when I see helpless ones, compassion does not arise.
When needy people come to me, I am tied up by a knot of
    miserliness.
Guru, think of me; look upon me quickly with compassion.
Grant your blessings so that my mind is mixed with the
    dharma.

I hold on dearly to futile saṃsāra.
For the sake of food and clothing, I completely abandon
    permanent objectives.
Though I have everything I need, I constantly want more
    and more.
My mind is duped by insubstantial and illusory things.
Guru, think of me; look upon me quickly with compassion.
Grant your blessings so that I am not attached to this life.

I cannot endure even the slightest physical or mental pain,
Yet I am so stubborn that I have no fear of falling into the
    lower realms.
Though I actually see unerring cause and effect,
Still I do not act virtuously, but perpetuate evil.
Guru, think of me; look upon me quickly with compassion.
Grant your blessings so that conviction in karma arises in
    me.

I am hateful toward enemies and attached to friends.
I am stupified in darkness as to what should be accepted and
    rejected.
When practicing the dharma, I fall under the influence of
    discursiveness, sloth, and sleep.
When acting against the dharma, I am clever and my senses
    are alert,
Guru, think of me; look upon me quickly with compassion.
Grant your blessings so that I conquer my enemy, the
    kleśas.

My outer appearance is that of an authentic dharma
    practitioner,
But inside, my mind is not mixed with the dharma.
Like a poisonous snake, the kelśas are concealed within me.
When I encounter bad circumstances, my hidden faults as a
    bad practitioner are revealed.
Guru, think of me; look upon me quickly with compassion.
Grant your blessings so that I can tame my own mind.

I don't realize my own bad faults.
I maintain the form of a practitioner while engaging in
    various nondharmic pursuits.
Because of the kleśas, I am naturally accustomed to
    unvirtuous actions.
Again and again I give birth to a mind of virtue, but again
    and again it falls apart.
Guru, think of me; look upon me quickly with compassion.
Grant your blessings so that I see my own faults.

As each day passes, my death is nearer and nearer.
As each day passes, my being is harsher and harsher.
Though I attend my guru, my devotion becomes gradually
 obscured.
Love, affection, and sacred outlook toward my dharma
 companions grow smaller and smaller.
Guru, think of me; look upon me quickly with compassion.
Grant your blessings so that I tame my stubborn nature.

I've taken refuge, aroused bodhichitta, and made
 supplications,
But devotion and compassion are not born in the depths of
 my heart.
I give lip service to dharmic action and spiritual practice,
But they become routine and I'm not touched by them.
Guru, think of me; look upon me quickly with compassion.
Grant your blessings so that I may be one with the dharma.

All suffering comes from desiring happiness for oneself.
Although it is said that buddhahood is attained by
 considering the welfare of others,
I arouse supreme bodhichitta but secretly cherish
 selfishness.
Not only do I not benefit others, I casually cause them
 harm.
Guru, think of me; look upon me quickly with compassion.
Grant your blessings so that I exchange myself for others.

The guru is buddha in person, but I regard him as an
 ordinary man.
I forget his kindness in giving profound instructions.
When he doesn't do what I want, I lose heart.
His actions and behavior are clouded over by my doubts
 and disbelief.
Guru, think of me; look upon me quickly with compassion.
Grant your blessings so that unobscured devotion will
 increase.

My own mind is the Buddha, but I never realize this.
Discursive thoughts are dharmakāya, but I don't realize this.
This is the unfabricated, innate state, but I cannot keep to
  this.
Naturalness is things as they really are, but I have no
  conviction in this.
Guru, think of me; look upon me quickly with compassion.
Grant your blessings so that my mind will be spontaneously
  liberated.

Death is certain to come, but I am unable to take this to
  heart.
The holy dharma truly benefits, but I am unable to practice
  it properly.
Karma and its result are certainly true, but I do not properly
  discriminate what to accept or reject.
Mindfulness and awareness are certainly necessary, but not
  stabilizing them, I am swept away by distractions.
Guru, think of me; look upon me quickly with compassion.
Grant your blessings to enable me to persevere in practice.

In the beginning I had no other thought but dharma.
But in the end what I have achieved will cause me to go to
  the lower realms of saṃsāra.
The harvest of freedom is destroyed by an unvirtuous frost.
Stubborn people like me have achieved bad consequences.
Guru, think of me; look upon me quickly with compassion.
Grant your blessings so that I will completely accomplish
  the holy dharma.

Grant your blessings so that I give birth to deep sadness.
Grant your blessings so that I maintain undistracted
  mindfulness.

Because of my former evil actions, I was born at the end of
  the dark age.
All that I have previously done has caused me suffering.

Because of evil friends, I am darkened by the shadow of evil
deeds.
My dharma practice has been sidetracked by my
meaningless chatter.
Guru, think of me; look upon me quickly with compassion.
Grant your blessings so that I completely accomplish the
holy dharma.

Grant your blessings so that I give birth to deep sadness.
Grant your blessings so that my worthless schemes are
curtailed.
Grant your blessings so that I take to heart the certainty of
death.
Grant your blessings so that conviction in karma arises in
me.
Grant your blessings so that the path is free from obstacles.
Grant your blessings so that I am able to exert myself in
practice.
Grant your blessings so that unfortunate circumstances are
brought to the path.
Grant your blessings so that I continually apply my
antidotes.
Grant your blessings so that genuine devotion arises in me.
Grant your blessings so that I glimpse the natural state.
Grant your blessings so that insight is awakened in my
heart.
Grant your blessings so that I uproot confusion.
Grant your blessings so that I attain buddhahood in one
lifetime.

Precious guru, I supplicate you.
Kind lord of the dharma, I cry to you with longing.
I am an unworthy person who relies on no one but you.
Grant your blessings so that my mind mixes inseparably
with yours.

I was first requested by some devoted monks to compose a supplication,
but I was delayed in fulfilling their request. Recently, Samdrup Drönma,

a lady practitioner of noble family, and Deva Rakṣita earnestly urged me. Therefore, I, Lodrö Thaye, who merely hold the appearance of a guru in this dark age, wrote this at the great meditation center, Dzongshö Deshek Düpa.[16] May virtue increase.

Translated by the Nālandā Translation Committee under the direction of the Vidyādhara the Venerable Chögyam Trungpa Rinpoche, © 1981 by Diana J. Mukpo and published by Shambhala Publications, Inc. Used with the permission of the Nālandā Translation Committee, 1619 Edward Street, Halifax, Nova Scotia, Canada B3H 3H9.

NOTES

1. Cāmara is one of the two islands next to the southern continent of Jambudvīpa. On this island, Padmākara (Padmasambhava) is said to now reside in a palace on the Copper Colored Mountain.

2. Yeshe Tsogyal is one of the two chief consorts of Padmākara (Padmasambhava), the other being Mandaravā. She is the author of a biography of Padmasambhava *(Padma thang yig).*

3. The kama lineage is the unbroken oral tradition that has been passed down from Vajradhara Buddha to one's present root guru. The terma lineage consists of sacred objects and teachings that were hidden by Padmākara and other teachers until the time was right for their unveiling. Then, they would be discovered and promulgated by teachers known as tertöns ("terma discoverers").

4. This is the name that was conferred on the famous Nyingma teacher, Longchen Rabjam (1308–1364), by Padmākara in a vision.

5. These four stages (snang bzhi) are: revelation of dharmatā, increasing experience, maturation of insight, and exhausting dharmatā.

6. Atīśa's (982–1054) spiritual son here is Dromtön (1004–1063), his main Tibetan disciple and the founder of the Kadampa school.

7. These are five great and early teachers in the Sakya lineage. They are Künga Nyingpo (1092–1158), Sönam Tsemo (1142–1182), Trakpa Gyaltsen (1147–1216), Sakya Paṇḍita (1182–1251), and Phakpa (1235–1280).

8. The Shangpa Kagyü is a sect of the Kagyü lineage founded by Barapa Gyaltsen Palzang (1310–1391). However, it traces its origin back to Shang Khyungpo Naljorpa (990–1139?), a follower of Bön who converted to Buddhism. He had many Indian gurus, one of them being Niguma, Nāropa's wife and disciple.

9. Thangtong Gyalpo (1385–1464) is famed throughout Tibet as a great siddha and builder of iron bridges.

10. Phadampa Sanggye (died 1117) is a South Indian teacher who brought the practices of shije (pacifying) and chö (cutting) to Tibet. His main disciple and consort was the Tibetan woman, Machik Lapkyi Drönma (1055–1149), who spread the lineage of the chö teachings in Tibet.

11. Tölpopa Sherap Gyaltsen (1292–1361) is the founder of the Jonangpa school, which mainly emphasized the *Kālachakra Tantra* and the teaching of tathāgatagarbha. The shen tong (gzhan stong, empty of other) view of mādhyamika that the Jonangpa evolved was quite controversial among the mainstream adherents of the rang tong (rang stong, empty of self) view; however, this shen tong view was a powerful principle for the Rime thought in general and in particular for Jamgön Kongtrül.

12. Tāranātha (born 1575) is one of the most famous teachers of the Jonangpa school, having written a well-known history of Buddhism in India as well as several important texts on the *Kālachakra*.

13. Jamyang Khyentse Wangpo (1820–1892) is one of the leaders of the nineteenth-century Rime movement in Tibet. He was the root guru of Jamgön Kougtrül Lodrö Thaye. Ösel Trülpe Dorje and Padma Do Njak Lingpa are the names given to him from a prophecy of Thangtong Gyalpo (see following two stanzas).

14. This image is used in ati teachings to describe the nature of primordial enlightenment. The youthful kāya is enlightenment which is always present. The vase contains all dharmas and gives rise to all phenomena.

15. The next four names all belong to the author of this text, Jamgön Kongtrül Lodrö Thaye. The first name he received when he took the vinaya vows, the second when he took the bodhisattva vow, and the third when he received abhiṣeka—formally becoming a student of the vajrayāna. The last name was given to him when he was formally recognized as a tertön, a discoverer of terma.

The reason Jamgön Kongtrül includes himself in the guru supplication is that he composed this text for his disciples' practice at their request.

16. This meditation center is northeast of Shigatse, located at Zambulung in upper Shang. Jamyang Khyentse Wangpo also resided here at one time and had an important vision of the eight manifestations of Padmākara.

ONE

The Tantric Practitioner

THE TANTRIC TEACHINGS of Buddhism are extremely sacred and, in some sense, inaccessible. Tantric practitioners of the past have put tremendous energy and effort into the study of tantra. Now we are bringing tantra to North America, which is a landmark in the history of Buddhism. So we cannot afford to make our own studies into supermarket merchandise.

A tantric revolution took place in India many centuries ago. The wisdom of that tradition has been handed down orally from generation to generation by the great mahasiddhas, or tantric masters. Therefore, tantra is known as the ear-whispered, or secret, lineage. However, the notion of secrecy does not imply that tantra is like a foreign language. It is not as though our parents speak two languages, but they only teach us English so that they can use Chinese or Yiddish when they want to keep a secret from us. Rather, tantra introduces us to the actuality of the phenomenal world. It is one of the most advanced, sharp, and extraordinary perceptions that has ever developed. It is unusual and eccentric; it is powerful, magical, and outrageous; but it is also extremely simple.

Opposite: Lodrö Thaye, Jamgön Kongtrül I (1813–1899). Often referred to as Jamgön Kongtrül the Great, Lodrö Thaye was a leader of the Ri-me movement (see chapter 10). This painting is from the lineage thangkas at Rumtek Monastery in Sikkim, India. PHOTO USED BY THE GRACIOUS PERMISSION OF HIS HOLINESS THE SIXTEENTH GYALWA KARMAPA, RANGJUNG RIKPE DORJE.

In order to understand the phenomenon of tantra, or tantric consciousness, we should be quite clear that we are not talking about tantra as a vague spiritual process. Tantra, or vajrayana Buddhism, is extremely precise, and it is unique. We cannot afford to jumble the vajrayana into a spiritual or philosophical stew. Instead, we should discuss tantra technically, spiritually, and personally—in a very exact sense—and we should discuss what the uniqueness of the tantric tradition has to offer to sentient beings.

In this book we will examine tantra theoretically. We are viewing the area that we might arrive at, at some point in the future. So it is a somewhat hypothetical situation, but at the same time we still could develop an experiential connection with it. The future of Buddhism depends on continuing to discover what the Buddha experienced and on sharing such experience with others. So there is a need to identify ourselves personally with tantric experience, rather than regarding tantra as one more spiritual trip.

Fundamentally, the vajrayana comes out of a complete understanding and comprehension of both hinayana and mahayana Buddhism. The development of the three yanas—hinayana, mahayana, and vajrayana—is one continuous process. In fact, the word *tantra,* or *gyü (rgyud)* in Tibetan, means "continuity." There is a continuous thread running through the Buddhist path, which is our personal experience and our commitment to the Buddhist teachings. Usually we think of a thread as starting somewhere. But according to the Buddhist teachings, the thread has no beginning, and therefore there is continuity. In fact, such a thread does not even exist, but at the same time, it is continuous.

At this point we are not yet in a position to discuss what tantra is. Since the continuity of tantra is based on personal experience, we first need to understand the person who is having the experience. That is, we need to know who is studying tantra: who is it, or what is it? So, to begin with, we have to go back to the beginning and find out who is perceiving tantra, that is, who is the tantrika or tantric practitioner.

We could say that some people are tantric by nature. They are inspired in their lives; they realize that some reality is taking place in the true sense, and they feel that the experience of energy is relevant to them. They may feel threatened by energy or they may feel a lack of energy, but they have a personal interest in the world: the visual world, the auditory world, the world of the senses altogether. They are interested in how things work and how things are perceived. That sense of enormous interest, that interest in perceptions, is tantric by nature. However, one problem with inspired, future tantric practitioners is that they are often too fascinated by the world of the senses. There is something lacking: although they are inspired, they may not have made a genuine connection to the world of the senses, which presents problems in understanding true tantra. Still, they could be regarded as tantric fetuses, or potential members of the tantric family.

When we begin to explore who the tantric practitioner actually is, our inquiry takes us further and further back, right to the basis of Buddhist practice, which is the hinayana teachings. From this point of view, hinayana *is* tantra. One of the inspiring glimpses or experiences of the hinayana practitioner is the absence of self, which is also the absence of God. When we realize that there is no individual being or personality who is perceiving external entities, the situation becomes open. We don't have to limit things by having a conceptualized divine being, traditionally known as God. We are simply examining who we are. In examining who we are, we find, according to both the hinayana and the tantric observation, that we are nobody—rather, nonbody. We might ask, "How is that possible? I have a name. I have a body. I eat. I sleep. I lead my life. I wear clothes." But that is precisely the point: we misunderstand ourselves, our nonexistent selves. Because we eat, we sleep, we live, and we have a name, we presume that something must be there. That common misunderstanding took place a long time ago, and it still takes place constantly, every single moment. Just because we have a name doesn't mean we have a self. How do we realize that? Because if we do not use such reference points as our name or our clothing, if we stop saying, "I eat, I sleep, I do such-and-such," then there is a big gap.

In a similar fashion, we often use reference points to show that we do not exist. We say we do *not* exist because of something else. We might say, "I do not exist because I am penniless." There is something wrong with that logic, because we still have a penny to be less of. However, this does not mean that we should try to destroy relative reference points. As an extreme example, during the 1960s some people made hysterical attempts not to exist. By destroying references and credentials such as draft cards and birth certificates, they hoped to become invisible. But creating their draft-card-less-ness was still a statement of deliberate individuality, and it was still fighting over the question of existence by struggling not to exist.

In the Buddhist tradition, discovering nonexistence, or egolessness, has nothing to do with destroying relative reference points. Whether we try to maintain such reference points or destroy them, we still have the same problem. The Buddhist approach is not to use any reference points at all—none whatsoever. Then we are not finding out whether we exist or not, but we are simply looking at ourselves directly, without any reference points—without even looking, we could say. That may be very demanding, but let it be so. Let us get to the heart of the matter.

When we attempt to see ourselves without reference points, we may find ourselves in a situation of not knowing what to do. We may feel completely lost, and we may think that what we are trying to do is very strange indeed: "I can't even begin. How can I do anything?" Then we might have an inkling of beginning at the beginning. Having to relate with the bewilderment of not knowing how to deal with ourselves without using reference points is getting closer to the truth. At the same time, we have not found the root of reality, if there is one at all.

We cannot find the beginning of the tantric thread unless we come to the conclusion that we do not exist. We might try to work out our nonexistence logically. However, the conclusion that we do not exist has to be experiential, and it also has to be beyond our stupidity and confusion. Our confusion at this point is not knowing how to begin. From that, we can start to feel the beginninglessness of the thread, and its endlessness as well. So we are getting somewhere, but we still might feel rather stupid, like jellyfish or robots. There is no sense of discovery at all, and the whole thing seems rather flat.

According to the tantric tradition, the only way to find our way out of that confusion, or our way in, is by having a sense of humor about our predicament. We are trying to find ourselves, but we are not able to do so, and we feel enormously flat and heavy and in the way. Something is being a nuisance, but we cannot put our finger on exactly what it is. Nevertheless, something, somewhere, is being a nuisance. Or is it? If we view this with humor, we begin to find that even the flatness, the lack of inspiration, the solidity, and the confusion are dancing constantly. We need to develop a sense of excitement and dance rather than just trying to feel better. When we begin to dance with our humor, our apparent stupidity becomes somewhat uplifted. However, we do no know for sure whether we are just looking at ourselves humorously while our stupidity grows heavier all the time, or whether we might actually be able to cure ourselves. There is still something that is uncertain, completely confused, and very ambiguous.

At that point, we finally could start to relate with the ambiguity. In the tantric tradition, discovering that ambiguity is called "discovering the seed syllable." Ambiguity is called a "seed syllable" when it becomes a starting point rather than a source of problems. When we accept uncertainty as the working base, then we begin to discover that we do not exist. We can experience and appreciate the ambiguity as the source of confusion as well as the source of humor. The discovery of nonexistence comes from experiencing both the energy of humor and the heavy "thingness" or form of confusion. But form or thingness does not prove the existence of energy, and energy does not prove the existence of form. So there is no confirmation, just ambiguity. Therefore, we still find ourselves at a loss. However, at this point that feeling of being lost has the quality of freedom rather than the quality of confusion.

This experience of ambiguity is a personal experience rather than an analytical experience. We begin to realize that actually we do not exist. We do not exist because of our existence: that is the punch line of our ambiguity. And the world exists because of our nonexistence. We do not exist; therefore the world exists. There is an enormous joke behind the whole thing, a big joke. We might ask, "Who is playing such a joke on us?" It is difficult to say. We do not know who it is at all. We are so uncertain that we might not even have a question mark to put at the end of our sentence. Nevertheless, that is our purpose in studying tantra: to find out who is the questioner, who set this question up altogether, if anyone at all.

The beginner's point of view is to realize nonexistence, to understand nonexistence, and to experience nonexistence. It is very important for us to realize that sight, smell, colors, emotions, formlessness, and form are all expressions of no-beginning, nonexistence, egolessness. Such nonexistence has to be experienced personally rather than analytically or philosophically. That personal experience is extremely important. In order for us to get into tantra properly, in order to become good tantra students, we have to go through the experience of nonexistence, however frustrating, confusing, or irritating it may seem. Otherwise, what we are doing is completely fruitless.

TWO

Vajra Nature

THE VAJRAYANA SEEMS to have been widely misunderstood in the West. People have projected a lot of ideas onto it, believing it to be an expression of wildness and freedom. However, the cultivation of vajrayana has to be based on a very subtle, definite, ordinary, and real foundation. Otherwise, we are lost. Not only are we lost, but we are destroying ourselves.

In talking about the tantric tradition, we are not talking about playing with sex or aggression or colors or the phenomenal world. At this point we are simply developing a basic understanding of how tantra works. We have to be very conservative. We have to be very, very concerned with the fundamentals. I could say: "Don't worry. If you worry, that's your problem. If you don't worry, everything is going to be okay. Let's dance together. Let's play music together. Let's drink milk and honey." But that does not work, not at all. Talking about tantra is not such an easy matter.

Working with the energy of vajrayana is like dealing with a live electric wire. We can use switches, gloves, and all sorts of buffers in handling this live wire, but we also have the choice of using our bare hands and touching the live wire directly—in which case we are in trouble. The institution of tantra, not only Buddhist tantra but Hindu tantra as well, has been presented very generously to American students by many competent and great teachers. Still, many students get into trouble. They can't take it. They simply can't take it. They end up destroying themselves. They end up playing with the energy until it becomes a spiritual atomic bomb.

We might feel that working with tantra is like planting a little seed: we nourish it, make it germinate and send out shoots of greenery, and finally it will blossom as a beautiful flower. That is wishful thinking. We cannot approach tantra in that way. Instead, we have to realize that taking care of such a plant is not ordinary gardening. An extraordinary process is needed. Dealing with our state of being, our state of mind, is extraordinary in many ways. Moreover, dealing with our state of mind from the subtle tantra point of view is extremely dangerous—highly dangerous and equally highly productive. Therefore we should be very careful and open when we talk about vajrayana. Nonexistence is the only preparation for tantra, and we should realize that there is no substitute.

The experience of nonexistence brings a sense of delightful humor and, at the same time, complete openness and freedom. In addition, it brings an experience of complete indestructibility that is unchallengeable, immovable, and completely solid. The experience of indestructibility can only occur when we realize that nonexistence is possible, in the sense of being without reference points, without philosophical definitions, without even the notion of nonexistence.

The development of indestructibility or immovability is extremely important to understand. Such indestructibility can only come out of the state of nothingness, egolessness, or nonexistence. According to the Buddha, tantra is greater liberation, greater discipline, and greater vision. But this greater liberation is based on working with the potentialities and energies that exist within us. Therefore, without having some understanding of nonexistence, there is no point in discussing indestructibility.

When we consider someone to be indestructible, we generally mean that he is well established in his discipline, such as a person who has mastered the art of warfare or studied philosophy in great depth. Because such a person has mastered all sorts of techniques and training, we therefore consider him to be immovable or indestructible. In fact, from the tantra point of view, the attempt to secure oneself with gadgetry is a source of vulnerability rather than indestructibility. In this case, we are not talking about indestructibility based on collecting information, tricks, or ideas. Instead we are referring to a basic attitude of trust in the nonexistence of our being.

In the tantra notion of indestructibility, there is no ground, no basic premise, and no particular philosophy except one's own experience, which is extremely powerful and dynamic. It is a question of being rather than figuring out what to be, how to be. Usually we rely upon reference points, conceptual ideas, and feedback to give us guidelines as to how to be good or bad boys and girls, but such dependence is questionable. If you say to your doctor, "I have insomnia; how can I fall asleep?" the doctor responds by saying, "Take these pills. Then you will have no problem." In America in particular that approach has become a problem. In tantra, the point is not *how* to handle ourselves, but that we simply have to do it. We cannot trick ourselves into realizing the state of immovability, or indestructibility. Indestructibility is based on our experience, which is solid, dynamic, and unyielding.

In that way, tantra discipline does not cooperate with any deception at all; therefore it is regarded as indestructible, immovable. The tantric approach of nonparticipation in the games that go on in the samsaric world, however, is something more than boycotting. When we boycott something, we do so in the name of a protest. We disagree with certain systems or certain ideas, and therefore we make a nuisance of ourselves. In this case, instead of boycotting the samsaric setup, we are fully and personally involved with it. We realize all the so-called "benefits" that the samsaric world might present to us—spiritual, psychological, and material goods of all kinds. We are fully aware of all the alternatives, but we do not yield to any of them at all. We are straightforward and hardheaded. That is the quality of immovability.

The word *hardheaded* is very interesting. When we say somebody is hardheaded, we mean that he is not taken in by anything. That is precisely what is meant by the term *vajra nature*: hardheadedness, vajra-headedness. Vajra is a quality of toughness and not being taken in by any kind of seduction. We also talk about "hard truth." Such truth is hard, unyielding, and uncomplimentary. When we receive news of someone's death, it is the hard truth. We cannot go back and say that it is not true. We cannot hire an attorney to argue the case or spend our money trying to bring the person back to life, because it is the hard truth. In the same way, vajra nature is hard truth. We cannot challenge or manipulate it in any way at all. It is both direct and precise.

The term *vajra* in Sanskrit, or *dorje (rdo rje)* in Tibetan, means "having the qualities of a diamond." Like a diamond, vajra is tough and at the same time extremely precious. Unless we understand this basic vajra

34

quality of tantra, or of the tantrika—this almost bullheaded quality of not yielding to any kind of seductions, to any little tricks or plays on words—we cannot understand vajrayana Buddhism at all.

Fundamentally speaking, indestructibility, or vajra nature, is basic sanity. It is the total experience of tantra, the experience of the enlightened state of being. This sanity is based on the experience of clarity, which comes from the practice of meditation. Through the meditation practice of the three yanas we discover a sense of clarity, unconditional clarity. Such clarity is ostentatious and has immense brilliance. It is very joyful and it has potentialities of everything. It is a real experience. Once we have experienced this brilliance, this farseeing, ostentatious, colorful, opulent quality of clarity, then there is no problem. That *is* vajra nature. It is indestructible. Because of its opulence and its richness, it radiates constantly, and immense, unconditional appreciation takes place. That combination of indestructibility and clarity is the basic premise of tantra Buddhist teachings.

We should understand how the vajrayana notion of brilliance differs from the notion of clear light as described in the *Tibetan Book of the Dead* and how it differs from the mahayana notion of luminosity. Clear light, according to the *Tibetan Book of the Dead,* is purely a phenomenological experience. You see whiteness as you die or as your consciousness begins to sink. Because the physical data of your body's habitual patterns are beginning to dissolve, you begin to enter another realm. You feel whitewashed, as if you were swimming in milk, or drowning in milk. You feel suffocated with whiteness, which is known as clear light. That is purely a phenomenological experience, not the true experience of clarity. On the other hand, the mahayana Buddhists talk about luminosity, called *prabhasvara* in Sanskrit, or *ösel ('od gsal)* in Tibetan. Ösel means seeing things very precisely, clearly, logically, and skillfully. Everything is seen very directly; things are seen as they are. Nevertheless, neither prabhasvara nor the notion of clear light match the tantric notion of vajra clarity.

Vajrayana clarity has more humor. It also has more subtlety and dignity. Moreover, it is utterly, totally outrageous. Things are seen as they are, precisely; but at the same time things are also seeing us precisely. Because we are totally exposed and open and not afraid to be seen, a meeting point occurs. Something makes us realize that we cannot chicken out and say that our life is just a rehearsal. Something makes us realize that it is real. That state of being is not merely a phenomenological experience. It is a real state of being, a true state of being that is full and complete. That indestructibility and clarity are vajra nature, which is superior to any other approach to spirituality, even within the Buddhist tradition.

The Mandala of Kalachakra. A two-dimensional representation of the mandalas of body, speech, and mind of the Kalachakra Tantra.

THREE

Mandala

THERE ARE THREE WORLDS presented in the tantric tradition: the world of perceptions, the world of the body, and the world of emotions. Our relationship with the world of perceptions is called the outer mandala; our relationship with the world of the body is called the inner mandala; and our relationship with the world of emotions is called the secret mandala.

OUTER MANDALA

We are constantly engaged in relationships with the ordinary world, that is, the world of ayatanas or the six sense perceptions: seeing, hearing, smelling, tasting, feeling, and thinking, the process which coordinates the other five. In Buddhism thinking is considered to be one of the senses. Our different perceptions are constantly being coordinated into a mandala. By mandala we mean interlocking relationships rather than an extraordinary magical circle. Mandala is simply the coordination of one point with another. For instance, in filmmaking the visual material is edited, and the sound has to be edited as well, so that the two work together.

The same thing happens in everyday life. When we enter a restaurant, we hear the clattering of pots and pans, and we begin to smell the food. At that point we may either get turned on or turned off by the restaurant's mandala. Or someone may introduce a friend to us: "This is a good friend of mine. I would like you to meet him." We say, "How are you?" and we sit down to talk with that person. That person speaks and behaves in a certain way, and we begin to feel that we like him, either on the grounds of our friend's recommendation or because we feel it is worthwhile to associate with such a person.

Perhaps our car is breaking down and we stop at a gas station. One of the passengers decides to step out and ask the attendant how far it is to the next motel. From the way that person behaves when he brings back the message, we can tell whether the answer is going to be favorable or disappointing. In that way, we always have a feeling about what is taking place.

According to tantra, that feeling, or intuitive setup, is a part of the external world. It is part of an actual relationship. Something is happening, or for that matter, something is not happening. Nevertheless, there is an actual relationship taking place constantly. Our experience of that relationship is not particularly based on superstition. We simply have a personal experience of the whole situation, a sense of the reality of mandala.

The outer mandala principle is the possibility of relating with a situation as a cohesive structure. Some setups are unpleasant, destructive, and unworkable; other setups are creative, workable, and pleasant. Mandalas are the general patterns, whether pleasant or unpleasant, that link us to the rest of the world, which is our world or our creation in any case.

When we begin to work with reality properly, an enormous relationship, a rapport, takes place between us and the external world. That rapport is taking place constantly, some kind of network or system of relations. It is as if something were circulating. For instance, when we are just about to catch the flu, we feel that the world is not particularly favorable to us. Whatever we experience and whatever we feel is somewhat strange. We feel that something is not quite clicking. We feel numb and unhealthy already. The world outside seems too solid, and we cannot relate that solidity to the softness or vulnerability in ourselves. The world seems hardened and heavy, and we cannot seem to make any connection with it. Those are the signs of a fever, an approaching flu. Although they seem to signal a discrepancy in our relationship with the world, that experience itself is an example of mandala principle.

According to the tantric tradition, the outer mandala principle is the external world and how we relate with it. However, the emphasis on relationship does not mean that the world is regarded as an intuitive or purely subjective world. It is simply the external world. For instance, the outer mandala is connected with how we relate with hot and cold. If we are outdoors in a hot climate and we walk into a highly air-conditioned building, we may get sick because we are not able to handle hot and cold properly. Our coordination with the world may not be quite right.

Usually, we experience such problems when we ignore the relationship between the world outside and our own world, our body. If we do not acknowledge our sense perceptions properly and thoroughly, we find ourselves in trouble—not because *what* we perceive is poisonous, but because *how* we perceive has become incompetent, haphazard, or confused, and therefore it has turned into poison. From that point of view, we cannot say that the phenomenal world we are living in—the traffic jams and the pollution and the inflation—is bad and devilish. We cannot condemn the world or put it into those kinds of conceptual packages. That approach does not work, because it means that we are fighting with our own phenomena.

Phenomena are ours: it is our country, our air, our earth, our food, our water, our electricity, our policemen. When we talk about the mandala setup we are speaking of an organic reality. We are not saying that we should reorganize the world, or that we should fight for it. We are talking about how we could look at it in an organic, natural way. The world could evolve *itself* according to our enlightenment—naturally. If you were a political activist, you might have difficulty in understanding this seemingly wishy-washy philosophy. You might say, "Don't we have to speak up? Don't we have to do something?" But when we talk about the tantric level of perception, we are not talking about concocting something. The outer mandala principle purely refers to actual, immediate relationships, visual, auditory, and conceptual relationships, with the so-called "world outside."

When we relate directly to the world, we can see that there is a thread of continuity. We can see the setup as a whole, rather than having only a partial view. According to the Buddhist path, there is nothing *other* than that whole world; therefore we could say that the tantric attitude toward reality is nontheistic. In the nontheistic approach to reality, the world is not divided between God and the Devil. The world is a totality in itself. It has its own muscles, its own brain, its own limbs, and its own circulation. The world has its own water system, electrical system, and sewage system automatically built in. They are already there. The problem we face is that we do not see that totality; we do not acknowledge it. We do not even get close to it, to see that it is actually true.

We are not talking about the totality of the world in the sense that everything should be good and perfect and fantastic, and nobody should acknowledge anything bad. We are talking about reality, in which good is made out of bad and bad is made out of good. Therefore, the world can exist in its own good/bad level, its self-existing level of dark and light, black and white, constantly. We are not fighting for either of those sides. Whatever there is, favorable or unfavorable, it is workable; it is the universe. That is why in the tantric tradition we talk about the world, or the cosmos, in terms of mandala.

Mandala is a totality; it has a universal quality. That totality is not a compromise, as if someone were to say, "If you tone down your badness and I tone down my goodness we will have a happy medium, with both good and bad toned down to a grey level." That kind of compromise is not a totality; it is just gray and depressing. In fact, that is one of the depressing aspects of some of the ecumenical movements taking place in this country and the rest of the world. They seem to be based on the feeling that everything should be okay and that everything is good. Badness should come up to the level of goodness, and goodness should come down to the level of badness, so that we can have some kind of happy medium. In that approach, there could be communist Buddhists or Nazi tantric practitioners. But somehow that does not work; it is too silly.

INNER MANDALA

We have been talking about the external world, or the world of perceptions, as a mandala that we are able to work with. The second type of world is the body, which is known as the inner mandala. This mandala is connected with how we handle our bodies in terms of our awareness, or sense of reality.

Developing awareness is quite deliberate. In the beginning we might feel that working deliberately with the body is too exaggerated a form of behavior. However, it seems to be necessary. We have never regarded our bodies as sacred property. The attitude of sacredness has been neglected, particularly in the Western world. Instead, life is regarded as a hassle. We were born, breast-fed or bottle-fed, and put into diapers. Those were our unpleasant facts of life. Now we can go to the toilet and drink our cup of tea—how victorious we are! We view it as a victory that we have survived all that. But we have not actually developed any art in our lives. We do not know how to care for our bodies.

Taking care of ourselves is regarded as an enormous hassle: getting up at a certain time, writing checks, going to the bank, going to a restaurant are all done humorlessly. Perhaps our only delight is to get drunk at a party. We have a fantastic time dancing with our partner, whoever it may be, and then we peacefully pass out. That is a very crude way of handling our bodies. There is no dignity in that, none whatsoever.

We may have been taught sophisticated table manners by our aristocratic parents. They may have taught us how to drink, how to use forks and knives, and how to sit properly and make good conversation. Still, there is some fundamental crudeness involved, because we have been taught a facade, rather than what should be felt. We could be extremely well mannered and able to pass through diplomatic circles immaculately and impeccably. Nevertheless, there could still be a crudeness of fundamentally not knowing how to relate with our cup of tea, our plate, our table, or our chair.

There are enormous problems with thinking that we can only trust in what we were told rather than in how we feel. When we have only been *told* how to handle ourselves, our behavior can become automatic. Automatically we pick and choose. We learn to be perfect actors. It does not matter how we feel. We might be in tears, but still we put on a gleaming smile and make polite conversation. If we cannot find anything good to talk about, we just talk about the weather. With that approach, we become very crude. In fact, we are trying to become perfect actors rather than real people.

Some students of meditation have a similar problem. They have been told to keep a good posture and that the more a person keeps perfect posture, the closer he or she is to enlightenment. If one takes that approach without a sense of personal connection, it can produce a situation similar to that of the children of aristocracy who are taught to have good table manners. In both cases, there is a body problem, an actual physical problem, which has nothing to do with politics or society.

The tantric tradition is fundamentally an intentional approach to life in terms of how we handle our body. How we speak, how we look, how we touch our cup, our fork or knife, how we lift things and carry them about—all those things are very deliberate. But such deliberateness is not presented in a manual or book on how to act according to the tantric tradition. The point is that there is no such thing as a real tantric diet or proper tantric behavior. Instead, we develop a basic attitude, so that when we begin to extend our arm, we simply do it. When we begin to touch, we touch; and when we lift, we lift in a very confident way. We just do it. We have a real experience of confidence. There is no tantric finishing school designed to train people for the tantric aristocracy or to develop a deceptive but well-mannered king. The tantric approach to body—how to handle our body and our sense perceptions, how to look, how to feel, how to listen, how to handle the whole situation—is very personal and real.

Tantra is deliberate, but at the same time, the heart of that deliberateness is freedom. The "crazy yogins" of the tantric tradition were not people who just hung out on street corners doing their crazy things. The freedom of tantra is something very real, dignified, and vajra-like. The sense of indestructibility is always there. There is intention, there is reality, and there are constant discoveries.

SECRET MANDALA

Then we have the third world, which is the secret mandala, or the mandala of the sacred realm. The sacredness and secretness of this mandala are not based on our being highly evolved and consequently looking down upon the outer mandala and the inner mandala. Rather, the secret mandala consists of simplifying our psychological behavior, our meditative behavior, into a sense of awareness and openness in which we have no hesitation, none whatsoever, in dealing with our emotions.

In the secret mandala, emotions are all interwoven and interconnected. Passion is connected with aggression, aggression is connected with ignorance, ignorance is connected with envy or jealousy, and so forth. There is a continuous web taking place that is quite obvious and real. Therefore a person at the tantric level should not regard any *one* emotion as a big deal, but all emotions are a big deal. All the emotions that exist in a person's mind are the same problem—or the same promise, for that matter. They contain the seed of freedom, or liberation, and as well, the seed of imprisonment. In the secret mandala we work with all our hidden corners, any little areas of irritation. In fact, those things that we regard as little problems may actually be our biggest problems. Those problems are completely interrelated, which is the notion of mandala here.

There is a sense of continuity in our emotions and a sense of openness at the same time. For instance, we lose our temper, we become outraged, we are about to strangle our partner, and in fact we begin to do so—that itself is a mandala display. We feel angry, we feel passionate, we feel jealous, and we feel ignorant—all those things are happening at once. That is a real experience. There is no "how to do it"; we did it already. That is our chance. In fact, that is our golden opportunity. We have manifested the secret mandala already.

On the other hand, we usually do not acknowledge or experience our emotions properly. When we need release we might make love; when we need release we might kill someone. That is not quite the proper way to approach our emotions. Exploding on the spot is not the way to express emotions directly. Emotions are sacred; they should be regarded as real and obvious things that can teach us something. We should relate with them properly, without "getting off" on something or other. We might say, "I'm bored. Let's go to the movies." That is not quite the way to deal with our boredom.

The tantric approach to emotions is much more disciplined and much more personal. It is highly personal; that is why this mandala is called the sacred mandala. It is very difficult to achieve, but it is also very important and extremely sacred. Normally, no one is able to achieve such perfection, or even to conceive of such a possibility. So we should respect the sacredness of the secret mandala.

The mandala principle is an important concept in the tantric teachings. The outer mandala is connected with the external world: how to relate to society, politics, organizations, domestic relationships, and so forth. The inner mandala is connected with our body, and how to handle it. The secret mandala is connected with how to deal with our emotions. We have to incorporate all three mandala principles simultaneously in our experience. We can't separate them; we can't practice each of them separately, at different times. We have to do it all at once. In that way things become much more real.

The mandalas *are* reality. It is as simple as that. Of course, reality is real, but our contact with reality is through our sense perceptions, our body, and our emotions—the three mandalas. The three mandalas are what meet, or mate, with reality. When we put our finger on a hot stove, it is our perceptions that get burnt by their meeting with reality. We have to communicate with reality; otherwise, there is no reality. We might try to get out of the whole thing by saying, "Who cares?" But *that* becomes reality at the same time. We cannot get away from it. It is very personal, and it is very haunting. It is all over the place.

FOUR

Nontheistic Energy

USUALLY WHEN WE TALK about energy, we are referring to an ongoing source of power, something that is able to generate power, such as an electric generator. In a similar manner, when we speak of an energetic person, we usually mean a vigorous person, someone who possesses enormous energy. When we are around such a person, we feel there is a bank of energy happening. That person works so hard that we feel guilty being idle around him or her. We feel that we should do something too, and we begin to work very hard. Then no one can say that we have been bad boys and girls, that we haven't done our chores, washed the dishes, or ironed the sheets. Because we feel that person's enormous energy, we begin to perk up, and we stop being idle. We begin to take part in the energy.

Then there is another kind of energy, which is self-existing. Self-existing energy is not dependent on something or somebody else; it simply takes place continuously. Although the source of such energy is difficult to track down, it is universal and all-pervasive. It happens by itself, naturally. It is based on enthusiasm as well as freedom: enthusiasm in the sense that we trust what we are doing, and freedom in the sense that we are completely certain that we are not going to be imprisoned by our own energy, but instead, freed constantly. In other words, we realize that such energy does come up by itself, and that we can work with it. This self-existing energy is the potentiality of *siddhi*, a Sanskrit word that refers to the ability to use the existing energies of the universe in a very special and appropriate way.

45

Self-existing energy is difficult to describe in words or concepts. When we try to describe this pattern of energy, we are only finger painting. Basically, it is the energy of the psychological realm. No matter what state of mind we are in, we experience a particular quality of life, that is, we experience an emotion. We begin to feel an electric spark taking place. That energy can come out of having a quarrel with our wife or out of having a severe accident or a love affair. It comes out of being either rejected or accepted.

This energy is created both when we fail to do something and when we accomplish something. Rejection or acceptance by the world does not mean that the energy is either invalid or valid. Rather, there is transparent energy happening all the time. Whether we are in an appropriate situation, in accordance with the laws of the universe, or we are in an inappropriate situation, not in accordance with the laws of the universe, energy is constantly taking place. This energy, from the vajrayana or tantric point of view, is simply the energy that exists. It does not mean being hard-working or extremely industrious, always doing things, being a busybody, or anything like that. This energy can come from all kinds of challenges, in the positive or negative sense. Such energy takes place constantly.

Self-existing energy permeates all of our emotional relationships: our emotions toward our relatives, our lovers, our friends, and our enemies. It also permeates our philosophical beliefs: either something is happening "right" according to our beliefs, or something has gone "wrong" according to our beliefs. Some situations try to dislodge us from our philosophical or religious commitments, and some situations try to draw us into certain commitments. All kinds of energies take place. So when we talk about energy, we are not talking about vigor alone but about that which exists in our lives. It is as though flint and steel were rubbing against each other and sparking constantly, again and again. That is, the phenomenal world exists, and we either rub against it or with it, and that rubbing is constantly creating a spark.

According to the tantric understanding of reality, energy is related to the experience of duality, the experience that you exist and others exist. Of course, both those concepts are false, but who cares about that?—at the time, anyway. The deceptive existence of you and other rubs together, nevertheless. Sometimes you are conquering the world and sometime the world is conquering you. It is like riding on a balloon in the ocean: Sometimes the balloon rides on you and you are underneath the ocean; sometimes you ride on the balloon and the balloon is underneath the ocean. That play of duality takes place constantly; that kind of electricity takes place all the time.

So the basic notion of energy is nothing particularly magical or miraculous. It is simply the rubbing together of the duality of you and the phenomenal world, you and other. We are talking about that spark, that fire. It is real fire, real water, real earth, and real air: The real elements are working with you. Still, at this point we have no idea who *you* are, actually. Let's just say we are talking about the basic *you*. Let's leave it vague at this point; otherwise it is going to get too complicated. Just leave it at *you*, this vague stuff that exists somewhere or other in the middle of the cosmos.

At this point the question arises of how we can handle, or utilize, such energy. In fact, that has been a question for a long, long time. For twenty-five hundred years the same question has been asked: How can we handle self-existing energy; how can we work with it? Fundamentally, that question is the question of how to handle duality, or the basic split.

The split between self and other is taking place constantly, constantly creating energy, and we are always trying to work with it. Our approach is usually to try to unify the split in order to avoid the energy. We may say, "I am a good man; I am a bad man; I am Joe; I am Mary." In doing so, we are trying to bring self and other together in a superficial sense, as if no energy existed at all, as though everything were going smoothly: "There is nothing to worry about; everything's going to be okay. I am Mary, and that's smooth. There is no gap between *I* and *am* and *Mary* at all." Or we try to avoid the split by refusing to say "I am." Instead we might say, "My *name* is Mary." Still we have a problem. That approach of smoothing things out and trying to make everything presentable and respectable brings enormous problems, enormous questions. In fact, instead of getting rid of the energy, it raises further energy.

The attempt to define who we are and who we are not is basically split into two approaches: the theistic approach and the nontheistic approach. In the nontheistic approach we simply acknowledge the dualistic gap rather than trying to unify it or conceal it. In the theistic approach, there is an ongoing attempt to conceal that gap completely. There is a notion of spiritual democracy. In fact, that approach is often used in dealing with political and social problems: "Blacks are not against whites—we are all the same species. Since we all live on the same earth, we should regard ourselves as a brotherhood."

That approach of covering up separateness, pretending that the black man is a white man, is the cause of all kinds of problems; but the theistic approach can go much further than that, to the point of covering up *any* differences: "Let us have real unity. We can conceal this problem. We can iron it out completely, like a cloth. Let us work in such a way that when we have ironed our sheet we can even conceal the seams. In fact, we can make the whole sheet seem to be made out of one big cloth. God is in us and we are in God. It's all one, so don't worry."

Another way to cover the gap is to try to eliminate discomfort. The modern world has provided us with all sorts of conveniences: television, beautiful parents, lots of toys to play with, automobiles, and so on. There are notices everywhere offering entertainment and telling us how to handle ourselves. Even while we are flying in an airplane, we have food to entertain us. The world has provided all kinds of entertainment to make us feel better, to make sure that we do not feel bad or lonely. When we board an airplane, the stewardess says, "Welcome, ladies and gentlemen. I hope you have a comfortable flight. Call us if you need any help." That is a theistic remark, and such remarks occur all the time.

On the other hand, we could act without guidelines. This possibility may be completely unappealing to people who are used to their luxury. Nevertheless, it is a very truthful way to relate with things, and there is no room for deception. In this approach there is no hospitality; we have to provide our own hospitality. We have to work on ourselves. We are provided with kits, K rations, booklets, and our own parachutes, and off we go. If we land on the top of a tree, we try to make the best of it; if we land in a gorge, we try to make the best of it. That is the nontheistic lifestyle: We can't do everything for one another. We have to make do for ourselves. We have to learn how to live with nature. So the nontheistic tradition is much harsher than the theistic tradition. It is very skeptical, unyielding, and somewhat outrageous.

We are not comparing Eastern and Western philosophies here, but theistic and nontheistic traditions, wherever they occur. We might hypothesize that Easterners think in a different way than Westerners, and that Eastern philosophy expresses this different style of thought. But philosophy is not that neatly divided into East and West. The basic thinking processes of the East and the West are the same. The only difference that exists is between the thinking style of ego and non-ego. Failing to acknowledge that difference in style becomes a tremendous problem.

The standard approach to ecumenicism is to try to pretend that theism and nontheism are not different. But this is another theistic attempt to conceal the discomfort or the energy that comes from experiencing duality. We should be aware that differences exist. Then true ecumenicism, or continuity, can come about because of the differences.

In comparing theism and nontheism, we are discussing different approaches to separateness. In the theistic approach, we know that things are separate, but since we don't like it, we feel we should *do* something about it. We don't like the separateness, so we try to overcome it to the best of our ability, and that becomes an enormous problem. In the nontheistic approach, we also know that things are separate; therefore things are unified. Things are different, but that is not regarded as a problem. Fire is hot and water is cold, but still they can coexist. Fire can boil water, changing it into steam, and water can kill fire. We should not be embarrassed about the functions of the universe.

We are still talking about energy—energy and reality. And we are concerned with what actual reality is. Is reality a gap, a crack, or is reality a big sheet of cloth, all-pervasive? In the nontheistic tradition of Buddhist tantra, when we begin to have a relationship with the world, we do not try to make sure that the world is part of us. In fact, the question of separation does not come up at all. According to the nontheistic tradition, we do not believe ourselves to be creatures. We are some kind of being—or nonbeing, for that matter—but we were never created, and therefore we are not particularly creatures. Nevertheless, there is a sense of continuity, without hysteria, without panic, without any congratulatory remarks or attempts to smooth things out. The world exists and we exist. We and the world are separate from that point of view—but so what? We could regard the separateness as part of the continuity rather than trying to deny it.

In the nontheistic approach, there is continuity, openness, and oneness—but in the sense of zeroness rather than even oneness. The nonexistence of a dualistic barrier does not quite mean that we are one, but that we are zero. Nontheism is the basis for understanding that. Tantra is continuity, so the thread of tantra runs through our life from beginning to end. In a sense, the beginning is part of the end, so a complete circle, or mandala, is formed. The beginning is the beginning of the end, and the end is the beginning of the beginning. That continuity is tantra. It is the continuous thread of openness that we could experience throughout our lives. Because of that, whatever sense perceptions or realms of experience come up, we can work through them.

From this point of view energy is very simple, extremely simple: energy is separate from you; therefore, energy is part of you. Without *you* separateness cannot exist. That is the dichotomy in Buddhist logic: you have form; therefore you do not have form. You cannot have form if you do not have formlessness, if you do not acknowledge or perceive formlessness. In the same way, you exist *because* you do not exist. Such riddles are regarded by Buddhists as the truth.

According to the tantric tradition of nontheism, energy is vital and important. Of course, in this approach we are viewing the world purely as a psychological process: if we do not have mind, we do not exist. The world comes out of our mind; it is created by our mind. From that point of view, working with energy, or developing siddhi, means that we do not have to depend on feedback but that we relate with life as straightforwardly and directly as possible. We relate directly to our domestic world, our enemies, our friends, our relatives, business partners, policemen, the government, or whatever happens in our life. We relate directly with energy as much as possible.

We are not talking about centralizing energy within ourselves, making ourselves into little atom bombs and then exploding. Working with energy in a tantric sense is a decentralized process. That is a very important point. We are talking about energy as something spreading, opening. Energy becomes all-pervasive. It is all and everywhere. If we centralize energy in ourselves, we are asking for trouble. We will find that we become like baby snakes who are vicious and angry but still very small. Or we may find that we are like extremely passionate, horny little baby peacocks. So it is important to remember that, in Buddhist tantra, energy is openness and all-pervasiveness. It is constantly expanding. It is decentralized energy, a sense of flood, ocean, outer space, the light of the sun and moon.

FIVE

Transmission

O UR NEXT TOPIC is the transmission of vajrayana teachings from teacher to student. Before we can discuss transmission, however, it seems necessary to go back a step and examine our level of sanity and discipline. We need to examine what we have accomplished in our relationship with the world. If we have not been able to make a relationship with our suffering, frustrations, and neuroses, the feasibility of transmission is remote, extremely remote, for we have not even made a proper relationship with the most basic level of our experience.

I could say to you, "Forget all that. Forget your pain and suffering; it is going to be okay." I could give you all kinds of antidotes: tranquilizers, mantras, and tricks. I could say, "Soon you'll feel good. Soon you'll forget your pain, and then you'll be in a beautiful place." But that would be an enormous falsity, and in the long run, such an approach is ungenerous and extremely destructive to the spiritual path. It is like giving our children tranquilizers whenever they begin to misbehave so that they will fall asleep. It saves us the trouble of getting a baby-sitter and changing diapers, but the child becomes a complete zombie. That is not the human thing to do, we must admit, and giving someone a spiritual tranquilizer is just as primitive as that. We suffer tremendously if we treat spirituality in that way, and we have to pay for it later on. Enormous problems arise—both resentment and discontent.

One approach that is used in presenting spirituality is to say that if we have any questions, we should just forget them. We should regard them as outside the circle of the spiritually initiated. We should forget

Jetsün Milarepa (1040–1123). The chief disciple of Marpa, Milarepa is renowned for his songs of devotion and realization. This statue was a shrine object of Gampopa, Milarepa's chief disciple.
PHOTO BY GEORGE HOLMES AND BLAIR HANSEN.

all our negativity: "Don't ask any questions; just drop them. It is important that you have hope, that you go beyond your questions. Only if you accept the whole thing will you be saved." That strategy is used to take advantage of the sanity of human beings—which is unlawful.

Someone may tell us that, if we commit ourselves to a particular practice or path, within four weeks we are going to be okay; we are going to be "high" forever. So we try it, and it works—but not forever. After six weeks, at most, or perhaps after only ten days, we begin to come down, and then we begin to panic and wonder what is going on. Usually the most faithful students blame themselves, feeling they have mismanaged the practice: "I must have some problem that I haven't cleared up yet. I must not have done my confession properly, or given in properly." But that is not the case at all. The problem is the way they were indoctrinated into their spiritual practice.

We accept what is presented to us with an open mind, which is beautiful, but then its truth does not hold up. Because of the basic deception involved in our initiation, all sorts of holes begin to develop. Unfortunately, we become the victims of those lies, deceptions, or charlatanisms, and we feel the effects constantly, over and over again.

So we have a problem with spiritual transmission, a problem of how to get real transmission from a competent master into our system. At this point, we are talking purely about the beginner's level and the preparations that might be needed in order for spiritual transmission to occur in the very early stages. It is necessary for us to sharpen our cynicism, to sharpen our whole critical attitude toward what we are doing. That cynicism provides a basis for our study and work. For instance, if we are building a bridge, we begin by constructing the framework. It could be made of timber or iron rods, but the skeleton must be built before we pour the concrete. That is an example of the cynical approach. It is absolutely necessary to have that kind of cynical attitude if we are going to build a bridge, and it is necessary to be cynical in our approach to spirituality as well.

We need to encourage an attitude of constant questioning, rather than ignoring our intelligence, which is a genuine part of our potential as students. If students were required to drop their questions, that would create armies and armies of zombies—rows of jellyfish sitting next to each other. But, to use a local expression, that is not so neat. In fact, it is messy. Preparing a beautifully defined and critical background for what we are doing to ourselves and what the teaching is doing to us is absolutely important, *absolutely* important. Without that critical background, we cannot develop even the slightest notion or flavor of enlightenment.

Enlightenment is based on both prajna, or discriminating awareness, and compassion. But without cynicism, we do not have either. We do not have any compassion for ourselves because we are looking for something outside of ourselves, and we want to find the best way to get it. We also do not have any prajna, or clarity. We become completely gullible, and we are liable to be sucked in without any understanding, none whatsoever.

Transmission is like receiving a spiritual inheritance. In order to inherit our spiritual discipline, in order to have a good inheritance, we should become worthy vessels. In order to become worthy vessels, we have to drop the attitude that we are going to be saved, that there is going to be a magically painless operation, and that all we have to do is pay the doctor's fee. We have the notion that if we pay the doctor, everything will be taken care of. We can just relax and let him do what he wants. That attitude is simple-minded. It is absolutely necessary to think twice. The questioning mind is absolutely necessary; it is the basis of receiving transmission.

I am not stressing the importance of critical intelligence because Buddhism is just now being introduced to America and the West. It is not that I think students here might be more gullible. Buddhism is a strong tradition that has existed for twenty-five hundred years, and throughout the ages students have been given these same instructions. Throughout the ages they have contributed their neuroses and their mistakes to help shape the methods and means of the Buddhist lineage. A learning process has been taking place for twenty-five hundred years, in fact, even longer. And we have inherited all of that experience. So this approach is ages old rather than a sudden panic. It is an old way, very old and very traditional.

One of the responsibilities of the lineage holder is not to give an inch, but to keep up the tradition. At this point, tradition does not mean dressing up in robes and playing exotic music or having dakinis dancing around us, or anything like that. Tradition is being faithful to what we have been taught and to our own integrity. From this point of view, tradition is being awake and open, welcoming but at the same time stubborn.

According to tradition, the teacher should treat his students in this stubborn way: He should require that his students practice properly, in accordance with the tradition of the lineage. There are problems when a teacher is too kind to students who do not belong to the teacher's race and upbringing. Some teachers from the East seem to be excited by foreignness: "Wow! Finally we are going to teach the aliens, the overseas people." Because of this fascination and out of a naive generosity, they make unnecessary concessions. Although such teachers may be liberal enough to include Occidental students, to take them to heart and be very kind to them, their extraordinary kindness may be destructive.

Such teachers regard Westerners as an extraordinary species, as if they came from the planet Mars: "Well, why don't we teach them, since we have a captive audience of living Martians here?" That misunderstanding is an expression of limited vision, of failing to see that the world is one world made up of human beings. A person who lives on this earth needs food, shelter, clothing, a love affair, and so on. We are all alike in that regard. Westerners do not need any special treatment because they invented the airplane or electronics. All human beings have the same psychology: They think in the same way, and they have the same requirements as students. The question is simply how one can teach students no matter where they come from.

In that respect we can follow the example of the Buddha, who presented the teachings to the Indians of his time in a universal fashion. It is much more enlightened to view the world as one global situation. Everybody is united: We are all samsaric people, and we all have the potential to become enlightened as well. We do not have to be particularly kind toward one part of the world or another, or for that matter, aggressive toward one part of the world or another. We are one world; we share one earth, one water, one fire, and one sun.

Wherever a student comes from, his or her attitude is very important. To receive transmission, a student should be humble and open but not wretched. Being humble in this case is being like a teacup. If we are pouring a cup of tea, the cup could be said to be humble. The cup has a sense of being in its own place. When we pour tea into a cup, the cup is at a lower level and the pot is at a higher level. This has nothing to do with spiritual trips, higher consciousness, lower consciousness, or anything like that. We are talking pragmatically. If we are going to pour tea into a cup, the cup obviously should be lower than the pot. Otherwise we would be unable to pour anything into it.

Water obviously has to flow down. It is very simple. Like a humble cup, the student should feel fertile and at the same time open. Because tea is going to be poured into this particular cup, the cup has a sense of open expectation. Why not? We are no longer wretched people who are not up to the level of receiving teaching. We are simply students who want to know, who want to learn and receive instructions. Also, one cup is not necessarily better or more valuable than another. It could be made out of many things—ordinary clay, porcelain, gold, or silver—but it is still a cup as long as it can hold water or tea.

To be a proper cup, we should be free from spiritual materialism, thoroughly ripened, and brought to spiritual maturity so that transmission can take place. Then, in our basic being, we feel the quality of "cupness"; we feel our whole existence thirsting to receive teaching. We are open to the teachings. That is the first step in transmission: Like the cup, we are on a certain level of experience that is not absolutely wretched or full of holes. We don't feel that we are deprived.

In fact, being a cup is an absolutely powerful thing: There is a sense of pride. Because our cup has such a strong quality of cupness, the teapot cannot help but fill it with knowledge or teachings. The teacher cannot wait to pour into us. We are seducing the teapot with our cupness: our pride, our self-existence, and our sanity. Two magnetic processes are taking place: The cup is magnetized by the teapot, and the teapot is equally magnetized by the cup. A love affair takes place; a fascination takes place.

Transmission means the extension of spiritual wakefulness from one person to someone else. Wakefulness is extended rather than transferred. The teacher, or the transmitter, extends his own inspiration rather than giving his experience away to somebody else and becoming an empty balloon. The teacher is generating wakefulness and inspiration constantly, without ever being depleted. So for the student, transmission is like being charged with electricity.

Transmission also requires the dynamic expression of the student's own emotions. As students, our aggression, our lust, and our stupidity are all included. According to vajrayana, everything we can think of, including the emotions, is workable. In fact, transmission cannot take place without emotions, because they are part of the food of transmutation. And since they are so energetic and powerful, we do not want to exclude any of them. As long as we separate our philosophy and our concepts of morality from our emotions, there is no problem. This does not mean that we should be completely loose, seemingly free from philosophy, morality, and ethics, but that self-existing ethics take place constantly. To receive transmission it is absolutely necessary to be an ordinary human being: confused, stupid, lustful, and angry. Without those emotional qualities, we cannot receive transmission. They are absolutely necessary. I do not think this is a particularly difficult requirement to fulfill. Everybody seems to have a pretty juicy helping of them.

Our emotions are regarded as the wiring or electrical circuit that receives transmission. We could say that we have three wires—one for passion, one for aggression, and one for naiveté, ignorance, or slothfulness. These three form a very busy electrical device that would like to receive transmission. We are hungry for it; we are dying for it. And on the other side, there is the electrical generator, which is somewhat smug, knowing that it is ready to transmit at any time.

So we have a good machine and we are beautifully wired: now we are just waiting for the generator to convey its charge—which in Sanskrit is called abhisheka. *Abhisheka* literally means "sprinkling," or "bathing," or "anointment." It is a formal ceremony of empowerment, a formal transmission from teacher to student. Abhisheka cannot take place unless the necessary wiring has already been set up, and to change our analogy slightly, abhisheka cannot take place without a good electrician, the teacher, or guru, who will know when to switch on the current.

In an abhisheka there is a sense of destruction, a sense of flow, and a sense of fulfillment. Those three principles of abhisheka are analogous to electricity in many ways: When we turn on a switch, the first thing that happens is that the resistance to the current is destroyed. Then, the current can flow through the circuit; and finally, the electricity can fulfill its purpose. If we turn on a lamp, first the electrical resistance is destroyed by turning on the switch, then the electricity flows, and finally the lamp is lit. In the same way, in receiving abhisheka, destruction comes first, right at the beginning. Anything that is disorganized or confused, and any misconceptions about receiving abhisheka, get destroyed on the spot—immediately.

According to the tantric tradition, it is better not to get into tantra, but if we must get into it, we had better surrender. Having surrendered, we must give up the idea of survival. Survival means that we can still play our games, play our little tricks on the world. We have our usual routines, the little gadgets that we play with, the little colors that we pull out of our personality to make sure that we exist. But in tantra, it is not possible to play any games. So at the beginning it is necessary to give in completely. We have to surrender to groundlessness: There is no ground for us to develop security. As well we surrender to the fact that we cannot hold on to our ego, which by innuendo means that we surrender to the enlightened state of being. Then, actually, we do not have to do anything. Once we open, we just open.

All that is part of the first principle of abhisheka: destruction. When that first level of abhisheka takes place, it kills any unnecessary germs in our system. At that point, we have no hopes of manipulating anything at all. Then the flow of energy can take place. And after that, there is fulfillment: we finally begin to see the reality of what is possible in tantric experience. It is necessary for anyone involved with the discipline of vajrayana to understand the three principles of destruction, flow, and fulfillment. I am glad we could discuss these principles publicly, so that you will have a chance either to prepare yourselves or to run away. That creates a very open situation.

The student always has a chance to run away. We seem to have the concept that tantric discipline imposes itself on us, but what we are discussing is entirely self-imposed. The student might freak out at any time; he might feel weighted down, overclean, and overfilled. But in order to receive transmission, he has to stay in his own place, which is not particularly pleasurable.

To conclude, the role of guru in transmission is to electrify the student's vessel, so that it becomes clean and clear, free of all kinds of materialistic germs, and then to pour the essence into it. And if he is to be electrified at all, to be cleaned out and filled up, the student must be waiting and ready. He has to be willing to be made into a good vessel. As a good vessel, the student feels that he is opening and taking part constantly. And as a good vessel, he could hold all sorts of heavy-handed liquids. In a good vessel, we could drink alcoholic beverages; that is, we could drink up dualistic thoughts. We could drink the blood of ego, which is killed on the spot.

SIX

The Vajra Master

MANY PEOPLE have heard fascinating facts and figures about tantra, exciting stories about the "sudden path." Tantra may seem seductive and appealing, particularly when it seems to coincide with modern notions of efficiency and automation. If we ask people whether they prefer to walk up the stairs or ride in an elevator, most people, if they are not used to working hard, will say they prefer to ride in the elevator. But that attitude is a problem in relating to tantra. If students believe that tantra is supposed to be the quick path, then they think they should get quick results. They do not want to waste their time. Instead they want to get their money's worth, so to speak, and quickly become buddhas. They become impatient, and not only that, they become cowardly. They do not want to face pain or problems, because then they won't get quick results. With that attitude, students have very little willingness to expose themselves and to face the state of panic of the tantric practitioner.

The student of tantra should be in a constant state of panic. That panic is electric and should be regarded as worthwhile. Panic serves two purposes: It overcomes our sense of smugness and self-satisfaction, and it sharpens our clarity enormously. It has been said by Padma Karpo and other great tantric teachers that studying tantra is like riding on a razor blade. Should we try to slide down the razor blade or should we just try to sit still? If we know how to slide down the razor blade, we might do it as easily as a child slides down a banister; whereas if we do not know the nature of the blade and we are just trying to prove our chauvinism, we might find ourselves cut in two. So the more warnings that are given about tantra, the more the student of tantra benefits. If the tantric master does not give enough warnings, the student cannot develop any real understanding of tantra at all, because he is not riding on the razor's edge.

Panic is the source of openness and the source of questions. Panic is the source of open heart and open ground. Sudden panic creates an enormous sense of fresh air, and that quality of openness is exactly what tantra should create. If we are good tantra students, we open ourselves each moment. We panic a thousand times a day, 108 times an hour. We open constantly and we panic constantly. That ongoing panic points to the seriousness of the tantric path, which is so overwhelmingly powerful and demanding that it is better *not* to commit ourselves to it. But if we *must* get into it, we should take it seriously—absolutely seriously.

It is possible that by following the tantric path we could develop vajra indestructibility and a sudden realization of enlightenment. But it is equally possible that we could develop an indestructible ego and find ourselves burnt up, as if we were an overcooked steak. We might find that we have become a little piece of charcoal. So there are two different possibilities: We could discover our inherent vajra nature, or we could become a piece of charcoal.

There is also a price on the head of the teacher. Those masters and teachers of tantra who teach students at the wrong time, who choose the wrong moment or say the wrong thing, or who are not able to experience accurately what is taking place may be condemned. They too may be reduced into pieces of charcoal. Such mistakes in teaching are called the offense of *sang drok (gsang sgrogs)*, which means declaring the secret at the wrong time. So there is a type of security system that has been set up in the vajrayana world.

If teachers feel that they can go outside the law, so to speak, outside the boundaries, or if they feel that they no longer need to commit themselves to the practice, they can be punished along with their students. It is because of this security system that the lineage of great tantric teachers has continued without interruption up to the present day. Everyone in the tantric lineage has panicked: The teachers have panicked and the students have panicked. Because of that healthy situation of panic, the tantric lineage has developed beautifully, smoothly, and healthily. Nobody has made mistakes. If anybody did make a mistake, he just vanished and became a piece of charcoal. Those who survived, both students and teachers, are those who developed vajra nature. Because of that they survived.

We might wonder why the vajrayana is kept secret at all. What is this famous tantric secret? The secret is not particularly exotic. It is not anything special. It simply refers to what we discover when we begin to play with the cosmos, the energy of the universe. As children we know that if we touch a naked wire we get a shock; we learn that by playing with our world. If we speed in our motorcar we will crash. We know that much. Here we are talking about the spiritual equivalent of that knowledge, which is a hundred times worse or a hundred times more powerful, depending upon how we would like to put it. We are talking about the energy that exists in the world. We first have a glimpse of that energy, we get completely fascinated by it, and then we begin to play with it. We are asking for trouble, as any sensible person would tell us.

This warning has been given hundreds of times: "Don't get into tantra just like that. Start with hinayana, graduate to mahayana, and then you can become a tantric practitioner. If you have already done your homework and finished your basic training, then you can become a tantric practitioner. But even then, it is still dangerous." That has been said many hundreds of times. Every book written on tantra, every commentary, every tantric text that has been recorded in the history of the cosmos, begins with that warning: "Be careful; think twice; pay respect; don't just take this carelessly—be careful." But interestingly enough, the more you put students off, the more interested they become.

The energy and power that exist in the tantric world are not different from what exists in the ordinary world. It is not that we suddenly wake up to a magical world. It is rather that developing a certain sensitivity exposes us to a different state of being. Often people who have taken hallucinogenic drugs claim that they have had a tantric experience, or people who have experienced extreme psychological depression or excitement claim that they have seen the tantric world. Those claims are somewhat suspicious.

When we talk about the tantric world, we are talking about *this* visual, auditory, sensory world, which has not been explored or looked at properly. Nobody has bothered to actually experience it. People just take it for granted. We may have been interested in our world when we were little children, but then we were taught how to handle it by our parents. Our parents already had developed a system to deal with the world and to shield themselves from it at the same time. As we accepted that system, we lost contact with the world. We lost the freshness and curiosity of our infancy a long time ago. And now, although the world is full of all kinds of things, we find that in communicating with the world we are somewhat numb. There is numbness in our sight, numbness in our hearing, numbness in all our senses. It is as though we had been drugged. The reality of the world—the brilliance of red, the brightness of turquoise, the majesty of yellow, and the fantastic quality of green—has not been seen properly. We have been indoctrinated, or we have indoctrinated ourselves. A state of numbness had developed, and we are not seeing our world properly.

The point of tantra is to reintroduce the world to us. Having developed a calmness of mind already in our practice of meditation, we can begin to re-view the world. We rediscover the world that exists around us, and we begin to find that this world is fabulous and fantastic. All kinds of exciting things are happening. Even people working nine-to-five jobs might find that their everyday life becomes fantastic. Every day is a different day rather than the same old thing.

The tantric approach to relating with the world is resharpening and reopening ourselves so that we are able to perceive our cosmos properly, thoroughly. We are keenly interested in and fascinated by the world. If we see a green light as we are driving, and it turns to amber and then red, it is fantastic. There is a world of self-existing messages and symbolism. For example, everybody dresses in his own colors and his own style of clothing. Some people decide to wear shirts and some people decide not to, but everybody wears a bottom part. Everybody has his own kind of hairdo. Some people wear glasses, and some do not. Everything makes sense. That is the whole point, that things make sense in their own right. Such truth does not have to be written in books—it is self-existing.

This may sound fantastic and enormously entertaining, but there is a catch. Along with that magic there is a naked sort of electricity. Once we are fascinated by this world and see the world without any filter or screen, then we are relating to the world so directly that it is as though we had no skin on our body. Experience becomes so intimate and so personal that it actually burns us or freezes us. It is not just that the world is becoming open to us, but we are shedding our skin as well. We may become extremely sensitive and jumpy people, and it is possible that we may panic more; we may react even more intensely. For instance, if we become too involved in the brightness of red, it could become poisonous. It is even possible that we could kill ourselves—cut our own throats.

The world is so magical that it gives us a direct shock. It is not like sitting back in our theater chair and being entertained by the fabulous world happening on the screen. It does not work that way. Instead it is a *mutual* process of opening between the practitioner and the world. Therefore tantra is very dangerous. It is electric and at the same time extremely naked. There is no place for our suit of armor. There is no time to insulate ourselves. Everything is too immediate. Our suit of armor is punctured from both outside and inside at once. Such nakedness and such openness reveal the cosmos in an entirely different way. It may be fantastic, but at the same time, it is very dangerous.

In addition to ourselves and the world, there is also a third element involved: the teacher who talks to us and introduces to us the possibility of such a true world. In the discipline of hinayana we relate to the teacher as a wise man who gives us constant instruction and guides us precisely. The relationship between teacher and student is very simple and clean-cut. In the discipline of mahayana, we regard the teacher as a kalyanamitra or spiritual friend who works with us and relates to us as a friend. He guides us through the dangerous and the luxurious parts of the path; he tells us when to relax and when to exert ourselves, and he teaches the disciplines of helping others. In the discipline of vajrayana, the relationship between teacher and student is much more vigorous and highly meaningful. It is more personal and magical than consulting a sage or, for that matter, consulting a spiritual friend.

The vajrayana teacher is referred to as the vajra master. The vajra master is electric and naked. He holds a scepter in his hand, called a vajra, which symbolizes a thunderbolt. The teacher holds the power to conduct lightning with his hand. By means of the vajra he can transmit that electricity to us. If the cosmos and the student are not connecting properly, the vajra master can respark the connection. In this sense the teacher has a great deal of power over us, but not such that he can become an egomaniac. Rather, the teacher is a spokesman who reintroduces the world to us: he reintroduces us to our world.

The vajra master is like a magician in the sense that he has access to the cosmic world and can work with it, but not in the sense that he can turn earth into fire, or fire into water, just like that. The vajra master has to work with the actual functions of the universe. We could say that the cosmos contains a lot of magic, and because the vajra master has some connection with the world and the happenings of the world, there is magic already. Therefore, the vajra master could be considered a supervisor of magic rather than a magician.

Relating with the vajra master is extremely powerful and somewhat dangerous at this point. The vajra master is capable of transmitting the vajra spiritual energy to us, but at the same time, he is also capable of destroying us if our direction is completely wrong. Tantra means continuity, but one of the principles of tantric discipline is that continuity can only exist if there is something genuine to continue. If we are not genuine, then our continuity can be canceled by the vajra master. So we do not regard our teacher in the vajrayana as a savior or as a deity who automatically will give us whatever we want.

The vajra master could be quite heavy-handed; however, he does not just play tricks on us whenever he finds a weak point. He conducts himself according to the tradition and the discipline: He touches us, he smells us, he looks at us, and he listens to our heartbeat. It is a very definite, deliberate process done according to the tradition of the lineage. That process—when the vajra master looks at us, when he listens to us, when he feels us, and when he touches us—is known as abhisheka or empowerment.

Abhisheka is sometimes translated as "initiation," but that does not actually convey the proper meaning. As we discussed earlier, *abhisheka* is a Sanskrit word that literally means "anointment." It is the idea of being bathed in holy water that is blessed by the teacher and the mandala around the teacher. However, abhisheka is not an initiation or rite of passage in which we are accepted as a member of the tribe if we pass certain tests. In fact, it is entirely different. The vajra master empowers us and we receive that power, depending both on our own capability and the capability of the teacher. Therefore the term "empowerment" is more appropriate than "initiation," because there is no tribe into which we are initiated. There is no close circle; rather, we are introduced to the universe. We cannot say that the universe is a big tribe or a big ego; the universe is open space. So the teacher empowers us to encounter our enlarged universe. At this point the teacher acts as a lightning rod. We could be shocked or devastated by the electricity he transmits to us, but it is also possible that we could be saved by having such an electric conductor.

In the vajrayana, it is absolutely necessary to have a teacher and to trust in the teacher. The teacher or vajra master is the only embodiment of the transmission of energy. Without such a teacher we cannot experience the world properly and thoroughly. We cannot just read a few books on tantra and try to figure it out for ourselves. Somehow that does not work. Tantra has to be transmitted to the student as a living experience. The tantric system of working with the world and the energy of tantra have to be transmitted or handed down directly from teacher to student. In that way the teachings become real and obvious and precise.

A direct relationship between teacher and student is essential in vajrayana Buddhism. People cannot even begin to practice tantra without making some connection with their teacher, their vajra, indestructible, master. Such a teacher cannot be some abstract cosmic figure. He has to be somebody who has gone through the whole process himself—somebody who has been both a panicking student and a panicking teacher.

We could say that the vajra master exists because he is free from karma, but that through his compassion such a teacher establishes a relative link to his world. However, in a sense no one is actually free from karma, not even the enlightened buddhas. The buddhas are not going to retire from their buddhahood to some heavenly realm. They have to help us; they have to work with us. That is their karma and our karma as well.

That is one of the interesting differences between the theistic and the nontheistic approach. In the theistic approach, when we retire from this world, we go to heaven. Once we are in heaven we do not have anything to do with the world. We have no obligations, and we can be happy ever after. But in the nontheistic tradition, even if we attain the state of liberation or openness, we still have debts, because the rest of our brothers and sisters in the world are still in trouble. We have to come back. We can't just hang out in nirvana.

So the vajra master is a human being, someone who has a karmic debt to pay as a result of the intensity of his compassion. The dharma cannot be transmitted from the sun or the moon or the stars. The dharma can only be transmitted properly from human to human. So there is a need for a vajra master who has tremendous power—power over us, power over the cosmos, and power over himself—and who has also been warned that if he misdirects his energy he will be cut down and reduced into a little piece of charcoal.

It is extremely important to have a living vajra master, someone who personally experiences our pain and our pleasure. We have to have a sense of fear and respect that we are connecting and communicating directly with tantra. Making that connection is a very special thing. It is extremely difficult to find a true tantric situation and to meet a true tantric master. Becoming a true tantric student is also very difficult. It is very difficult to find the real thing.

SEVEN

Visualization

IN TANTRA THERE is a sense of continuity, there is a sense of existence, and there is a sense of reality. If we are deeply involved in our experience, then there is a total and profound sense of experiencing reality. Whereas if we have a halfhearted approach to experience, then obviously we get halfhearted results in understanding reality. The tantric approach is complete involvement, which begins with a basic sense of being grounded: in our body, in our house, in our country, on this planet Earth. We are not talking about taking trips to Mars or Jupiter or even to the moon. We are working right here, on this planet Earth. Whether we like it or not, we are here and we have to face that.

This suggestion might seem rather depressing, if we do not want to keep relating with the earth. Of course, the earth has been glorified by descriptions of its beauty: the beautiful flowers and greenery that the earth nurtures, the waterfalls and rivers and fantastic mountains that the earth has provided. But apart from that, the earth seems to be rather hopeless. It is just a solid lump of rock.

We may try to cheer ourselves up by saying: "Wow! Fantastic! I took a trip to the Himalayas and I saw the beautiful mountains of Kanchenjunga and Mount Kailasa." Or we may say: "I saw the Rocky Mountains. I saw the Grand Canyon. Great!" Such remarks are just comic relief. In fact we feel that we are stuck with this earth, and therefore we should glorify it; we should appreciate it. But deep in our hearts, we would like to take off. We would like to fly away into the cosmos, into outer space. We really would like to do that. In particular, anyone seeking spiritual

Chakrasamvara and Vajravarahi. Two of the principal yidams, or "personal deities," of the Kagyü school of Tibetan Buddhism, used in tantric visualization practice. This statue was a shrine object of Naropa, Marpa's guru.
PHOTO BY GEORGE HOLMES AND BLAIR HANSEN.

materialism or spiritual entertainment feels that way: "Wouldn't it be much better if we could leave this earth, our home ground, if we could swim across the galaxies of stars? We could feel the cosmos bubbling, and we could dance in the darkness, and occasionally we would relate with the sun or the planets." The problem with that approach is that we want to neglect our home ground and the familiarity of our highways, our plastic world, our pollution, and all the mundane happenings in our lives. But they are all part of the adornment of living on this earth—whether we like it or not.

What is familiar becomes a part of tantric study, because it is basic to our state of being. Our state of being is grounded in a sense of continual experience, a sense of continual landmarks of all kinds. For instance, our body is a landmark. It marks the fact that we were born on this earth. We do not have to refer back to our birth certificate to make sure that we were born. We know that we are here, our name is such-and-such, our parents are so-and-so. We were born in Louisiana, Texas, Colorado, New York City, Great Neck, or wherever. We were born, and we were raised in our hometown. We went to school and studied and did our homework. We related with other people: We began to play and to fight with the other students, and we began to develop into real boys or girls. Eventually we went to a bigger school, called a university. Then we really began to grow up: We began to take part in politics and philosophy and to experiment with life. We developed opinions of all kinds. Finally we grew up and became men and women—real individuals. Now we are people of the world. As grownups, we might be looking for marriage partners or business contacts, or we might be dropping out of the world and becoming free spokesmen, who do not believe in this crazy society. In any case, as men and women of the world, we make our statements; we develop our philosophy. In tantric language, that experience is called samaya.

Samaya is a basic term in the language of tantra. The Tibetan translation, *tamtsik (dam tshig)*, literally means "sacred word." The fact of life, the actual experience of life, is samaya. Whatever we decide to do, all the trips we go through, all the ways we try to become an individual are personal experience. Fighting for personal rights of all kinds, falling in love or leaving our lover, relating with our parents, making political commitments, relating with our job or our church—all these things are the expression of samaya.

At a certain point in our life, we begin to live on our own. We may try to reject any interdependence as fast and as hard as we can. Although it is impossible to be completely independent, we still try to be so. We try to get any factors out of our system that seem to bind us. We feel that we have been imprisoned by our parents, by society, by the economy, or by our religion. So we try to get out of those prisons and we try to get into expressing our personal freedom. On the other hand, rather than rebelling, we might choose to get into a certain church or a particular social environment based on a sense of our own personal choice. That could also express our freedom, because we were never told to do that—we just decided personally to do it. When we commit ourselves to the world, whether as a reaction to constraints or as a decision to get into something new, that is called samaya, sacred word, or sacred vow.

Whether we are pushed, and we begin to give in and then slowly we get into the system, or whether we are pushed and we reject the system completely, that is an expression of independence in our personal mental functioning. Any move we make to join a society, organization, or church is based on our own personal experience rather than just tradition or history. On the other hand, breaking away from anything that we feel entraps us is also based on personal experience. Therefore, the commitments and choices that we make are called sacred word, or sacred bondage—which are saying the same thing. Samaya can be interpreted as sacred bondage, although literally it means sacred word, because we are bound by certain norms, certain processes that organize our experience. When we accept those boundaries as our own, that is the sacred bondage of samaya.

In the tantric practice of visualization, we visualize what is known as the samayasattva. *Sattva* literally means "being," "individual," or "person." Samaya, as we discussed, means acknowledging connections and being willing to bow down to the experience of life. Sattva is the being who experiences the situation of samaya. So in visualizing the samayasattva we are acknowledging our experience of life and our willingness to commit ourselves to it. We acknowledge that we are willing to enter fully into life.

Visualization is a central practice of tantra. It not only encompasses visual perception, but it is also a way of relating with all sense perceptions—visual, auditory, tactile, mental—with the entire range of sensory experience, all at the same time. As well, it should be obvious from our discussion of samaya that visualization is a way of relating to our state of mind and a way of working with our experience.

In order to begin the tantric practice of visualization, we must have gone through the disciplines of hinayana and mahayana already, and we must have done preliminary vajrayana practices as well. Then when we receive abhisheka, we are given a deity to visualize, a samayasattva connected with our own makeup, our basic being. Whether we are an intellectual person, or an aggressive person, or a passionate person, or whatever we are, in accordance with our particular qualities, a certain deity is given to us by our vajra master, who knows us personally and is familiar with our particular style. The deity that we visualize or identify with is part of our makeup. We may be outrageously aggressive, outrageously passionate, outrageously proud, outrageously ignorant, or outrageously lustful—whatever our basic makeup may be, that complex of emotions is connected with enlightenment. None of those qualities or emotional styles are regarded as obstacles. They are related with our personal experience of a sense of being, a sense of existence. If we must exist in lust, let us abide in our lust; if we must exist in anger, let us abide in our anger. Let us live in our anger. Let us do it. Let us be that way.

Therefore, we visualize a deity that is connected with our own particular qualities and our commitment to ourselves and to our experience. Having visualized that deity, called the samayasattva of our basic being, then we invite what is known as the jnanasattva. The jnanasattva is another being or level of experience that we are inviting into our system; however, it is nothing particularly extraordinary or fantastic. Jnana is a state of wakefulness or openness, whereas samaya is an experience of bondage, or being solidly grounded in our experience. The samayasattva is basically at the level of body and speech, whereas the jnanasattva is an awakening quality that comes from beyond that level. Jnanasattva is the quality of openness or a sense of cosmic principle. At the same time, jnana is a fundamentally cynical attitude toward life, which is also a humorous attitude.

In this case humor does not mean being nasty or making fun of people. Instead it is constantly being fascinated and amused in a positive sense. We may be amused at how somebody eats his spaghetti. He does it in such a personal way, and the way he eats his spaghetti seems to be very healthy and, at the same time, humorous. It is not that the person is funny in a cheap sense, but that the person has the courage to eat his spaghetti in a direct and beautiful way. He actually tastes the spaghetti, and he uses it properly, productively. There is a sense of healthiness in seeing that person handle his universe properly.

Jnana is experiencing a feeling of humor and fascination about everything and realizing that everything is being handled properly—even on the inanimate level. Flowers grow, rocks sit, pine trees are there. These things are unique, personal, and very real. So the humor of jnana is entirely different from the basic bondage of samaya. With jnana there is a real feeling of upliftedness and appreciation. When we see somebody doing something, we appreciate that he is not just conducting his affairs, but he conducts them fully, artfully, and humorously.

Jnana literally means "wisdom" or, more accurately, "being wise." Wisdom implies an entity, a body of wisdom that we could learn or experience, such as "the wisdom of the ages." But jnana is the *state* of being wise, a spontaneous and personal state of experience. In the term *jnanasattva, jnana* is this state of wisdom, and *sattva* again is "being." But in this case *sattva* expresses the sense of being at a humorous and open level.

The goal in all tantric traditions is to bring together the lofty idea, the jnanasattva of humor and openness, with the samayasattva, which is the bodily or physical orientation of existence. The practice of visualization is connected with that process of combining the jnanasattva and the samayasattva. In a sense, the level of jnanasattva is free from visualization. We do not have to visualize jnanasattvas as such: They just come along. They just float down from the sky and join our own cluttered and clumsy visualization; they simply dissolve into our clutteredness.

EIGHT

Body, Speech, and Mind

AN IMPORTANT PRINCIPLE in the tantric tradition is the role of body, speech, and mind in our relationship with the cosmos or the world. The vajrayana teachings place great importance on these principles. In fact, the notion of vajra nature is developing vajra—indestructible—body, vajra speech, and vajra mind. We all have certain ideas about what body is, what speech is, and what mind is, but we should examine the tantric understanding, which could be quite different from our ordinary associations.

The sensory world of the body obviously includes shapes, colors, and sounds. That is quite simple. We all know that. At the same time, the body has a divine or transcendental aspect. There is a transcendental aspect because bodies are not really bodies, shapes are not really shapes, and sounds, sights, colors, and touchable objects are not really there. At the same time they *are* actually there. That kind of phenomenal play between existence and nonexistence takes place all the time, and we are pushed back and forth. In general, either we say that we are *not* there and we hold on to that particular metaphysical argument, or else we say that we *are* there and we try to hold on to *that* metaphysical standpoint. But in tantra we cannot hold on to either of those views. We cannot hold on to any of our sense perceptions or experiences.

Things are there because they are not there—otherwise they could not exist. They are there because they are dependent on their nonexistence. Things cannot exist unless they can not-exist. A white poodle crossing the highway is *not* a white poodle, because her whiteness de-

73

pends on blackness. Therefore the white poodle *is* a white poodle, because the whiteness depends on blackness. A white poodle crossing the highway is definitely a white poodle because she is not a black poodle. At the same time there is no highway. It is very simple logic; in fact it is simple-minded: The crescent moon is a crescent moon because it is not a full moon. But on the basis of that very simple logic we can build fascinating and sophisticated logic: I exist because I do not exist; you exist because you do not exist; I exist and you exist because I do not exist; and you and I exist because we do not exist. To understand that type of logic requires training, but it is actually true. Once we look into that system of thinking, the sun is black because it is bright, daytime is nighttime because it is daytime, and so forth.

The experience of body or shape or form is usually such a hassle for us that we cannot solve problems of logic. At the tantric level, the logic of believing in being or form, believing in the actuality of physically existing here right now—I have my body and I am fat or I am thin—begins to become a problem, and at the same time, it becomes a source of study. The body exists because of its bodyness. That might be our psychological attitude. But when we again ask what bodyness is, we discover it is nonbodyness. We cannot find an answer, because answers always run out. That is both the problem and the promise.

The vajra mandala of body refers to that back-and-forth play: Things are seemingly there, but at the same time they are questionable. That play gives us enormous ground to work with. We do not have to work our hearts and brains to their extreme limits so that we finally become mad professors of tantra. Instead we can work and relate with that play of experience. At the level of the vajra mandala of body, our experience of the world becomes entirely phenomenological. It is a much more personal experience than even existentialists talk about. It is entirely phenomenological, and yet it transcends the notion of phenomenological experience, because the phenomena do not actually exist.

Next is the role of speech. We are considering speech from the same phenomenological perspective as body. We are taking the same logical stance, but we are approaching our experience from a slightly different angle. At the level of speech, there is much more movement, much more shiftiness and dancelike quality than in our experience of the body. The vajra mandala of speech refers to the mandala of letters, which are traditionally seen as symbols and seed syllables. Relating to the mandala of letters does not mean being literate, or being an educated person. Instead it is the notion of seeing the world in terms of letters: A-B-C-D. The phenomenal world actually spells itself out in letters and even sentences that we read, or experience.

Through the mandala of speech, the world is seen as a world of syllables, a world of letters. My friend is made out of *A*. My lover is made out of B-X. My sister is made out of B-B. My brother is made out of B-A. Everybody has his own symbol. Everything stands for its own point of reference, which we can read. But at the same time it is a subtle language. Today is a B-day because the sun is shining and it is hot. Tomorrow might be an X-day if it is raining. The next day might be a Y-day if it is partly cloudy and partly clear. Or, today is an extremely K-day because it is so cold and snowy. Hopefully tomorrow will be an N-day, which is partially warm and partially cold. The entire world, every experience, is made out of letters from that point of view. According to tantric Sanskrit literature, the world is made up of fourteen vowels and thirty-three consonants. But we have to have a personal experience of that.

Understanding the mandala of speech is basic to how we raise children. From the beginning of their infancy, children begin to read us. They read mommy, they read daddy, and they read how we handle ourselves. They read us opening a bottle or a can. They read how we undo a box of chocolates. They can read the world in the same way that we do. The whole process starts right at the beginning, in infancy. We were all children once upon a time. In fact we still may be children in some sense, because we are all learning to read the world. We learn to read books; we learn to read highways; we learn to read motorcars; we learn to read our own minds. Reading takes place constantly. Because we read a face, the next time we see someone we recognize that person; because they also read us, they know who we are as well. In the same way that we read books, we read each other. We read constantly.

But a problem occurs when we do not have any new reading material and when the reading material that we already have has been memorized by heart. When something is interesting or challenging to us, we don't just skip over it quickly; we pause to read carefully. But when we find that we are reading something familiar, we are dying to get on to the next paragraph, and we rush. We are constantly looking for entertainment. We don't really want to read the pages of life properly and we panic; we actually panic tremendously. From the tantric perspective, that panic is called neurosis. We run out of reading material and we panic. Or we begin to find spelling mistakes. When we finally become smart enough to notice them, we cease to take a humorous attitude and we begin to panic. We begin to criticize the editor of the journal of the world.

On the spiritual level, when people experience the neurosis of speech, sometimes they think they have opened their sound chakras: "Now I can be verbose and accurate in what I have to say, and I can speak very fast." But there is some kind of problem with that approach; it is actually a reading impediment. When somebody has opened his sound chakra, he does not have to speak so fast. He does not have to write poetry suddenly or become a completely verbose person. There is something fishy about that, something sacrilegious. That is disregarding the world-mandala of letters and syllables.

Next is the level of mind. Mind in this case is very simple; in fact, it is simple-mindedness. We are not talking about the mind that thinks, but the mind that feels in a haphazard way. Such mind does not depend on whether we are educated or not. We are simply talking about the mind that feels different things in different ways. On the naive or ignorant level, the functioning of mind brings an experience of nonexistence in the negative sense. We are afraid, and we do not have enough guts to realize that the phenomenal world is magical. At the tantric level, the positive experience of nonexistence comes about when the mind is completely turned into the magical possibilities of life. At the level of the vajra mandala of mind, subconscious gossip, or the continual background chatter and ongoing commentary of our thoughts, is completely cut through. Mind is completely open. This vajra experience of mind creates a continuous celebration in dealing with life directly and simply. At the vajra level of mind, every situation takes place very simply, on its own, and mind relates with whatever arises quite simply.

NINE

The Five Buddha Families

TANTRA IS extraordinarily special, and extremely real and personal. The question in this chapter is how to relate our own ordinary existence or daily situation to tantric consciousness. The tantric approach is not just to make sweeping statements about reality and to create calmness and a meditative state. It is more than learning to be creative and contemplative. In tantra we relate with the details of our everyday life according to our own particular makeup. It is a real and personal experience. But in order to relate to our lives in the tantric fashion, there are certain technical details of tantric experience that we have to understand.

The tantric discipline of relating to life is based on what are known as the five buddha principles, or the five buddha families. These principles are traditionally known as families because they are an extension of ourselves in the same way that our blood relations are an extension of us: we have our daddy, we have our mommy, we have our sisters and brothers, and they are all part of our family. But we could also say that these relatives are principles: our motherness, our fatherness, our sisterness, our brotherness, and our me-ness are experienced as definite principles that have distinct characteristics. In the same way, the tantric tradition speaks of five families: five principles, categories, or possibilities.

Those five principles or buddha families are called vajra, ratna, padma, karma, and buddha. They are quite ordinary. There is nothing divine or extraordinary about them. The basic point is that at the tantric level people are divided into particular types: vajra, ratna, padma, karma,

Vajra and ghanta (bell).
PHOTO BY GEORGE HOLMES.

and buddha. We constantly come across members of every one of the five families—people who are partially or completely one of those five. We find such people all through life, and every one of them is a fertile person, a workable person who could be related with directly and personally. So, from the tantric point of view, by relating directly with all the different people we encounter, we are actually relating with different styles of enlightenment.

The buddha family, or families, associated with a person describes his or her fundamental style, that person's intrinsic perspective or stance in perceiving the world and working with it. Each family is associated with both a neurotic and an enlightened style. The neurotic expression of any buddha family can be transmuted into its wisdom or enlightened aspect. As well as describing people's styles, the buddha families are also associated with colors, elements, landscapes, directions, seasons—with any aspect of the phenomenal world.

The first buddha family is the vajra family, which literally means the family of sharpness, crystallization, and indestructibility. The term *vajra* is superficially translated as "diamond," but that is not quite accurate. Traditionally, vajra is a celestial precious stone that cuts through any other solid object. So it is more than a diamond; it is complete indestructibility. The vajra family is symbolized by the vajra scepter, or *dorje* in Tibetan. This vajra scepter or superdiamond has five prongs, which represent relating to the five emotions: aggression, pride, passion, jealousy, and ignorance. The sharp edges or prongs of the vajra represent cutting through any neurotic emotional tendencies; they also represent the sharp quality of being aware of many possible perspectives. The indestructible vajra is said to be like a heap of razor blades: if we naively try to hold it or touch it, there are all kinds of sharp edges that are both cutting and penetrating. The notion here is that vajra corrects or remedies any neurotic distortion in a precise and sharp way.

In the ordinary world, the experience of vajra is perhaps not as extreme as holding razor blades in our hand, but at the same time, it is penetrating and very personal. It is like a sharp, cutting, biting-cold winter. Each time we expose ourselves to the open air, we get frostbite instantly. Intellectually vajra is very sharp. All the intellectual traditions belong to this family. A person in the vajra family knows how to evaluate logically the arguments that are used to explain experience. He can tell whether the logic is true or false. Vajra family intellect also has a sense of constant openness and perspective. For instance, a vajra person could view a crystal ball from hundreds of perspectives, according to where it was placed, the way it was perceived, the distance from which he was looking at it, and so forth. The intellect of the vajra family is not just encyclopedic; it is sharpness, directness, and awareness of perspectives. Such indestructibility and sharpness are very personal and very real.

The neurotic expression of vajra is associated with anger and intellectual fixation. If we become fixated on a particular logic, the sharpness of vajra can become rigidity. We become possessive of our insight, rather than having a sense of open perspective. The anger of vajra neurosis could be pure aggression or also a sense of uptightness because we are so attached to our sharpness of mind. Vajra is also associated with the element of water. Cloudy, turbulent water symbolizes the defensive and aggressive nature of anger, while clear water suggests the sharp, precise, clear reflectiveness of vajra wisdom. In fact, vajra wisdom is traditionally called the mirrorlike wisdom, which evokes this image of a calm pond or reflecting pool.

Incidentally, the use of the term *vajra* in such words as *vajrayana, vajra master,* and *vajra pride* does not refer to this particular buddha family, but simply expresses basic indestructibility.

The next buddha family is ratna. Ratna is a personal and real sense of expanding ourselves and enriching our environment. It is expansion, enrichment, plentifulness. Such plentifulness could also have problems and weaknesses. In the neurotic sense, the richness of ratna manifests as being completely fat, or extraordinarily ostentatious, beyond the limits of our sanity. We expand constantly, open heedlessly, and indulge ourselves to the level of insanity. It is like swimming in a dense lake of honey and butter. When we coat ourselves in this mixture of butter and honey, it is very difficult to remove. We cannot just remove it by wiping it off, but we have to apply all kinds of cleaning agents, such as cleanser and soap, to loosen its grasp.

In the positive expression of the ratna family, the principle of richness is extraordinary. We feel very rich and plentiful, and we extend ourselves to our world personally, directly, emotionally, psychologically, even spiritually. We are extending constantly, expanding like a flood or an earthquake. There is a sense of spreading, shaking the earth, and creating more and more cracks in it. That is the powerful expansiveness of ratna.

The enlightened expression of ratna is called the wisdom of equanimity, because ratna can include everything in its expansive environment. Thus ratna is associated with the element of earth. It is like a rotting log that makes itself at home in the country. Such a log does not want to leave its home ground. It would like to stay, but at the same time, it grows all kinds of mushrooms and plants and allows animals to nest in it. That lazy settling down and making ourselves at home, and inviting other people to come in and rest as well, is ratna.

The next family is padma, which literally means "lotus flower." The symbol of the enlightened padma family is the lotus, which grows and blooms in the mud, yet still comes out pure and clean, virginal and clear. Padma neurosis is connected with passion, a grasping quality and a desire to possess. We are completely wrapped up in desire and want only to seduce the world, without concern for real communication. We could be a hustler or an advertiser, but basically, we are like a peacock. In fact, Amitabha Buddha, the buddha of the padma family, traditionally sits on a peacock, which represents subjugating padma neurosis. A person with padma neurosis speaks gently, fantastically gently, and he or she is seemingly very sexy, kind, magnificent, and completely accommodating: "If you hurt me, that's fine. That is part of our love affair. Come toward me." Such padma seduction sometimes becomes excessive and sometimes becomes compassionate, depending on how we work with it.

Padma is connected with the element of fire. In the confused state, fire does not distinguish among the things it grasps, burns, and destroys. But in the awakened state, the heat of passion is transmuted into the warmth of compassion. When padma neurosis is transmuted, it becomes fantastically precise and aware; it turns into tremendous interest and inquisitiveness. Everything is seen in its own distinct way, with its own particular qualities and characteristics. Thus the wisdom of padma is called discriminating-awareness wisdom.

The genuine character of padma seduction is real openness, a willingness to demonstrate what we have and what we are to the phenomenal world. What we bring to the world is a sense of pleasure, a sense of promise. In whatever we experience, we begin to feel that there is lots of promise. We constantly experience a sense of magnetization and spontaneous hospitality.

This quality of padma is like bathing in perfume or jasmine tea. Each time we bathe, we feel refreshed, fantastic. It feels good to be magnetized. The sweet air is fantastic and the hospitality of our host is magnificent. We eat the good food provided by our host, which is delicious, but not too filling. We live in a world of honey and milk, in a very delicate sense, unlike the rich but heavy experience of the ratna family. Fantastic! Even our bread is scented with all kinds of delicious smells. Our ice cream is colored by beautiful pink lotus-like colors. We cannot wait to eat. Sweet music is playing in the background constantly. When there is no music, we listen to the whistling of the wind around our padma environment, and it becomes beautiful music as well. Even though we are not musicians, we compose all kinds of music. We wish we were a poet or a fantastic lover.

The next family is the karma family, which is a different kettle of fish. In this case we are not talking about karmic debts, or karmic consequences; karma in this case simply means "action." The neurotic quality of action or activity is connected with jealousy, comparison, and envy. The enlightened aspect of karma is called the wisdom of all-accomplishing action. It is the transcendental sense of complete fulfillment of action without being hassled or pushed into neurosis. It is natural fulfillment in how we relate with our world. In either case, whether we relate to karma family on the transcendental level or the neurotic level, karma is the energy of efficiency.

If we have a karma family neurosis, we feel highly irritated if we see a hair on our teacup. First we think that our cup is broken and that the hair is a crack in the cup. Then there is some relief. Our cup is not broken; it just has a piece of hair on the side. But then, when we begin to look at the hair on our cup of tea, we become angry all over again. We would like to make everything very efficient, pure, and absolutely clean. However, if we do achieve cleanliness, then that cleanliness itself becomes a further problem: We feel insecure because there is nothing to administer, nothing to work on. We constantly try to check every loose end. Being very keen on efficiency, we get hung up on it.

If we meet a person who is not efficient, who does not have his life together, we regard him as a terrible person. We would like to get rid of such inefficient people, and certainly we do not respect them, even if they are talented musicians or scientists or whatever they may be. On the other hand, if someone has immaculate efficiency, we begin to feel that he is a good person to be with. We would like to associate ourselves exclusively with people who are both responsible and clean-cut. However, we find that we are envious and jealous of such efficient people. We want others to be efficient, but not more efficient than we are.

The epitome of karma family neurosis is wanting to create a uniform world. Even though we might have very little philosophy, very little meditation, very little consciousness in terms of developing ourselves, we feel that we can handle our world properly. We have composure, and we relate properly with the whole world, and we are resentful that everybody else does not see things in the same way that we do. Karma is connected with the element of wind. The wind never blows in all directions but it blows in one direction at a time. This is the one-way view of resentment and envy, which picks on one little fault or virtue and blows it out of proportion. With karma wisdom, the quality of resentment falls away but the qualities of energy, fulfillment of action, and openness remain. In other words, the active aspect of wind is retained so that our energetic activity touches everything in its path. We see the possibilities inherent in situations and automatically take the appropriate course. Action fulfills its purpose.

The fifth family is called the buddha family. It is associated with the element of space. Buddha energy is the foundation or the basic space. It is the environment or oxygen that makes it possible for the other principles to function. It has a sedate, solid quality. Persons in this family have a strong sense of contemplative experience, and they are highly meditative. Buddha neurosis is the quality of being spaced-out rather than spacious. It is often associated with an unwillingness to express ourselves. For example, we might see that our neighbors are destroying our picket fence with a sledgehammer. We can hear them and see them; in fact, we have been watching our neighbors at work all day, continuously smashing our picket fence. But instead of reacting, we just observe them and then we return to our snug little home. We eat our breakfast, lunch, and dinner and ignore what they are doing. We are paralyzed, unable to talk to outsiders.

Another quality of buddha neurosis is that we couldn't be bothered. Our dirty laundry is piled up in a corner of our room. Sometimes we use our dirty laundry to wipe up spills on the floor or table and then we put it back on the same pile. As time goes on, our dirty socks become unbearable, but we just sit there.

If we are embarking on a political career, our colleagues may suggest that we develop a certain project and expand our organization. If we have a buddha neurosis, we will choose to develop the area that needs the least effort. We do not want to deal directly with the details of handling reality. Entertaining friends is also a hassle. We prefer to take our friends to a restaurant rather than cook in our home. And if we want to have a love affair, instead of seducing a partner, talking to him or her and making friends, we just look for somebody who is already keen on us. We cannot be bothered with talking somebody into something.

Sometimes we feel we are sinking into the earth, the solid mud and earth. Sometimes we feel good because we think we are the most stable person in the universe. We slowly begin to grin to ourselves, smile at ourselves, because we are the best person of all. We are the only person who manages to stay stable. But sometimes we feel that we are the loneliest person in the whole universe. We do not particularly like to dance, and when we are asked to dance with somebody, we feel embarrassed and uncomfortable. We want to stay in our own little corner.

When the ignoring quality of buddha neurosis is transmuted into wisdom, it becomes an environment of all-pervasive spaciousness. This enlightened aspect is called the wisdom of all-encompassing space. In itself it might still have a somewhat desolate and empty quality, but at the same time, it is a quality of completely open potential. It can accommodate anything. It is spacious and vast like the sky.

In tantric iconography, the five buddha families are arrayed in the center and the four cardinal points of a mandala. The mandala of the five buddha families of course represents their wisdom or enlightened aspect. Traditionally, the buddha family is in the center. That is to say, in the center there is the basic coordination and basic wisdom of buddha, which is symbolized by a wheel and the color white. Vajra is in the east, because vajra is connected with the dawn. It is also connected with the color blue and is symbolized by the vajra scepter. It is the sharpness of experience, as in the morning when we wake up. We begin to see the dawn, when light is first reflected on the world, as a symbol of awakening reality.

Ratna is in the south. It is connected with richness and is symbolized by a jewel and the color yellow. Ratna is connected with the midday, when we begin to need refreshment, nourishment. Padma is in the west and is symbolized by the lotus and the color red. As our day gets older, we also have to relate with recruiting a lover. It is time to socialize, to make a date with our lover. Or, if we have fallen in love with an antique or if we have fallen in love with some clothing, it is time to go out and buy it. The last family is karma, in the north. It is symbolized by a sword and the color green. Finally we have captured the whole situation: We have everything we need, and there is nothing more to get. We have brought our merchandise back home or our lover back home, and we say, "Let's close the door; let's lock it." So the mandala of the five buddha families represents the progress of a whole day or a whole course of action.

Without understanding the five buddha families, we have no working basis to relate with tantra, and we begin to find ourselves alienated from tantra. Tantra is seen as such an outrageous thing, which seems to have no bearing on us as individuals. We may feel the vajrayana is purely a distant aim, a distant goal. So it is necessary to study the five buddha principles. They provide a bridge between tantric experience and everyday life.

It is necessary to understand and relate with the five buddha principles *before* we begin tantric discipline, so that we can begin to understand what tantra is all about. If tantra is a mystical experience, how can we relate it to our ordinary everyday life at home? There could be a big gap between tantric experience and day-to-day life. But it is possible, by understanding the five buddha families, to close the gap. Working with the buddha families we discover that we already have certain qualities. According to the tantric perspective, we cannot ignore them and we cannot reject them and try to be something else. We have our aggression and our passion and our jealousy and our resentment and our ignorance—or whatever we have. We belong to certain buddha families already, and we cannot reject them. We should work with our neuroses, relate with them, and experience them properly. They are the only potential we have, and when we begin to work with them, we see that we can use them as stepping-stones.

TEN

Abhisheka

I N AN EARLIER CHAPTER we discussed the basic meaning of transmission. At this point we could go further in our understanding and discuss some of the details. Basically, transmission is the meeting of two minds. Understanding this is absolutely necessary. Otherwise, there is no way out and no way in—there is no way to enter the vajrayana, even if we have already been trained in the basic Buddhist teachings. The formal experience of transmission takes place at a ceremony that is called an abhisheka. The particular form of the abhisheka that we receive is suited to our own basic being or basic psychological state, and it also depends on the particular level of tantric practice that is appropriate for us. So altogether there is a need to respect the nature of transmission itself, the form of transmission, and also a need to respect our own attitude in receiving transmission.

In order to receive transmission, we must be willing to commit ourselves to the fundamental trust, or the potential for trust, that exists as the working basis of the student-teacher relationship. This attitude of trust is extremely important in tantra. When we speak of trust in the tantric sense, we mean the actual experience of trusting in ourselves. There is a sense of genuine compassion toward ourselves, but without any self-indulgence. We are gentle and straightforward, but we are no longer playing the game of idiot compassion, using false kindness to protect ourselves unnecessarily. We also are completely free of spiritual materialism. There is a sense of one hundred percent fresh air: Things are clear and there is circulation, freshness, and understanding in our system.

Our life feels quite okay. There is nothing to worry about, nothing to be that concerned about. That does not mean that all our problems have been solved and that everything is milk and honey. There is still a sense of struggle, but it has become very healthy. It is a learning process, a working process. In fact, struggle becomes the fuel for the bright burning flames of our energy.

When we have that attitude of trust, we can go further with the discipline of tantra and enter the samaya, or sacred bondage, of receiving abhisheka. When trust has been established as the working basis between student and teacher, mutual understanding and mutual openness take place constantly. There is openness to the tradition that exists, to the lineage, to ourselves, to our fellow students, and to our root guru—the actual performer of the abhisheka. The root guru is our vajra master, and he is the person who actually initiates us and gives us the abhisheka. So once we have that basic background of trust and openness, and once we have prepared ourselves properly, then we can receive abhisheka.

There are several divisions or levels of transmission that are part of an abhisheka. Each level is itself called an abhisheka, because it is a particular empowerment or transmission. Here we will discuss the first level, the first abhisheka, the abhisheka of form, which is a process of thoroughly training the student so that he is prepared and can enter the magic circle or mandala of the abhisheka properly. The abhisheka of form is a process of bringing the student up, raising him or her from the level of an infant to a king or queen. We will discuss this process in detail a little further on.

Traditionally, in medieval India and Tibet, the date for an abhisheka was set six months in advance. In that way students would have six months to prepare. Later the tantric tradition became extremely available, and some of the teachers in Tibet dropped that six-month rule—which seems to have been a big mistake. If we do not have enough time to prepare ourselves for an abhisheka, then the message doesn't come across. There is no real experience. That suspense—knowing that we are just about to receive an abhisheka but that, at the same time, we are suspended for six months—is extremely important. We have no idea what we are going to do. The text of the abhisheka may have already been presented to us, but still we have no idea what we are going to experience. In the meantime, we have six months to study how to handle ourselves and how to relate with the experience of abhisheka, which is described and explained in minute detail in the text.

The number of people who are going to receive a particular abhisheka is also very important. A certain chemistry takes place within a group of individuals and between certain types of people. Maybe twenty or twenty-five students should receive abhisheka, or maybe only three. It is at the discretion of the vajra master to decide on the number of students and to choose the particular students to be initiated, because he knows the students' development and their understanding. Receiving abhisheka is an extremely precious event. And the psychology that happens between the people involved and the environment that such people create together is right at the heart of the matter.

Receiving abhisheka is not the same as collecting coins or stamps or the signatures of famous people. Receiving hundreds and hundreds of abhishekas and constantly collecting blessing after blessing as some kind of self-confirmation has at times become a fad, a popular thing to do. This was true in Tibet in the nineteenth century as well as more recently in the West. That attitude, which reflects the recent corruption in the presentation of vajrayana, has created an enormous misunderstanding. People who collect successive abhishekas in this manner regard them purely as a source of identity and as a further reference point. They collect abhishekas out of a need for security, which is a big problem.

Jamgön Kongrül the Great, a Tibetan teacher who lived in the nineteenth century, was raised and educated as an enlightened student of vajrayana. Because he received so many transmissions, it might seem that he was doing the same thing—collecting abhishekas. But in his case it was an entirely different process because he felt, he experienced, and he understood what he studied. After he finished his basic training, he studied under and received all the teachings from more than one hundred and thirty-five teachers. Then he initiated a reformation of Buddhism in Tibet, which he called the Ri-me school. The term Ri-me literally mans "without bias," an "ecumenical approach." The Ri-me school brought together the various contemplative traditions of Tibetan Buddhism to create a powerful practicing lineage, which we ourselves belong to. My predecessor, the tenth Trungpa tulku, also belonged to that lineage.

The Ri-me school made an enormous impression. For one thing, it generated a great deal of sarcasm and jealousy on the part of some practitioners: "Why make a big deal out of nothing? Why can't we just go on as we were and continue to buy abhishekas? What's wrong with what we are doing?" But Jamgön Kongtrül had seen that something was wrong with the tradition and practice; something was wrong with receiving a succession of abhishekas purely as collector's items. He pointed out that problem by saying that if we have no understanding of the practicing lineage then we are just collecting piles of manure, and there is no point in that. A pile of manure may be ripe, smelly, and fantastic, but it is still a pile of shit. If we were manure experts, we could utilize it. But when we are actually collecting such manure to try to make it into food, that is out of the question.

This kind of spiritual materialism was present in Tibet from the nineteenth century onward. Tibet had lost its communication with the outside world and was no longer hosting great teachers from other countries. It had become just a little plateau, a little island that had to survive by itself. Consequently, it became too inbred. In that atmosphere spiritual materialism began to develop. Abbots and great teachers were more concerned with building solid gold roofs on their temples, constructing gigantic Buddha images, and making their temples beautiful and impressive than with the actual practice of their lineage. They sat less and they did more business.

That was the turning point of Buddhism in Tibet. Tibet began to lose its connection with dharma, and it slowly, very irritatingly and horrifically, began to turn into ugly spiritual materialism. Jamgön Kongtrül the Great was like a jewel in a pile of manure. His wisdom was shining. He saw that it was necessary to call upon the eight great traditions of Buddhism in Tibet—which included the Geluk tradition, the Sakya tradition, the Kagyü tradition, and the Nyingma tradition—and bring them together: "Let us unite; let us work together within this contemplative tradition. Let us experience this tradition for ourselves, instead of inviting hundreds of artists to build glorious shrines. Let us experience how it feels to sit on our meditation cushions and do nothing." This reintroduction of practice, which had long been forgotten, was the focus of the contemplative reformation of Tibetan Buddhism during the nineteenth century.

As part of his effort to revitalize the contemplative tradition and bring together practice and experience, Jamgön Kongtrül compiled and edited many collections of the sacred teachings of the practice lineage of Buddhism in Tibet. One of these works is entitled *Dam Ngag Dzö*, which literally means "The Treasury of Oral Instructions." In it he describes how a person can properly experience abhisheka. In this commentary he also describes how tantric students should be treated in such a ceremony of empowerment. It is not purely that the ritual and ceremony should inspire awe in the students. In fact, they may be awed simply because they have no idea how to behave, how to handle themselves, or how to handle their state of mind in that situation. Consequently they become bewildered and feel overwhelmed. Jamgön Kongtrül explains that this mixture of inadequacy and awe is not the experience of the meeting of two minds.

You cannot take advantage of students if they do not know how to deal with the ceremony. When students feel freaked out, they have no handle or stepping-stone, so they should be treated gently, freely, and kindly. They should have some understanding of the steps in the process they are about to go through: "This ceremony has such and such levels. First you relate with this, and then you can go on to the next level." Students should be guided as a mother raises her infant. She starts out by nursing her child, then she feeds him milk from a cow, then she feds him broth, and finally she begins to introduce solid food. When the infant has been raised into a proper child, he knows how to drink liquid and how to chew and swallow meat. He even knows how to drink soup and eat vegetables at the same time.

Initiating tantric students in an abhisheka is precisely the same process. At the beginning of the ceremony the students are not capable of doing anything; they simply experience oneness. They are like infants who have not yet learned to drink cow's milk instead of their own mother's milk. Then the students begin to realize that their openness allows them to relate to the world and to emotions. At that stage they are fascinated by the ceremony and fascinated by the tantric tradition altogether. Finally, the students begin to feel that they are actually grasping the teachings and that the teachings make sense. They mean something personally, experientially. The students then can relate with the principles of the five buddha families. At that point in the abhisheka, the teacher presents, or confers, what are known as the five abhishekas of form, which are directly related to the five buddha families. Each one is an empowerment, and together they make up the first abhisheka.

This presentation of the first abhisheka is based on the tradition of anuttara yoga, which is the pinnacle of the three lower tantric yanas. According to the tradition of anuttarayoga, the first abhisheka of form is the abhisheka of the jar or vase. Actually, this abhisheka is symbolic of bathing. According to the custom in medieval India, when a person wanted to bathe himself, he would go out into a river with a jar, scoop up a jarful of water, and pour it over himself. So the jar abhisheka is a process of purifying. We are cleaning out the hidden corners of the body, seeing that our ears are clean and our armpits are clean. Any hidden corners in our basic makeup have to be cleansed.

In this case, the purification is obviously psychological. Psychologically we have smelly armpits that generate lots of odor for our neighbors and ourselves. We begin to dislike that psychological odor, and our neighbors might begin to dislike it as well. In fact, we feel completely revolted, which is a very positive step at this point because we actually have the means to clean up properly.

You may remember that the word *abhisheka* literally means "anointment." Through the vase abhisheka, we are cleaned out completely. It is similar to the Christian tradition of baptism or christening, which also makes use of water as a symbol of psychologically cleansing oneself. If we go to the bathroom just before we have lunch, we wash our hands. That is a basic and sensible law of human conduct: We should taste our food rather than our excrement when we eat. The vase abhisheka is the same kind of sensible approach. It is connected with the vajra family. Water is a symbol of the sharpness and the clarity of vajra, which cleanses us of any psychological dirt. Then, when we are cleaned out and fundamentally purified, we can put on our clean clothes.

In an abhisheka, the students are regarded as princesses and princes who are coming to court. They are just about to sit on the throne and relate with their subjects, that is, with their subconscious gossip, their mind, their samsaric world. So the idea of abhisheka is receiving royal treatment. The Tibetan word for abhisheka is *wang (dbang),* which simply means "empowerment." The student is empowered as the royal ruler, the majestic one.

Before he gives an audience to the public, a king first bathes and puts on his clothes. Then he puts on his crown. That is the second abhisheka, the crown or coronation abhisheka. In this abhisheka, the student is presented with a crown which has five prongs and is inlaid with jewels. Each prong represents a different buddha family: vajra, ratna, padma, karma, and buddha. Finally we are coronated: We are made into a tantric master, or at least a confident practitioner, a confident person. The crown abhisheka is connected with the ratna family. There is a sense of being enriched and a sense of plentifulness, lack of threat, openness, and generosity.

At this point in the abhisheka we are like a young king who is very ambitious and youthful, but still does not know how to handle his subjects. Although we have been coronated, our hands are just resting in our lap and we have nothing to hold on to. In that condition we could feel quite self-conscious: there is a big crown sitting on our head and we are dressed up in robes but our hands are just loose. We could pick our nose or scratch our chin, but we still feel awkward. At this point we are presented with the third abhisheka, the abhisheka of the vajra. The idea is to give a royal toy to this little prince or princess. The first toy we receive, which should be given to us in the right hand, is the vajra scepter, or dorje, which we discussed earlier as the symbol of indestructibility. It represents immense power. Seven qualities characterize the vajra: It cannot be cut, it cannot be disintegrated, it cannot be obstructed, it is penetrating, it is fearless, it is open, and it is utterly destructive. According to tradition, the vajra is a weapon as well as a scepter. Each time the king throws the vajra, it goes out, it fulfills its deadly purpose, and it comes back into his hand.

The abhisheka of the vajra is related to the padma family. Padma here is the sense of being a beautiful lover. In this abhisheka you are acknowledged as a powerful person and at the same time you are told that you can make love without destroying somebody else. Rather, you could create by making love. So holding the vajra brings a feeling of compassion, warmth, and hospitality.

In the next abhisheka, the abhisheka of the bell, not only does the student have a scepter in the right hand, but as a royal personage, he or she also receives a musical instrument, a bell, in the left hand. The musical instrument signifies that we are not only concerned with our own compassion, our own crown, or our own cleanliness, but we have something to say. Rather than playing by ourselves with all our toys, we have something to proclaim. The bell, or *ghanta* in Sanskrit, is a karma family symbol, and this abhisheka is connected with the karma family. Karma is the fulfillment of action. Here, it is the utterance of sound which cannot be blocked, sound which can be heard by anybody anywhere. If we are around the corner we can hear it; if we are far away we can hear it; if we are close by we can hear it. The karma sound of this bell is unobstructed: We cannot hide underneath our chair pretending we did not hear anything. The bell is heard and understood completely and thoroughly. It pierces our ears. The sound of this bell is also very high-pitched, which invokes wakefulness: We cannot fall asleep anymore, because the sound of the bell is too penetrating to our ears.

The fifth abhisheka also uses the vajra and bell, but in this abhisheka the bell and the vajra are fastened together at right angles with a silk ribbon. The king already has a clean body and beautiful clothes; he has a crown; he holds a scepter as a sign of power; and he has a bell for proclaiming—so what is lacking? He does not have a name. We do not yet know which king we are. Who are we? That is a problem: If we do not know who we are we have very little to say. We may try to say something but we have no idea what our name is or what our status is—whether we are literate or illiterate, or even whether we are actually a human being.

The first thing we usually say to people is, "How do you do?" which is like ringing the bell. Then we introduce ourselves: "My name is Jack Parsons, Julie Smith, or whatever." Similarly, in this abhisheka we introduce ourselves to the world. So this abhisheka is called the abhisheka of name. In this abhisheka our vajra master rings the bell with the vajra attached to it above our heads, and at the same time as the bell is rung, we are given a tantric name, which is traditionally known as our secret name. This name is not publicized as is our ordinary name, but when we need to use our power or to wake someone up, we say our vajra name, our tantric name. The name abhisheka is connected with the buddha family. It is the sense of complete spaciousness and openness that comes when we finally, thoroughly, take our place in the vajra mandala.

These five abhishekas make up the abhisheka of form, which is the first of four levels of transmission that traditionally make up the complete ceremony of empowerment in anuttara yoga. When we have received the abhisheka of form, there is a sense of enormous psychological progress and psychological change. We have gone through a whole process of being accepted and acknowledged: We have our scepter, we can proclaim, and now we know our name as well. We actually become a ruler of some kind.

A problem with many religious traditions is that they make a point of condemning us. They talk about how wicked we are or how terrible we are and how we have to pull ourselves together. And if we do so, they promise us some candy or reward. But the vajrayana is an entirely different approach. The tantric tradition builds us up so we do not have to relate at the level of a donkey reaching for a carrot anymore. The donkey has the carrot already, so the donkey should feel good.

The basic point of abhisheka is not to zap us with magical power but to bring us up slowly and gently so that we can experience and relate with ourselves simply. Because we exist and we have a body, therefore we can bathe ourselves. Having bathed, we can put our clothes on. Having dressed, we can put on our crown. Then we have something to hold in our hand and something to say. We can make a statement about why we are doing all this. And we have a name as well. This is the basic process of graduating from the ordinary world into the world of continuity, the tantric world. We finally become a real person. That is the basic meaning of abhisheka.

The ceremony of abhisheka is actually based on the example of the Buddha. It is said that Shakyamuni Buddha was once invited by King Indrabhuti to teach the dharma. The king said, "I would like to relate with my sense perceptions and my emotions. Could you give me some teachings so that I can work with them?" The Buddha said, "Oh, you want to hear tantra." And the king said, "Yes." Then the Buddha replied, "If that is the case, let me excuse my arhats and my hinayana and mahayana disciples from the room." So he asked his disciples to leave. Then the Buddha appeared to the king in royal costume and taught the first tantra, the *Guhyasamaja*. That was the first presentation of tantra.

So the Buddha is seen in different ways at different levels of practice. Unlike hinayana and mahayana, at the vajrayana level the Buddha is dressed as a king: He has a crown, he has a scepter in his hand, he has a royal gaze, and he behaves like a king. This is quite a different approach than the traditional hinayana or mahayana view. In fact, the vajrayana approach could be quite shocking to practitioners of the lower yanas. That is why the Buddha excused all his other disciples from the room before he introduced the tantric teachings.

Abhisheka, or empowerment, plays an extremely important part in tantric literature, tantric ceremony, and the tantric tradition altogether. One of the reasons that tantra is so rich is because it actually relates with human experience as a physical situation rather than as a lofty idea. In the hinayana we are struggling to maintain our awareness, and in the mahayana we are trying to be kind to our neighbors. Vajrayana Buddhism respects those disciplines, but it also transcends them and becomes the greatest idea of all.

Vajrayana deals much more directly with ego than the previous two yanas. In the abhisheka of form, we actually bathe ego, coronate ego, and give ego a scepter. Finally, when ego finds itself with everything it wants, it begins to flop. It begins to be so embarrassed that it becomes nonexistent. Then we can begin to build a new kingdom of egolessness. That is the tantric way. Sometimes I wonder who thought up tantra. It constantly amazes me. But it happened; it exists. Somebody actually thought up such an idea and transmitted it to people—and it actually works. It is very amazing. I suppose we could call it magic.

In going through the landscape of the tantric tradition, I have been very careful not to introduce the juicy tidbits at the beginning. I am being very faithful and orthodox and presenting the tradition in the same way that it was presented to me. To begin with, we need panic. We need that sense of nervousness or uncertainty. It is absolutely necessary. And then, having gone through such a period already, we arrive at the point at which we are capable of receiving abhisheka. Then we are much more at home, and we are complimented by our teacher and our world. I experienced this myself in my training in Tibet.

In my education, I was constantly criticized. If I leaned back I was criticized and told that I should sit up. I was told that I should always make pleasant conversation with visiting dignitaries and that I should be hospitable to them. At that level, the training was very simple and not particularly tantric. Every time I did something right—or I thought I was doing something right—I was criticized even more heavily. I was cut down constantly by my tutor. He slept in the corridor outside my door, so I could not even get out. He was always there, always watching me. He would be serving me and watching me at the same time. My other teachers would all work through him so that they themselves did not have to put embarrassing pressure on me. Instead, they could pressure my tutor, and in turn my tutor would pressure me—which I thought was very clever. It was also very claustrophobic and somewhat painful.

I was constantly cut down. I had been brought up strictly since infancy, from the age of eighteen months, so that I had no other reference point such as the idea of freedom or being loose. I had no idea what it was like to be an ordinary child playing in the dirt or playing with toys or chewing on rusted metal or whatever. Since I did not have any other reference point, I thought that was just the way the world was. I felt somewhat at home, but at the same time I felt extraordinarily hassled and claustrophobic. It did not feel so good.

At the same time I knew that there were little breaks, like going to the bathroom—which was an enormous relief. The only time I was not being watched was when I went to the bathroom. It was my one free time. Usually I would feel an enormous rush of fresh air, because bathrooms were built overhanging cliffs and had big holes in the floor. I would feel the fresh air coming up, and at the same time I would know that nobody was watching me, telling me how to defecate properly. Apart from that, I was always watched. Even when I ate, I was watched and told how to eat properly, how to extend my arm, how to watch the cup, how to bring it to my mouth. If I made a big noise while swallowing, I was criticized for eating "crocodile style." I was told that rinpoches, or other important tulkus, were not supposed to swallow crocodile style. Everything was very personal from that point of view—to say the least.

Then, very interestingly, I stopped struggling with the authorities, so to speak, and began to develop. I just went on and on and on. Finally that whole world began to become my reference point rather than being a hassle—although the world was full of hassles. At that point, my tutor seemed to become afraid of me; he began to say less. And my teachers began to teach me less because I was asking them too many questions. I was interested in what they had to say and I pursued them for more and more, so that they began to have a more relaxed approach than even I wanted.

My tutor was frightened because he did not know exactly how to handle me. I thought that maybe this was all some kind of joke, and that my teachers would leave me alone for ten days and then catch me again. But ten days went by, and a month went by, and finally six months—and nothing changed. The situation just went on and on. Something was actually working. Something was finally beginning to click. The discipline had become part of my system. My tutors and my teachers were pushed by me instead of my being pushed by them. I wanted to know more and more about what was happening, and they began to run out of answers. They were hassled by me because I was so wholehearted. They became afraid that they could not keep up with me anymore.

I'm telling you this because there are parallels between my own experience and that of other tantra students. It is a question of interest. Once you are really into something, you become part of that experience, or it becomes part of you. When you become part of the teachings, you are no longer hassled. You are no longer an entity separate from the teachings. You are an embodiment of them. That is the basic point.

ELEVEN

Being and Manifesting

THE TANTRIC APPROACH is not mystical experience alone, but it is concerned with how we can perceive reality in a simple and direct way. In our normal confused, or samsaric, way of perceiving and handling the world, we perceive reality on the level of body, on the level of emotions, and on the level of mindlessness, which is traditionally known as basic ignorance. Body refers to basic self-consciousness, which includes the various sense perceptions: thought, vision, sound, taste, touch, and smell. Emotion includes aggression, passion, ignorance, jealousy, pride, and all other emotions and feelings. Mindlessness, or basic ignorance, refers to a state of total bewilderment: Fundamentally we have no idea what we are doing or what we are experiencing, and we are completely missing the point all the time. Those three major principles—body, emotions, and mindlessness—are how we experience our life.

By "body," to begin with, we mean an actual physical body. Bodies may be well shaped, fat or thin, functional or nonfunctional. Some bodies see but cannot hear. Some bodies hear but cannot see. Some bodies feel but cannot see or hear. Some bodies hear and see but cannot feel, and some bodies can do the whole thing. There are all kinds of bodies, and there are all kinds of physical experiences, depending on whether we are lame or deaf or dumb or completely healthy. Still, we all have the same basic experience, that is, the experience of the body, the experience of reality at that very simple level.

In the sutras, the Buddhist scriptures, Buddha once said to Ananda:

Vajradhara. The dharmakaya buddha. A tantric manifestation of the Buddha,
Vajradhara is depicted as dark blue.
PAINTING BY SHERAPALDEN BERU.
PHOTO BY GEORGE HOLMES AND BLAIR HANSEN.

"Ananda, if there is no body, there is no dharma. If there is no food, there is no dharma. If there are no clothes, there is no dharma. Take care of your body, for the sake of the dharma." Relating with the body is extremely important in the tantric tradition. However, we don't make a personal "trip" out of it. We could become a vegetarian and sneer at meat eaters. We could wear pure cotton clothing and renounce wearing any leather. Or we could decide to search for a country to live in that is free from pollution. But any of those approaches could be going too far. When someone becomes a vegetarian, he stops eating meat, but he still might take a bloodthirsty delight in peeling bananas and crunching his teeth into peaches and cooking eggplants as meat substitutes. So our attempts to relate with the body can become very complicated.

I'm not particularly advocating eating meat or otherwise at this point. Rather, I am pointing out that we do not accept our body as it is, and we do not accept our world. We are always searching for some way to have an easy ride. When we feel unhappy or uncomfortable, we think that we would like to go somewhere else, up or down or wherever. Some people call it hell, some people call it heaven, but whatever it is, we would like to have an easy ride somewhere.

It is actually quite humorous how we view the cosmos, our world. We view it as if it were not a real world at all, but a world we could control. Sometimes we treat the world as a problem child who is trying to suggest all kinds of evil things to us. Sometimes we treat our world as a priest or master who is telling us that everything is good, that whatever we do is fine: There are flowers, there are meadows, there is wildlife, and the world is a fantastic place. But fundamentally, we haven't really made up our mind what this world is all about. Sometimes we think we have, but there is still a flicker of doubt. Whenever a temptation comes up, we regard it as fantastically evil or challenging and we jump sideways, like a temperamental horse. There is a big problem with that: we have not accepted our world thoroughly, properly, and fully.

The world we are talking about is a very simple world, an extremely simple world which is made out of concrete, plastic, wood, stones, greenery, pollution, and thin air. Actually, every one of us is sitting or standing on that world. Shall we say this is the real world or should we pretend that the world is something else? You and I are both here. If we feel guilty, it's too late. This is our world, here, right now. We could say, "Hey, that's not true. I can go out in my car and drive up in the mountains. I can camp out in the mountains in my sleeping bag." But sleeping in our sleeping bag is the same as sitting on a rug or carpet. Somehow we cannot get away from the world. This world is the real world, the actual world, the world we experience, the world in which we are thriving. This is the world that communicates to our sense perceptions. We can smell incense or tobacco or food cooking; we can see and hear what is around us. This is our world.

Wherever we are, we carry this world with us. If we go out to a lecture, we see the stage, the backdrop, the podium, the speaker; we smell the musty air in the hall; and we hear the seat creaking under us. When we go home, we take this world with us. We look back again and again, remembering where we have been, so we can't get away from this world. By the time we look back, of course, "this world" has become "that world," which is the world of the past. But our memory is still of this world, nevertheless. Otherwise we could not have a memory. So we are still in this world, this real world made out of thisness, in fact, made out of us. If somebody asks what this world is made out of, what the substance of it is, it is 75 percent "I" and 25 percent "am." So this is our world: "I am" is our world, and we cannot get away from it.

The next level is the world of emotions. It is not exactly a different world, but it is a different perspective, seeing things from a different angle. There are many ways that emotions color our experience. When we are depressed and angry, we begin to feel a grudge and to grind our teeth. We find our world fantastically aggressive: Everything is irritating, including fence posts in the countryside that have harmlessly placed themselves there with barbed wire or electric wire going across them. We feel that we have been invaded, raped. We feel so bad about this world.

When we experience aggression we feel that everything is an expression of injustice. There is too much concrete, too much steel, too much grease, too much pollution, and we feel very angry and frustrated. We are so involved with this world of emotions that, although we might have a beautiful sunny day, fantastic weather, and a fantastic view, we still grind our teeth. We feel that the world is trying to mock us. The clear blue sky is trying to mock us or insult us. The beautiful sunshine is embarrassing to look at, and the fantastic full moon and the beautiful clouds around it are an insult. There is constant hate, enormous hate, so much so that it is almost unreal. We feel that we are actually levitating off the ground because we are so angry. We feel that our feet are not attached to the ground, that we are hovering above the world, because there is such a sense of aggression taking place.

On the other hand, if we are passionate, if we are in love or in a lustful state, we begin to feel that there is an enormous amount of glue sprayed all over the world that is trying to stick to us. Our only frustration is that we do not have enough money to buy all the beautiful clothes we see in shop windows, all the beautiful antiques we see in the shops, and all the beautiful food or wealth that exists. We may try to project an image of aloofness or specialness: "I'm not going to be like the rest of my countrymen. When I buy clothes, I'm going to buy special ones, not like the rednecks." But that is just a sidetrack. Fundamentally, the juice of the juice is that we *want* so much, and we begin to spray our own glue all over things. We want to be stuck to things, to persons, objects, wealth, money, parents, relatives, friends, or whatever. So we begin to spray this crude glue all over the place. We are asking to be stuck.

Hopefully, we think, we can pull things or people back into our territory: "Once I get stuck to something, I've got enough sanity and enough power to pull it back to me. I want to make sure, to begin with, that my glue is strong enough. Then when I am stuck to my friend, I can step back, and my friend will be so stuck to me that I will not have to worry. He or she is always going to be with me, because my glue is so powerful, so strong, and so tough." That is the game we play. But the problem is that things get turned around, and we find ourselves stuck. The ground we create is too solid, too powerful, and we cannot step back. Then we might scream and begin to worry. But that panic connected with passion is another matter altogether, beyond the subject we are discussing at this point.

Another emotional style is called stupidity or ignorance. It occurs when we are so absorbed in our world that we miss the sharp points. For example, if somebody is yelling at us, calling our name, we might answer him and we might not. We want to shield ourselves from the world. The world makes us blush, and we begin to hide behind a timid smile. If somebody insults us, we try to walk away. We are trying to save face by ignoring reality. If somebody is irritating us, we feel we can't be bothered: "Let's change the subject. Let's talk about something else—my fantastic trip to Peru. I took photographs there when I was with the Indians. It was fantastic!" We become very skillful at changing the subject of conversation. Sometimes we shield ourselves with a little sense of humor, but the humor is usually somewhat superficial. Fundamentally we are ignoring the situation. The sharp edges that come up are pushed away or ignored. We play deaf and dumb.

There are many different emotions, but these three—aggression, passion, and ignorance—are the basic emotions or basic styles that make up the second level of perception.

The third level of perception is the ultimate idea of bewilderment or confusion. It is much more fundamental than the emotional style of ignorance that we just discussed. Basic bewilderment or mindlessness is experiencing things as if the world did not exist and we did not exist. We could almost view this level of perception as mystical experience because it is so solid and pervasive. It is like being entranced by the shimmering reflection of light on a pond: There is a sense of being stunned, fixed solid—so fixed that the experience is extremely confusing, but nevertheless, we do not want to let go of our fixation; we do not want to let go of the phenomenal world. We would like to hand on to it, to keep ourselves attached to the world, as though we had tentacles with suction cups on the ends.

We are determined to ignore the possibility of any spaciousness in our experience. This level of bewilderment is the fundamental style of ego. Space is completely frozen into mindlessness. In such a state, it is impossible to step out or to step in. There is a sense of being fixed, being part of a rock or a mountain. It is like flat air, which doesn't have any energy. We begin to feel that our head is being flattened on top, as though we were wearing a cast-iron frying pan on our head. Our head is stuck to that pan, and we are constantly carrying that big flat metal object on our head. Our head is not even stuck to a sheet of corrugated iron—that texture would be too interesting. This is completely flat. We do not feel exactly squashed, but we feel that we are being weighted down by the force of gravity.

This kind of heavy-handed mindlessness makes us feel that we shouldn't worry about anything at all. On the one hand, everything is there and at the same time it is confusingly not there. We can't be bothered to talk about anything at all. We are carrying a cast-iron head, our shoulders are stiff, our neck is stiff, and in fact, our whole body is made out of cast iron. Since our legs are cast iron, we can't even move. But we still have a heartbeat, which is a reference point. The only things functioning are our lungs and heart. We breathe in and out, and our heart beats: That is the ultimate level of stupidity or bewilderment.

We have been discussing the samsaric way of handling our world, in terms of the three levels of samsaric perception: body, emotions, and mindlessness. There is a definite tantric approach to those three levels of perception, which is known as the principle of the three kayas, or the trikaya. Kaya is a Sanskrit word that simply means "body." There is a correspondence between the three levels we have discussed and the three kayas. In the language of tantra, the level of body corresponds to the kaya or body of manifestation, the nirmanakaya. The level of emotions corresponds to the body of complete joy, the sambhogakaya, and the level of bewilderment or ignorance corresponds to total space, the dharmakaya. There is no tension or contradiction between the samsaric and the tantric descriptions. Rather the tantric principle of the three kayas shows how we could relate to the levels of body, emotions, and bewilderment that already exist within our state of being.

Traditionally, dharmakaya is the first kaya, corresponding to the samsaric level of mindlessness. *Dharma* means "law," "norm," or "truth," among other definitions. The teachings of the Buddha are called the dharma, the truth. The first kaya is called dharmakaya, the "body of truth," because the dharma speaks completely and totally in accordance with the language of ignorant people. The starting point for hearing the dharma is confusion. If we are not ignorant and confused—thoroughly, utterly, and completely—then there is no dharma. At the same time, dharma speaks the language of intelligence, which is the opposite of ignorance. The dharma is able to communicate the truth by relating to the confusion of sentient beings.

Dharmakaya is the original state of being, which transcends our basic state of mindlessness. It is the opposite of having a cast-iron pan on our head. It is a state of complete freedom. It is so free that the question of freedom does not even apply. It is complete and it is open—thoroughly open, utterly open, magnificently open. Dharmakaya is so completely open that the question of openness does not apply anymore at all, and so completely spacious that reference points do not make any difference.

The second kaya is the level of emotional manifestation. This is called *sambhogakaya*, which literally means "body of joy." The dharmakaya, as we have discussed, is completely open and completely free. At the level of sambhogakaya we are looking at the emotions that are manufactured or manifested out of that. The emotions that manifest out of this state of openness transcend the samsaric emotions, including aggression, passion, and ignorance. In the sambhogakaya, emotions manifest as the transcendent or completely enlightened versions of the five buddha families that we discussed in chapter nine. When they manifest in this way, the emotions provide tremendous capability and enormous scope for relating with the universe. There is accommodation for dualism, for relating with this and that if necessary, because from this point of view duality is not particularly regarded as a threat or unkosher. This accommodation provides tremendous freedom. There is a sense of celebration in which emotions are no longer a hassle.

The third kaya, the nirmanakaya, is the "body of emanation," the body of existence or manifestation. It is the manifestation of our mind and our body. It is also the manifestation of the bodies of those who have already experienced or gone through the other two kayas, and who then manifest on the third level, the nirmanakaya. In that sense the nirmanakaya refers specifically to the vajra master or teacher who is here on earth. Such a teacher has achieved the dharmakaya and the sambhogakaya, but in order to communicate with our body, our food, our clothes, and our earth—that is, with our sense perceptions—he needs a manifested body. It is necessary that the teacher manifest in the nirmanakaya in order to communicate with us and to teach the vajrayana and the entire buddhadharma.

In studying tantra, we relate with all three kayas simultaneously by relating to the vajra master, who embodies all three. The three kayas are not abstract principles, but we can relate to them experientially, personally, spiritually, and transcendently, all at the same time. As we develop to the level of the teacher's body, the level of nirmanakaya, then we begin to experience the sambhogakaya. At that level emotions are transmuted and are workable. Beyond that, we also begin to tune in to the dharmakaya, which is open, all-pervading space.

If we are going to study tantra, it is necessary to understand the trikaya principle of being and manifesting. In tantric practice the first step is to realize the level of body, the nirmanakaya. Then we see that the five buddha families are related with the sambhogakaya or the level of emotions. Beyond that it is necessary to transcend both the bodily and the emotional level, which is the dharmakaya, high above. When we discuss maha ati in the closing chapter, you may understand more about dharmakaya. But first it is necessary to understand the importance of relating with the body, or earthly existence, and relating with the vajra master, the great teacher who exists on earth. In some sense such a teacher is a magician, a conjurer: He has achieved total space, conquered the level of emotions, and he actually exists in an earthly body.

T W E L V E

The Question of Magic

THE SANSKRIT WORD for magic is *siddhi*, which means actualizing or working with the energy that exists in the realm of experience and the realm of physical being. Unfortunately, in the Western world, the concept of magic seems to be associated with mysteriousness and impossible powers, such as turning fire into water or the floor into the sky. So magic is considered to be possible only for those few chosen people who develop mysterious magical powers. In comic books, for instance, magical things happen because a person possesses a certain power that he exercises over other people, either destroying them or helping them. Such a magician can change a giant into a dwarf, a mute into a bard, a cripple into a runner, and so forth.

In the West, we often treat spirituality with that comic-book approach, and we view spiritual discipline as the process through which we will eventually end up as magicians. We feel that, although we may have a few little problems as beginners, when we become highly accomplished persons, we won't have these problems. We will be able to shake them off and do anything we want. That is the simple-minded concept of spiritual practice and the simple-minded concept of magic: that once we are accomplished persons we will be able to do anything. We will be able to shake the universe, to change the shape of fleas and the habits of mice, to turn tigers into cats and cats into tigers.

Genuine mystical experience, according to either the Judeo-Christian tradition or the Buddhist tradition, has nothing to do with that kind of mysteriousness. It is not that the mysteriousness finally manifests, and then we realize that spirituality has some value after all: "Now we don't need to ride elevators; we can just levitate." That is the ultimate idea of automation, the true American dream. From that point of view, the world is a nuisance; it is problematic; it gets in our way. So we hope we can change its course once we graduate to a higher level. Obviously, there is a problem with that approach to spirituality.

A deeper problem is that this approach is based on misunderstanding the world of ego. We think that ego can achieve enormous power beyond its present ability, which is called "magic." In that case, we do not have to give up anything at all. We can just latch on to some greater power and expend further energy in the direction of ego. That is an enormous problem, an enormous blockage, and that is precisely why it is necessary for potential students of tantra to go through a gradual process and to give up any idea of the rapid path. It is necessary to start slowly, very slowly, to start at the bottom and grow up slowly. In that way our simple-minded version of the cosmos or the universe changes and becomes more real, more personal, and more direct. Our world becomes workable; it no longer remains separate from our basic being at all. The world contains invitations for us to participate, and we in turn extend our invitation and willingness to participate to the world. In that way, the world can come into us and we can get into the world.

Beyond that, there *is* a magical aspect of the world. That magic does not have to be sought, but it happens by itself. It is not as sensational as we might expect. The greatest magic of all is to be able to control and work with ego, our mind. So we could say that magic begins at home, with our own minds. If we couldn't practice magic at home, we would be at a loss. We would have no place to begin. So magic begins at home.

We might ask: "What is so magical about all this? We have been working with ego all along, throughout our Buddhist training. What is so special about this magic?" We don't see anything particularly extraordinary about it. That is true. It is quite ordinary. In fact, the ordinary aspect becomes so powerful that it *is* magic. If something is extraordinary, it is usually a mechanical invention, something sensational but feeble. But because of ordinariness, magic is possible.

As far as tantra is concerned, magic is relating with the world on as ordinary a level as possible: We make flowers grow; we make the sun rise and the moon set. If we stay up long enough we will see the moon set and the sun rise. If we would like to watch the sun rise, we have to stay up so late that it finally becomes early. There is some discipline involved with that. We can't give up and go to bed to take a rest. If we do, quite possibly we will miss the sunrise.

The question of magic at this point is completely relevant to our life, to our path, to our actual practice. Magic is very real, direct, and personal. It is so personal that it becomes excruciating. It is at the level of excruciation that we have a glimpse of magic. We find ourselves on a threshold, and at that point, we can, in fact, push ourselves one step further. That threshold occurs when we think we have gone too far in extending ourselves to the world. There is some kind of warning, and at the same time a faint invitation takes place. Quite possibly we chicken out at that point because it requires so much effort and energy to go further. We feel we have put in enough effort and energy already, and we don't want to go beyond that. So-called sensible people wouldn't take such a risk: "Oh no! We have gone far enough; we mustn't go too far. Let's step back."

According to the *Tibetan Book of the Dead,* when a brilliant light comes to us in the bardo, or after-death state, we shy away from it. When a pleasant, faint, soothing light comes to us, we go toward it. In choosing the dimmer light we come back to square one, which is samsara. The point at which we can either extend ourselves further and go toward an unfamiliar brilliance, or return to a more soothing and familiar dimness is the threshold of magic. It is very personal. We feel pushed, hassled, and exposed through our practice. All kinds of irritations and all kinds of boundaries begin to come up, and we would like to stay within our territory, within those boundaries. We don't really want to step beyond them. We fear that in stepping beyond those boundaries we might do something beyond the boundaries of the teachings, something beyond the level of basic human sanity. Basically, we fear that we might destroy ourselves if we go beyond the territory of survival.

Such boundaries or thresholds always come up, and we really do not want to push anymore. But some kind of push is necessary. We might say, "Well, we have given our income and our possessions to the church. We have committed ourselves. We have signed our names on the dotted line. We pay our dues. We subscribe to your magazine. We do everything." But there is still something left behind. We are still missing the point. Those commitments are very easy to make. At this point, it is a question of giving up our arms and our legs. Even that might be easy to do. We can give up our hair, we can give up our beard, we can take off our clothes. But we have no idea, none whatsoever, how to give up our heart and brain.

Once we give up our heart and brain, the magic begins. It actually does. That is the spark. We give up our little heart, our little brain, and then we get greater nothingness. That is where the magic begins. We do not get anything back in return, as such, because we actually have given up; but still something happens. Actual magic begins there. The magic cannot begin unless we are willing to step over the threshold. We have to step on the electric fence that has been keeping us inside the corral, and then we have to step over it. We might get a mild shock or a violent shock in the process, but that is absolutely necessary. Otherwise there is no tantra; there is no magic.

According to the tantric tradition, there are four levels of magic. The first is *one-pointedness*. In this case, we are not talking about one-pointedness as it is often described in hinayana meditation practice. "We are not talking about a highly sharpened, pointed needle that pierces through discursive mind, enabling us to develop our mindfulness. The vajrayana version of mindfulness or one-pointedness is like a dull needle, a dagger made out of stone rather than efficient stainless steel. When we sew fabric with a sharp needle, the needle sews through the texture of the fabric without damaging it. The needle just goes in and out, and consequently our clothes are made very efficiently with almost invisible seams. In vajrayana one-pointedness, we are not only going through the web of the fabric, but we are crushing what is there. When we crush the fabric, there is no obstacle. It is thorough penetration, very, very personal and very real.

So one-pointedness, or the first level of magic, is a particular kind of penetration. Wherever there are obstacles, they are acknowledged, and then they are cut through very bluntly. Therefore there is a hole, a gate, or an entrance point. A sharp needle is sneaky and efficient and keeps apologizing to each strand of fabric, making each one feel better. With such a needle, one piece of fabric can be joined to another quite beautifully, without destroying or damaging the fabric. It is a very polite approach. Tantric one-pointedness, on the other hand, is blunt and not at all polite. Emotions occur and are experienced; they are not suppressed in a neurotic fashion, but instead they are dealt with directly, in their own place.

The second level of magic is called *simplicity* or noncomplication. Literally, it is nonexaggeration. Usually we find ourselves exaggerating. This exaggeration takes the form of spiritual materialism, trying to acquire all kinds of spiritual techniques and disciplines, and it also takes the form of psychological materialism, or trying to acquire all kinds of little metaphysical theories and experiences. The point here is that, having already been penetrated by the vajrayana one-pointedness, the phenomenal world has been related with properly, fully, and thoroughly. It can exist in its own way; therefore simplicity is there already. In this case, simplicity does not mean being a harmless person who lives in a hermitage and is so kind and good that he would not kill a flea. Simplicity is noncomplication rather than romantic simplicity. This means, again, that there is no need for further exaggeration.

Often, when we refer to somebody as simple, we mean that the person is slightly dumb or naive. He is so simple that he does not know how to be sophisticated or complicated. We might find that type of energy very refreshing, but such simplicity is regressing rather than progressing in any way. In this case, simplicity is self-existence. Something is simple because of its own magical qualities. For instance, fire burns by its own simplicity but still has its energy. A rock has its magic because it sits still and never gets bored. A river keeps flowing in a simple way; it never gets bored and never gives up its course. So the qualities of self-existence are directness and simplicity, rather than purely being naive or good or kind.

The next level of magic is known as *one taste*. Because things have a self-existing simplicity, they do not need any reference point. That is one taste: no need for further reference point. It is direct, one flavor. Usually, sugar is sweet because salt is salty, but such reference points do not apply. One taste is a one-shot deal. If you feel extreme pain and frustration, you *feel* it. Often, I find students saying that they feel extremely pained and frustrated, but they cannot understand why. There is some element of truth in that. There may be magic in that, in fact. The students are not being analytical but direct. They feel the nowness of the pain—or of the pleasure—as it is, personally, directly, simply. That magic is very powerful, very important.

The fourth level of magic is known as *nonmeditation*. In this case, meditation is the idea of contemplating some object, such as visualizing a candle, a rose, or a clear pond. We find ourselves associating with what we have visualized: We become a living rose. When we have finished meditating on the rose, we begin to feel like a rose—rosy. But in non-meditation, we do not meditate *on* anything. It is beyond reference point of subject and object. It is just simple, direct personal experience.

Nonmeditation provides a contrast to our expectations and constant sense of wanting. We always want something. We want to bring something in constantly, all the time. We want it badly, seemingly, but that is questionable. What is this wanting? "I would like a blah blah blah. Could I do blah blah blah blah?" We manifest our wanting in all kinds of ways, but it is all the same thing. "I want to eat. I don't even want to chew. Once I get food inside my mouth, I just want to swallow." The magical level of nonmeditation is entirely different from that constant wanting. Nonmeditation is not necessarily *not* wanting as such, or being dispassionate and cool and good. Rather, we are not particularly hungry. We are not particularly full either; nonetheless, we are not particularly hungry. We can accommodate food if something to eat comes up. It is welcome, even fantastic, but let us eat properly, in a nonmeditative way.

That is the greatest magic of all. At the final or fourth level of the magical process, we do not just perform magic because our magic wand works. When an angry soldier fires his machine gun at his enemies, each time the machine gun operates properly and kills his enemies, he licks his lips with enormous satisfaction. Somehow magic doesn't happen that way. Magic is an expression of total nonaggression and an expression of total energy and power at the same time.

The question at this point might be whether what we have discussed is magical enough. It feels slightly toned-down and too sensible. But at this point we haven't experienced those four levels of magic personally, so we have no idea how powerful they are. The little glimpse of energy we experience by studying tantra is perhaps one-hundredth of the tantric energy taking place—and even then we might experience it as too much. But there is more to come. There is a great deal more to come, indeed. The great Indian pandit Naropa once said that practicing tantra is like trying to ride a burning razor. Maybe he was right.

THIRTEEN

The Tantric Journey

YANA IS A SANSKRIT WORD that literally means "vehicle." The three major yanas or vehicles of practice are, as we know, hinayana, mahayana, and vajrayana. Then there are further subdivisions, or subtleties. There are six yanas within vajrayana: kriyayogayana, upayogayana, yogayana, mahayogayana, anuyogayana, and maha ati. Before discussing any of the tantric yanas specifically, we need to examine the basic idea of yana or path in connection with the tantric idea of continuity.

From our earlier discussion we know that tantra means continuity or thread. The tantric notion of continuity is quite special. Continuity obviously cannot take place without some means to continue ourselves. So the question is, "Who is continuing? What is continuing?" When we become tantric practitioners, we have discussed and studied the hinayana and mahayana levels of Buddhism already, but we still do not know completely who or what is making the journey. According to the vajrayana, nobody is making the journey; but if there is no traveler, how is it possible to have a path? Of course there is the possibility that there is no path, no yana. But we cannot just *say* that there is no path. We have to acknowledge the phenomenological-experiential level: We have to relate to our own experience rather than simply making metaphysical assumptions such as that path does not exist.

We have to come back to square one: "What is this? Who am I?" The simplest way to approach this question is by realizing that it does not really matter who asks the question, but we need to see whether the question *itself* exists or not. Where does the question come from? It seems to come from curiosity and fascination, wanting to find the original truth. But where does that curiosity come from? How is it possible for there to be a question at all? From the point of view of the questionless state of being, questions are only fabrications; and since the question does not exist, therefore the questioner does not exist either. We have to work backward using this type of logic.

For instance, we say that since there is no sun, it must be nighttime. That is proper logic. We could say that it must be nighttime because it is dark, which in turn means that there is no sun, but that is weak logic. The questioning process has to work back to the first flash of reality. After that first flash of reality is experienced, *then* one begins to question reality and whether reality exists in its own right or not. In fact it doesn't, because reality depends on the perceiver of reality. Since such a perceiver does not exist, therefore reality itself does not exist either. We have to work with that kind of logic; otherwise our understanding becomes too linear, too theistic.

So the question of a perceiver and the question of being is purely a phantom of our experience, purely a phantom, and it is questionable whether this phantom exists or not. On the one hand, the phantom does exist because of its phantomlike quality; but on the other hand, the phantom does not exist, also because of its phantomlike quality. We are cutting our throat if we discuss it, as if we were swallowing a razor blade.

With that understanding of egolessness or nonexistence, we begin to develop what is known as the knowledge of egoless insight, *lhakthong dagme tokpe sherab (lhag mthong bdag med rtogs pa'i shes rab). Lhakthong* means "insight," *dagme* means "egoless," *tokpe* means "realization," and *sherab* means "knowledge." Without that knowledge there is no way of understanding vajrayana or tantric experience at all. Egolessness may seem to you to be just another concept, but it is absolutely necessary.

A sense of nonexistence or egolessness is the essential background for understanding the difference between nontheistic and theistic traditions. In comparing theism and nontheism we are not arguing about the existence of God, but about whether the *perceiver* of God exists or not. Having understood very clearly and precisely that the perceiver does not exist, we therefore conclude that God does not exist either. In the tantric tradition continuity has nothing to do with divine providence, since the notion of divinity has already been discarded. The continuity of tantra is simply the sense of path or journey, which takes place constantly. This journey is by no means an illusion. It is a real journey, a journey that takes place on the planet Earth in this particular solar system, in this particular country, for that matter.

When we refer to a journey, it seems to be quite clear that we are not talking about struggle or ambition. On the other hand, maybe we *are* talking in terms of struggle and ambition: ambition in the sense that we are inspired into the nowness, this very moment; and struggle in that a sense of exertion or discipline in the practice is necessary. This seems to be a contradiction. On the one hand we are talking about nonbeing, no world, nonexistence; and on the other hand we are discussing the process of the path, how we could proceed along a path and exert ourselves. Isn't there a hole in our logic? If we split hairs in that way, there is no truth anywhere, none whatsoever. Let it just be that way; let us have contradictions.

At the same time, let us be suspicious of the nature of the path. That is great; that is precisely what is needed. We should not become so gullible that if we are asked to lick our teacher's bottom we are willing to do so. That becomes somewhat ugly and too gullible. It is good that we have questions in our mind, that we have such suspicion and such unyielding pride. Such suspicion is required for the study of tantra in particular, as well as for studying the rest of the Buddhist teachings. We are not asked to take anything at its word.

For the tantric practitioner the point is that a sense of journey takes place. Whether the journey is regarded as a hypothetical journey, a cynical journey, or an actual spiritual journey, some kind of journey is taking place continually, and we have to acknowledge it. It might seem that our own journey is a backward journey; we might feel that we started with a point of reference in which we had confidence but that now we find ourselves quite uncertain. Or we may be uncertain whether we are going forward or backward.

In tantra, it is necessary to have pride that we are taking a journey; it does not really matter whether it is a forward or a backward journey. A journey is actually taking place—that is what counts. It is like aging. We know that we are getting physically older all the time. We might find ourselves becoming infantile psychologically, but in that case, we are an old person being infantile rather than actually a baby. We know that we are getting physically older as long as we have a body. We are developing gray hair, we are becoming somewhat inaccurate in our physical behavior, our sight is becoming blurry, our speech is becoming slightly old-fashioned, our hearing system is degenerating slightly, and our taste in food and our interest in excitement or entertainment is becoming somewhat numb and dulled. We are getting old. Whether we regard that as going backward, becoming infantile, or going forward, approaching our death, something is happening to us. We could consider that process of aging as a metaphor for the spiritual journey. Whether we like it or not, we *are* moving forward.

When we become a Buddhist, we become a refugee: We take the refuge now and commit ourselves to the Buddhist path. We make the preliminary decision to call ourselves Buddhists. After that we slowly begin to develop the confidence that we are not only working on ourselves but that we can also work with others. Then we take another vow, called the bodhisattva vow. As we proceed further, we are ready to take tantric transmission, or abhisheka. We are still making a journey. We might feel that we are going backward or forward—but that is simply the play of emotions. If we feel we are becoming infantile, we are learning; if we think we are an insignificant old man, we are still learning. A learning process takes place constantly, throughout the whole path.

It would be very difficult to go through each of the tantric yanas in detail since many of you are beginning practitioners. So I would like to take a more general approach in discussing the tantric journey. We could discuss the beginning, the middle, and the end of the path, that is, kriya-yoga, the first yana; anuttaratantra, the culmination of the first three; and atiyana, the final yana. The main point is that the same psychological attitude permeates all the tantric yanas, the same continuity based on the nonexistence of ego. There is a continual sense of journey throughout the path. We have developed a sense of egolessness at the hinayana level, we have understood the compassionate activities that might take place at the mahayana level, and now we are approaching the vajrayana level. There is the continuity of an inspired student who is well-disciplined, highly inspired by working with others, and who now is coming to grips with reality properly and thoroughly.

The first tantric yana is kriyayoga. *Kriya* literally means "action," so kriyayoga is the yoga of action. The basic approach of kriyayoga is that of purity or cleanliness, which in this case means understanding reality from the sharpest possible perspective, the clearest possible point of view. In order to see the vajra world or the tantric world properly, thoroughly, and clearly, we have to see it in a highly purified way. Otherwise, rather than creating the clear vision of kriyayoga, we will begin to fixate on spots of dirt all over the place. Actions such as vegetarianism, taking baths frequently, and leading a very pure life are recommended in kriyayoga, but they are by no means "trips," because before we begin such actions we already have been trained. We already have been educated in the hinayana and mahayana. Therefore we are able to practice the disciplines of kriyayoga properly. We are not just presented with kriyayoga suddenly out of nowhere, as though our mother decided to wean us by abruptly taking away her nipples.

One of the basic notions of kriyayoga is that there is both purity and dirt in emotions. Initially, emotions occur in a spontaneous way. Then we interpret those spontaneous emotions to our own advantage. Having done so, we begin to possess our emotions as territory: We have our logic and our arguments, and other people's interpretations seem illogical or unreasonable. We feel that our emotional approach is accurate because we *feel* it; we feel that we are experiencing our emotions properly and thoroughly. So we begin to take pride in our emotions, and finally we begin to find ourselves so righteous that it is upsetting. We are extraordinarily passionate, proud, jealous, and justified because we have worked out our logic completely. But that process is problematic. At the beginner's level, we experience pure emotion; but then we dilute it; we try to control it. In the end, we find ourselves swimming in a pool of sewage, which is extraordinarily irritating, to say the least, and somewhat hellish, in fact.

The *Vajramala,* a text on kriyayoga, talks a great deal about working with the emotions. According to the *Vajramala* and its commentaries, kriyayoga separates emotions into two types: pure and impure. Pure emotion, which is the original flash of instantaneous experience, could be called wisdom, which is *jnana* in Sanskrit or *yeshe (ye shes)* in Tibetan. With that first flash, we experience emotions properly and thoroughly, without preconceptions. At that level, emotion is insight. Then, as our emotions begin to deteriorate, as we begin to dilute them, they become ordinary passion, ordinary aggression, and ordinary ignorance. At that point they are regarded as dirt or impurity.

There is a definite division of experience into black and white in kriyayoga. The first impulse is regarded as purity, the true experience of reality in its fullest sense. Then we begin to water it down and mask that experience with all kinds of interpretations in an attempt to possess it. In doing so, the emotion becomes a confused one. So there is direct experience and there is a neurotic overlay, both happening at once. That original purity is vajra nature, which is inherently pure and cannot be contaminated—it cannot be destroyed *at all*. It is fundamental toughness. The moon might be behind a cloud, but the moon in itself is still pure. The cloud is the problem—if we sweep away the cloud the moon is sure to be a good moon.

One should see the neuroses clearly, look at them and study them, and finally flush them down the toilet. The way to do that is through various purification ceremonies and visualization practices. Purification in kriyayoga is a very personal experience, but solving our neurotic problems is not the point at all. Purification is learning to relate with the problems. Does a problem exist or not? Is the problem a problem, or is the problem a promise? We are not talking about how to get rid of problems or impurities here, as though we were suddenly surrounded by piles of garbage that we want to clean up. That is not the point. The point is to discover the quality of garbageness. Before we dispose of our garbage, first we have to examine it. If we approached purification as simply trying to get rid of our garbage, we would do a great job of emitting spiritual pollution into the atmosphere.

Having related with our garbage, the question of how we can purify ourselves is a question of surrendering. But all kinds of tricks are possible in this approach as well. We might say, "If I accept the whole thing and regard it as no big deal, then will I be free of any problems?" Those little tricks of ego, overlapping tricks of all kinds, go on constantly. The idea is to surrender completely.

The visualizations of kriyayoga are highly developed. They are very transparent visualizations, rather than simply imagining that we are a great guy or thinking of ourselves as a good person. In kriyayoga, visualization is identifying with our inherently pure psychological state of being, the part of us that is inherently innocent. The deities are visualized in the name of our innocence—or through the experience of our innocence. That innocent quality or pure aspect of our being is seen as a deity, as the embodiment of living enlightenment.

So kriyayoga's approach to life is segregation: certain parts of our life are good and pure, and certain parts of our life and our experience are impure, that is, diluted and contaminated by egocentricity. In kriyayoga we take the attitude that we are going to experience things very clearly and properly. We are not purely trying to relate with some abstract divinity or deity, but we are willing to relate with real experience.

Evam. The personal seal of Chögyam Trungpa and the Trungpa tulkus (see chapter 14).
DESIGN BY MOLLY K. NUDELL.

FOURTEEN

Anuttarayoga

THE FIRST THREE tantric yanas, kriyayoga yana, upayoga yana, and yoga yana, are called "lower tantra." And the last three tantric yanas, mahayana yana, anuyoga yana, and atiyoga yana, are called "higher tantra." Anuttarayoga brings together the teachings of the lower tantra. It is usually not regarded as a separate yana but as the culmination of the first three. In some ways it acts as a bridge between the lower tantra and the higher tantra. The word *anuttara*—in Tibetan, *la-me (bla med)*—literally means "nothing higher." As far as the lower tantras are concerned, anuttara is the highest tantric achievement. Many tantric practices, such as Kalachakra, Chakrasamvara, and Guhyasamaja, are based on anuttarayoga.

Earlier we discussed the principles of body, speech, and mind. It is through body, speech, and mind that we relate with the phenomenal world. Such a relationship is not necessarily spiritual; it is physical, bodily. It is a question of being a person of sanity, a person of openness. In fact, we could almost approach the whole path in a secular way and call it the nontheistic discipline of developing sanity and openness, rather than regarding it as purely a religious tradition.

In anuttarayoga, there is particular emphasis on speech. Speech is not only voice or verbal description, but any speechlike experience that brings a sense of rhythm or movement. In other words, it is energy or circulation rather than sound alone. We are not using speech here in the narrow sense, but we are speaking of speechlike situations, any interchange that exists, related with hearing, seeing, smelling, and the general sensory system of the body. As the basic communication that takes place in human society, speech is not limited to newspapers, television, and radio shows. More basically, it is a link between us and our body, a link between us and our mind. As such, speech brings mind to the cognitive level and body to the energetic level. Such a link, either with the mind or with the body, takes place constantly. That kind of movement and energy is speech.

Some kind of interchange takes place in our life constantly, which is known as energy. We are not talking about energy as a gigantic "voom!" that suddenly zaps us and makes us feel electrified. That kind of expectation seems to be a spiritual version of playing cowboys and Indians. When a local bandit swings open the bar door and walks in, suddenly tension builds up—there is obviously the possibility of a gunfight. We are not talking about energy at that level, even spiritually. Energy here is the self-existing energy that exists in every one of us. It is not particularly a sensation of electrified vibrations of energy. Such a sensation is very rare, if it happens at all. It could happen when we are at the height of our temper, but that is just one of those things that we do when we feel weak. When we don't feel so good, we might lose our temper to try to recharge ourselves. But energy is not necessarily so pathetic. Rather there is self-existing energy that goes on constantly, purely at the survival level. We exist, others exist, and therefore energy takes place constantly. There is energy of aggression, energy of passion, energy of depression, energy of excitement, energy of uncertainty, and so on.

According to the tantric tradition, beginning with upayoga, yoga-yana, and anuttarayoga, such energy is divided into three parts. The anuttarayoga model that we are going to discuss is based on *Kalachakra Tantra. Kala* means "time" and *chakra* is "wheel." So *Kalachakra* means "the wheel of time." *Tantra* in this context is used to designate a root text of vajrayana teachings. This tantra, as well as many others, describes three types of energy: nadi, prana, and bindu.

Nadi is like a channel. Energy has to have a channel, a way to journey, its own specialized path. Nadi is like a railroad track in that it provides a certain path or pattern that our energy follows. In this case, the phenomenal world has already created the sense of pattern for us. At this point the phenomenal world is not regarded as particularly radical or extraordinary. Rather, the phenomenal world has set up the system for us, so we personally do not have to set it up; the system is already there. We can build railroad cars with wheels, but the railroad tracks already exist. Taranatha, one of the Kalachakra tantric masters, likened the existence of nadi to putting boiled milk out in the cold air: The milk is sure to form its own skin. Boiling-hot milk has learned how to deal with reality by forming a skin. That is the railroad track that exists already. We don't have to try to find a transcendental world, a better world, or a world suited to tantra at all. This world exists as what we experience already, which is the notion of nadi.

The metaphor for prana is a horse looking for a rider. Such a horse has to be a good horse, well fed and strong. We are not using the horse as a metaphor for speed, but we are talking in terms of conviction, strength. Again, we are willing to relate with the existing world that has been set up for us. There is a highway already built for us, a supermarket built for us, shopping centers already built for us—there is already some kind of energy and pattern. So prana is the horse that rides on that energy, that rides on the existing tracks of the world, the nadi, that have already been set up.

Then there is bindu, the rider of the horse of prana. Bindu is a particular type of consciousness. The inquisitive quality of mind that tries to explore or to set up the universe is called *sem (sems)* in Tibetan. The definition of sem at this point is that which responds to reference points. Such a mind is willing to survey, willing to look into areas of energy. But sem purely responds to reference points, while bindu is the quality of mind that relates with the sense of journey. When we ride a horse, the horse just walks for us. We can't quite say the horse takes the journey; it just moves. The rider takes the journey, in that the rider controls the horse. It is the rider who looks right and left, ahead and behind, and appreciates the sights. This rider is bindu, which we could simply call consciousness.

So consciousness or bindu is journeying through the energies of the world. Consciousness is the awake quality that doesn't have to refer to immediate reference points alone, but has greater scope, like a radar system. Such a radar system has to be mounted in some kind of mechanical framework, which in this case is functional mind, sem. And that mounting has to be connected to the track by a wheel, which is prana. In other words, we have a radar system on a mounting that has a wheel that goes along a railway track. The radar system is called bindu, its mounting is sem, the wheel is prana, and the rail is nadi. In this case, it is bindu, the radar system, that guides or controls the journey. And the whole process is based on energy, obviously.

The tantric practices that work with nadi, prana, ad bindu are based on hatha yoga, pranayama practices, and certain concentration and visualization experiences. But there is something more than that. In the application of nadi, prana, and bindu, there is still a sense of taking a journey, cranking up our machine along our railroad track. We can perceive our world in terms of nadi, prana, and bindu, and using them, we can take our journey. But then, at the highest level of anuttara yoga, we begin to transcend that journey; we go beyond using those three types of energy. We go on to something more than that, something beyond consciousness and mind, and our experience of the world alone. We begin to expand ourselves, and a greater openness begins to take place. It is like the unfolding of a flower: we don't even feel a sense of journey anymore. In anuttara yoga, that greater openness is symbolized by the monogram EVAM.

Discovering the existence of evam transcends hatha yoga and pranayama experience. E is the level of basic accommodation in which the attainment of buddhahood and the state of sentient beings are no longer different. At this point, naming somebody as a buddha or naming somebody as a sentient being is saying the same thing. When we say somebody is a buddha, that automatically is saying that he or she is no-buddha. In that sense, even the Buddha is no-buddha as well. A buddha exists only by the grace of somebody being no-buddha, or the reference point of somebody who is no-buddha. So sorting out buddhas and confused persons at this point is irrelevant. That is E. When you say E, it comes from your heart. You just breathe out—*ehhh*. It is a sound of opening up, without any particular definition or definite reference point. So E symbolizes the nonexistence of buddha, and the nonexistence of sentient beings as either confused or enlightened beings.

Having that enormous space of E already, then you have VAM. Vam is called the seed or the vajra-holder principle. Basically, VAM is the son and E is the mother. When you have a mother, you have a son. That might mean that the son and the mother are separate, that they conflict with each other. However, the VAM principle is that energy exists within the E of nonduality. Within the E of non-samsara and non-nirvana, there is still basic energy.

Real energy exists as a sense of having a certain discipline, a certain experience, and a certain openness. If you had too much E you would space out and you wouldn't find anything anywhere; you wouldn't have any discipline. So EVAM brings the discipline of VAM together with the spaciousness of E. Altogether, having transcended the three disciplines of nadi, prana, and bindu, you have a sense of openness or E, and then you have a sense of one-pointedness with concentrated energy or VAM. The combination of E and VAM brings together openness or spaciousness with indestructibility and one-pointedness. EVAM is a central monogram or basic symbol of *Kalachakra Tantra.*

One of the basic points of anuttara tantra is that we are able to use any form of confusion or hallucination that we experience in ordinary everyday life. Actually, echo may be a better word than hallucination. First there is an experience and then there is the echo, the doubt or questioning: "Did I or didn't I?" Anuttara yoga brings out the constant doubt that goes on in the mind: "Am I or am I not? Did I experience that or didn't I experience that? Maybe something is just about to happen to me, maybe not." Such chatterings of mind take place all the time, but they are never legitimized in the Buddhist teachings of the hinayana and mahayana.

In the lower yanas, such questions are ignored. Such tentative explorations are ignored: "If you have any questions, regard them as your mind. Just say it's your mind; you're just confused. Just come back to your practice." But *Kalachakra Tantra* says such confusion is legitimate. In fact, such confusion has enormous potential. We have the potential of becoming an enormously successful—if we could use such a word— tantric student because we have such creepy questions about ourselves. Such double thinking, double hearing, and double vision are legitimate. They are already included. When we experience this double vision, the first vision is sharp and then there is a shadow around that. The first vision is VAM, and the second vision is E. That is exactly the process of EVAM: We have a sharp vision first and then we have a shadow around it. So we are seeing EVAM constantly. That is the basic approach of anuttara: allowing doubt, and including that doubt as part of our progress.

FIFTEEN

Maha Ati

THE NINTH YANA, maha ati or atiyoga, is the final stage of the path. It is both the beginning and the end of the journey. It is not final in the sense that we have finished making a statement and we have nothing more to say, but final in the sense that we feel we have said enough. At this level, if there are any further words, they are the creations of space rather than idle remarks.

The tantric journey is like walking along a winding mountain path. Dangers, obstacles, and problems occur constantly. There are wild animals, earthquakes, landslides, all kinds of things, but still we continue on our journey and we are able to go beyond the obstacles. When we finally get to the summit of the mountain, we do not celebrate our victory. Instead of planting our national flag on the summit of the mountain, we look down again and see a vast perspective of mountains, rivers, meadows, woods, jungles, and plains. Once we are on the summit of the mountain, we begin to look down, and we feel attracted toward the panoramic quality of what we see. That is ati style. From that point of view, our achievement is not regarded as final but as a re-appreciation of what we have already gone through. In fact, we would like to retake the journey we have been through. So maha ati is the beginning of the end and the end of the beginning.

Ati teachings talk of enormous space. In this case, it is not space as opposed to a boundary, but a sense of total openness. Such openness can never be questioned. Atiyana is regarded as the king of all the yanas. In fact, the traditional Tibetan term for this yana, *long gyur thap kyi thekpa (klong gyur thabs kyi theg pa)*, means "imperial yana." It is imperial rather than regal, for while a king has conquered his own country, in order to be an emperor, he has to conquer a lot of other territories and other continents as well. An emperor has no need for further conquests; his rule is beyond conquering. Likewise, ati is regarded as "imperial" because, from the perspective of atiyoga, hinayana discipline is seen as spaciousness; mahayana discipline is seen as spaciousness; and the tantric yanas, as well, are seen as spaciousness. If you review what we have been discussing throughout this book, you will see that we have been taking that point of view. We have discussed everything from the perspective of ati. Because of that, we have been able to view the characteristics of the various yanas and tantric disciplines in terms of openness and spaciousness and inevitability. That notion of wakefulness we have been discussing constantly is the final wakefulness of atiyoga.

Atiyoga teaching or discipline is sometimes defined as that which transcends coming, that which transcends going, and that which transcends dwelling. This definition is something more than the traditional tantric slogan of advaita, or "not two." In this case, we are looking at things from the level of true reality, not from the point of view of slogan or belief. Things are as they are, very simply, extremely simply so. Therefore things are unchanging, and therefore things are open as well. The relationship between us and our world is no relationship, because such a relationship is either there or not. We cannot manufacture a concept or idea of relationship to make us feel better.

From the perspective of ati, the rest of the yanas are trying to comfort us: "If you feel separate, don't worry. There is nonduality as your saving grace. Try to rest your mind in it. Everything is going to be okay. Don't cry." In contrast, the approach of ati is a blunt and vast attitude of total flop, as if the sky had turned into a gigantic pancake and suddenly descended onto our head, which ironically creates enormous space. That is the ati approach, that larger way of thinking, that larger view.

Buddhism has a number of schools, primarily divided into the hinayana, mahayana, and vajrayana traditions, and squabbling goes on among all of them. They all speak the language of totality, and every one of them claims to have the answer. The hinayanists may say that they have the answer because they know reality. The mahayanists may say that the bodhisattva is the best person that we could ever find in the world. Tantric practitioners may say that the most fantastic person is the powerful and crazy yogi who is unconquerable and who has achieved siddhis and magical powers of all kinds. Let them believe what they want. It's okay. But what do those things mean to us personally, as students who want to practice and who want to experience the teachings?

The maha ati practitioner sees a completely naked world, at the level of marrow, rather than skin or flesh or even bones. In the lower yanas, we develop lots of idioms and terms, and that makes us feel better because we have a lot of things to talk about, such as compassion or emptiness or wisdom. But in fact, that becomes a way of avoiding the actual naked reality of life. Of course, in maha ati there is warmth, there is openness, there is penetration—all those things are there. But if we begin to divide the dharma, cutting it into little pieces as we would cut a side of beef into sirloin steaks, hamburger, and chuck, with certain cuts of beef more expensive than others, then the dharma is being marketed. In fact, according to Vimalamitra, the reason maha ati is necessary is because throughout the eight lower yanas the dharma has been marketed as a particularly juicy morsel of food. The maha ati level is necessary in order to save the dharma from being parceled and marketed; that is, it is necessary to preserve the wholesomeness of the whole path.

Actually, if we could make an atiyoga remark, all the yanas are purely creating successively more advanced and mechanized toys. At first, when a child is very young, we give him mobiles to look at, rings to suck, and rattles to shake. Then, when the child is more sophisticated, we give him more sophisticated toys, "creative playthings," and brightly colored bricks and sticks to put together. We provide even more sophisticated toys as the child becomes more and more inquisitive and sophisticated, and his mind and body are better coordinated.

Finally, at the level of adulthood, we continue to buy toys for ourselves. When we are old enough, we may buy ourselves a set of *Encyclo-*

paedia Britannica, or a stereo kit that we can put together. We may even build ourselves a house—the ultimate creative plaything. Or we may invent some new gadget: "I designed a new kind of motorcar, a new kind of airplane, a new kind of submarine. I built it and it actually worked. Isn't that fantastic?" We feel that our abilities are becoming much greater because not only can we build fantastic toys and enjoy them ourselves but we learn how to sell them, market them. When we become really sophisticated, we might design a zoo or even an entire city, and be accepted as important people in our society. It feels fantastic, extremely powerful and encouraging. But we are still fascinated by our toys.

According to atiyoga, going through the yanas is similar to that process of collecting more and more toys. The more sophisticated and fascinated we become, the more we are actually reducing ourselves to a childlike level. Somehow we are not yet at the level of the maha ati if we are still fascinated by our toys, our occupations, no matter how extensive or expansive they may be. At the maha ati level, those little tricks that we play to improve ourselves or to entertain ourselves are no longer regarded as anything—but at the same time they are everything, much vaster than we could have imagined. It is as though we were building a city or a zoo, and suddenly the whole sky turned into a gigantic pancake and dropped on us. There is a new dimension of surprise that we never thought of, we never expected. We never expected the sky to drop on our head.

There is a children's story about the sky falling, but we do not actually believe that such a thing could happen. The sky turns into a blue pancake and drops on our head—nobody believes that. But in maha ati experience, it actually does happen. There is a new dimension of shock, a new dimension of logic. It is as though we were furiously calculating a mathematical problem in our notebook, and suddenly a new approach altogether dawned on us, stopping us in our tracks. Our perspective becomes completely different.

Our ordinary approach to reality and truth is so poverty-stricken that we don't realize that the truth is not one truth, but all truth. It could be everywhere, like raindrops, as opposed to water coming out of a faucet that only one person can drink from at a time. Our limited approach is a problem. It may be our cultural training to believe that only one person can get the truth: "You can receive this, but nobody else can." There are all sorts of philosophical, psychological, religious, and emotional tactics that we use to motivate ourselves, which say that we can do something but nobody else can. Since we think we are the only one that can do something, we crank up our machine and we do it. And if it turns out that somebody else has done it already, we begin to feel jealous and resentful. In fact, the dharma has been marketed or auctioned in that way. But from the point of view of ati, there is "all" dharma rather than "the" dharma. The notion of "one and only" does not apply anymore. If the gigantic pancake falls on our head, it falls on everybody's head.

In some sense it is both a big joke and a big message. You cannot even run to your next-door neighbor saying, "I had a little pancake fall on my head. What can I do? I want to wash my hair." You have nowhere to go. It is a cosmic pancake that falls everywhere on the face of the earth. You cannot escape—that is the basic point. From that point of view, both the problem and the promise are cosmic.

If you are trying to catch what I am saying, quite possibly you cannot capture the idea. In fact, it is quite possible that you do not understand a word of it. You cannot imagine it in even the slightest, faintest way. But it is possible that there are situations that exist beyond your logic, beyond your system of thinking. That is not an impossibility. In fact it is highly possible.

The earlier yanas talk about the rug being pulled out from under our feet, which is quite understandable. If our landlord kicks us out of our apartment, the rug is pulled out from under our feet, obviously. That is quite workable, and we find that we can still relate with our world. But in ati we are talking about the sky collapsing onto us. *Nobody* thinks of that possibility. It is an entirely different approach. No one can imagine a landlady or a landlord who could pull that trick on us.

In maha ati we are not talking about gaining ground or losing ground, or how we settle down and find our way around. Instead we are talking about how we can develop headroom. Headroom, or the space above us, is the important thing. We are interested in how space could provide us with a relationship to reality, to the world.

I do not think we should go into too much detail about maha ati. I have basically been finger painting, but that is as far as we can go at this point. However, we could discuss another topic that is closely related to ati yana: crazy wisdom.

Using the word *crazy* from the English language to describe tantric experience is very tricky because of the various ideas we have about craziness. In the American Indian tradition there was a warrior named Crazy Horse. He was a crazy, old, wise eccentric, who was a great warrior and had tremendous courage. Being crazy is also associated with the idea of being absurd, on the verge of lunacy. There is also a notion of craziness as being unconventional. And sometimes we talk about somebody being crazy about music or crazy about honey or sugar. We mean that somebody takes excessive pleasure in something or has an excessive fascination, to the point where he might destroy himself by being so crazy about whatever it is.

We might also say that someone is crazy if he doesn't agree with us. For instance, if we are trying to form a business, we will approach somebody to be our business partner who agrees with our business proposals. We tell him that the two of us can make lots of money. And if we approach this "uncrazy" person properly, he will accept our logic and he will love the idea of going into business with us. Whereas if we approach an intelligent "crazy" person, he will see through us. He will see any holes in our plan or any neurosis that our business might create. So we don't want to approach such a person as a business partner: "I won't talk to him. He's crazy." What we mean is, "He will see through me. He won't buy my simplistic logic, my trip." That description of craziness comes somewhat close to the tantric idea of craziness. Still, such craziness has a sense of basic ground. There is a lot of room, a lot of trust, but there is also a lot of solidity.

We might also view our grandparents' orthodoxy as crazy. They are so soaked in their own culture and their own norms that they don't understand our culture at all. Their crazy ways make them practically unapproachable to us. We cannot shake their faith and their convictions, and we feel frustrated when we have something to say to them and they don't respond as we want. So we might regard them as semi-crazy.

I don't think crazy wisdom fits any of the examples above. Instead crazy wisdom is the basic norm or the basic logic of sanity. It is a transparent view that cuts through conventional norms or conventional emotionalism. It is the notion of relating properly with the world. It is knowing how much heat is needed to boil water to make a cup of tea, or how much pressure you should apply to educate your students. That level of craziness is very wise. It is based on being absolutely wise, knowing exactly what to do. Such a wise person is well-versed in the ways of the world, and he has developed and understood basic logic. He knows how to build a campfire, how to pitch a tent, and how to brush his teeth. He knows how to handle himself in relating with the world, from the level of knowing how to make a good fire in the fireplace up to knowing the fine points of philosophy. So there is absolute knowledgeability. And then, on top of that, craziness begins to descend, as an ornament to the basic wisdom that is already there.

In other words, crazy wisdom does not occur unless there is a basic understanding of things, a knowledge of how things function as they are. There has to be a trust in the normal functioning of karmic cause and effect. Having been highly and completely trained, then there is enormous room for crazy wisdom. According to that logic, wisdom does not exactly go crazy; but on top of the basic logic or basic norm, craziness as higher sanity, higher power, or higher magic, can exist.

One attribute of crazy wisdom is fearlessness. Having already understood the logic of how things work, fearlessness is the further power and energy to do what needs to be done, to destroy what needs to be destroyed, to nurse what should be nursed, to encourage what should be encouraged, or whatever the appropriate action is.

The fearlessness of crazy wisdom is also connected with bluntness. Bluntness here is the notion of openness. It is a sense of improvising, being resourceful, but not in the sense of constantly trying to improvise the nature of the world. There are two approaches to improvising. If we have a convenient accident and we capitalize on that, we improvise as we go along. That is the conventional sense of the word. For instance, we might become a famous comedian, not because of our perceptiveness, but purely because we make funny mistakes. We say the wrong things at the wrong time and people find us hilarious. Therefore we become a famous comedian. That is approaching things from the back door, or more accurately, it is like hanging out in the backyard.

The other approach to improvising, or bluntness, is seeing things as they are. We might see humor in things; we might see strength or weakness. In any case, we see what is there quite bluntly. A crazy wisdom person has this sense of improvising. If such a person sees that something needs to be destroyed rather than preserved, he strikes on the spot. Or if something needs to be preserved, although it might be decaying or becoming old hat, he will nurse it very gently.

So crazy wisdom is absolute perceptiveness, with fearlessness and bluntness. Fundamentally, it is being wise, but not holding to particular doctrines or disciplines or formats. There aren't any books to follow. Rather, there is endless spontaneity taking place. There is room for being blunt, room for being open. That openness is created by the environment itself. In fact, at the level of crazy wisdom, all activity is created by the environment. The crazy wisdom person is just an activator, just one of the conditions that have evolved in the environment.

Since we are reaching the end of our tantric journey together, so to speak, I would like to say something about how you could relate to all of this information that you have received. You don't have to try to catch the universe in the same way that you would try to catch a grasshopper or a flea. You don't *have* to do something with what you have experienced, particularly. Why don't you let it be as it is? In fact, that might be necessary. If you actually want to use something, you have to let it be. You cannot drink all the water on earth in order to quench your thirst eternally. You might drink a glass of water, but you have to leave the rest of the water, rivers, and oceans so that if you are thirsty again, you can drink more. You have to leave some room somewhere. You don't have to gulp everything down. It's much nicer not to do that; in fact, it is polite.

If you are terribly hungry and thirsty, you want to attack the universe as your prey all at once: "I'll have it for my dinner or my breakfast. I don't care." You don't think about anybody else who might have just a humble request, who might just want to have a sip from your glass of milk or a piece of meat from your plate. If you are told that you should be devotional, you might think that means that you should be even more hungry and try to get every possible blessing into your system. Since you are hungry, you suck up everything, all the systems and resources that exist, including your own. You don't find yourself being a productive human being; instead you find yourself becoming a monster.

There are a lot of problems with that, unless you have the umbrella notion of maha ati, which says: "It's okay. Everything is okay. Just take a pinch of salt, a spoonful of soy sauce. Just take one shot of whiskey. Don't rush; everything is going to be okay. You can have plenty of room if you want. Just cool it." You don't have to do a complete job, all at once. If you go too far, if you are too hungry, you could become a cosmic monster. That message is very courageous, but very few people have the courage to say that.

I am actually concerned and somewhat worried about how you are going to handle all this material. You could overextend yourselves and get completely zonked or completely bewildered. Or you could use this as just another clever reference point, a new vocabulary or logic to manipulate your friends and your world. What you do with this material is really up to you. I hope that you will feel grateful for this introduction to the tantric world, and I hope that you will realize from this that the world is not all that bad and confused. The world can be explored; it is workable, wherever you go, whatever you do. But I would like to plant one basic seed in your mind: I feel that it is absolutely important to make the practice of meditation your source of strength, your source of basic intelligence. Please think about that. You could sit down and do nothing, just sit and do nothing. Stop acting, stop speeding. Sit and do nothing. You should take pride in the fact that you have learned a very valuable message: You actually can survive beautifully by doing nothing.

Lord Marpa's Praise to the Gurus

Lord Akṣobhya, Mahāsukhakāya,
United with Vajraḍākinī,
Chief of ḍākas,
Śrī Heruka, I praise you and prostrate.

Collector of commands and secret mantras,
Possessor of the Secret,
Propagator of the holy dharma in the world of men,
Lord Nāgārjuna, father and son, I praise you.

You who bring down the overwhelming vajra thunderbolt,
The kind one who protects from fear,
Tilopa, lord of the three levels,
Who has attained supreme siddhi, I praise you.

Undergoing twelve trials attending the guru,
All the piṭakas and tantras
You realized in an instant;
Lord Buddha in human form, I praise you.

Indestructible form of mahāmudrā,
Possessing the uncontrived primordial essence,
Realizing the truth of the bliss of simplicity,
Lord Prince Maitrīpa, I praise at your feet.

Expounding the doctrine of the command lineage,
Attaining the siddhi of the profound Guhyasamāja,
You are endowed with compassion and wisdom,
Jñānagarbha, I praise at your feet.

Dwelling in charnal grounds, solitudes, and under trees,
A kusulu savoring potency,
Possessing the miracle of traveling in space,
Kukkurīpā, I praise you.

Having realized the truth of abundance,
Possessing the potency of moonbeams,
You satisfy and bring bliss to those who see you,
Yoginī, I praise you.

Resting in the shade of the excellent umbrella
Adorned with golden ribbons,
Seated in the sky, attaining mastery over the sun and moon
Jetsüns of Nepal, I praise you.

Overcoming the worldly attachment of grasping and
    fixation,
Possessing the benefit of attending the guru,
Holding principally to the practice of enlightenment,
Preserving the learning of mahāyāna,
Clearing away obstructions as well as obstacles caused by
    agents of perversion,
The friend who introduces one to the good guru,
Guiding masters, I praise you.

The merit of praising the guru
Is equal to offering to the buddhas of the three times.
By this merit of praising the masters,
May all beings attend spiritual friends.

"Lord Marpa's Praise to the Gurus" is excerpted from The Life of Marpa the Translator, *translated by the Nālandā Translation Committee under the direction of Chögyam Trungpa,* © 1982 *by Diana J. Mukpo, published by Shambhala Publications, Inc.*

THE LION'S ROAR

An Introduction to Tantra

Edited by SHERAB CHÖDZIN KOHN

Editor's Foreword

THE TWO SEMINARS that make up this book were given by Vidya-dhara the Venerable Chögyam Trungpa Rinpoche, in May 1973 in San Francisco, and December 1973 in Boulder, Colorado, respectively. Each bore the title "The Nine Yanas." *Yana* is a Sanskrit word meaning "vehicle." It refers to a body of doctrine and practical instruction that enables students to advance spiritually on the path of buddhadharma. Nine yanas, arranged as successive levels, make up the whole path. Teaching nine yanas means giving a total picture of the spiritual journey.

To give this total picture in 1973 meant a new departure for the Vid-yadhara Trungpa Rinpoche in his teaching in the West. It meant intro-ducing tantra, or vajrayana, because the last six of the nine yanas are tantric yanas. Until the San Francisco seminar, though students under-stood that the Vidyadhara's ultimate perspective was tantric, and though he often spoke in general terms about the tantric approach, specific de-tails were taboo. He turned aside prying questions about tantra with humor, derision, intimidation, evasion, or whatever other means was handy.

Then he embarked on a new phase in his teaching. In May he gave the San Francisco seminar, introducing tantra for the first time as a level of teaching that could actually become available to his students if they worked through the preceding levels. In the fall he taught the Vajradhatu Seminary, the first in a long series of yearly three-month practice-and-study intensives that took the form of detailed instruction on the nine yanas. The seminaries were not public. Here students who had already received appropriate training were prepared to enter upon tantric prac-tice. Immediately after that first seminary, in December, the Vidyadhara taught the nine yanas to the public again in Boulder, once again holding out the possibilities of the complete path. This time, after each of his own talks, he had one of his students fresh from seminary explain something of what he had understood and experienced there.

Tantra is an astonishing doctrine. It seems to come out of primordial depths of experience and run at all kinds of odd angles to convention and conceptual thinking. It eludes these two would-be stabilizers of human experience; therefore the presentation of it is shocking and raw. One of the slogans that comes out of the tantric Buddhist tradition of Tibet is *tampe tön ni jikpa me,* which the Vidyadhara chose to translate, "The proclamation of truth is fearless." He made that the motto of Vajradhatu, the religious organization he founded, and that motto strongly characterizes the seminars we have before us.

Traditionally the elements of a situation in which the dharma is transmitted are enumerated as the right teacher, teaching, place, time, and students. All five shape the event. The last three factors shaping these two seminars can be evoked most simply by recalling that this was the time in America of hippies and the "spiritual supermarket." It was a period that was a crack between periods. One social minibubble of manners and outlooks had been punctured and let, another had yet to inflate. It was a moment of openness, of exuberance and candor.

Perhaps these elements provide a partial explanation of the extraordinary qualities of the Vidyadhara Trungpa Rinpoche's teaching. In it, there is a near absence of protective reserve. Guarding and cherishing the essence of tradition, he steps beyond its stone walls to meet his students on open ground. He does not rely on established doctrinal formulations, but speaks from a nonconceptual, essential understanding of things and explains them in terms experiential for his audience. After he has already made an experience clear, he might say, "In fact the traditional metaphor is . . ." or "The traditional term for this is . . ." He sometimes referred to his unique style of displaying the inner heart of the teaching without focusing on its outer details as "finger painting." This book is an excellent example of how his "finger painting" can directly communicate insight far beyond the pale of conventional understanding. He does not present us with airtight rehearsals of doctrine. To any audience, then or now, such presentations can become like displays in a glass case in a museum, remote though perhaps fascinating. Instead, here, the complete teachings of buddhadharma are presented fresh and raw, with their odor intact, as personal experience. They are the mighty roaring of a great lion of dharma. Many of those who first heard them are tantric practitioners today.

In this book I have put the Boulder seminar first, because it seemed to provide an easier leg-up for the general reader than the San Francisco one. Chronological purists may want to read them in the other order. I have provided a few explanatory notes for the general reader. Readers with some specialized knowledge can skip them without loss.

> *May the sound of the great drum of dharma*
> *Eliminate the suffering of sentient beings.*
> *May the dharma be proclaimed*
> *Through a million kalpas.*

SHERAB CHÖDZIN KOHN
Nova Scotia, 1991

Part One

NINE YANAS SEMINAR

BOULDER
DECEMBER 1973

ONE

The Journey

THE BUDDHIST JOURNEY is a journey from beginning to end in which the end is also the beginning. This is the journey of the nine yanas, the nine stages that students go through on the path. *Yana* means "vehicle" or "mode of transport." Once you get onto this particular bandwagon, it is an ongoing journey without reverse and without brakes. You have no control over the horse that is pulling this carriage. It is an ongoing process. Beginning this journey is committing yourself to a particular karmic flow, a karmic chain reaction. It is like being born. When you are born, nobody can say, "That was just a rehearsal," and take the whole thing back. Once you are born, you keep on growing up, growing up, getting older, becoming aged, more aged, and then finally you die. When you are born, there is a certain amount of commitment involved—to be born as a human child from a mother's womb, with parents, with a house, and so on.

This journey is a very definite one, absolutely definite, and that is why it is called Buddhism. Although *-ism* is a rather ugly suffix, it is a definite "ism." It is a "Buddha-ism," because we are trying to imitate Buddha's journey. And when we try to imitate Buddha's journey, it just so happens that what we are doing becomes an "ism." It is a real journey, and it involves a real commitment. It also involves some kind of dogma. It means associating yourself with a certain doctrine, a certain formulation of truth. We are not embarrassed to call ourselves Buddhists. In fact we take pride in it, because we have found a way, a path, that makes it possible for us to associate ourselves with Buddha, the

Awakened One. *Awakened* here means highly awakened, fully awakened, awakened to the point of being entirely sane, to the point where there is no neurosis to confuse our journey. Ours is a completely sane approach. Thus there is room for pride, room for dogma, room for real commitment. That is the quality of the nine-yana journey.

There is a subtle difference between doctrine or dogma or commitment that is based purely on one's own interest in awakening and the same based on defending oneself against somebody else's belief. Buddhism's approach is the former, and in that respect it can be called a path of nonviolence. We are not interested in putting down any other spiritual journeys taking place elsewhere in this universe. We concentrate on the journey we ourselves are taking.

If we were driving on a highway and became fascinated by the oncoming traffic on the other side of the highway, we might become blinded by the glare of headlights coming toward us, lose track of our own steering, and end up in an accident. But we are interested in this one, direct journey. We keep our eyes on the dotted white line that goes with our direction. We might change lanes, of course. There are faster lanes and slower lanes, but we do not try to get on the *other side* of the road. That is unlawful. There are no U-turns allowed.

So the journey is definite, absolutely definite, definite to the point of being dogmatic. It is dogmatic in the sense that there is no room for insanity or confusion.

You might ask, "If there is no room for confusion, since we are all confused, how can we go on this journey? Are you saying that there is no hope for us to travel on this path? Do we have to get rid of our confusion first in order to embark on this journey?" As far as I know, the answer is no, you do not have to get rid of your confusion first. Precisely because of your confusion, because of your bewilderment and the chaos that you experience, this is the most unconfusing journey you can ever take.

If you are utterly confused, you are confused to the point of seeming to yourself to be unconfused. This is what we call "spiritual materialism"—you have your ideas of the good way, the higher path, and so on, and you think you are beyond confusion.[1] In that case, you might try to cross over to the other side of the road, make U-turns. Because you think you are an unconfused person, you presume you have all kinds of leeway. But in our case, since we know we are confused, we stick to our one journey. Since we know we are confused, this becomes the true confusion, which you can walk on—drive along—as the true path. Working on confusion is the basic point. Since we are highly confused, we have a better chance of getting into this kind of direct and real path. Since we are so very confused without a doubt, we have a big chance, tremendous possibilities. The more confused we are, single-mindedly confused, the more we have one direction, one path, one highway.

Sometimes it seems there is an opportunity to interrupt our confusion by taking a break, taking a rest here and there. As you drive along the highway, you see a rest area. How about turning in to that, pulling in for just a few minutes? Or there's a sign, "food, gas, lodging." How about taking a little rest? Those advertisements for a break, those signposts, in Buddhist terms are called the daughters of Mara. They slow your journey. Suppose you stopped for every one of those signposts, you turned off and stopped and then came back to the highway. Your journey would be delayed, would double and triple in length. You wouldn't get to your destination on time at all. You would be delayed. As a matter of fact, you might not only be delayed. You might be seduced into stopping at a particular motel and fall asleep forever. Go to the Holiday Inn, celebrate life; go to the Ramada Inn, enjoy the salad bar of the spiritual feast. There are an infinite number of places where you can eat food and fall asleep forever.

What we are saying is we should try to be very practical—get on the highway and don't stop anywhere. Before you begin your journey, fill up your gas tank to the top. Make the journey and don't get tired. If you get tired of driving your vehicle, turn to your friends. Ask them to take the wheel. You become the passenger and *go on*. There's no point in stopping at these places. This is the yana, this is the journey. None of those little seductions of spiritual materialism that are presented to us are worthwhile. Each one of them says to us, "Don't go too far. Stay here with us. Stop at our place. Spend your money here."

In this respect, the Buddhist path is ruthless, absolutely ruthless, almost to the point of being uncompassionate. What we could say is that we are not looking for pleasure. The journey is not particularly geared for finding pleasure; it's not a pleasure trip. It is a visiting trip rather than a pleasure trip. By no means is it a vacation, a holiday. It is a pragmatic journey. You want to see your mother, your father. You undertake the journey to see them, and you keep driving constantly, maintaining your speed. You don't make any of those roadside stops. You just go, you drive straight to your parents' home.

One of the greatest misunderstandings people have is regarding the spiritual journey as a vacation trip with all kinds of nice things happening on the side. It is a direct journey, visiting our relatives. We don't actually want to see them, but at the same time we are intrigued, fascinated by the possibility of seeing them. "I wonder what they're doing. I wonder how they're getting on." That is precisely what our journey is about.

There is a Buddhist term, *dharmata*, which means dharma-ness, the isness of reality. Isness is the parents we are trying to visit. This isness might turn out to be chaotic, terribly embarrassing, or maybe fantastically beautiful and enlightening. All the same, we make our journey back home, back home somewhere, wherever it is.

We left our home a long time ago. We dropped out of college, and we've been wandering here and there, hitchhiking. We are leading our life of a hippie or a tripper, or whatever. We've been here, there, and everywhere. Some time ago, we started to think, "I wonder what my mother's doing. Maybe I should phone her and find out." We phoned her, and then we thought, "Now that I've heard her voice on the phone, I'm more intrigued to see her. Maybe I should pay her a visit. Also, maybe my grandmother would be an interesting person to meet again after all these years. Maybe I should go back and pay her a visit. Grandfather, too, maybe I should visit him." That is exactly what our journey is like. Going back to our heritage, our origin, that is the meaning of "journey" here. So it is not a pleasure trip.

A journey like this can be painful. You wonder why you are taking such a journey. It was not long ago that you felt embarrassed by your family. They gave you enormous pain, real pain. There were all kinds of hassles connected with your parents and grandparents. Your memory of them and your memory of yourself in connection with them is painful.

That is the neurosis of our own basic being. It is highly neurotic, completely confused. We carry a fat body or a skinny body, and we have this big dictionary that we carry with us. Each time we open the dictionary we find a word, which is a piece of our subconscious gossip. And each time we find a word, we close down—we get anxious about the whole situation. Then we open this book again and find another word. This produces further anxiety, more subconscious gossip. We're hampered: We're completely crowded, confused, and claustrophobic with all the passion, aggression, and all kinds of other things going on in our minds bouncing back on us.

Sometimes, of course, we try to put this off on somebody else—kick somebody or make love to somebody. These involvements provide further fuel for the constantly ongoing fire of our emotions. Even trying to get away from it, to turn our minds toward the higher truths, only adds further fuel. We say, "Now I am getting rid of all that, because I'm getting involved with a higher truth. Whew!" But it comes back again. "Oh-oh," we say, "here I go again." And the same trip goes on again and again and again, constantly. An awareness of unending confusion begins to develop heavily in our state of mind.

We might say, "I'm a happy person. I've got my life worked out. I've found a certain truth that I can rest my mind in. I don't have a problem anymore. My existence is very simple. I've paid my debts materially, psychologically, and spiritually." The more we say and think things like that, the more there is a very subtle but fundamental pin piercing our heart. It says, "Am I doing the right thing? Maybe I'm doing the wrong thing."

An endless journey of this and that, that and this, is going on all the time. We may think that we have encountered a greater truth, the greatest doctrine of all, or we may tell ourselves that we are just beginners— "I'm just a beginner, but I have found a solid point to begin from"—but whatever we think, whatever we tell ourselves, the whole thing is chaos, absolute chaos. We have question after question happening constantly, all the time. We have even lost track of where we're going or of whether we're coming or going. Having heard the truth, we think, "Is that really the truth?" We ask ourselves, "Do I exist or don't I?" Or, "Who am I, what am I?" This kind of experience is not necessarily restricted to LSD trippers, not at all. Even people who are absolutely normal, in the ordinary sense of the term, who think they're doing okay and are on the right track, have the same kind of confusion, a complete mingling and mix-up of this and that, continually woven into each other. It is fantastically confusing, absolutely confusing. We are confused to the extent that we do not even know who we are or what our journey is about.

This is particularly the case with well-known poets, writers, and psychologists. They seemingly work out their trip purely by writing a book or doing a poetry recital or by adopting the role of a teacher and instructing people. That is the only reference point they have. The rest of their mind is completely in turmoil.

The point is, we have to acknowledge this confusion. Let us acknowledge that it is actually there, that it is happening with us all the time. No matter how much we are confused, no matter how chaotic our experience is, we have some reference point that enables us to know that this is happening. There is some little secret corner in us that says, "This is actually happening to me." That is there, even though we do not want to admit our confusion or tell anybody about it. Publicly or privately, we do not want to admit that this is happening, but personally, we know it. It's because of this little secret of ours that we might get offended in the supermarket. The cashier says, "Thank you and take it easy. Take it easy, now." We think, "How could he know? He doesn't really know who I am and what I am. That was just a common phrase he used."

What I'm saying is that though we think our confusion is highly secret, it's actually highly public. In fact the secret is a secret only for us privately; the fact that such a secret is being kept is public. The self-deception is as outrageous as that. Our private parts are common knowledge, whether we believe it or not.

In Buddhist terms, that private-parts kind of pain is known as *duhkha,* which means suffering—the fundamental suffering. So you don't have to ask anybody, not even a teacher or master, what is meant by pain, duhkha, suffering. You just have to refer to things as they are, this thing that we have, our familiar thing that we have. It's this thingy-ness, which seemingly should be kept private and unseen and unknown even to ourselves. But it is public knowledge.

We should admit this infamous, familiar pain. This is the pain that is actually happening. We cannot say that it is just nothing. It is the biggest thing that we have to hide. We plan all kinds of ways to hide it, thinking that nobody will know. It is like the story of the man who was stealing a bell. He covered his own ears so that nobody would hear anything. A lot of people, including those who are supposed to be the smartest, do that. They turn out not to be so smart. We are so very subtle, therefore we end up being so very obvious. It is really very, very embarrassing; and that embarrassment is pain, duhkha, suffering. Trying to hide our private parts does not work out the way we wanted it to.

Realizing this fundamental suffering, the private parts that we stupidly try to hide—being so intelligent and so stupid at the same time—is the first step of the journey, the first step of Buddhism. Buddha taught about this in his first sermon, calling it duhkha satya, the truth of suffering. This is the first of the four noble truths. To realize it is a very noble thing, fantastically noble. It is the highest thing you can discover. This most terrible thing that we are trying to hide more than anything has been exposed as the truth, as dharma, as doctrine. The absolute truth we have discovered is that hiding it doesn't work. Discovering that this hidden factor is exposed already is the highest thing of all. It is the real truth, and if we acknowledge it, it is a beautiful truth, a fantastic truth. The hypocrisy of the whole universe, not just of this world but of the whole universe, of this entire cosmic system, has collapsed—by realizing its own hypocrisy. Acknowledgment of our thingy factor as pain is the highest truth, the most powerful weapon of all. It is a fantastic discovery. Once we have acknowledged that, we have no solid ground to stand on anymore. That is the starting point of all the yanas, the foundation.

Student: You seem to advise against resting when you are tired and want to rest. But pushing yourself is spiritual aggression. Where is the medium between those two?

Trungpa Rinpoche: Taking a proper rest is quite different from taking a break from your embarrassment. Usually when we want to take a rest, it means we don't have enough strength to continue our hypocrisy. But taking an ordinary proper rest is quite different from maintaining the showmanship of your hypocrisy. While you are taking a proper rest is the best time to expose your hypocrisy. You can expose your hypocrisy by falling asleep. You can expose yourself simultaneously with whatever else you are doing all the time.

The point is that there is a very abstract feeling that the whole world is my embarrassing private parts and that I don't want to let go of relating to things that way. So I just take a rest so I can maintain my shield, the curtain of my hypocrisy. A person cannot rest in that properly. People work hard even while they sleep, maintaining their hypocrisy. A real rest, a real break, comes from letting go of that heavy labor.

Student: So we try to maintain the fiction that we're not suffering, that we're okay?

Trungpa Rinpoche: It's more than that. When you say you're okay, that means you've been able to conceal yourself. Nobody has seen your private parts, therefore you're okay. This is all because you don't want to expose yourself. Real okay would be the result of letting go. That is the meaning of the truth of suffering. It is painful to see yourself letting go and everything being exposed. This is not particularly pleasant. We wouldn't call it blissful, but it is blissful to the extent that it is being truthful. When you realize the indestructibility of the truth, you connect with an entirely different dimension of reality and security. You have nothing to lose, therefore you're okay. This contrasts with the sense of having lots to gain.

Student: Then why does pain and suffering intensify so much as you progress along the path?

Trungpa Rinpoche: Because you are continually realizing that you have further subtle games; you keep uncovering them all the time.

Student: You spoke about going along the highway not looking at the opposite lane, not getting sidetracked. Isn't that a sacrifice of the panoramic awareness you often talk about?

Trungpa Rinpoche: Looking at the opposite lane could hardly be called panoramic awareness. With panoramic awareness, you see the whole scene. There are no sidetracks. Looking at the opposite lane is just one-sided vision, being distracted by one highlight. You lose the rest of the panoramic vision, which can cause an accident.

Student: Does the pride in being a Buddhist that you talked about at the beginning of the lecture have anything to do with the discovery or unmasking of suffering?

Trungpa Rinpoche: That pride is a kind of conviction, a sense of certainty, the sense that you are taking a definite, particular journey, one which does not provide false hospitality or false pleasures, because it's so real. In that perspective, the sense of security is a sense of the groundlessness of security as opposed to a sense of security based on ego's clinging. You have pride in that kind of security, because you begin to have a sense of the looseness of the air you are flying in as you fall to the ground. You begin to realize that the air is a very secure place; the air is what makes it possible that you *can* fall.

Student: Is that the kind of pride that makes the discovery so real?

Trungpa Rinpoche: Definitely, because then you have no trust in anything else besides the fact that you have nothing to lose.

Student: It seems to me that there is far less pain today than there was thousands of years ago when the Buddha taught. Is his teaching that existence is pain still applicable?

Trungpa Rinpoche: We are not talking so much about physical pain but about this thingness in us that creates pain, which is the pain. This is a universal thing, always up-to-date. Creating happiness in us is beyond technological means. In the midst of trying to create happiness technologically, that sense of thingness will be present all the time. Thus Buddhism is completely up-to-date, therefore it is dogma, rather than being religion or philosophy. It is like telling a child, "Those electric burners on your stove may look beautiful, so nice and orangey-red, but if you put your finger on them, it will get burned." Buddhism is as simple as that.

S: Is it not the nature of ego that it is always suffering?

TR: The ego suffers even without its expressions, its manifestations. Ego suffers bluntly, itself.

S: It sounds like when you discover suffering as your foundation, it's like building your foundation on sand, or even worse, in the air, like a castle in the air. It leads automatically to a sense of impermanence, to insecurity. It seems strange that that should be the beginning of the path. You have to put up with complete insecurity. The only security you get through discovering truth is insecurity.

TR: Well said. That is what is called in Buddhist terminology *egolessness*. Discovering that is discovering another truth, which is a firm foundation on which you can build the nine stories of the nine yanas, a tremendous castle of enlightenment.

Student: Where does joy come into the path?

Trungpa Rinpoche: Joy can only come when you realize that there's nothing to be joyful about.

S: That sounds morbid.

TR: What do you mean by morbid?

S: It seems to me that joy is as real as pain, and when you feel joy, to say all that there is is pain is to spit in the face of the joy that you feel.

TR: Are you saying that you feel joy when you don't feel pain? Or do you feel pain when you feel joy?

S: Yes.

TR: That's it. Real joy comes when you experience that something is actually there. That is real joy as opposed to something flowery and sweet. The problem of pain is that there is nothing secure; you're about to lose your ground. Usually when we experience joy, it is purely superficial joy with pain going on beneath the whole thing. Real joy comes when you realize the superficiality of that experience. Then you begin to realize that there is something really happening, whether in the form of pain or pleasure. Then you have the real security of a real discovery of truth. That is actually solid. Joy is related with the solid experience of securing one's ground. Real security could be either pain or pleasure—it is that something real is happening. That is why joy is synonymous with truth. From that point of view, the discovery of the first noble truth, the truth of suffering, is the discovery of real fundamental joy. Because suffering is real; it's absolute. There is nothing other than suffering, and it is very solid and fundamental. It is heroic, indestructible, and beautiful.

Student: Can you explain again what you mean by suffering?

Trungpa Rinpoche: The idea of suffering here is the thingness in us, which is very lumpy and slightly inconvenient. It is the awkwardness in us, which is not very nice or pleasant or flowing. There is something that is in the way that doesn't allow us to be free-flowing. There is a vast thing that is in the way somewhere. That's the fundamental suffering. It is not particularly painful in the ordinary sense of physical pain. But it is in the way. It stops us from flowing. In that sense, suffering could be regarded as synonymous with the idea of a "hang-up."

S: It seems that you don't always have to be suffering, though.

TR: Well, you always have a thing with you, whatever you do. You don't have to be suffering all the time, but you have a thing all the time. The thingy-ness is suffering, though it's true you don't have to be experiencing painfulness all the time.

S: Should you just forget about distinguishing between pain and pleasure?

TR: It's not particularly a question of distinguishing pain and pleasure. The only thing that matters is to begin to realize your thingness, your beingness, that fundamental and deep feeling of awkwardness. That seems to be the point. You might experience pain and pleasure as two or as one, or you might feel that either is okay, you don't care. But still there is this thing that says that pain and pleasure are one. This thingness is happening there—as if you swallowed a lump of rock and it's still in your stomach.

S: Is that real?

TR: It's up to you. It's real as far as you are concerned, if you are talking about it. In that sense, of course it's real. The more you discuss it, the more real it gets. In fact, it becomes a belief, a hang-up. It is definitely there.

Student: A moment can be a warming thing and feel good, and it can also be a burning thing—

Trungpa Rinpoche: It doesn't matter. The dichotomy is there.

Ego and pain is a mystical experience, actually, which transcends both pleasure and pain and thingness and thinglessness. But still there is this thing there that is happening. Right there. That could be called spiritual experience, if you like. What I mean by spiritual experience is the indefinable, ineffable experience of thingness. It is beyond words, beyond concepts. But it is definitely there, hanging on there. It is a mystical experience that everybody has.

TWO

Hopelessness

WE HAVE DISCUSSED the nature of pain. That leads us to the subject of commitment, or discipline. What is meant by these words is committing ourselves to what is there, which is pain. The discipline is realizing that this commitment is self-existing. There is no way we can get out of this commitment, so we can make it a wholehearted one.

At this point, we have to understand the origin of pain. As we said, there is that sense of thingness that is hanging out with us all the time. It is part of our shadow. It constantly speaks to us the unspoken word of embarrassment, of inconvenient confusion. As we said, this thingness is connected with suffering and pain. Acknowledging that is our starting point.

It is more than just a starting point, because it inspires us to look further. It inspires us to discover what is behind that awareness of thingness. For example, I personally cannot say I love you or I hate you. There is something that holds us back, that is preventing us from saying such things. It is a sense that we do not want to commit ourselves to becoming involved with embarrassing private parts. And that thingness there that is holding us back has a back and a front. It is just a face, a mask. If you examine it, if you look at somebody who has a mask on and look behind it, you find all kinds of strings and knots. You begin to understand how this person keeps his mask on—with all the bundles of knots in back. Exposing this mask is discovering the origin of pain, of suffering.

The unmasking process is connected with the second yana, the pratyekabuddhayana. The mask develops when we try to trace our origins, trace back and back to the origin of the origin. The mask develops from our wanting to ignore ourselves as a confused person to begin with. There is a traditional image for this process of ignoring. It is called the blind grandmother.

The blind grandmother was the creator of our whole family, the whole race. She is also a professional in relating to all the functioning of mental games, ideas, objects, and so forth. But at the same time, she's blind. She can't see what's happening right *there*, right *now*.

When we begin to understand the blind-grandmother principle, we realize how our process of ignoring, of not relating to the blind-grandmother-ness, is constantly creating further karmic chain reactions. Further levels of this process develop. The image for the next level is the potter. The potter makes a pot. He spins his potter's wheel around. He throws mud, a dough made of mud, on his wheel, and in accordance with its speed and how he holds his hands, the potter makes a pot. He makes a pot out of the feeling, which is the volitional action of karma.

We have this thingness, this embarrassment, hanging out in our state of being. It is extremely embarrassing and inconvenient. When we look back, we want to ignore this; we don't want to know anything about it. We might say, "It's not me; it has nothing to do with me. It's somebody else's doing. She did it. He did it. I'm clean. I'm in the clear. My only duty is to stick to this thingness." So we expand ourselves based on this thingness. We explore further and further and further. Having created these karmic situations, we go on with all twelve links of the karmic chain of existence, of our basic makeup: ignorance, volitional action, consciousness, name and form, sense perceptions, touch, sensation, desire, grasping, the further grasping that is copulation, birth, old age, and death. And we are back to square one. We go through all those processes, and each one has its traditional image.[1]

This entire map has been seen clearly, thoroughly, and completely by Buddha. Because of Buddha's teaching, we know this entire map of our basic psychology and the origin of that thingness of ours in all the twelve causal links of karma. That thingness is created by going around and around through these twelve again and again. There is birth and death, which leads to a further birth, then ignorance and karma again. It is like a whirlpool, continually circling. That is what is called samsara. We go around and around and around in a circle. The end is the beginning.

Each time we look for the end of the beginning, we create the beginning of the end. Each time we look for the beginning of the end, we create the end of the beginning. Each time we look for the end of the beginning, we create the beginning of the end. We go on and on in this way. We are in samsara, constantly going around and around trying to catch our shadow. The shadow becomes us, and we become the shadow again. It's a constant circling, an endless game. Endless game after endless game after endless game. There are so many games happening.

What we are discussing at this point is the hinayana level, which involves making a complete study of the four noble truths. We are discussing the second noble truth, which is the truth of the origin of suffering. The origin of the suffering of our thingness is circling with speed. The origin of the suffering is the speed. Graspingness, re-creating one karmic situation after another. That is the basic point here.

This is all pretty ironic, maybe even funny. We could laugh at it—there is such foolishness taking place. It is such a foolish thing that we do. Isn't it ironic? Isn't it funny? Isn't it actually absurd? Ha ha! But it is we who are ha-ha, and it turns out to be very grim actually. We might think, "Ha ha," but it is not all that ha-ha, because it is *our* psychological portrait the way Buddha described it, which happens to be highly accurate. It's very scientific. It's very funny.

What's next? Your guess is as good as mine. What's next after what's next after what's next? What's next? Could we get out of this? Trying to get out would be another circle? Sure we could get out of this. We could get out, and then we could get back in, and then we could start all over again.

You are expectant: "Tell us more" [your expressions say]. Sure. By telling you more, we could get into it, then we could get out and get into it and then we could get out and get into it again.

As a matter of fact, the situation is pretty scary, haunting, frightening. In fact there's no ground except the speed itself. No ground, and we go on and on. We could discuss the next subject and give birth to the next thing; then we'd have volitional action, karma, pain and suffering, touch, desire, copulation, death and old age, birth, ignorance all over again. All over again.

"Tell us about freedom, enlightenment." Sure. By all means. But then: all over again. You get out, you get in. You're liberated. You get onto the liberator's bandwagon, and you take a journey, and you come back. You want to be victorious, win a war of some kind: Then you go around all over again, all over again.

We are not making fun of the samsaric world, not at all. We are taking the whole thing very seriously. This is a serious matter. It is a life-and-death matter, very serious. We are talking about reality, freedom, enlightenment, buddhahood, if I may be so presumptuous as to use these words. We are talking about something that is actually happening to us. But so far we haven't touched upon the *heart* of the thing at all. So far we have just discussed the nature of our reality, the confusion that goes on in us all the time. "Nothing new," you say. That's true.

Ladies and gentlemen, you are so faithful and so honest and so straight-faced. I appreciate your seriousness and your long faces, listening to me. That's beautiful—in a way. On the other hand, it's rather grotesque seeing you with your long faces trying to find out about enlightenment.

From this chair, I see lots of faces without bodies, serious faces. Some are wearing glasses, some are not wearing glasses. Some have long hair, some have short hair. But in all cases, it's a long face, made out of a skull wall. These faces—if I had a big mirror behind me, you could see yourselves—are so honest, earnest. Every one of you is a true believer. Every bit of even the glasses you are wearing is a true believer. It is very cute and nice and lovable. It's beautiful—I'm not mocking you at all. I appreciate your patience. You had to wait for a long time and it's late, and now there are all kinds of other things. You're hungry. Probably you had planned to eat after the talk. Probably you are not used to sitting on the floor and would like a nice comfortable chair. All kinds of things go into making up that earnestness. But there is one thing that we haven't touched upon yet, which is that the whole thing is completely hopeless.

Hopelessness. There's no hope, absolutely none whatsoever, to be saved. Hopelessness. Let me define the word *hopelessness*.

Hope is a promise. It is a visionary idea of some kind of glory, some kind of victory, something colorful. There are trumpets and flags, declarations of independence, all kinds of things that are hopeful. Nevertheless, we want to find out the truth here. Discussing the twelve nidanas, the twelve causal links in the karmic chain reaction that goes on all the time, and all the time, *and* all the time, we see that we have no chance, none whatsoever. As long as we possess a body and our face, our face and our facade, we have no chance at all of being liberated, none whatsoever. It is as hopeless as that. There is no hope, absolutely no hope. We are going to be drawn into, and drowned in, a deep pool of shit, an ocean of shit, that is bubbling, gray in color, but smelly at the same time. We are drowning in that all the time. This is true; and the situation is hopeless, absolutely hopeless.

We might think, "I'm very smart, extraordinarily smart. I've read all the books on Buddhism, about the twelve nidanas and about everything else. I have the answers. I've read about tantra. I've read about Naropa and Milarepa.[2] I've read Meister Eckhart, the medieval mystic who talks about beautiful things. And I've even read about Don Juan, who says wonderful things about the nature of reality.[3] I've read Krishnamurti, who is very sensible. I'm hopeful, obviously. There's *got* to be a way out somewhere. There must be something. Things can't be all that gray and hopeless."

But what authority do we have? We've just read the books. Maybe we have a friend who has also read the books, and we comfort each other: "Hey, did you read that book? Isn't that great?" "Sure. I agree with you." We build up a whole organization of believing each other and we make each other feel good. However, there's no lineage, no authority. There's no transmission of information from somebody else's true experience. We have no idea whether Don Juan exists. Maybe he's purely Carlos Castaneda's trip. For that matter, we also have no idea whether the books *Meditation in Action* or *Cutting Through Spiritual Materialism* were really written by myself. Maybe they're somebody else's idea of how things should be. The whole thing is subject to question. Possibly all the miracles described in *The Life and Teaching of Naropa*, translated by Herbert Guenther, supposedly translated by Guenther, were just made up. Do we really know that there was such a person as Naropa at all? How do we know there was such a person as Meister Eckhart? And is it possible that what he said was not true, even if there was such a person? And we have no idea about the actual origin of the *Bhagavad Gita*, which contains divine instructions concerning warfare. We have no idea.

Sometimes one wonders who is fooling whom.

Who thought of the idea of enlightenment, actually? Who dreamed up God? Who proclaimed himself as god over all the earth? It seems that the whole thing is full of shit, actually, if I may use such language. Full of dung.

Sometimes we ask questions because we are really frustrated and we hope to get something out of asking them. Sometimes it is because we are feeling slightly relaxed and want to expose any intrigues that may be going on. Maybe some people are playing a game at our expense, and we would like to expose it. Such trips are constantly going on in our minds. But one thing we haven't come up with is a real understanding of those trips. This is because we haven't fundamentally faced ourselves and the notion of hopelessness. All these messages in scriptures, textbooks, information media, magical displays—whatever we have—are not going to help us. They will just reinforce our blind-grandmother principle of complete ignorance, because we haven't given up any hope. We're still looking around to see if somebody's cheating us. We still believe everything might be okay if we could beat that cheating. That is actually our problem. Nobody has given up hope of attaining enlightenment. Nobody has given up hope of getting out of suffering. That is the fundamental spiritual problem that we have.

We should regard ourselves as helpless persons. That is the first spiritual step we can take. Taking this step is entering what is called the path of unification.[4] It is giving up hope; it is the step of hopelessness. The first path, which comes before this, is called the path of accumulation, in which we gather a lot of materials around us. Then comes the second path, the path of unification, which is giving up hope, totally, and at the same time realizing our helplessness. We have been conned by all kinds of trips, all kinds of spiritual suggestions. We've been conned by our own ignorance. We've been conned by the existence of our own egos. But nothing that has been promised is actually happening. The only thing that is going on is karmic volitional action, which perpetuates our desires and our confusion. Relating with that is the second path, the path of unification.

The reason it is called the path of unification is that there is a sense of uniting ourselves with ourselves. There is a path, there is a goal, and there is a practitioner of the path; but we realize that at the same time those are purely stage props, and the situation is utterly hopeless. We have no way of getting out of this misery at all. Once we realize that there's no way of getting out of this misery, we begin to make a relationship with something.

If we end up in prison with a life sentence, we decorate our cells with pinups and graffiti and make ourselves at home. We might begin to have more gentle feelings about the prison guard and start to enjoy the meals that are presented to us in prison.

Our problem all along has been that we have been too smart, too proud. Our feeling is: I want to stick my neck out all the time. I don't want to relate with anybody else; I want to get enlightened. I'm going to be higher than the rest of you. I don't want to have anything to do with you at all.

That kind of attitude has been the cause of slowing down our spiritual journey. We would do better to take the attitude of the prisoner. Once we realize that we are trapped in our twelve nidanas, imprisoned, we begin to relate much more. We give birth to compassion in our prison cells. And our existence begins to make much more sense based on what we actually are.

I'm afraid this is very, very depressing. Still, it's heroic at the same time. As you acknowledge the basic situation, you become a drummer of the dharma; you fly the flag of the dharma in your prison cell. You understand that your prison cell is made out of walls: this wall, that wall, this wall and that wall. And you have a simple floor and a simple meal. But those things become an interesting monastic situation. It is exactly the same as being in a monastery. Being in prison is the same thing.

That is why this yana is called the pratyekabuddhayana. *Pratyekabuddha* means "self-enlightened buddha." You care about your environment, which is necessary, important, very basic, and also tremendously fun. The fun of hopelessness is very powerful, fantastic.

I'm afraid this is very boring. You see, Buddhism is the only nontheistic religion. It doesn't contain any promises, or doesn't permit any. It just suggests the basic necessity of working with ourselves, fundamentally, very simply, very ordinarily. It is very sensible. You have no complaint when you get to the other end of the trip of Buddhism. It's a very definite journey.

Perhaps we could have a discussion, if you don't feel too depressed.

Student: From what you were saying about hopelessness, I guess it could help one relate to one's environment better, but there is something else. Maybe I'm thinking of another kind of hopelessness, but it seems that hopelessness takes away the inspiration to practice at all. And the same thing in relation to the teacher. If you see him as not being able to save you either, it takes away your inspiration for relating to the teacher.

Trungpa Rinpoche: What's the problem?

S: That seems to me to contradict what you were saying about hopelessness being a way to make a true relationship with the teaching.

TR: Hopelessness is getting into the teaching more because you have no choice. When we think about hopefulness, that involves choices of all kinds. But when you realize that there's no hope at all, the way we were talking about, you end up with just yourself. Then you can generate teachings or expressions of teachings within yourself.

Student: What influences you to slow down if you find yourself speeding?

Trungpa Rinpoche: Hopelessness, obviously. The more you speed, the more frustrated you get. So there's no point in speeding. It's hopeless.

Student: Could you distinguish between hopelessness and despair?

Trungpa Rinpoche: Despair is still hopeful, and hopelessness is utterly hopeless. There is no ground to hang on to. You are completely wiped out, therefore you might hang on to your basic being.

Despair is a resentful attitude. You are in despair because you have a sense of retaliation against something or other. Hopelessness is a very genuine, beautiful, simple act. You're hopeless—it's a fantastic thing. You really *are* hopeless then, you know. There's no trips about it. It's clean-cut.

Student: Rinpoche, does this mean that a person has to experience a lot of suffering before he becomes really hopeless? Or could it just happen on the spot?

Trungpa Rinpoche: Both.

Student: Rinpoche, it would make no sense to try to give up hope. If you did that, you would be hoping not to hope. How do you give up hope?

Trungpa Rinpoche: You don't. You're stuck with hope. And then you're disgusted with it.

Student: If there's no trick to giving up hope, how do you manage not to shoot yourself?

Trungpa Rinpoche: Shoot yourself?

S: Yes.

TR: I don't see the connection.

S: When you're faced with being a fake, that causes panic for sure.

TR: But shooting yourself is creating more pain.

S: Not for long.

TR: Really? How do you know? If you regard the body as the problem, then obviously you might be able to destroy your body. But the whole point here is that your mind is the problem. And you can't get a gun that will shoot your mind. Let us know if you find such a gun.

Student: It seems you're saying that the only hope is hopelessness.

Trungpa Rinpoche: That's true.

Student: But that's a contradiction.

TR: No, the only hope is hopelessness. "Only hope" means that the ground, our sense of security, is the only hope, which is hopeless—you have no ground. You don't make yourself into a target [for the pain] in any way at all, which is hopeless. The only hopelessness is not to provide yourself as a target.

Student: Isn't that true because when you have no hope, there are no expectations? You cease making judgments, so you like whatever you've got?

Trungpa Rinpoche: That could be said.

S: Isn't that the beginning of joy?

TR: Let's not rush too fast.

Student: Hopelessness is: Mind and body are equal? If body and mind are both dropped . . . hopelessness doesn't become. So without hope and with hopelessness, would—

Trungpa Rinpoche: Please don't try too many angles. It is hopeless *straight*. You can't get around it. It will bounce back on you.

Student: Is seeking the mind of a pratyekabuddha still in the realm of hope?

Trungpa Rinpoche: What I have been trying to say is that the mind of a pratyekabuddha is hopeless. We have gotten as far as that, the second yana. The first yana is the acknowledgment of pain. The second yana is the pratyekabuddha realizing hopelessness, realizing the hopelessness of the circle of samsara.

Student: Does the experience of hopelessness always have to be painful? It would seem that after a while you couldn't keep up the pain or the pain would change to something else.

Trungpa Rinpoche: In the beginning it's painful, but in the end, it's reality.

Student: Do you have to realize the truth of your own death before you can become hopeless?

Trungpa Rinpoche: No, your own death is also hopeless. They go together. Your death is hopeless.

Student: At one point, you talked about discipline. You said getting at the origin of pain involved discipline. How does that discipline relate with how you get to hopelessness?

Trungpa Rinpoche: Being faithful to your hopelessness is discipline.

THREE

The Preparation for Tantra

SINCE OUR TIME is too limited to take a slow, extended journey through the nine yanas, we are going to make a jump. We are going to discuss now the preparation for tantra, which is the mahayana path. First we prepare ourselves in such a way that we have a chance to know just ourselves. Then we begin to know otherness, and then we know everything in mandala perspective.[1]

This approach is based on a sense of individuality and on a sense of egolessness at the same time. What happens with the sense of our individuality here is that, in giving up hope, in reaching a state of hopelessness, complete and total hopelessness, a sense of openness begins to develop simultaneously [which contains an element of egolessness]. Because we have given up hope completely, utterly, totally, there is a sense of opening. That particular sense of openness is called faith or devotion. We have completely tired ourselves out, exhausted ourselves beyond our hopefulness. We realize that life is hopeless and that any effort we put in to gain further experience is also hopeless. Then we get into a real understanding of the space between us and our goal. That space is totally and completely full. And that fullness is what is called faith.

Let me give you a Buddhist-dictionary definition, the definition of faith. *Faith* here means dedication to and conviction in one's own intelligence, which permits one's own intelligence to begin to manifest as one's guru, teacher, spiritual friend. You have trust in the basic truth of what you are, who you are. You have some understanding of that, and therefore there is tremendous trust. Trust in oneself in turn radiates further trust toward the other. In this case, the other is your spiritual friend, guru, your master, your teacher. The other acknowledges your existence, and you acknowledge the other's existence and that provides a very solid base of security and well-being. There is a sense that finally you are completely and fully taken care of. That is the definition of faith.

Let me go over that to clarify it further. The definition of faith is: You recognize your existence, which is in turn based on somebody else acknowledging your existence at the same time. This is not a matter of blind faith. It is awakened faith, real faith. You have pain, you are hopeless, and you have somebody else who says, "That's you." This validates your hopelessness. As a result of the agreement that happens between you and the other—your spiritual friend or guru—you realize that something constructive is happening.

It is not purely guesswork. There is a sense of faith based on realizing your hopelessness and having that hopelessness acknowledged by your spiritual friend. You feel secure in the absence of security. There is a sense of trust there.

This is the mahayana path we are discussing here.

Then we have a second category after faith, which is called vigor. The Tibetan word for that is *tsöndrü*.[2] Vigor here has the sense of energy. You are not tired of yourself and you are not tired of working with your spiritual friend or the rest of your friends either. Out of the hopelessness comes inspiration, which brings vigor and a sense of joy—after all, there is something out there that is workable. So you have a feeling of inquisitiveness, an interest in rediscovering your hopelessness [from a different angle]. You have faith in your hopelessness and the communicative relationship you have established with your spiritual friend. In other words, you have devotion. And then beyond that, there is a sense of energy. You are intrigued by the whole thing. You feel something highly intriguing: "Maybe after all there is something in this." It is true, maybe there is something happening. Something's cooking. This sense of intrigue or mystery also ignites your energy, your vigor.

This is like a mad archaeologist who finds a spot to dig. He digs faster and faster and faster. He employs more people to help him. He thinks, "Maybe I'm going to discover gold or a tomb, a temple or a hidden city." It's possible. Here's actually something taking place. But this doesn't turn out to be so much on the fantasy level. There is something realistic happening.

That's vigor. *Virya* is the Sanskrit word for this. The definition of *virya,* our second Buddhist-dictionary term, can be understood like this: A person becomes highly inspired, therefore highly inquisitive; therefore he does not become tired of his task. He's inspired, intrigued, tickled. That's the definition of *virya, tsöndrü.*

The great Indian teacher Shantideva talks about tsöndrü in his writings.[3] His definition of it is "taking delight in the virtue of rediscovering oneself." There is this sense of delight and inquisitiveness.

The next category, number three, is *trenpa* in Tibetan, which means awareness, intelligent awareness. At this level [the mahayana] one practices the six perfections or transcending actions (Skt. *paramita*), which are generosity, discipline, vigor (energy), patience, meditative awareness, and knowledge. All six of those happen with awareness. In talking about awareness, we don't mean that you have to meditate on a certain thing you've been told to meditate on. It is not a question of sitting down and gazing at a candle in order to try to develop awareness, or sitting listening to the traffic trying to daze yourself with that sound. Awareness here is pragmatic awareness of what is actually taking place in the realm of your consciousness, in the realm of your intelligence connected with your sense of being.

You are what you are. You have sense consciousness, six of them according to the Buddhist tradition. The sixth one is mind-consciousness, and the other five are sight, sound, smell, hearing, taste, and touch. The sixth one, mind-consciousness is also regarded as a sense organ—brain and heart work together. And the sense of being takes place there. The awareness that we are talking about here is definitely connected with that sense of being.

As you sit listening to me talk here, you also realize that you are sitting on the floor, which is padded with cushions. The temperature of the room is agreeable. It does not distract your attention. There is no distracting noise to keep you from listening, no traffic sounds, no babies crying. You have a sense of being here, which is also a sense of well-being. You feel well clothed; your clothes are appropriate and suited to the temperature. You can sit here and listen with that sense of well-being, which is awareness. There's an overall awareness of a relaxed state. Things are physically okay, psychologically conducive.

You might feel a bit overstuffed from dinner, or somewhat hungry, looking forward to going home and eating. But those discomforts and desires have become relatively distant, and your main fascination and intrigue can function properly here in this room. That is awareness of well-being that is happening to you right now.

If we want to define that for our Buddhist dictionary, we could say that awareness means a person can tune himself in to certain mental objects and also to a sense of being, or well-being, thoroughly and without distraction. The Sanskrit for the Tibetan *trenpa* is *smriti*. Literally it means "recollection." This is not particularly recollection in the sense of going back to the past. It has more to do with renewing one's habitual patterns, habitual patterns that do not require your further attention. You can be as you are in your basic form. There is a sense of relaxation, which is necessary in order to proceed on the bodhisattva path.

The next is number four, meditation; in Tibetan, *samten*. Here meditation is an extension of the sense of well-being, or awareness, that we've been talking about. There is a feeling of understanding and a feeling of security, which enables you to let go of your mind. The definition of meditation here is the ability to be as you are without further contrivances to make yourself comfortable. The definition of meditation is just a sense of being, a sense of isness that is happening.

Here you are listening to me, listening to this particular "broadcast." You are listening to Radio Peking. You are listening to Radio Peking, but suppose you turn off your radio. Then you find yourself suspended somewhere. You were listening, then that radio was turned off that you had become accustomed to listening to, and you are still there listening to the silence.

It's like television watchers late at night, who will watch up till the very little last dot that appears on their screen. They will watch up till the last little thing when the whole thing dissolves. (In England, an announcer tells you not to forget to turn off your set when the broadcast is over—a very domestic touch.) You turn off your set and you're suspended somewhere, still inquisitive and awake and watchful. That is the state of meditation that we are talking about here. Having turned the set off, you're still watching, but watching nothing. You know you have turned off your set, but you are still there, very awake and ready for something. At the same time, you know that you are not going to get into any entertainment anymore. You've had enough of it. That sense of suspension and of vacancy. Meditation in this sense is like that vacant aftereffect of watching television or listening to the radio. The set is *off*, and you are still fully awake and fully there.

Suppose I said now, "This lecture is over. This is the end. I bid you good night." The moment you heard those words, you would have a sense of your antennae beginning to retract into your basic being. "Wow, the whole thing's gone, finished." And you'd have a sense of well-being taking place. That is the meaning of meditation, samten.

The Sanskrit word for this is *dhyana*, which is the equivalent of *zen*, a sense of meditative absorption without anything in your mind at all to grasp on to. Your television set is turned off, your antennae are retracted: no further entertainment. Yet you are there, definitely there.

There is something very ironical, very funny about this. There is some kind of humor involved here. One catches a glimpse of one's own seriousness: "Now I have turned off this set, and I am still here." You are very serious—something very real is taking place. Empty space. There is a sense of beingness that takes place there that is the essence of meditation. It is not a matter of getting into a spiritual absorption, a higher trance, or anything of that nature. It's a sense of being there, and then being there providing no ground. No entertainment. Blank.

Number five, the fifth category, is *prajna*, which means "knowledge." *Jna* means "intelligence" and *pra* means "premium," "higher," "greater." That's the Sanskrit word, and the Indo-European word comes from that. [*Know, gnosis, cognition,* etc., are etymologically related to *jna.*] Prajna is the premium knowledge, the highest and greatest knowledge of all. It's premium in the sense of premium gas that you can ask for at the gas station. There is a gas shortage these days, but I'm sure there is no shortage of prajna. It's ongoing stuff. Prajna, discriminating knowledge.

Prajna, to make a further entry in our Buddhist dictionary, is a process of looking. It is the highest way of looking at reality. It is like making an acquaintance (in the sense of picking a colleague, a fellow worker). You are working hard enough so you hire your own intelligence to work with you. You create a colleagueship with yourself, you make an acquaintance to work with you—knowledge.

We run into a conflict here with the Christian tradition concerning mystical wisdom. According to the Christian tradition, or any theistic tradition, wisdom comes first and knowledge comes afterward. But in Buddhism, knowledge comes first and wisdom comes later.

Once I watched a television program on Italian classical art—

Michelangelo and Leonardo da Vinci, and so on. It was beautifully done. It was presented by some English lord or other, who spoke very beautifully. A point he made was that in order to understand art in the Western world, you have to look in order to see. That is the approach of a theistic mystical experience: Look in order to see. Seeing is regarded as a discovery; looking is the primary method. It seems obvious: If you want to see, you have to look first. Very sensible; very scientific. Before you draw conclusions, you gather information with the computer. When the computer says thus-and-such and so-and-so is the case, then you begin to see. You look in order to see. But in the nontheistic traditions, such as Buddhism (and at this point, the only nontheistic traditional religion we have in this universe is Buddhism), the idea is to see in order to look. Looking is regarded as much more important, because you can't abandon the world, you can't abandon relationships.

First you have to see. Projections are necessary in order for you to work with yourself. Having related with your projections properly—clearly and thoroughly—having seen things as they are, you start to scrutinize, you start to look. When you look, you discover all kinds of subtle qualities of things as they are, subtleties upon subtleties, fantastic details of things as they are, fantastically colorful.

Saying that you have to see in order to look is a tantric statement. It is very subtle and very precise.

What might happen to us is: We look in order to see. We look first and have a flash of something fantastically beautiful. We look at something and get dazzled by it. We get dazzled and begin to see psychedelic visions of the universe. Fantastic! Wow! Then we are supposed to see whatever it is. But seeing isn't important anymore, because we have already looked. We lost so many subtle little details, because we looked. The Buddhist approach toward perceiving phenomena is to see in order to look, not look in order to see.

This is a definition of prajna that leads toward tantra.

Understanding this is important when it comes to translating certain terms. We translate *jnana* as "wisdom" and *prajna* as "knowledge." A lot of scholars translate *prajna* as "wisdom" or *prajnaparamita* as "wisdom gone beyond." The idea of seeing in order to look is closer to Don Juan's teaching, the American Indian approach.

First you see things, perceive things. I see a lot of faces here. Heads without glasses, heads with glasses. Then I look to see who they are. They are listening to this talk.

Castaneda talks about seeing a jackal or a coyote. Don Juan placed a white cloth somewhere, then later moved it, and in doing so removed a whole landscape. It had something to do with the coyote principle. It's very interesting, very close to tantric Buddhism. The whole thing is based on seeing. For instance, in relation to the idea of choosing a spot, a place where you are going to sit and be yourself. In doing this, once you begin to look, you become very awkward. If you see a spot, you should arrange yourself suitably in it and then begin to look. That seems to be the point in discussing prajna as a preparation for discussing tantra. The pertinent experience of prajna also takes place on the mahayana level.

Looking is demanding, if you look prematurely. But seeing is undemanding if you do it properly. The sense of well-being that we talked about takes place.

Having accomplished faith, vigor, awareness, meditation, and prajna, then we begin to become somewhat proud of ourselves. We feel good. There is a sense of well-being. We do not have to reduce ourselves to the level of bullshit. We are Mount Meru.[4] We are the great mountains of the Himalayas. We are worth being proud of. We have understood faith, energy, awareness, meditation, and knowledge. We have gone through all those with the help of the six paramitas. We now begin to feel that maybe we could stick out our necks again, once more. We are noble sons and daughters of Buddha. We *are* Buddha. We have Buddha in us. Why should we crunch ourselves down and deform our state of being? Why don't we just expand ourselves into our perfect form, our perfect being? We have perceptions and energies and inspirations. We have everything. We have a spiritual friend, we have the teaching. We have everything. What more do we want? We have everything in this whole universe. We have everything there. We have intelligence and understanding and the materials to understand. We have everything. We can afford to extend ourselves a bit more. That is why this approach is called the mahayana, the great vehicle, the bodhisattva path.[5] It is heroic.

We beat the drum of dharma, sound the trumpet of wisdom and compassion, celebrate the feast of intelligence. It is very joyous. And the reason that it is so joyous is because the whole thing is so hopeless. It doesn't provide us with any hope. Once we become hopeful, we are taking the approach of poverty. We are adopting a penniless mentality. We are locking ourselves into the ghettos of the samsaric world.

We have an enormous sense of delight. There are wonderful things taking place in us. That is the sense of the bodhisattva path. That is also connected with tantra, because in tantra, the whole thing is based on pride, vajra pride, as we call it, indestructible pride, adamantine pride. An enormous sense of delight begins to take place. There is no room, absolutely none whatsoever, for misery.

This has nothing to do with being "love-and-lighty." We don't have to furnish ourselves with goodness, whiteness, cleanness. We don't have to adopt the conviction that finally we are good and beautiful, loving and lighting. Rather we are what we are. We are sons and daughters of noble family, in the direct line of the Buddha. We have our heritage, our lineage. We can take pride in ourselves. It's fantastic.

That is the preparation for tantra. I suppose we could talk about it in terms of looking. We have seen already; then we begin to look.

Student: I didn't quite get the difference between seeing and looking. It seemed that looking involved discrimination and seeing didn't. Is that the distinction?

Trungpa Rinpoche: Looking is premature discrimination, and seeing is discriminating wisdom. But you can look once you have seen.

Student: How do you see if you don't, at some point or other, make the effort to look?

Trungpa Rinpoche: You don't deliberately try to see. That would be looking. You perceive, you just perceive. And having perceived things as they are, as we say, you begin to find yourself looking at them. It's very much like buying an antique. You don't look at the details of the piece you want to buy. If you start looking, you're going to be a loser. You're going to make wrong decisions. If you want to be a good buyer, a competent buyer, you see the antiques. You see antiqueness. You just see it, you feel it. Seeing is feeling. Then, having seen it, you begin to look. You begin to question the state of that particular antique—whether it is worth buying, whether it has been corrupted, restored, whatever. You see the piece, then you look at it, then you buy it.

If you go to an antique auction and you look at the pieces, you make the wrong choices. You bid at the wrong time. You hit yourself, hurt yourself. When you go to an antique auction, don't look, see.

Student: Seeing is more panoramic, Rinpoche?
Trungpa Rinpoche: Yes.

Student: It's intuition as opposed to thought?
Trungpa Rinpoche: Well said.

Student: If you don't get sucked into looking—you know, it does occasionally happen that you don't—and you find yourself seeing instead, at that point are you still in the five skandhas?[6]
Trungpa Rinpoche: I think you are.
S: In?
TR: Yes, both. You are in and out.
S: Could you expand on that?
TR: You are already subject to the skandhas. But there is the possibility of being free from them at the same time.
S: In other words, it's like life and death happening continuously.
TR: Continuously, yes.
S: Do you find you yourself personally in and out of the skandhas all day long?
TR: Sure. As long as you have a body. As long as you have to shit and eat and make love.

Student: The hopelessness is about certain goals, isn't it? It's not a total hopelessness about yourself.
Trungpa Rinpoche: Whenever there's hopefulness about yourself, there's also a problem related to a goal. Hopelessness is hopeless all over. But there are some gaps. What's the Jewish word for that? *Chutzpah,* yes. There's still chutzpah.[7]
Believe it or not, hopelessness is encouragement. It's fantastic. From our point of view, it means we are starting on a new dimension of reality. With vigor, virya, chutzpah.

Student: Isn't that because you have nothing left to defend, so you have nothing left to fight against?
Trungpa Rinpoche: Yes, that's right.

S: So you can do anything you want.

TR: Precisely, sure, yes. It's your universe. It's your world. Let's celebrate.

Student: But still you have to keep an awareness all along of being in an ocean of gray shit? If you began to think that you weren't in it, then you would begin to fear falling back into it. You'd be back in hope and fear again. So do you have to continue to be aware that you're in the gray shit anyhow?

Trungpa Rinpoche: And take pleasure in it. I'm afraid the whole thing is as gross as that. It's far from the three *H*'s: happy, healthy, and holy.

Student: Is there any separation between daily life and art in terms of seeing?

Trungpa Rinpoche: No. Everybody's an artist.

Student: Do you learn to trust yourself from feedback you get from people and situations around you, or does it just come from yourself?

Trungpa Rinpoche: Both. You relate to situations as well, obviously; otherwise you have no reference point. Your guru is your situation as well.

Student: I still don't understand about seeing and looking.

Trungpa Rinpoche: Do you see me?

S: I think so.

TR: You do see me. Unless you're blind, you see me. But you haven't looked yet. Until you look, you're color-blind.

FOUR

The Basic Body

W ITH THE PREPARATION we have made in the foregoing talks, perhaps at this point we could discuss tantra.

Fundamentally, tantra is based on a process of trust in ourself that has developed within us, which is like a physical body. Tantra involves respect for our body, respect for our environment. Body in this sense is not the physical body alone; it is also the psychological realization of the basic ground of sanity that has developed within us as a result of hinayana and mahayana practice. We have finally been able to relate with the basic form, the basic norm, basic body. And that body is what is called *tantra*, which means "continuity," "thread." That body is a sense of a working base that continues all through tantric practice. Thus tantric practice becomes a question of how to take care of our body, our basic psychological solidity, our solid basic being. In this case, the solidity is comprised of sound, sight, smell, taste, feeling, and mind. Body here is the practitioner's fundamental sanity. The practitioner has been able to relate with himself or herself to the extent that his or her basic being is no longer regarded as a nuisance. One's basic being is experienced as highly workable and full of all kinds of potentialities. On the tantric level, this sense of potential is called *vajra*, which means, "adamantine," or "diamond," or "indestructible." A sense of indestructibility and a strong continuous basic body has developed.

The notion of mahamudra is prominent in tantric teaching. *Maha* means "great" and *mudra* means "symbol." *Maha* here means "great" not in the sense of "bigger than a small one," but in the sense of "none better." And "better" even has no sense of comparison. It is "none-better," on the analogy of "nonesuch." And mudra is not a symbol as such. It refers to a certain existence we have in ourselves, which is in itself a mudra. Eyes are the mudra of vision and nose is the mudra of smell. So it is not a symbol in the sense of representing something or being an analogy for something. In this case, mudra is the actualization of itself. The idea is that physical activity has been seen as something workable; it is something very definite and at the same time highly charged with energy.

Particularly in Buddhist tantra, a lot of reference is made to the idea that pleasure is the way, pleasure is the path. This means indulgence in the sense perceptions by basic awakened mind. This is the mahamudra attitude. Things are seen clearly and precisely as they are. One does not have to remind oneself to be in the state of awareness. The sense objects themselves are the reminder. They come to you, they provide you with awareness. This makes awareness an ongoing process. Continuity in this sense does not need to be sought but just is.

Nobody has to take on the duty of bringing the sun up and making it set. The sun just rises and sets. There is no organization in the universe that is responsible for that, that has to make sure that the sun rises and sets on time. It just happens by itself. That is the nature of the continuity of tantra that we have been talking about. Discovering this is discovering the body.

We have a basic body, which is very intelligent, precise, sensitive to sense perceptions. Everything is seen clearly and the buddha-family principles are acknowledged. There is vajra intellect, ratna richness, padma magnetizing, karma energy of action, and the basic, solid, contemplative being of buddha.[1] We have acquired such a body, which is not a new acquisition. It is the rediscovery of what we are, what we were, what we might be. With the rediscovery of that, a sense of being develops, a sense of vajra pride, to use tantric language. That is, there is a sense of dignity, of joy, a sense of celebrating the sense perceptions, sense consciousnesses, and sense objects, which are part of the coloring of the mandala experience.

Now the dawn has awakened us. We see light coming from the east. We see the reflections on our window, showing that the light is coming out. It is about to be daytime, and we begin to wake up. That is the discovery of the basic body. In the tantric tradition, it is called the dawn of Vajrasttva. The basic discovery has been made that daylight is just about to come, and one is ready to work with one's sense perceptions.

We wake up and then we get out of bed. The next thing, before eating breakfast, is to take a shower. That corresponds to what is called kriyayoga, the first tantric yana, which is connected with cleanness, immaculateness. You have woken up and discovered that you have a body, that you're breathing and are well and alive again and excited about the day ahead of you. You might also be depressed about the day ahead of you, but still there is daylight happening, dawn is taking place. Then you take a shower. This is the kriyayoga approach to life, which has to do with beautifying your body, taking care of your body, that is, the basic body we've been talking about.

The basic idea of kriyayoga is to purify our being of anything unnecessary. Such dirt does not provide any necessary steps toward enlightenment, but is just neurosis. Here of course we do not mean physical dirt. This is a psychological, psychosomatic type of dirt. It is neither transmutable nor workable. So we jump in the shower.

You can't take a shower with fire and you can't take a shower with earth or air. You have to take a shower with water, obviously. In this case water is the basic crystallization of one's consciousness of waterness, the water element, which is connected with basic being. The chillness of water, the coldness of water, and its sparkliness are also a process of cleaning oneself, cleaning one's body. When you take a cold shower you wake up. You're less sleepy when the water from a cold shower pours over you. So this is also a waking-up process as well as a cleansing one.

You can't take a shower with just water pouring on your body. You also have to use soap of some kind. The soap that you use in this case is mantras, which go between your mind and your body. Mantras are an expression of unifying body and mind. The Sanskrit word *mantra* is composed of *mana*, which means "mind," and *traya*, which means "protection." So the definition of *mantra* is "mind protection." Here protecting does not mean warding off evil but developing the self-existing protection of beingness. You are proclaiming your existence. You proclaim that you are going to take a shower because you have soap and water and body there already. Water as a symbol is related with consciousness in general; and body is the thingness, the continuity of thisness, solid basic sanity; and mantra is the tune, the music you play. When you dance, you listen to music. And you dance in accordance with the music.

At a certain point, mantra becomes a hang-up. It becomes another form of dirt. Like soap. If you don't rinse it off, soap becomes a hang-up, a problem, extra dirt on your body. So you apply the soap thoroughly and then you rinse it off with water.

The idea here is that mantra is the communicator. You make a relationship between the elements and basic sanity. The elements are the sense perceptions, the projections. This is the water. The projector is your state of mind. That which relates the projection and the projector is the energy that the mantra brings. When communication between those two—or rather those three, including the energy of mantra—have happened properly, then the soap—the mantra—has already fulfilled its function. Then you have a rinse. You take a further shower to clean away the soap, clean away the method. At some point the methodology itself becomes a hang-up, so you rinse it away.

Having brought mind, body, and energy together properly, one begins to develop the appreciation of one's basic being further. Your body is already clean, immaculate, and beautiful.

Now we come to the next situation, which is putting on clean clothes. That corresponds to the next yana, upayoga—putting clean clothes on your naked body, which has been beautifully cleaned and dried and is in absolutely good condition. Upayoga is basically concerned with working with action. Action here is connected with fearlessness. You are no longer afraid of relating with sense perceptions, sense pleasures, at all. You are not ashamed of putting a beautiful garment on your body. You feel you deserve to put on beautiful clothes, clothes that are beautifully cleaned and pressed, straight from the dry cleaners. The action of upayoga is further excellent treatment of one's body, one's basic sanity.

There is a need to be clothed, rather than presenting oneself naked all the time. Exposing one's body without clothes becomes purely showmanship, chauvinism. It becomes another form of ego-tripping. So the body has to be wrapped in the beautiful garment of action. This involves a sense of awareness. Every action you take is noticed; you have awareness of it. None of the actions you take is a threat to your basic sanity. Every action you take in your life situation is highly workable—there's no conflict between the mind and the body at all. In fact, your action is another way of glorifying the beauty of your body.

This kind of appreciation of action is not a matter of watching yourself act, but rather of taking pride in your basic being in action. You don't have a prefabricated attitude; your action is spontaneous action. In this case the point of action is dealing with emotions. Aggression arises, passion arises, jealousy arises—let them be as they are. Purified aggression is energy, purified passion is compassion, purified ignorance is wisdom, inspiration. Your clean body is the best of your existence. On top of that you put clean clothes, which are a further adornment of your body. This is the action aspect. There is some sense of reality at this point, and that reality is that you are no longer afraid to perform your actions. You are no longer afraid of your emotions at all. The emotions are further fuel for your inspiration.

The next tantric yana is yogayana. You have bathed and put on clean clothes, and you look magnificent. You have realized your own beauty, but putting on clean clothes does not express it fully. You should take a further step, which is to put on ornaments—a beautiful necklace, beautiful rings, beautiful bracelets. Adorning your body in this way is a further way of taking care of it and appreciating its beauty, a further way of celebrating the continuity of your basic sanity. That is the yogayana.

The sense of cleanness and the sense of being beautifully clothed produce the sense of ornament. They are a definite statement of the purity of basic sanity. In putting on these ornaments, you begin to associate yourself with the buddhas, the tathagatas, the bodhisattvas of the higher realms. You put on crowns and tiaras, earrings and necklaces. You behave like a king or queen on the throne. There is a complete sense of trust, a complete sense of the obviousness of your basic sanity. That is why the Buddhist tantra is pleasure-oriented.

The pleasure orientation is very important, very powerful, and very basic. If you are not pleasure-oriented, you can't understand tantra. You have to be pleasure-oriented, because otherwise you are pain- and misery-oriented. But this is not a psychological trick of convincing yourself through positive thinking. It is an obvious, reasonable, and real thing. When you treat yourself well, you feel good. When you feel good, you dress yourself in good clothes and adorn yourself with beautiful ornaments. It is a very natural and basic way of relating to oneself.

The main qualities of tantra that come out here are basic trust and basic elegance. Elegance here means appreciating things as they are. Things as you are and things as they are. There is a sense of delight and of fearlessness. You are not fearful of dark corners. If there are any dark, mysterious corners, black and confusing, you override them with our glory, your sense of beauty, your sense of cleanness, your feeling of being regal. Because you can override fearfulness in this way, tantra is known as the king of all the yanas. You take an attitude of having perfectly complete and very rich basic sanity.

Ordinarily, this is very hard to come by. When we begin to appreciate our richness and beauty, we might get trapped in ego-tripping, because we no longer have enough hinayana and mahayana discipline related to pain and hopelessness. Pain and hopelessness have to be highly emphasized, if possible to the level of 200 percent. Then we become tamed, reduced to a grain of sand. The saint knows that he is a grain of sand and therefore is no longer afraid of ornamenting himself with all kinds of beautiful things. There is a sense of dignity, of sophistication, a sense of celebration. So one of the basic points of tantra is to learn how to use pleasure fully.

Here we are not just talking about sexual pleasure. We're not just talking about the pleasure of being rich, or about pleasure in terms of getting high in a cosmic way. We are talking about pleasure in the sense that everything can be included. There is a sense of reality involved in pleasure. There is a sense of truth in it. As we said in talking about mahamudra, it is nonesuch, nothing better. It's self-existingly great, not in a comparative sense. As it is, it is great and dynamic.

Student: It seems that it could be misleading to have even an intellectual understanding of this tantric material, because it would make you want to get out of your pain and suffering. So what use is it at this point?

Trungpa Rinpoche: You cannot get into it unless you have a good and real understanding of pain and hopelessness. Without that, you are nowhere near it. It would be misleading if we presented it right at the beginning and you had no idea at all of hinayana and mahayana. That would be misleading and very dangerous. You would turn into an egomaniac. But once you have an understanding of the necessity and simplicity of pain and the necessity and simplicity of compassion of the bodhisattva's path, you can begin to look into other areas. Hinayana and mahayana are necessary and very important.

Student: Rinpoche, what is the relationship between negativity and the energies that are transformed into the five wisdoms?[2] I've been becoming more aware of the energy of negativity and how alive it is, but I don't see where it fits into the pattern of the five wisdoms.

Trungpa Rinpoche: The whole point is that within itself, negativity is self-existing positive energy. If you have a really clear and complete understanding of negative energy, it becomes workable as a working base, because you have basic ground there already. Do you see what I mean?

S: No.

TR: Negative energy is no longer regarded as threatening. Negative energy is regarded as fuel for your fire, and it is highly workable. The problem with negative energy is that negative energy does not enjoy itself. It doesn't treat itself luxuriously—sybaritically, one might say. Once the negative energy begins to relate to itself sybaritically in its own basic being, then negative energy becomes a fantastic feast. That's where tantra begins to happen.

S: Okay. So much for negativity in itself. What then is the relationship to the five wisdoms?

TR: The five wisdoms begin to act as the clear way of seeing your negativity. In mirrorlike wisdom, vajra, aggression is seen as precise, clear-cut intellect. The wisdom of equanimity, ratna, is related with a sense of indulgence and richness; at the same time, everything is regarded as equal, so there's a sense of openness. In discriminating awareness, padma, passion is seen as wisdom in that passion cannot discriminate itself anymore, but this wisdom does perceive it discriminatingly. In the wisdom of the fulfillment of action, karma, instead of being speedy, you see things as being fulfilled by their own means, so there is no need to push, to speed along. In the wisdom of dharmadhatu, all-encompassing space, which is related with the buddha family, rather than just seeing stupidity, you begin to see its all-encompassingness, its comprehension of the whole thing.

The wisdoms become a glorified version of the emotions, because you are not a miser. One of the problems is that in relating with the samsaric emotions, we behave like misers; we are too frugal. We feel that we have something to lose and something to gain, so we work with the emotions just pinch by pinch. But when we work on the wisdom level, we think in terms of greater emotions, greater anger, greater passion, greater speed; therefore we begin to lose our ground and our boundaries. Then we have nothing to fight for. Everything is our world, so what is the point of fighting? What is the point of segregating things in terms of this and that? The whole thing becomes a larger-scale affair, and ego's territory seems very cheap, almost inapplicable or nonexistent. That is why tantra is called a great feast.

Student: Is the thing that prevents us from relating to the world in a tantric way right now the fact that we have a sense of self? Are you saying that we have to go through the hinayana and the mahayana first in order to break down our sense of self so that we can relate to tantra?

Trungpa Rinpoche: If you think on a greater scale as vajrayana, or tantra, does, you have no idea of who is who and what is what, because no little areas are kept for a sense of self. Mahayana works with more developed people, hinayana with people who are less developed but still inspired to be on the path. Each time they relate with the path, they lose a pinch of self, selfishness. By the time people get into vajrayana, the selfishness doesn't apply anymore at all. Even the path itself becomes irrelevant. So the whole development is a gradual process. It is like seeing the dawn, then seeing the sunrise, then seeing the sun itself. Greater vision develops as we go along.

Student: How can you have a sybaritic relationship with negativity.

Trungpa Rinpoche: That's the greatest of all

S: I'm sure it is, but I don't understand it.

TR: It's like putting seasoning on your food; if you don't, you have a bland meal. You add color to it, and it's fantastic. It's very real and alive. You put salt and spices on your dish, and that makes it a really good meal. It's not so much a sense of indulgence as of appreciating the meal.

Student: So far in this seminar, you have skirted the use of the word *shunyata.*[3] I was wondering about the shunyata experience, which you have characterized in the past as appalling and stark. How does that relate with the sense of isness or being? I had a nihilistic feeling about shunyata. It seemed very terrifying and claustrophobic, whereas the idea of isness seems very comfortable and expansive.

Trungpa Rinpoche: Isness feels good because you know who you are and what you are. Shunyata is terrifying because you have no ground at all; you are suspended in outer space without any relationship at all to a planet.

S: Shunyata is characterized in some literatures as ultimate point, a final attainment.

TR: That's a misunderstanding, if I may say so. Shunyata is not regarded as an ultimate attainment at all. Shunyata is regarded as no attainment.

Student: I'm wondering about the transition to tantra from the earlier discipline. It seems one might get hung up on the hinayana and mahayana. The hopelessness begins to have a kind of dignity, and you might get attached to it. It seems to be a very abrupt kind of transition, and it could be very hard to switch over.

Trungpa Rinpoche: You are able to switch over because of your sense of sanity. You are no longer interested in whether the different yanas are going to be kind to you or unkind. You don't care anymore. You are willing to face the different phases of the various yanas. And you end up with vajrayana.

S: That takes a lot of bravery.

TR: That is the whole point. Relating with the samaya vow and the vajra guru takes a lot of discipline and a lot of bravery.[4] Even the high-level bodhisattvas supposedly fainted when they heard the message of vajrayana.

Student: When you reach the point of transition between mahayana and vajrayana, do you have to give up your cynicism about the teachings and the teacher and about yourself that you have during hinayana and mahayana?

Trungpa Rinpoche: I think so. A that point you become very clear, and cynicism becomes self-torture rather than instructive and enriching. At that point, it is safe to say, there is room for love and light. But it is sophisticated love and light rather than simple-minded lovey-lighty.

FIVE

The Crazy-Wisdom Holder
and the Student

WE ARE GOING TO TRY to go further with our understanding of vajrayana, or tantra. Something has been missing so far in our discussion of tantra. The tantric experience can only come about through a transmission from your guru, from a vidyadhara (which means a holder of crazy wisdom). Such a transmission can take place but involves enormous trust and enormous sacrifice. This sense of trust and sacrifice can come about at the time of receiving an abhisheka.

Abhisheka is a Sanskrit term that is usually translated "initiation." But initiation here is not just the idea of being accepted into a tribe by going through a certain ceremony. Here there is a sense of complete and total surrender. Surrendering in this way is very unreasonable from an ordinary point of view; but this sacrifice and the bond that arises from it have to be established before we can trust the universe as a potentially enlightened situation. From the tantric point of view, we have to go through this in order to be enlightened. And in order to get enlightened, one has to go through tantric training in any case. And enormous surrendering and enormous trust are involved.

Trust on this level means one cannot maintain one's ego. One cannot maintain one's basic existence as "myself." This self has become completely dedicated, it has completely opened up in surrendering to the world created by the guru. The world that the guru creates is not particularly a pleasant one. It might be very unpleasant, horrific. It might also be beautiful at the same time. The reason the world created by the guru tends to be an irritating one is that the guru goes beyond the role of spiritual friend at this point and begins to act as a dictator. He minds your business completely; he minds every inch of your life.

Your guru has the ability to do such a thing, because he knows every inch of your life, of your state of consciousness. He knows the tiniest fragments of your subconscious gossip, he knows all the little freckles in your mental functions. The guru has a complete understanding of all this. Therefore you are highly exposed, fully exposed.

For this reason, the tantric tradition is considered very dangerous. The traditional format is that you can either make love to your guru as a divine being or kill him. The analogy is that of a snake in a bamboo tube. When you put a snake in a bamboo tube, the snake has to face either up or down. Relating with the guru is very powerful, too powerful. It is too much having somebody mind your business in that fashion. From that point of view, it is extremely horrific. Nevertheless, at the same time it is an extremely delightful gift.

Tantric transmission cannot take place without a guru, without a spokesman of the mandala perspective. That is a very basic point that we should be very clear about. Entering tantra is hellish, shall we say. When the guru begins to manifest himself as somebody minding your business two hundred percent, you are bound to feel extraordinarily claustrophobic. He not only minds your business, he minds the business of your business. He sees inside out, outside in. This is a very powerful and a very paranoid situation.

Without the guru's consent, without his acknowledgment of you as a good vessel for the vajrayana, you don't get anything out of it at all. The guru acts as a channel for both creative and destructive happenings. He can destroy you instantly or instantly build you up. And this becomes very obvious, very definite.

When you approach tantra, you are approaching the magical aspect of the cosmos more and more. Magic in this sense has nothing to do with miracles as such. There is magic in the sense of certain energies, certain mysteries, that you have never tapped before. You haven't understood them, or you haven't had enough gaps in your experience to relate to them. Now you are getting into tantra, and your guru is going to initiate you into the tantric situation. You are going to begin to tap untapped areas, which we usually leave alone, which we usually daren't work with. You are getting into a very powerful situation here.

In this powerful role, the guru is referred to as he who presents the samaya vow. *Samaya* is a Sanskrit word that is translated in Tibetan as *tamtsik (dam tshig)*. Samaya is a certain kind of bond that is like the kind of electric fence that's used to keep cows in. In this case, it is highly electrified, and if you touch it or begin to play with it, you are going to get a shock. And if you try to get out of it, you're going to get destroyed.

Destruction does not mean just death. You will end up in what's called vajra hell, which is a very powerful hell. From there, even the greatest spiritual strength cannot rescue you. That hell is neither up somewhere nor down somewhere. It is self-existing imprisonment in which your neuroses are vibrating constantly, all the time. You're trapped in that hell, and there's no remedy and no freedom at all. Pleasure and pain both become part of the imprisonment. That is why tantra is regarded as a very dangerous thing and very powerful thing to get into.

Only tantra can produce enlightenment in one lifetime. There is no other doctrine or teaching in Buddhism—including the sudden teachings of Zen, which is part of the mahayana tradition—that can deliver enlightenment in one lifetime. Tantra is the only path that enables us to attain enlightenment in one lifetime. That's true.

Getting into tantra is like taking a supersonic jet. Either it will destroy your life because it is so fast, or it will deliver you to a more advanced place. You have breakfast in Tokyo and lunch in London and dinner in New York. It's very fast and powerful. If it destroys you, you won't even have a chance to be aware of your death. You're just dead on the spot, in midair.

I am not going to explain all the aspects of how it is powerful, but you can find out.

The holder of such a doctrine is also very powerful. The holder of the doctrine is in league with death. At the same time, he is in league with Buddha. Not just an ordinary buddha, but the highest of all the buddhas, the dharmakaya buddha.[1] The vajra guru has enormous power over your life and complete control over the phenomenal world. He has the power to destroy you or make you an enlightened person, so it is a very powerful commitment one makes when one enters tantra.

I say this, because I want people to think thrice about getting into it, if it is even possible for them to get into it at all. It is very dangerous, and without having gone through hinayana and mahayana discipline, getting into it is completely out of the question. But even if you go through hinayana and mahayana, it is still dangerous to get into this vajrayana discipline, and very powerful, magnificently powerful.

Committing oneself to the vajrayana teaching is like inviting a poisonous snake into bed with you and making love to it. Once you have the possibility of making love to this poisonous snake, it is fantastically pleasurable: You are churning out anti-death potion on the spot. The whole snake turns into anti-death potion and eternal joy. But if you make the wrong move, that snake will destroy you on the spot.

During the early years of my teaching in America, I was very hesitant even to discuss the subject of tantra. I felt I should be conservative and keep to basic Buddhism. But the development of my students has provided me with a lot of hints [to go ahead]. They are beginning to stick their necks out and their eyes are beginning to light up. Maybe it is time to proclaim the vajrayana victory. I feel very fortunate to be able to discuss this subject. I feel we are making headway toward establishing one hundred percent Buddhism in this country. Without vajrayana we don't have a head. Hinayana is the feet. Mahayana is purely heart. But Buddhism without a head is dead. Therefore I feel very happy about the possibility of sharing my understanding with you. It is like discovering a new friend. It is a very moving situation for me personally.

Nevertheless, we should be very careful of the danger we are getting into, which is enormous. I am not going to take the responsibility alone. Everyone of you is going to take the responsibility, if I may say so.

What we are discussing is one of the most secret and sacred things ever heard on this earth. It is very dangerous and powerful. People think the atomic bomb is powerful. Maybe physically it is. But we are talking about a psychological atomic bomb, which is millions of times more powerful than the physical bomb. I want you to appreciate this and become terrified of this opportunity. It's a very serious matter.

You are in a unique position having the opportunity to hear this teaching, which has never been proclaimed in this country. You should regard yourselves as very fortunate people. I am not saying this because I want to intimidate you particularly, but I want to share my responsibility with you. I feel that I can relate with every one of you, within your understanding, in terms of the complete teachings of Buddhism.

Another aspect of this is what is know as "open secret." This teaching is self-secret. You may not be able really to hear it or understand it because of your own trips, your speed, your confusion. That is a safety precaution that has already been developed. If you are not ready to hear such a thing, you don't hear it. What I have to say becomes purely gibberish.

Let us discuss the remaining three yanas of vajrayana.

The next three yanas are described as the ultimate yanas. These yanas are as far as we can go as far as Buddhism is concerned, as far as enlightenment is concerned altogether. They are called mahayogayana, anuyogayana, and atiyogayana. These yanas provide the most advanced teaching Buddhism can ever present to you. They are the dead-end point at which you *should* attain enlightenment. It is demanded of you: You are required to be enlightened at that point. You are guaranteed to be enlightened once you reach the highest point of atiyoga. You have no choice. And you will become enlightened in the fullest way of all.

As an analogy for the lower tantric yanas, we talked about bathing, getting dressed, and putting on ornaments. At this point, in the mahayogayana, you no longer put on ordinary clothes: It's more like going back to ape instinct. Instead of putting on a crown of jewels and gold, now you put on a headdress of skulls. Instead of an ordinary skirt, you wear a tiger-skin skirt. Instead of an ordinary shawl, you wear a shawl of human skin. You begin to change your perspective on the world and get back to a more organic approach.

There is a hint of savagery, a hint of craziness. A hint of crazy wisdom begins to appear. Having bathed, purified, now you wear skins and bone ornaments. At this level of mahayogayana, consciousness begins to change. Some kind of dignity begins to appear—fearlessness. Fearlessness of blood, fearlessness of earth, fearlessness of human skulls and skin. We strip away all kinds of purified levels that we have gone through before in previous yanas.

Previous yanas have taken a very genteel approach. We tried to make ourselves into an emperor or king. We bathed, we wore beautiful clothes and jewelry of all kinds. Now we develop a sense of reality of a different nature. Neurosis as such is no longer regarded as bad at all. It is regarded as an ornament, a delightful ornament, a real ornament. We can wear such ornaments, we can adorn ourselves with all sorts of neuroses that we have. This is a fantastic proclamation of sanity in fact.

This approach explains why vajrayana is very dangerous, very freaky. Nevertheless, here it is. At this point, we are willing to swim in the shit pile once again, willing to adorn ourselves with bones and skulls and skins. It is very organic. We might even say it is macrobiotic in the ultimate sense. We begin to realize, totally without fear, that we are divine beings.

The next yana is anuyogayana. Here the sense of indulgence just described has become a trip. Abiding in the fermented manure of neurosis becomes a problem. Maybe we have indulged ourselves too much in the organic trip. Now we don't even care about that. We take off our costumes, strip. There is no need to dress up as vampires or imitate them. We begin to lose that kind of perspective. We begin to relate more with our heart and brain. The *Tibetan Book of the Dead* describes how the wrathful herukas come out of your brain and the peaceful herukas come out of your heart. This takes place now. More coordination is developed between the vajra type of heart and brain. You develop an enormous sense of being the conqueror of the whole universe. You transcend apeness altogether, or maybe you become a transcendental ape. It is very powerful. You see a panoramic openness and there is a fantastic sense of already having conquered. The conquering has already taken place and you're just revealing it.

The next and last level is atiyogayana. At this level you don't need any kind of outfit at all. Dressing or undressing is irrelevant. Once again you expose your naked body. No clothes at all, none whatsoever. You don't even have to bathe anymore—you are what you are. The only relationship that you have at this point is to your sense perceptions of sight, sound, smell, touch, and taste. Those sense perceptions become guidelines. When you hear a sound, you relate with that very simply as part of a reminder. When you see colors, you see them that way, very simply. This is an extraordinarily high level of perception.

There we are. We have come back to where we were, back to square one. We realize that the journey never need have been made. All the journeys are a way of fooling ourselves. The journey becomes an endless journey, so there is no point in making journeys at all.

Student: Rinpoche, you talked a great deal about the dangers that attend the vajrayana path. I am very puzzled by that, since the whole exercise is supposed to be about getting out of and annihilating ego, and in that case, what dangers can there be? As I see it, the only dangers there can be would relate to what's left of the ego.

Trungpa Rinpoche: You said it. The only danger is getting back to ego and ego's being fortified by all kinds of techniques that you acquired.

S: I read a *chö* ritual in which you offer yourself, your flesh and your bones, to the hungry ghosts.[2] And apparently there's a possibility you might freak out, but that is a danger only to ego.

TR: The danger is that, having performed such a sacrifice, you might feel self-congratulatory about this magnificent act of yours.

Student: What you said about atiyoga seems to have been that you see what you see and you hear what you hear. But it seems to me that we can do that right now.

Trungpa Rinpoche: Sure, we could do it right now, but we don't want to believe in that. Therefore we need a path to lead us to that.

S: We need to develop courage, get rid of doubt?

TR: You need some kind of feeling that you have put in enough energy to arrive at that point.

Student: You spoke of the vajrayana path as one that could lead to enlightenment in this lifetime. Yet in the bodhisattva vow, we vow not to enter enlightenment until all sentient beings have become enlightened. That seems to present a contradiction.

Trungpa Rinpoche: I don't think so at all. That's the trick of the mahayana path; it helps you to give up. You're not going to attain enlightenment at all; you're going to work with sentient beings. And the idea in vajrayana is that you're going to attain enlightenment in one lifetime. Both work together. In mahayana, the idea that you're not going to attain enlightenment cuts your speed, your ambition. In the vajrayana, you develop pride, vajra pride, and dignity. Actually, both amount to the same thing. *You* can't become buddha in any case at all. Youless, unyou, nonyou, is going to attain enlightenment. That logic holds true all the way along. *You* can't attain enlightenment. Maybe nonyou can attain enlightenment. Good luck!

Student: I think you said you can only get enlightened by going through tantric transmission. Have enlightened people from the Zen tradition gone trough tantric transmission?

Trungpa Rinpoche: In some cases. Sure. I think so.

S: In that case, would you say that Suzuki Roshi was a tantric master?

TR: Absolutely. Good for him.

Student: You suggest thinking thrice. About what? What's the other choice besides the path?

Trungpa Rinpoche: Nothing.

Student: Have you experienced vajra hell?

Trungpa Rinpoche: Sure. But I'm not in it. I experienced enough to tell people what it's about. Which is very hair-raising.

S: But you said that once you got in, no amount of spiritual strength could get you out again.

TR: Yes. True.

S: So you're still in it, then.

TR: You can experience a glimpse of it. But once you get into it, nobody else can rescue you. You're stuck there.

Student: You said that the hinayana and mahayana were prerequisites for tantric practice. You also labeled the American Indians' spirituality tantric. But the American Indians haven't heard of hinayana and mahayana. How does that work?

Trungpa Rinpoche: Very simple. The terms don't matter, really. The American Indians have an equivalent discipline of basic sanity in their domestic affairs and in their tribal life. You know: Be on the earth, learn how to cook a good meal on a fire, learn how to share with your fellow tribesmen. It's very simple. They don't have to relate with the terms *hinayana* and *mahayana,* which are purely labels.

S: Okay. You say tantra is the only way to attain enlightenment in this lifetime. How can we know what we've been doing in previous lifetimes?

TR: In previous lifetimes, you may have been working toward this. Maybe that's why you're here. Maybe that's why you're one of the fortunate persons who has had the opportunity to hear the dharma properly. Maybe in a previous life you were a good cat who heard the dharma. Or maybe you were a dumb kid who heard the dharma at his parents' knee. And now you're here. It could be anything. But there is no reason why you are not here, because you are here.

Student: At what level do you transcend birth and death?

Trungpa Rinpoche: At the level of no speed. Speed is karmic relational action.

Student: Rinpoche, why are you telling us this?

Trungpa Rinpoche: This what?

S: This doctrine that we can't understand.

TR: The point is, if you can't understand it, that's the beginning of your understanding.

S: Yes, you could tell us about something that's only one or two steps ahead of where we are and we still wouldn't understand it.

TR: But it's still good. It holds true because you don't understand it. The point here is that you have to tap your own potential. If there were no possibility of that, you wouldn't be here. You might even fall asleep on the spot. I'm telling you these things for the very reason that you have not fallen asleep here.

SIX

Alpha Pure

A s w e s a i d a t t h e beginning, the journey through the nine yanas is a process of rediscovering oneself. As you move along the path, you have a feeling of particular locations. You are traveling through a dense forest or through heavy snow; you are climbing mountains or crossing fields; you encounter rainstorms and snowstorms. You have to stop each night to eat and sleep, and so on. All those experiences make up your journey. In a sense we could say that the rainstorms are your rainstorms, the snowstorms are your snowstorms, and the dense forests are your dense forests. It's your world. As you move through the nine yanas, it is yourself that you are rediscovering—more and more clearly.

At the beginning there is a vague idea that something is not quite right. There is something wrong with oneself. Things are questionable, and one begins to look into the question, to relate with the pain, the chaos and confusion. That is the hinayana level. Then at a certain stage some of the answers that arise out of the search begin to create further hunger, further curiosity. One's heart becomes more and more steeped in the teachings. Then the mahayana experience of intense dedication to the path begins to take place. Dedication to the path in this case also means compassion, a loving attitude toward oneself and others. One begins to find one's place in the universe, in this world. Being on the bodhisattva path is finding one's place and one's sense of dedication in this universe. At that point, the universe is not threatening or irritating anymore. This is true for the very simple reason that one has developed a style for working with the universe; meditation in action has begun to develop.

As you go on then, you rediscover the brand-new world of tantra. An enormous surprise takes place. You recognize the magical aspect of the universe, which means yourself as well as everything else. You rediscover the redness of red, the blueness of blue, the whiteness of white, and so on. You rediscover the meaning of passion and the meaning of aggression, their vividness, their aliveness, and also their transcendental quality. Rediscovering this new world is the vajrayana path.

At that point, not only do you realize the meaning of pain and confusion, and not only do you realize you have a place in the world, but you also develop a sense of dignity. In fact, you are the emperor of the universe, the king of the world. Your sense of dignity is related to the experience that you have an enormous place in this world. In fact, you are the maker of the world.

As the tantric experience develops through the lower tantras to the higher tantras, even the notion of being the emperor of the universe becomes unnecessary. You are the universe. You have no reference point, none at all. Everything is on the level of complete oneness. In higher tantric terms, this is known in Tibetan as *kadak*. *Ka* is the first letter of the Tibetan alphabet, *dak* means pure. So it means "pure right at the beginning," or you might say "alpha pure." Purity in this case has nothing to do with the relative reference point of pure as opposed to impure. Purity here has the sense of being really without comparison to anything, without any relative reference at all. That seems to be the state of development we are working toward. That, finally, is the level of the maha ati teachings, in which there is no reference point, none whatsoever. Therefore, in that state we find millions of reference points everywhere, which do not conflict with each other. Therefore we become precise and open, very general and very specific at the same time. That is the state of enlightenment, if it can be described at all in words. That's a sort of finger painting of the enlightenment idea.

The whole journey that we have discussed has its roots in overcoming spiritual materialism to begin with, then developing friendship toward oneself and others, and finally developing vajra pride, or a sense of dignity.[1] Those three steps are the general guidelines for the hinayana, mahayana, and vajrayana, or tantra. And those experiences cannot come about without a teacher or master to begin with, on the hinayana level;

a spiritual friend who minds one's business intensely on the bodhisattva or mahayana level; or, on the vajrayana level, a vajra master or vajra guru, who holds one's life strings in his hand.

There is a story about the abhisheka that the great tantric master Padmasambhava received from Shri Simha, the great sage of maha ati. Shri Simha reduced Padmasambhava to the form of the letter HUM. Then he ate it, he put it in his mouth and swallowed it. And when Padmasambhava came out the other end of Shri Simha, that completed his abhisheka. This is an example of the action of the vajra master. He is more than a teacher alone, more than a spiritual friend. The vajra master eats you up and shits you out, having completely processed you in his vajra body. That is the kind of power we're talking about. Without such a relationship, without this kind of communication, vajrayana cannot be presented. Without this, one cannot even come near to understanding it. So relationships with the various levels of teacher are definitely requirements for progressing on the path.

Then, of course, there is the practice of meditation, which is another important part of the journey. One must practice meditation on the hinayana level in order to develop the basic sanity of relating to one's mind as a working basis. The satipatthana methods of mindfulness developed in the Theravada tradition are very powerful and important.[2] The methods developed in the Sarvastivadin hinayana tradition that exists in Tibet, Japan, and China are identical.

When I was in India, I discussed meditation techniques for awareness practice with a Burmese master who was the disciple of a very great Burmese meditation teacher. When I told him about the vipashyana meditation technique that we used in Tibet, he shook his head and asked me, "When did you go to Burma?"[3] So the methods seem to be identical.

It is necessary to begin at the beginning with the hinayana practice. Without that, we do not develop proper sense perception, so to speak. We have to have good eyesight and good hearing to read and listen to the teachings. And we have to have a good body in order to sit and meditate. Good sense perceptions here mean sense perceptions that are no longer distorted. We can have real understanding, no longer distorted by neurosis. That is absolutely necessary; there's no other way at all, according to Buddha anyway.

Having that solid rock bed for a foundation, that solid, sane, open, fresh ground, you can begin to build, to put up walls. That corresponds to the mahayana discipline of the six paramitas and friendliness to oneself and others. This gives us a sense of direction about how to act as good citizens, which is the bodhisattva path. After one has become a good citizen, there is an enormous possibility of becoming a genius. Basic sanity has developed and a proper lifestyle has been established. There are no hassles, no obstacles at all. Then you become a genius, which is the vajrayana level.

You become a fantastic artist, musician, sculptor, or poet. You begin to see the workings of the universe in its ultimate, last details. You are such a genius that you see everything completely. That's the final level.

This genius is described as jnana, wisdom. There are five types of genius, five wisdoms. There is mirrorlike wisdom, which is clarity. There is the wisdom of equality, which is seeing everything at once in a panoramic vision. There is the wisdom of discriminating awareness, which is seeing details on an ultimately precise level. There is the wisdom of all-accomplishing action, in which speed does not have to be included in one's working situation, but things fall into your pattern. Then there is the fifth wisdom, the wisdom of dharmadhatu, or all-encompassing space, which develops enormous basic sanity and basic spaciousness in the sense of outer space rather than space that is related to the reference point of any planet. That is the kind of cosmic level of genius that we find in the vajrayana.

I suppose this seminar cannot be any more than a teaser for you. But at least you should know that millions of great people have been produced by this path; and not only have they been produced, but they all say the same thing. They've all gone through the same process that is being presented here. And we are not excluded from the possibility of becoming one of them. According to the Buddha, one out of every four people in the sangha becomes enlightened.

What we have done very roughly in this seminar has been to give a complete description of the path from the beginning stages to enlightenment. I hope you will have a sense of aspiration and feel joyful about what we discussed. The other possibility is that you might feel depressed, because you have heard about so many possibilities and good things, but none of them seem to apply to you. Well, okay, be that way—and use your depression as realization of the truth of suffering. Then you will have accomplished the first step already. Or if you are inspired, then buddha fever, the fever of buddha nature, has already possessed you. So let it be that way. It seems that whatever we do, we can't go wrong.

Student: I have a question about inspiration or motivation. It seems that in the hinayana, the motivation is suffering. In mahayana at some point this is transformed into compassion, so that one continues because one has a sense of working, not for oneself, but for all beings. But, going beyond that, I don't understand the motivation or inspiration for vajrayana. Why would one go further?

Trungpa Rinpoche: One of the interesting points about vajrayana is that it does not need to be nursed. It just happens that once you have developed the fullest level of compassion as an accomplished mahayanist, you find yourself being a vajrayanist. That's the general pattern that applies. There's no particular motivation as such. The only thing is a sense of transcendental fascination with the universe and the play of its energy, its emotions, and so on. Everything is such a magnificent display of the mandala pattern, and you can't keep yourself from looking at it.

Student: If mahayana is "gone-beyond" wisdom, the wisdom of the paramitas, then would going beyond that, beyond the paramitas, be vajrayana?

Trungpa Rinpoche: You could say that, yes.

S: So in some sense, it's the natural conclusion of the mahayana.

TR: You could say that too, yes.

S: Thank you.

TR: Anything you say.

Student: Rinpoche, where is the spirituality in tantra? It feels like tantra could be very materialistic?

Trungpa Rinpoche: How is that?

S: One thing is relating to one's sense perceptions as real. Couldn't that just be spiritual materialism, perhaps? It just seems to me that after mahayana, the spirituality becomes vague.

TR: If we just started with tantra, we might end up cultivating Rudra, which is very dangerous. Tantra can only develop by going through the other yanas first, destroying all kinds of spiritual materialism.

It's very interesting: You can't say tantra is a spiritual thing exactly, nor is it a worldly thing. That's why tantra is said to transcend both samsara and nirvana. There is a term in Tibetan that Herbert Guenther translates "coemergent wisdom." The idea of coemergence here is that you are on neither side; you are not on the side of ignorance nor on the side of wisdom. Because of that, a lot of hinayanists and mahayanists panicked about tantra—because it's completely unspiritual. On the other hand, they can't say tantra is worldly, because there is nothing worldly about tantra either—because of the craziness.

Student: What advice would you give for dealing with somebody who is in vajra hell?

Trungpa Rinpoche: Let me go over the idea of vajra hell once again, if I may. Having heard the vajrayana teachings, instead of becoming awakened, you become deaf and dumb to the teachings. The medicine turns into poison. And there's nothing one can do for such a person. The only thing is to imprison them in a vajra den, which is vajra hell. It's like you have a prison cell made out of books about the vajrayana all around you. They imprison you. But you might be interested some time or other just in pulling one out, and maybe you might read it. Sheer claustrophobia brings some kind of hope. It is a rather horrific place to be.

S: Would an ordinary prison be any kind of comparison to vajra hell?

TR: I don't think so. It's much more than that. It's a total experience, like having cancer throughout your whole body. But you can't even die out of it. You're fed by the disease.

Student: Does it have an eternal quality? You said there's no escape from it.

Trungpa Rinpoche: Claustrophobia is eternity in this case. There's no windows and no doors. You can't even exist, but this threat of nonexistence becomes the food that keeps you alive.

S: There's no possibility of a future way out in terms of a bardo?

TR: The *Tibetan Book of the Dead* describes two types of advanced rebirth that can take place. Either you go up to the level of dharmakaya without a bardo experience or else you go down to vajra hell, also without a bardo experience. Because a bardo is some kind of chance or opportunity you have.

Student: Would it be beneficial to try to help somebody in vajra hell?

Trungpa Rinpoche: Helping doesn't particularly change the karma of that person.

S: So it's best to avoid such people?

TR: Best to leave them as they are.

S: But how does that relate to the bodhisattva vow?

TR: In taking the bodhisattva vow to save all sentient beings, you could add "except those who are in vajra hell." Even bodhisattvas can't reach the helpless.

Student: Can a person in vajra hell ever get out by becoming aware of himself, say, by reading those books that make up his prison?

Trungpa Rinpoche: Yes, that's the only possibility. Through sheer claustrophobia, you might be able to squeeze something out of yourself.

Student: You said that at the end of this journey, there is the realization that there was never a need to make this journey at all. But at the same time, isn't the journey absolutely necessary?

Trungpa Rinpoche: It is necessary in order to realize that your journey was futile. It is called a path, but it is not really a path, because you are really neither coming nor going. But still there is an illusion of a journey. That's why the various levels are called yanas, which means "vehicles." You think you are moving. But maybe it is the landscape that is moving.

Student: Doesn't the analogy of vehicles also contain the idea that you are being carried by the energy of the path rather than you yourself making any progress?

Trungpa Rinpoche: That is also possible. That depends on how much you are identified with the teachings personally. Once you are identified with the teachings personally, then development is sort of like wine fermenting. It ferments by itself.

Student: You used the analogy of an electric fence around a cow pasture. If the cow tries to go beyond the fence, it gets a shock. There's some kind of painful situation. I take that to mean that once a person is on the path, there is some kind of safeguard that the guru, through his insight, provides. Then, in order to flip out and go to vajra hell, it is necessary to make some sort of egoistic assertion to the effect that the guru is no longer able to discriminate properly what is right and what is wrong for us. Is that what this vajra hell thing is about? And then you are left to go off on your own?

Trungpa Rinpoche: Are you asking if that kind of a development is the cause of vajra hell?

S: Yes.

TR: I think so. Some sort of alienation takes place between the teacher and the student. There is the story of Rudra, one of the first persons to go to vajra hell. He and a fellow student, a dharma brother, were studying with the same master. They had a disagreement about how to interpret the master's instructions. They were taking opposite extremes in carrying out their practice, and each of them was sure that he was right. They decided to go to the teacher and ask for his comment. When the teacher told Rudra that he was wrong, Rudra became so angry that he drew his sword and killed his teacher on the spot. Then he ended up in vajra hell. It is that kind of alienation.

Student: Is going to vajra hell the equivalent of attaining egohood, or are they two different things?

Trungpa Rinpoche: Vajra hell is not quite complete egohood. It's still part of the journey. But when you come out of vajra hell without any realization, then you attain the real egohood, which is the state of Rudra. You turn yourself into a demon.

S: So you're not in vajra hell when you attain egohood.

TR: No, egohood seems to be quite difficult to attain. As difficult as enlightenment. Doing a really good job on it is very difficult.

Student: It seems to me that some act of surrendering is definitely necessary. But is that something you can try to do, or do you just have to wait and let it happen? Is it something you have to stop trying to do?

Trungpa Rinpoche: The general policy seems to be that you have to surrender artificially to begin with. You have high ideals, some inspiration about what the possibilities might be, but you can't quite click into those possibilities spontaneously at the beginning. So you have to start by creating artificial openness, by surrendering artificially. This is precisely what taking the refuge vow or the bodhisattva vow is. It is artificial actually—you are not up to it. But the commitment involved begins to have an effect on your state of being, for the very reason that you cannot wipe out your past. That artificial gesture becomes part of the landscape of your life; then something there begins to ferment, begins to work.

Part Two

NINE YANAS SEMINAR

SAN FRANCISCO
MAY 1973

ONE

Suffering, Impermanence, Egolessness

THE NINE YANAS of the Buddha's way were developed to enable people—psychologically, personally, physically—to surrender themselves to the Buddha's teaching. The nine yanas seem to be an absolute necessity. If we did not have the first yana, nothing could be achieved at all. We have to start with the first step, which is the shravakayana, in which everything is looked at in terms of a human situation, a physical situation. Here the Buddha is regarded as son of man who still had a physical obligation to this earth. He was also wise. He saw everything in our life situation as consisting of pain. But at the same time the nature of pain is characterized by impermanence, and the experiencer of the pain is regarded as nonexistent. So there are these three points: The nature of life is pain; the nature of pain is impermanent; and the experiencer of pain is nonexistent.[1]

You might ask, if the experiencer of pain is nonexistent, how come there are situations in which we feel that we do experience pain and pleasure, very solid situations? How do we know that this nonexistence is the case? If the Buddha said that being is nonexistent, how do we experience pain and how do we experience impermanence?

We simply say, "I don't know about everything else, but I still feel pain. I do feel pain. I do feel frustrated. I do feel unhappy, I really do. I don't know about the impermanence or nonexistence of my being, but I simply do experience pain, I sure do." Well, in some sense, that's great. At least you have found some relationship with the teaching. If you really do experience pain and suffering in its own way, that's wonderful, fantastic.

Are you sure, though, that you are really experiencing pain, experiencing it in the fullest way? "Well, I'm not even certain of that, but I do feel some kind of discomfort. I do experience pain when I'm pushed into a corner, but during the rest of my life, I'm not so certain whether I actually experience pain or not. I do experience pain when somebody hits me, cheats me, or insults me. Then I do feel extreme pain, discomfort, anger, and so forth. But the rest of the time I'm not so sure whether I feel pain as a continual thing happening to me. All the same, I feel that there's something hanging out that's bugging me; and I don't feel absolutely free either. Particularly when I check up on what's happening with me, I feel funny. I feel some sense of being trapped, but I don't know what it's all about. Maybe this is happening, but maybe also I'm just imagining it. I can't say. Something is happening. Sometimes I feel haunted, and sometimes I feel I'm just being silly—I should forget the whole thing. I should just go out and enjoy myself and do my own thing, whatever I want. But even if I try to do that, I can't really do it, because I still stop and look back at myself and what I'm doing. And once I begin to check what I'm doing, I feel uncomfortable. Something is bugging me somewhere. Something is happening behind my back, as if I had a huge burden that I'm carrying all the time. But I'm not sure if this is the thing that's happening to me or I'm just imagining it. Maybe I should stop thinking altogether. But I already thought of that and tried it. The more I try to shake off the watcher, the more I feel I have to make sure that I have shaken him off. I couldn't shake him off because I was being watched all the time by my shaking-off project that was happening to me."

Maybe Buddha had similar experiences, even identical ones. There was a sense of ambition to become a spiritual or religious person. Buddha went so far as to leave home. He left his parents and his wife and infant child. He fled from his palace and plunged into the world of yogic teachers, Hindu masters. But still something didn't work, because in some sense he was trying too hard, trying to become great, the greatest spiritual warrior of the century. He was trying to achieve something; he was concerned with achieving and with saving himself.

That seems to be the problem that we encounter all the time. We feel uncertain because, though we feel we know what direction we should go in, when we try to follow that direction, that itself seems to become a source of ignorance. The direction we were following seems to turn into clouds and clouds of darkness. Finally we begin to lose our sense of direction. But that seems to be the basic point: In relation to that, we discover pain, duhkha. That pain is a self-existing thing that we cannot escape. Beyond the pain, we try to find the source of the pain, the origin of the pain, but we don't find it. We find bewilderment and fogginess, uncertainty of all kinds. But that *is* the discovery of the origin of pain, which is a very important discovery indeed.

Discovering the origin of pain does not necessarily mean that we should give up hope, or that we should give up fear, for that matter. Giving up means disregarding the whole thing rather than working with it.

Pain is constantly existing. Even if we find the origin of pain, it is a constant discovery, a very powerful one. Pain exists all the time whether we feel happy or sad. The happiness is superficial; pain is behind the happiness all the time. The pain goes on constantly; the self-existing pain, the pain of self-consciousness, the pain of ambition, and so on. All of those go on all the time regardless of the superficialities of what we feel. The facade is different, but behind it is the fundamental pain that is happening constantly.

The experience of pain thrives on its own fickleness. It is like a lamp burning or a candle flame. The flame has to breathe very fast to remain solid and still. It has to get fuel from the candle as it burns. It is continuously breathing, so the stillness of the flame is based on the continuity of discontinuity. Constant death and constant birth are taking place simultaneously. We cannot hang on to life as though it were something solidly continuous like a pipe. If life wasn't changing, if life was a solid thing happening solidly, then we couldn't have pleasure and we couldn't have pain. We would be frozen into jellyfish or robots, reduced into rocks. Because we are able to experience our pain and pleasure, our highs and our lows, depressions and excitements, all kinds of things can develop in our life situations. That means that there is automatically some sense of change or shifting happening all the time.

A bridge wouldn't be built if a river was still. Because a river is dangerous and turbulent and passing all the time, because the current is happening constantly, therefore we build a bridge. Otherwise we could just put a huge boat there and walk across that. The sense of discontinuity is important. Impermanence is important.

But before getting into impermanence further, we should mention that there are different types of pain. There are three types of pain. The first is pain as a natural condition. This is the pain that is always there. Even when we are indulging in the pleasure, extraordinary sybaritic pleasure—delightful, beautiful, fantastic, deep, profound pleasure, pleasure that is physical, psychological, reassuring, solid, textural—even that contains a tone of suspicion constantly. Even if we have millions of guards to protect our pleasure domain, still there is a tone of pain happening. However extraordinarily happy we may be, there is still a tone that suggests that the whole pleasurable situation might possibly be extraordinarily painful. There is a sense that we are dwelling on, digging, the pleasure for the sake of the pain or digging the pain purely for the sake of the pleasure. It feels questionable—our mind is completely intoxicated, so we are uncertain whether we are digging the pleasure to defend against the pain or digging the pain to defend against the pleasure. That is the quality of self-existing pain. Pain is definitely not fun, not particularly pleasurable.

The second kind of pain is the pain of change. You think you have pleasure happening in your existence. You feel you are involved in a real, good, solid, organic situation of pleasure. The pleasure feels extremely definite, even to the point where you no longer feel you have to defend your pleasure or compare it with pain at all. You are out on a sailboat, enjoying yourself, sunning yourself on the deck. The water is beautiful. The sea is smooth. The wind direction is good. You had some nice food before you went out, and you have a nice companion who sparks your wit and takes care of you. It is an absolutely ideal situation. Suddenly a storm comes, a hailstorm. You don't have a chance to get yourself together, to protect yourself. Your boat is tipped over. Your wittiness is unable to continue. Instead of wit, aggression now becomes a problem. You blame your companion. You feel it is his fault, because he didn't take precautions against such a thing. You regret that you didn't have a life jacket on board. You are just about to die. You've sailed too far out into the ocean, because you wanted to be alone and enjoy your friend's companionship. You have sailed out too far for anyone to rescue you. You regret that. You have killed yourself.

That is pleasure changing to pain. By the way, the traditional analogy for that is being at your wedding party and suddenly having the house collapse due to earthquake, or whatever. That is the second type of pain. The first type was self-existing pain, within pleasure.

The third one is the pain of pain. In this case, you are already caught up in pain, extreme pain. Real, juicy, good pain. For example, you are experiencing the acute pain of just having been in an automobile accident. Your ribs have been fractured, and you can hardly breathe, let alone talk. Even if somebody makes a joke, it is painful to laugh. You are in extreme pain. Then you catch pleurisy or pneumonia. You can't talk because of your rib fracture, and now you catch pleurisy or pneumonia, and you can't even breathe without extreme pain. Or it is like having leprosy, being ridden with leprosy, and then having a car accident on top of that. Or you are already bankrupt, and then on top of that you are kidnapped, and the kidnappers demand more money.

Those three types of suffering are part of the display of impermanence. Suffering happens because impermanent situations exist. Suffering cannot exist on solid ground. Suffering has to dwell or develop in a situation, and situations can develop because situations are constantly changing. We die so that we can be reborn. We are born so that we can die. Blossoms bloom in the spring so that there will be seeds in the autumn. Then the winter gives the seeds time to adapt to the soil. Then spring comes again. The seeds are awakened after their hibernation. Having settled down to the ground, the seeds are reawakened. Then the plants grow, and there are more seeds. Then another spring comes, another summer comes, another autumn comes, and so forth. Things change constantly, always.

We think we can keep a record of things if we write them down in our notebooks. "On this particular day, such-and-such a thing happened. I heard a word of wisdom on this particular day. I'll write that down." You write that down today for the sake of what you experience now. But then you walk out of this situation and you relate with yourself tonight, tomorrow, the next day, the next week. When you read your note again after that, it is not going to speak to you as you thought it would when you wrote it down tonight, right now. The inspiration and the impact are going to change, change constantly. Let's see what happens if you write something down: that the pain of pain is acute and powerful. Then you'll walk out of this hall and spend your time: tonight, tomorrow, the next day, the next day, the next day, and so on. You will begin to develop self-consciousness concerning the fact that you wrote this thing down rather than relating to the idea or the philosophical implications that inspired you.

Things are like that constantly. Statements that we hear and things that we experience are not as solid as we would like. For that matter, even the experience of enlightened mind flashing is not all that permanent. It is a temporary situation. Fundamentally, we are distrustful people, all of us. We can't trust ourselves at all. We get one impression one moment and another impression the next, and so forth. We cannot repeat what we experienced the previous hour, thirty minutes ago—at all. We are untrustworthy persons because we are subject to impermanence.

Moreover, if we keep changing to the next subject, it's because we have no substance to hang on to. This is what we call egolessness, if I may introduce that subject as well. The notion of egolessness refers to the fact that we don't have any central headquarters. We do not have a definite thing, definite ground, to maintain—me, mine, my existence as such. We have been fooled by the play back and forth [into thinking that there is such a thing]. It's purely that we have been fooled by the back-and-forth, by impermanence, thrown back and forth between this and that, that and this, past and future, future and past. People are thrown back and forth constantly like a Ping-Pong ball. So in conclusion I would like to point out that we do not have a heavy basic solid soul or ego as we would like to have. We do not have that at all. Because of that, we are so frivolous that we are unable to grasp any teachings, any solid situation of basic sanity at all.

If we had some basic ego, a solid thing with aggression and passion happening to it, then we might be able to grasp onto that as a monumental expression of some kind. We could say: "Once I killed myself. I would like to make that into a monument, a reference point for praise. I would like to show that to other people: 'This is my monument—my having killed myself.'" But that won't work. You are not around anymore if you have killed yourself. Yet it seems that that is what we are asking for: "I have become an extraordinary person because I have given up what I was and have become what I would be, and this is my image for the future, which is independent of the present." That [making a monument out of hanging on to your projection of yourself] seems to be one of the biggest problems that has happened. So egolessness at this point means that you cannot hang on to anything; you cannot hang on to any experience.

Student: Is the trouble and pain of samsara potentially the same for everybody?

Trungpa Rinpoche: I think it's the same for everybody, yes. If somebody values pleasure, then pain automatically comes along with it as its shadow. If somebody asks for light, a shadow will be there along with that.

Student: I thought you said that pain was there regardless of the pleasure, that it was not just a complement to the pleasure but was continuous in the background in any case.

Trungpa Rinpoche: Yes, the background is also pain, painful. It is not a matter of choice; it is a constantly painful situation. But the background is also asking for an ideally pleasurable background, asking for the whole thing to be smooth. This asking for smoothness is trying to defend against roughness, which automatically invites pain.

Student: We seem to be using pain for a lot of different things. I understood that the background pain is not the same as the other pain that we invite when we try to insist on pleasure.

Trungpa Rinpoche: Yes, you are right. There are several types of pain. The background pain is very low key, backgroundish. It has a basically paranoid quality, a quality of being haunted. Then there's the actual pain that challenges your pleasure. Then there's more actual pain [the third type], which invites chaos. It is a suicidal thing. You have one pain and you invite another pain on top of that.

Student: Is understanding the pain that you call the background pain the Buddha's teaching?

Trungpa Rinpoche: All the pains are teachings. That alone is nothing particularly extraordinary. But you should also realize that you were born out of pain and dwell in pain as far as the way of samsara is concerned. So any element that is related with the pain is the truth of duhkha, suffering, the first noble truth. Just experiencing the pain is not quite the point; the point is acknowledging that such pain does exist in your being. Acknowledging the pain is the teaching.

Student: It's easy to acknowledge the pain. I just say, "Well, the root of everything is suffering." But it's another thing for me to be aware of the experience.

Trungpa Rinpoche: You don't particularly have to stop in order to experience it. You have the experience first. That seems to be why you are here attending this seminar, which is in itself a very positive action. You have decided to come here and discuss the whole thing, which is a very inviting situation, a hopeful situation, a pleasurable one, we might even say. Your being here means that you have decided to work on your pain. That's great, wonderful. But that doesn't mean that we here are going to undermine your pain. We are going to accentuate the meaning of your pain. The teaching does not provide a possible hope, the possibility of a pleasurable situation. The teaching provides intelligence to relate with the pain.

Student: Does the background pain lack coherence in the way you were talking about with the candle flame? Does the background pain exist as a kind of moment-to-moment thing, rather than—?

Trungpa Rinpoche: It's always there, always there. The front part of the pain is depression, excitement, and so forth [it is more fickle]. But the background pain goes on all the time, simply because you have experience of some kind. Experience is pain. Your human functioning—any kind of intelligence that goes on in your mind—*is* pain, because you feel uncomfortable about the whole thing. Even if you have a tremendous insight to the effect that you are going to conquer the world, make yourself a million dollars, still there is something not quite fitting. There is some kind of hole somewhere that is not quite comfortable. That is the original pain. There is a very mystical experience of pain, something not quite comfortable.

Student: Why do we decide to continue to exist? Some people say that the ego is body-consciousness, so it seems that the body could decide to keep on living even when the ego has decided not to live anymore. But if you really decided you didn't want to be on this planet, couldn't you just leave it when your body was sleeping?

Trungpa Rinpoche: You can't.

S: Why not?

TR: You can't, because you begin to notice yourself. No other logic is necessary. Because you notice yourself, you let the rest of it come along as well. Anyhow, committing suicide does not solve the whole problem. You killed yourself. There is someone watching you being killed.

S: The ego isn't body-consciousness, then?

TR: The ego is self-consciousness. And self-consciousness is automatically the relative reference point for other at the same time. In that sense, you cannot destroy the law of relativity. So you have to live.

That is precisely the idea of enlightenment: transcending the barrier between this and that [self and other]. But enlightenment does not mean suicide, killing this or that. That doesn't work. Purely removing the barrier between this and that is the only solution.

Student: Is pain a kind of energy?

Trungpa Rinpoche: Yes, pain is energy.

S: Then pain brings energy.

TR: If it weren't for that, I wouldn't be here. Buddhism wouldn't be here on this continent if there wasn't enough pain. Your pain has brought fantastic energy. That's why I'm here. That's why Buddhism, buddhadharma, is here. That's why tantra is here. Without pain there is no energy. That pain is an indication that you are serious, that you want to relate with your situation in the space of truth, if I may say so.

Student: Rinpoche, it seems that pain brings on a certain inspiration. For example, when things get very painful, there's a shift from the background to the foreground. This means that you can be aware of the pain, and somehow that begins to change the energy. But then inspiration goes. It leaves once the pain goes back to the background. It goes back and forth again. How do you sustain the inspiration?

Trungpa Rinpoche: Inspiration shouldn't be regarded as a cure or as medicine. Inspiration shouldn't be regarded as an enlightened state. The inspiration is to bring out more shit and piss and being willing to face that. If you are into that, then no doubt you will get more pain, more frustration, more inspiration, more wisdom, more insight, and more enlightenment in your life. That's up to you.

T W O

Competing with Our Projections

T HE FIRST YANA, shravakayana, which we discussed yesterday, is the starting point. It is the starting point in the sense that in it we begin to realize the meaning of life; or, we might say, we discover the stuff that life consists of. Life consists of pain, transitoriness, and nonsubstantiality. Discovering that could be said to be discovering the first truth about life. You might find that rather depressing, but nevertheless, that's the way things are.

The first step, which happens in the shravakayana, is realizing the form of manifestations, realizing the nature of manifestations; realizing the nature of sound, objects, colors, movements, and space; realizing the nature of shapes and their characteristics.

The next yana is called the pratyekabuddhayana. This means the yana or path of self-enlightenment or self-contained enlightenment. This involves starting on oneself before getting involved with anything else. As they say, "Charity begins at home." One has to start with oneself. It is because of this that the approach of hinayana as a whole has been referred to as a self-centered approach. Christianity has often looked down on Buddhism as being too self-centered. Christians have said that there isn't enough charity in Buddhism, or there aren't enough charitable organizations in Buddhism. In some sense that is the shortcoming of the hinayana. There's too much emphasis on oneself. But on the other hand, that is the virtue of the hinayana. There's no fooling around with anything else. One does not need encouragement or reinforcement from elsewhere, from any foreign element. We don't have to introduce foreign elements in order to prove our existence. We just simply work with the stuff we have. We start right on the point where we are.

The pratyekabuddhayana could also be described as a yana of the psychological understanding of the meaning of life. In the shravakayana, we related to the physical structure of the meaning of life. We related to impermanence and the dissatisfaction produced by impermanence, and the fact that basically things have no substance; they are empty; there is no watcher, no observer, therefore there is egolessness.

In the pratyekabuddhayana, the approach to psychological development is that of the five skandhas.[1] The first is the skandha of form. Form in this case is basic being, which is ignorance from the samsaric point of view. It is that which causes duality, the split between subject and object, between projector and projection. But at the same time that kind of ignorance is very intelligent and very definite and full of all kinds of tactics and schemes. It has already developed the scheme, the policy, of ignoring any possible threats. The meaning of ignorance here seems to be ignoring the threats of any possibilities of realizing egolessness. In other words, it means ignoring that its own game is a foolish one. In that sense, ignorance is effortless. It is a kind of natural ape instinct in which, wanting to hang on to something, we don't even have to think about hanging on to it. Ignorance holds it automatically. It senses that there are possibilities of letting go, but it doesn't want to face them. If you let go, then you no longer have pain or pleasure to occupy yourself with, so you stay on the edge of the straight path. Straightforwardness is seen, but instead of going ahead right onto the path of straightforwardness, you stay on the edge. That is basic ignorance.

It seems that we all have that tendency. We know that there are possibilities of loosening up, of freeing ourselves, but we don't really want to give in to them, because it would be too humiliating in the sense that we would no longer have any weapons to wave. We would no longer have any stuff to entertain ourselves with.

There is a sort of hunger for pain. Usually when we think of pain, we don't regard it as something we want. The conventional idea of pain is something that any sensible person would regard as undesirable. But actually and fundamentally, that's not true. There is a very profound unreasonableness that ignorance has created, which makes it so that we want to hang on to pain. At least having the experience of pain reassures us of our existence. We have a chance to play with it as though we didn't want it, which is a game. We are playing a game with ourselves.

All those schemes and projects involved in maintaining ego and pain are unconscious or subconscious ones. There is an inbuilt reaction that happens that even the watcher doesn't see. It happens on an instinctive level; therefore it is ignorance. It is a self-contained administration.

And then we have another skandha beginning to develop, which is the skandha of feeling. Feeling also is on a somewhat semiconscious level. We are beginning to be aware of ourselves, of our existence, and because of that we start to survey our territory and check our security to see whether the environment around us is threatening or welcoming or indifferent. The area around us in this sense is comprised of our basic fear or paranoia of ego's possibly losing its grip. This sends out a kind of magnetic field, and feeling is the messenger that tests out that magnetic field of ego. It tests whether the mechanism of ego will work or not, whether we will be able to survive or not.

Beyond that, a cruder level than that of the subconscious mind develops. This is the actual manifestation onto the solid level, which is perception [the third skandha]. Perception is another form of feeling but on the more active level of perceiving, of sharpening sense-consciousness. Having developed a way of detecting whether the area around us is desirable or undesirable, now we have to survey the projections more. We look to see if there is a way of seemingly changing the projections to make them constitute a more favorable situation, to make them into more favorable perceptions. This is a kind of intuition, the highest form of intuition, in which we try to see whether we can maintain ourselves or not in terms of relationships.

The next skandha is intellect, intellect in the sense of that which labels things, gives them a name, and puts them into certain categories.[2] It does this in such a way that these categories fit with what we checked out by means of feeling and studied through perceptions. Now finally we make an official statement that things fit into this category or that category in relation to oneself and one's productions. This is a work of art, an intellectual one. So the intuition of perception is general sensing, and intellect is finalizing.

Then the fifth skandha is consciousness, which contains emotions, thought patterns of all kinds. Emotions come from frustration. The meaning of emotion is frustration in the sense that we are or might be unable to fulfill what we want. We discover our possible failure as something pathetic, and so we develop our tentacles or sharpen our claws to the extreme. The emotion is a way of competing with the projection. That is the mechanism of emotion.

The whole point is that the projections have been our own manifestations all along. Naturally, we have put out our own projections. We put them out as our allies, our subjects, our guards who could bring back messages and let us know what's happening. But at the same time, the ruler [the projector] is very suspicious of anything other than himself. There is the possibility that your ally might turn into your enemy; your closest friend might become your enemy; your bodyguards might assassinate you. That kind of suspicion is always happening, and because of this uncertain relationship with the projections, emotions begin to arise as another way of undermining the projections. In other words, the ruler himself has to have a weapon in case he's attacked. That is emotion.

Emotion is uncertainty regarding the projections, and the projections have also been put out by us. What we label things makes the projections. The buildings or the houses or the trees or the people as such are not the projections. What we make out of them is the projections—our version of the buildings, our version of the landscape, the people, the trees. It is the new coat of paint that we put on them, the reproductions we make of them. And there is the possibility of not being able to relate with those, since we are uncertain of ourselves [and thus uncertain of our own projections].

Basically, we are uncertain of who we are, so there is a huge, gigantic fear in the back of our minds, which is hidden very neatly behind the veil of ignorance, of ignoring. But even though it is hidden, we are still uncertain—as though there were a huge, cosmic conspiracy happening. Whether the bomb is going to explode from the inside or the outside is uncertain. But we don't talk about the inside bombs. On that side, we pretend that nothing has gone wrong at all. At least we have to have some place to sit, to live, dwell. So we decide to blame everything on the outside situation.

So that is the psychological state of the pratyekabuddha; that is his worldview on the psychological level. There seem to be two aspects to the meaning of life. There is the meaning of life from the point of view of the outside, which is characterized by the three marks of existence:

pain, impermanence, and egolessness; and there is the internal way of seeing the meaning of life, which is in terms of the five skandhas.

It seems to me that we can't be charitable to anyone, even ourselves, if we do not know who we are and what we are, or who we are not and what we are not—whether we exist or not. This is a very important point to understand before we begin to practice. We have to find out who is actually practicing and what we are practicing for.

Those two yanas, the shravakayana and the pratyekabuddhayana, are purely hinayana. They constitute the hinayana level of philosophy and practice. The role of the hinayana in the dharma is to define life, to lay the ground, establish a foundation. That foundation is a real understanding of the practitioner and a real understanding of the basic meaning of practice.

The meditation practice in the hinayana goes right along with what we have been describing philosophically. Meditation practice at this level is establishing a relationship with yourself. That is the aim of meditation. There are various techniques for doing that. It is not a question of achieving a state of trance or mental peace or of manufacturing a higher goal and a higher state of consciousness at all. It is simply that we have not acknowledged ourselves before. We have been too busy. So finally we stop our physical activities and spend time—at least twenty minutes or forty-five minutes or an hour—with ourselves.

The technique uses something that happens in our basic being. We jut choose something very simple. Traditionally, this is either the physical movement of walking or sitting or breathing. Breathing seems to have the closest link with our body and also with the flux of emotions and mental activities. Breathing is used as the basic crutch. This is the hinayana way of relating with oneself to begin with.

When we talk about making a relationship with ourselves, that sounds quite simple. But in fact it is very difficult. The reason we are unable to relate with ourselves is that that there is fundamental neurosis that prevents us from acknowledging our existence—or our nonexistence, rather. We are afraid of ourselves. However confident or clever or self-contained we may be, still there is some kind of fear, paranoia, behind the whole thing.

Neurosis in this case is inability to face the simple truth. Rather than do that, we introduce all kinds of highfalutin ideas—cunning, clever, depressing. We just purely bring in as much stuff as we like. And that stuff that we bring in has neurotic qualities. What "neurotic" finally comes down to here is taking the false as true. The illogical approach is regarded as the logical one. So just relating with ourselves in meditation practice exposes all this hidden neurosis.

That may sound fantastic. We might think there has to be some secret teaching, some semi-magical method—that we can't expose ourselves just by doing something simple like breathing or just sitting and doing nothing. But strangely enough, the simpler the techniques, the greater the effects that are produced.

The sitting practice in hinayana is called shamatha. This literally means "dwelling on peace" or "development of peace," but let us not misunderstand *peace* in this case. It does not refer to tranquillity in the sense of a peaceful state. *Peace* here refers to the simplicity or uncomplicatedness of the practice. The meditator just relates with walking or breathing. You just simply be with it, very simply just be with it.

This technique is especially designed to produce exquisite boredom. It is not particularly designed to solve problems as such. It is very boring just to watch one's breathing and sit and do nothing; or walk, not even run, but just walk slowly. We may think we have done that many times already. But usually we don't just breathe and sit and walk. We have so many other things happening at the same time, millions of projects on top of those things. But in this case we relate to the boredom, which is the first message of the nonexistence of ego.

You feel as if you are in exile. You are a great revolutionary leader. You had a lot of power and schemes and so on, but now you are in exile in a foreign country and you're bored. Ego's machinations and administration have no place in boredom, so boredom is the starting point of realization of the egoless state. This is very important.

Then at some point, within the state of boredom, one begins to entertain oneself with all kinds of hidden neuroses. That's okay, let them come through, let them come through. Let's not push neurosis away or sit on it. At some point, even those entertainments become absurd—and you are bored again. Then you not only draw out the discursive, conceptual side of hidden neurosis, but you begin to become emotional about the whole thing. You're angry at yourself or at the situation you managed to get yourself into. "What the hell am I doing here? What's the point of sitting here and doing nothing? It feels foolish, embarrassing!" The image of yourself sitting on the floor and just listening to your breathing—that you let yourself be humiliated in this way—is terrible! You are angry at the teacher and the circumstances, and you question the method and the teaching altogether.

Then you try more questions, seeking out another kind of entertainment. This involves believing in mystery. "Maybe there is some kind of mystery behind the whole thing. If I live through this simple task, maybe it will enable me to see a great display of higher spiritual consciousness." Now you are like a frustrated donkey trying to visualize a carrot. But at some point that becomes boring as well. How many times can you seduce yourself with that? Ten times, twenty times? By the time you have repeated the same thing seventy-five times, the whole thing becomes meaningless, just mental chatter.

All those things that happen in sitting meditation are relating with ourselves, working with ourselves, exposing neuroses of all kinds. After you have been through a certain amount of that, you master the experience of breathing in spite of those interruptions. You begin to feel that you actually have a real life that you can relate to instead of trying to escape or speed [along without having to connect with it]. You don't have to do all those things. You can be sure of yourself, you can really settle down. You can afford to slow down. At this point you begin to realize the meaning of pain and the meaning of egolessness and to understand the tricks of ignorance that the first skandha has played on you.

So shamatha meditation practice is very important. It is the key practice for further development through all the yanas of Buddhism.

Student: Is the experience of boredom also an experience of egolessness?

Trungpa Rinpoche: It is an experience of egolessness rather than an egoless state.

S: The ego is experiencing the boredom?

TR: Yes, ego is experiencing its own hollowness. This is still experience, not achievement. If there is achievement, you don't experience egolessness, but this is the experience of egolessness.

Student: Doesn't the boredom just become another form of entertainment?

Trungpa Rinpoche: I don't think so. It's too straightforward, too frustrating to be entertaining. I mean the idea of it might be entertaining now, but when you are actually experiencing it . . .

S: Well, you were talking about pain being entertaining.

TR: That's different. In pain, something's happening; in boredom, nothing's happening.

Student: Sometimes I'm sitting meditating and I notice strange neurotic things happening to me. I try to understand them, but as soon as I try to understand, I just get confusion. Is it best to just drop it?

Trungpa Rinpoche: You don't have to try to do anything with it, particularly. Just let it arise and fall away of its own accord. One of the important aspects of the proper attitude toward meditation is understanding that it is a very simple process that does not have any schemes in it. Of course sitting and breathing is a scheme to some extent, but in order to remove dirt we have to put soap on the body. So something has to be applied. You have put another kind of dirt on in order to remove the existing dirt. But it's not very much and it's the closest we can get to [no schemes at all].

Student: What do you do with your emotions when they arise? What about anger, for example? Suppressing it just seems to be a cop-out.

Trungpa Rinpoche: If, when you're angry, you just go out and have a fight with somebody, that's also a cop-out. That's another way of suppressing your anger. You can't handle it, therefore you try some other way. Whether you do that or suppress, you are not relating with your emotions completely. The real way of relating with an emotion is just to watch it arise, experience its crescendo, and then find out if that emotion is threatening you in any way. You can do that if you are willing to do that. Of course, you could say you didn't have time to do such a thing-before you knew it, you just exploded—but that's not quite true. If you are willing to do it, you can relate with your emotions.

Emotions are not regarded as something that you should throw away; they are regarded as very precious things that you can relate with. The final frustration of the ego is the emotions. It can't cope with itself, therefore it has to do something—become extremely jealous or extremely angry, or something like that. But one can really watch the emotion: Instead of relating with the end result of the emotion, relate with the emotion itself.

S: Not watch what it does to the object of the emotion?

TR: Yes, that's right. You see, usually in talking about emotions, we completely misunderstand the whole thing. We just talk about the end results, which is also an expression of frustration that doesn't solve your problem. It doesn't release anything; it just creates further chain reactions.

Student: Your emotion can be telling you things.

Trungpa Rinpoche: Yes, but you don't listen to it. You are just hypnotized by the emotion—that's the problem. The emotion is telling *you* things. It is talking to you, but you are not talking to it. You just become something the emotion manipulates by remote control. You don't have access back to its headquarters. That's the problem, always. That's why emotion is so frustrating. It finally gets hold of us and controls us completely. We are reduced to just an animal. That is why we usually find emotions uncomfortable.

Student: How do you relate to the energy of your emotions?

Trungpa Rinpoche: You see, there are two ways of relating to energy. You build up energy and then you spend it, or you build up energy and regenerate it. The second way, if you relate to the qualities of the emotions completely, you are able to retain the inspiration of the emotions, but at the same time you see the neurosis [that occasioned them] as blindness. Particularly in the tantric teachings, emotions are not regarded as something to get rid of but as something necessary. Also in the bodhisattva path, emotions are regarded as necessary. They become the seeds of the bodhisattva's paramita practices.³ Those practices are based on the chemistry of the different emotions and how they can be transformed into different things. In tantric practice, the emotions are transmuted into different inspiration. Emotions are the seed of compassion and wisdom. They are a way to attain enlightenment. So one wouldn't try to get rid of them; one would try to relate to them. That's the whole point.

Student: You mentioned watching your emotions. Even at the time of the emotion's crescendo, there's still a very strong watcher. Is it like riding them or watching them from the outside?

Trungpa Rinpoche: It is not so much a matter of looking at them from the outside. It's a matter of embracing them as something together with you. In other words, it's trying to build a bridge. There's a big gap [between you and the emotion], that's why the emotion becomes uncomfortable. There's a tremendous gap; the emotion becomes separate entertainment. It becomes a separate entity that is going to hit you back. You become small and the emotion becomes huge and begins to manipulate you.

S: The larger the gap, the more it's out of control?

TR: Well, the more frustrating it becomes, anyway, because you can't reach it, even though you are controlled by it. So the idea is to build a bridge, or take down the barrier between you and your emotion.

As long as you regard the problem as separate from you, there's no way of solving the problem, because you are actually contributing toward the separateness. Your enemy becomes more and more terrifying. The more you relate to it as an enemy, the more the enemy can do to you.

Student: I feel that my experience of boredom is very close to panic, like it has panic on the borders or is the other side of panic.

Trungpa Rinpoche: Yes, obviously boredom is panic in the sense of not having a sufficient supply of entertainment. That's why you panic, sure. But that sounds like a very good sign.

Student: Rinpoche, how do you transform emotions?

Trungpa Rinpoche: Transform? You don't do it, it happens. If you are willing to do it, it happens.

Student: When you talk about relationship with emotions, does that mean attention looking at the meaning of the emotions?

Trungpa Rinpoche: It seems to be some kind of feeling of putting out a sympathetic attitude toward the emotions as being yours.

S: Would you call that attention or awareness?

TR: I think you could call it awareness. When the texts describe this practice, they speak of the emotions being self-liberated. In fact there's no difference between you and the emotion, so the emotion is liberating itself. The sense of separateness is just illusion.

I think one of the biggest problems is that we are unable to develop compassion or a sympathetic attitude toward our projections, let alone toward things outside our projections—other people, other life situations.

We can't even take a sympathetic attitude toward ourselves and our own projections, and that causes a lot of frustration and complications. That is the whole point we are trying to deal with here. The boredom of meditation demands your attention; in other words, the boredom becomes the sympathetic environment in relation to which you can develop compassion. [In that boredom] you have no choice but to relate directly to what is happening to you.

THREE

The Dawn of Mysticism

T HE HINAYANA APPROACH, which we discussed in the previous two talks, is generally very factual. There is no room for mystical inspiration. It is very down to earth and very definite. In the third yana, the mahayana, which is also called the bodhisattva path, or path of the Buddhist warrior, some sense of a mysticism, just an element of it, begins to develop. Of course when we get to tantra, or the vajrayana, the mysticism becomes more obvious.

Let us discuss the meaning of mysticism from the Buddhist point of view. Here mysticism has more to do with the depth of the potentiality for enlightenment than with any sense of uncovering something mysterious. Mysticism is often associated with a mysterious secret doctrine. The relative truth cannot measure the absolute truth, and therefore the whole thing becomes mysterious. From a simple-minded, conventional point of view, mysticism is the search for magic, maybe not witchcraft or voodoo, but still magic in the sense that things will be changed from the ordinary way we perceive them. Another part of the conventional idea of mysticism is that ordinary human beings cannot achieve the heights of it, cannot create this highest work of art. Only a talented and highly skilled person is capable of that. This achievement is regarded as powerful and mind-boggling, like someone changing water into fire and going on to drink it and have it quench his thirst. These are the kinds of things we read about in the books about Don Juan. They are involved with the mystery of hidden forces and things like the magical transference of objects. We also read about that kind of thing in the stories of saints and great spiritual masters: Water is changed into wine, Milarepa flies through the air, Padmasambhava causes earthquakes.[1] These kinds of ideas of powerful magic that mystics can develop are widely found in the mysticism of Christianity, Buddhism, Judaism, et cetera. Everybody looks forward with excitement to the possibility of becoming a super-practitioner, a complete adept of the practices, so that they can perform miracles. Wouldn't that be fun? There is such a sense of envy!

Scientists also look for proof of spirituality in the same terms. If there is such a thing as high spirituality, if there is a supreme achievement like enlightenment, someone who has accomplished that should be able to perform a miracle. That would be regarded as proof of their spiritual attainment. Scientists prefer to remain skeptical, scientifically objective, but at the same time they look for such proofs.

There is great excitement and a tremendous sense of confirmation associated with this kind of magic. One imagines students comparing notes as to which guru performs the most sophisticated kinds of miracles. But from the Buddhist point of view, mysticism is not concerned with this kind of magic. We might describe the mahayana as the dawn of mysticism and the vajrayana as the sunrise of mysticism. And naturally mysticism in the mahayana and the vajrayana does have to do with uncovering the unknown. But it is not a question of receiving training in order to perform magic in the sense just described.

There seem to be two different approaches to magic. We could say that the attainment of enlightenment is also magic. Working on ego, which is anti-enlightenment, produces enlightenment, which is extraordinarily magical. But this is not magic in the style of the cartoons, involving supermen and so on.

Mahayana is the dawn of mysticism because here we begin to get a hint that there is something more than the five skandhas that we experienced on the hinayana level. Different views of this were taken by the two main mahayana philosophical schools, the Yogachara and the Madhyamaka schools.

The Yogachara approach to the discovery that there is something more than the five skandhas focuses on the notion that there is a discoverer of the existence of ego. Did the ego discover itself? Did the ego discover its own deception, or is there something else [that made that discovery]? Ego did discover its own deception, but there is some kind of intelligence that enabled ego to see its own emptiness. Ego's perception of its own emptiness, ego cutting through ignorance, is not ego as such; it is intelligence. So at this point we have to be clear about the difference between ego and wisdom.

Ego is that which thrives on the security of your existence. Beyond that there is intelligence that sees the foolishness in trying to thrive on your security. It sees that insecurity is the ego's problem. The intelligence that sees that is called *tathagatagarbha* in Sanskrit, which means "buddha nature." Every act that perceives pain and impermanence and egolessness and the five skandhas, and even that which perceives meditation itself, is an act of non-ego. In other words, we could say that ego has two aspects: One is the honest and solid, sincere ego; the other is the critical surveyor of the whole situation, which is somewhat intelligent and more flexible and spacious. That aspect that is spacious and flexible, intelligent, is regarded as non-ego and called tathagatagarbha.

The first dawn of the bodhisattva path is based on a sense of the continuity of intelligence in spite of ego, of some intelligence functioning beyond the security level, an awakened state of mind. Still, however, this is called *garbha,* which means "essence" or "seed," something embryonic. Whenever there is a doubt, some uncertainty, whenever there is boredom, that is an expression of tathagatagarbha shining through in the form of a complaint.

That complaint is that ego's administration is no good. This is like having a revolutionary party criticizing the establishment. In this case the revolutionary approach is much more intelligent than that of the establishment. So it is trying to throw off the government, trying to find its holes, its shortcomings, its points of ignorance, and so forth.

The first step on the bodhisattva path, and the reason why mahayana exists at all, consists simply in seeing that the mechanism of the five skandhas and the mechanism of the three marks of existence are not quite enough—that there is something more. The bodhisattva's approach is like that of an underground or revolutionary movement that studies the ego and also the deception of ego in its fullest sense. The ego is not indispensable. Tathagatagarbha, buddha nature, is the starting point of the bodhisattva's inspiration. You could say in some sense that the bodhisattva path is based on hope, on the conviction that the enlightened state of mind exists and that there are techniques of all kinds [to attain it].

Then there is the Madhyamaka approach to the bodhisattva path, which says that tathagatagarbha, or buddha nature, does not need any encouragement, because it is self-existing. It calls for the act of a warrior rather than an act of hope or positive thinking. This is more advanced than the Yogachara.

Historically, the two schools, Yogachara and Madhyamaka, coexisted. The Yogachara influence of hope and positive thinking produced tremendous inspiration in China and Japan. Buddhist art has been highly influenced by the Yogachara school, because it is aesthetically positive and hopeful as well as philosophically positive and hopeful. The Yogachara was also a major influence on the practice of Zen. For instance, the [third] Chinese patriarch's [Seng-ts'an's] work, *On Trust in the Heart*, is the epitome of the Yogachara approach of negating everything, that is, of transcending dualistic comparison. This transcending is the hope, the promise, held out by the Yogacharins. Transcending a promise is a promise. Transcending the extremes of both good and bad produces ultimate goodness; it is a promise. But from another angle the Yogachara point of view is a slightly weak one, to speak euphemistically. In spite of transcending dualistic concepts of all kinds, it still speaks as though God's on your side, as it were. What it says is comparable to saying we transcend both God and the devil and that that very transcendence is a noble action, an action toward the highest, the ultimate goodness.

There are some problems in that. What I want to get across here is that, to begin with, the bodhisattva's approach, the mahayana approach, is a very positive and very hopeful one. It is also very profound. The discovery of buddha nature is a very profound and accurate one. But when we make a big deal out of buddha nature as a promise, there is a possibility of falling into eternalism.[2] There is a possibility of going against the transitoriness of life and experiences, of going against the original discoveries of the hinayana level. In the hinayana level, we discovered that everything is impermanent, and now we are looking for hope.

The Madhyamaka, which is the highest philosophical approach every developed in Buddhism, cuts the hope. Instead of being hopeful, you develop another attitude, which is that of the warrior. If a warrior lives within hope, that makes him a very weak warrior. He is still concerned with his success. If the warrior no longer has the hope of achieving success, he has nothing to lose. Therefore enemies find it very difficult to attack him. The warrior will also regard a defeat as a victory, since he has nothing to lose.

This approach is called "luring an enemy into your territory." You lure enemies into your territory by giving in to defeat constantly. The enemies finally find that there is nothing to attack, and they feel they have been fooled. They keep on conquering more territory, but their opponent places no value on the territory and does not put up a struggle. This eventually causes the enemies to lose heart.

At the same time, however, it seems to be necessary to have some kind of hope. We seem to need some positive thinking. In this case that thinking is that there is a definite, very solid basic mind that provides the basis for the warrior mentality. There is something more than ignorance, something more than just the big joke that ego has created. The bodhisattva path is characterized by great vision, great action, and great realization. The great vision here is the hope or positive thinking that the bodhisattva warrior does not need any further reinforcement or confirmation. You are already awake. So when you take the bodhisattva vow to devote your life to liberating all sentient beings, you also renounce your own liberation.[3] The idea is that in some sense the warrior has already achieved his goal. The very existence of the warrior has already defeated the enemy.

The warrior has no dreams of becoming a king. Being a warrior is both the path and the goal at the same time. Psychologically, the warrior's conviction transcends ego: There is nothing to lose and nothing to gain; therefore the petty games that ego plays do not apply anymore at all. This notion of a warrior is one of the basic themes of the mahayana. The scriptures often compare the bodhisattva to an athlete who has the highest physical training. The bodhisattva can regain his balance if he slips through the very process of slipping, so he never falls. The slipping itself becomes a way for him to gain strength. It becomes just another exercise for him.

The main practice of the bodhisattva is the six paramitas, or transcendent actions.[4] These are generosity, discipline, patience, energy, meditation, and knowledge. Generosity is the starting point. The reason it is the starting point is that if you think you are a warrior, you could become very self-contained and uptight. If you think you have nothing to lose and nothing to gain, you could in fact become very obnoxious. Generosity is a way of softening the bodhisattva's warriorlike quality, of preventing him from indulging in the warrior mentality. This is an important point.

Generosity here is not the conventional notion of being charitable. The idea is giving without demanding anything in return. You are willing to receive people into your territory, to offer hospitality and appreciate their existence and their presence—and then make no further demands. It could be very irritating and even terrifying to be a bodhisattva's guest because of his way of being generous. You might think there is something fishy behind it: "Why should this guy be extremely kind and friendly to me and not demand anything? Maybe it's a Mafia plot or something." But if you come across such a thing, you should not be afraid. Usually one finds a genuine act of generosity more terrifying than partial generosity, because there is nothing to hang on to. If it is partial generosity, we can play games with it. We could give half an inch in exchange for the other person's half an inch—it becomes a kind of bartering. But that element is absent here.

The next practice of the bodhisattva is discipline. This is self-existing discipline, discipline that need not be contrived or manufactured. It is something very spontaneous, a totality, total awareness, completeness. Situations demand discipline and you work with those situations. Discipline in this case is really more like fundamental awareness of things, of challenges in situations. Nothing is regarded as a temptation. Temptation is self-presenting, therefore you work with the temptation rather than becoming the victim of it or the villain of it. There's no pick and choose; the very existence of temptation is a reminder.

If you had a person with this kind of discipline as a guest, it might be hard to relate with him. He just sits there and acknowledges your hospitality, but nothing happens. The discipline of a bodhisattva in relating with hospitality or any kind of luxury is to accept the whole thing fully and completely. He also gets more satisfaction out of it than you would, because there is no impulsiveness involved. He is very straightforward, very close, very human. There is no flattering, but he takes advantage of your hospitality fully and completely, and he likes it. He eats your food and drinks your wine and likes them, but there is no frivolity. Sometimes it's so smooth that it seems too good to be true, but the ruggedness of the bodhisattva's human quality prevents him from being oversmooth, like a con man.

Patience is the next bodhisattva action—patience or forbearance, a quality of bearing discomfort. However, the fact that a bodhisattva is very forbearing in relating with discomfort does not mean that he has a higher pain threshold or a thick skin. This has nothing to do with his biological makeup—the bodhisattva does experience irritations. That is the most interesting thing about the bodhisattva's patience—he is extremely sensitive to all kinds of irritations. His intelligence is so enormous that he experiences *all* the irritations and sees all kinds of possible things wrong, as well as everything that is not in accordance with his or her taste. All the expressions of chaos and all the problems around a bodhisattva are acknowledged and seen. He is supersensitive and very efficient, but he does not regard the things going on around him as a personal threat, as we so often do. Even if something has nothing to do with us, we may regard it as a personal threat. Air pollution or rush-hour traffic is something that generally happens in a city, but everybody individually takes it as a personal threat or insult. Let alone the personal relationships that go on in our lives! They are of course a personal problem, but we take them as more than that—as a personal threat! If we were able to experience all the sensitive areas where things do not go in accordance with our expectations, we would become complete nutcases. We would relate to everything as a personal threat. But strangely enough, the bodhisattva manages to stay sane in spite of his higher perceptions [his greater sensitivity].

By the way, what I am describing to you are the practices of a bodhisattva rather than a myth that is being retold. I'm not describing a superman. These are practices we can do ourselves.

Patience is very interesting. Usually when we talk about patience, we have in mind someone who doesn't react to some problem or does not even see the problem, because he is *above* the problem. We think of an unperturbed person who is above all the nitty-gritty and hassles, someone who is raised above all that. We think of somebody like a nun or a jellyfish. If you had such a person in your car, that person would sit beautifully and quietly in the back seat or at the wheel, and if there was a traffic jam, he would still be grinning with enjoyment, not noticing the traffic jam. Then when the cars started to move again, he would go along happily.

This kind of approach is superficial. We have to think twice [rather than go for a simple-minded approach like that]. The bodhisattva is highly aware of the air pollution or the traffic jam or other problems going on in the world that could cause a mental freak-out. But he regards these as facts of life. He is not being philosophical particularly, not just philosophizing the whole thing. He also does not shield himself with a sense of humor, as if to say the whole thing is a big joke. Everything for him is very direct and human. At the same time, he is unmoved by these problems. Being unmoved involves intelligence as well as tremendous space within the intelligence. Intelligence is no longer conditioned by speed. When there is no speed in intelligence, it becomes factual understanding, almost photographic memory, so to speak, of every detail. Nevertheless there is room to relate to things, room to appreciate them. Also, there is no point in screaming if you're caught in a traffic jam. Bodhisattvas are very reasonable. If you scream and freak out in your car, you may cause another traffic jam. He knows that. He's very patient because he knows about the whole thing. And as a result of his patience, the bodhisattva is not a nuisance to society. In fact, he is a sane, good citizen. He is highly reasonable and wise and intelligent, and at the same time, irritable as well.

Then we have energy. This is not really a good translation. We don't have a good one for this. The Sanskrit is *virya,* which literally means "working hard" rather than purely "energy." Energy seems to be the product of the hard work of egolessness. "Vigor" might be better.[5] It is taking delight in your life situation of a bodhisattva and working hard. If we enjoy doing something, then we usually work hard. For the bodhisattva, every event is great fun, workable, wonderful. Not that the bodhisattva is on a love-and-light trip and so everything is wonderful, beautiful, and sweet. Rather, at all times everything is workable. At all times whatever happens is a learning situation that can be related with. This is possible because you relate to your knowledge as part of you rather than as information coming to you from the outside, as from some other culture or approach, or as part of some other style. Whatever you perceive—information, ideas, challenges—whatever you encounter is a learning situation, a workable situation, a highly workable situation. So there is a tremendous feeling of being human, of things being very personal. This is nothing pious, nothing philosophical as such. It is very direct. The whole point here seems to be that there is no speed involved in how you deal with your life, therefore you can't be bombarded with demands. Usually the problem is not that we are bombarded with demands; the problem is that we're speeding so much that we think we are being bombarded by things. In fact we are bombarding ourselves, and there's no room for movement or intelligence or breathing.

The next bodhisattva action is meditation. In this case, meditation is almost, we could say, aesthetic appreciation. This means awareness of body, awareness of colors, awareness of things around you, awareness of people's different styles. There's always room for everything that comes up. Everything is treated reverently, respectfully. Nothing is regarded as rubbish. Even the garbage heap is a work of art. Things have their own place, and you appreciate this, which is meditation in the broader sense. Both the relevant and the irrelevant are respected, so you don't have to economize on your time and energy. Because of that, everything becomes an object of meditation, of greater awareness, panoramic awareness. You take tremendous interest in different styles, people's different approaches, and the different physical situations of objects around you, and the different emotional states within yourself. For the bodhisattva, the whole thing is constantly meaningful and workable.

Aesthetic appreciation does not mean looking for beauty alone. It means looking at things with space around them. When things are seen with space around them, they have their own pictorial quality, so to speak. Things are seen in perspective rather than as representing demands or expectations. So bodhisattvas make a wonderful audience for the theater of life and death. This is meditation. But at the same time, the bodhisattva takes part in this theater, so the whole things does not become merely a matter of impersonal observation.

The last of the bodhisattva's six actions is prajna, or knowledge, which is a governing element in relation to all the paramitas, all the transcendent actions of the bodhisattva. In this case prajna is clear perception. Generosity, discipline, patience, energy, and meditation each have their own precise intelligence, their own clarity. That element of precision and clarity that exists within the other five paramitas is the merit of prajna. Prajna is referred to as that which is able to perceive the unbiased nature of the world, which is seeing it in its nonduality. Objects of mind are not seen as mind's trip but are seen in their own right. An object is seen as what it is rather than what it might be or what it hopefully ought to be. Prajna perceives the shunyata experience of nonduality. That is perceived with the eyes and precision of prajna.

So we could say that the precision that exists in the six transcendent actions is transcendent knowledge, prajna, and the relationship to details involved in these actions can be regarded as the bodhisattva's skillful means. So all the bodhisattva's actions are an expression of the indivisibility of skillful means and knowledge.

Student: Since you say the bodhisattva has already achieved his goal, it seems there is no evolution on the bodhisattva path. When you take the vow, it seems you are announcing that you can accomplish all the bodhisattva actions already. So how can you take that vow without being an instant pious fraud?

Trungpa Rinpoche: It seems that you have to make some statement that sets up a landmark for you, and that is taking the bodhisattva vow. But taking the vow does not necessarily mean congratulating yourself.

S: But it seems that when you take the vow, you're saying that you can already manage everything the bodhisattva is supposed to do.

TR: Not necessarily. It's not as magical as that.

S: I thought you implied that the bodhisattva path was not evolutionary.

TR: The evolution here is that in the hinayana you have realized the nuisance quality of life, and now you begin to realize the possibilities of life as well. At that point you have to be pushed into the Yogachara kind of positive thinking to begin with. So you take the bodhisattva vow. Then you have no choice. You commit yourself to looking ahead. As a result, though you may not think you will be a good warrior, you become one anyway. It's like being drafted into the army.

S: I thought the Madhyamaka point of view was that you don't hope for something in the future, you just assume it's there.

TR: Yes. And in order to do that, you need tremendous assurance that it is there already. So instead of relying on somebody to talk you into it, you just commit yourself and take the bodhisattva vow. Then you have no choice; you've been cornered. You begin to pull yourself out on your own then.

Student: You said that the bodhisattva sees all situations as workable. How do you work with violence and aggression that is directed toward you? How would that be workable?

Trungpa Rinpoche: There must be some reason for it to be happening. Nothing happens without any logic. Even if the roof falls on your head, there has to be some logic in it. You can't generalize, but somehow if you are realistically in tune with what is happening, without being uptight and overemotional, there is a way. But, you know, there is no general prescription. You have to improvise as you go along.

Student: If the bodhisattva is devoted to all sentient beings and also notices everything that's irritating to him and goes against his taste— when you relate to everything so equally, how do you decide what to be involved in? How do you decide what to be devoted to?

Trungpa Rinpoche: It's very simple logically what should be your priority. You see all kinds of things on different levels and scales, and you pick up what the priority is. That's prajna. Prajana is precisely what susses out that kind of thing.

Student: Wouldn't the priority be the thing you're already in, whatever that is?

Trungpa Rinpoche: Not necessarily. The thing you are in might already be taken care of.

Student: I understand how you can have something called generosity that is giving with no thought of getting anything in return. But even if you don't get anything in return, just having this conception of generosity and knowing, "I'm a good generous person"—that is a return.

Trungpa Rinpoche: The approach of generosity is just being giving, and there's appreciation of the process rather than watching yourself do it. That's the whole point. The meditation of the fifth paramita cuts through that, so there's no watcher involved. You just appreciate things and just do them.

Student: I was wondering how generosity would be different from anything else a bodhisattva would do.

Trungpa Rinpoche: In fact the six categories of transcendent action are not six categories: This is one life action. You could be talking to somebody and there would be the expression of all six paramitas happening simultaneously. You could help an old lady across the street, and the expression of all six paramitas could be there as well.

Student: What is the determining factor in whether a person is ready to take the bodhisattva vow?

Trungpa Rinpoche: If you're inspired to put yourself into such an awkward situation.

S: Well, it seemed to me that it depended in some way on having successfully completed the hinayana. Does that inspiration depend on having completed the hinayana?

TR: Yes, I think that's necessary. That is why the hinayana comes first. First you have to cut through your spiritually materialistic attitude. Hinayana cuts things down completely, you know: Spirituality in the hinayana consists of experiencing pain, impermanence, the lack of your ego, and all the ego's problems. That is very important before you get into anything more than that. You have to have completely understood those warnings. This does not necessarily mean actually being completely free from spiritual materialism, but at least you have to have had those questions transplanted into your heart. That in itself might even be spiritual materialism, but nobody can just start with a complete achievement. You cannot wait for a complete achievement before going on to the next step—that would take centuries. So one has to trust that one can do it.

Student: Is that the point that you have described as taking a leap?
Trungpa Rinpoche: Taking the bodhisattva vow?
S: Yes.
TR: Well, that is a kind of mini-leap before going into tantra.

Student: How does the warrior resist temptation without giving birth to an even larger ego? It seems that when you try to discipline yourself, if in fact you succeed at it, the ego just gets larger.

Trungpa Rinpoche: You don't try too hard to secure yourself. You don't try to act perfectly. When you try to look for perfection in transcending ego, too much accuracy creates more chaos. So the whole thing has to be somewhat freestyle, if we could use such an expression. Fundamentally, you have to be willing to be a fool. You are not ashamed to be a fool.

Student: In describing the paramita of meditation, you mentioned an attitude of reverence and appreciation. Would that be an attitude to cultivate in our meditation, rather than simply watching, simply watching our thoughts and our breathing?

Trungpa Rinpoche: And in the everyday situation as well, not in sitting practice alone. Whatever happens in your life situation you don't just dismiss as being ordinary and casual. Rather, everything has its own place, and there is a balance there already. You don't have to create a balance.

Student: What selects the object of meditation?
Trungpa Rinpoche: One doesn't select the objects of meditation. They come to you.
S: Always?
TR: Mmm-hmm.
S: The content comes to you?
TR: That's saying the same thing.

Student: But I thought each person had his own particular version of the story.
Trungpa Rinpoche: Sure, but there's no censor. There's no censorship. Things don't have to be purely dharmic. They come to you. *It* comes to you.

Student: You say the breath is a crutch, meaning it's something that doesn't come to you, but you have to sort of grab onto *it.*
Trungpa Rinpoche: Yes. That's kind of first-grade level.
S: Don't we sort of make crutches out of everything?
TR: No. Usually one doesn't manufacture crutches, but crutches are given to one.
S: We don't manufacture other objects of meditation?
TR: I hope not. Well, what else can you meditate on? It seems the technique is so spare; there's just walking and breathing. The rest is just nothing—it comes to you. The technique should be very spare. There shouldn't be too many techniques. There should just be one or two techniques at the beginning.

Student: I'm beginning to see that the nine yanas are stages it's possible to go through one after another. I'm so over my head already, I'm wondering what the practical value is of learning about nine yanas.
Trungpa Rinpoche: It is so you can identify with the path and understand that it is not only a myth but something you can do yourself. And

also, once you're told about it, there's no mystery. The whole map is at your disposal. You can buy it. You can have it.

S: So as I go along the path, I'll always be able to—

TR: To identify with it, sure. That's what's supposed to be happening. That's why they are called yanas, or vehicles. You can't have a vehicle without passengers. Or without a driver, for that matter.

Student: Is that how the bedroom and the kitchen sink come together, in meditation?

Trungpa Rinpoche: Precisely! That's good thinking! That's the marriage of skillful means and wisdom, the bedroom and the kitchen sink.

FOUR

The Juncture between Sutra and Tantra

WE DISCUSSED THE transition from the hinayana level to the mahayana level in terms of the perception of reality involved. At this point I would like to emphasize once again that egolessness, impermanence, and suffering are a prominent part of the path, an important part of preparation for the mahayana. The basic idea of the mahayana is to realize shunyata, emptiness, through the practice of the six paramitas. But at the same time we should not lose our valuation of impermanence, egolessness, and suffering, which remain definite and important.

Egolessness can be approached from all kinds of different angles. Self is not applicable anymore, because you have realized selflessness. From the student's point of view, what is experienced is the irrelevance of the self. This leads to the basic practices of the bodhisattva's way, which bring further realization of impermanence and the nonexistence of self. Ego is regarded as a collection of stuff related with the five-skandha process, as we have said. It is purely a collection and does not amount to anything else. Therefore those five stuffs or skandhas depend for their sense of existence on relative reference points.

From the point of view of impermanence, anything that happens within that realm that depends on the existence of self is also subject to decay and death. Life is a constant process of death and decay. Life consists of a process containing birth, illness, old age, and death. Life contains fundamental bewilderment, in which you don't even recognize the bewilderment as it is anymore.

Today we are trying to understand the basic meaning of shunyata.

The shunyata experience could develop as a sense of the basic emptiness of life and the basic suffering of life, and at the same time, as a sense of nondualistic wisdom, inspiration. I feel that it is extremely important before discussing tantra to realize the nature of the juncture between the tantra and the sutra teachings, which is what we are joining together at this point, to realize what is the continuity there and what is not.[1] It is very important to realize that.

Self, ego, tries to maintain itself and develop its territory. Should that be encouraged or discouraged? Should we try to maintain ourself or should we not? What would you say?

Student: Who should?
Trungpa Rinpoche: I beg your pardon?
S: Who should try to maintain itself?
TR: Who is he?
S: Should we? Who?
TR: Who is we or who?
S: Should we try to maintain ourselves? Who is we?
TR: I'm asking you.
S: I don't know.
TR: Who is that? Who is that?
[*Silence*]
TR: Did you say you don't know?
S: Well, I . . . I suppose who is that.
TR: Yes, but who isn't that?
S: Who isn't that?
TR: Moreover, what are you talking about?
[*Laughter, then silence*]
TR: Who are you?
S: I don't know.
TR: Why don't you? Why?
S: There's no way of answering the question.
TR: Why not?
S: Nothing works.
TR: Why should it work?
[*Silence*]
TR: It's not a matter of con-manship. Things don't have to work. Let's warm up. Why should it work? Who are you? Why should it work? Who are you? Why should it work?

S: It just stopped.

TR: Stopped?

S: The questioning.

TR: Where does it stop? Where? Where?

[*Silence*]

TR: How come it stopped there?

S: I guess you can't focus anymore. Other things start happening.

TR: Understand that. We all show that common symptom. So much is happening that we find the whole thing bewildering, are unable to focus on any one particular thing. The whole thing is bewildering, bewildered. Constantly. Bewildered constantly all over the place. So we are confused, bewildered. Subject to confusion. We are a victim of confusion. What shall we do? Shall we stay? Try to get some sleep? Get some food? Or shall we try to get out of it? If you try to get out of it, it means putting in a lot of energy. Trying to get out means creating some kind of scheme so that you *could* get out of this prison. Could we do that? Couldn't we do that? How can we do that? Do you want to get out or do you want to stay in?

It's a very inviting, smooth nest. Like being a worm. You could regenerate your next generation. You could retain yourself constantly by being a worm. Or you could stick your neck out by being a crocodile. You could.

Something coming up there? [*The Vidyadhara invites a question from the audience.*]

Student: When you ask how can we get out or whether we want to get out, maybe the thing to do is just be aware of the mess we're in.

Trungpa Rinpoche: Aware of what?

S: Aware of confusion.

TR: How would you get out of that? How would you do it?

S: Why would you want to?

TR: Precisely, why should you want to? Why?

Student: It's not secure.

Trungpa Rinpoche: Yes, it's so secure.

S: It's *not* secure.

TR: Well, it seems to me it's secure, because the whole thing is set up for you. You can swim in your amniotic fluid, and—

S: Well, for a while.

TR: You have your placenta, and along with the placenta, beautiful swimming pools have been created.

S: Yeah, it's fine as long as it works.

TR: It seems to work as long as the mother eats enough food. I mean there's no point at which we have to come out of the womb. If we are happy, we could remain there eternally. If the mother eats appropriate food, we eat and we get to survive. Moreover, we get the fun of swimming around in the water, behind the placenta, inside the womb. We feel happy. Great!

Student: But isn't that a problem?

Trungpa Rinpoche: That is a problem, of course. But how do you see the problem? How could we maintain that situation? We could stay there. What prevents us from staying in our mother's womb? What prevents us? What triggers off our leaving?

Student: At some point it's painful.

Trungpa Rinpoche: You don't know, because you haven't been there yourself. You've forgotten the whole thing. When you're an infant, you have no idea of it. You have to purely guess. If the baby had a reference point of relating with an open situation as opposed to the claustrophobia of being in the womb, obviously the baby would want to come out. But the baby has forgotten the reference point. It has forgotten being pushed into the womb and developing as an embryonic being. It has no reference point, so where would you start? How would you relate with the whole thing? How would you?

Student: Is there a choice?

Trungpa Rinpoche: As far as the baby is concerned there's no choice. It is just so. That's the whole point. [For there to be a choice, there has to be a reference point that sets up alternatives.] So why would there be an alternative? There is no reference point, absolutely no reference point.

Student: Did we create that alternative?

Trungpa Rinpoche: I suppose so. But there is no reason for creating a reference point as far as the baby is concerned.

Student: People make the reference points for the baby, don't they?

Trungpa Rinpoche: What?

S: The parents or other people make the reference points for the baby. The baby doesn't have a choice.

TR: How? How?

S: By having selves. By having egos of their own. They make reference points for the baby, and the baby takes them on. He doesn't have any choice but to take them on.

TR: Yeah. That sounds interesting. Yeah. How do they do that?

Student: Doctors say something about the cortex connecting up with the hypothalamus. There's a different brain structure when the baby's in the womb.

Trungpa Rinpoche: Yes. How do we do that? As a mother—

Student: You tell the child how to relate to the pain.

Trungpa Rinpoche: Well, that's at a more developed stage. It has already related with the pain; that means it has already made its mind up. But before that? How do we work with the birth?

Student: It's what you said about emotions being the result of our projections onto the outside. The mother has all of those, so she's already giving them to the baby from the moment the baby is conceived. Even if the baby has no thought, he's already got the mother's—

Trungpa Rinpoche: That's true, it seems. That's how we come to the conclusion. Duality happens—through a demand to go from one extreme to the other extreme. Duality constantly happens, going from one extreme to the other extreme. Duality is not basically a set pattern, but it has its momentums [that move it] from one extreme to relate to the other extreme. It's not preprogrammed as such, but it is related with a reference point that creates [a movement from] one extreme to the other extreme. Which is a very important point.

Student: There's no memory without duality?

Trungpa Rinpoche: Yeah, there's no memory without duality. Yeah.

S: Then how could Padmasambhava say there is one mind with continuous memory? In Evans-Wentz's book *The Tibetan Book of the Great Liberation,* it's stated that your memories continue.

TR: That's primarily in reference to the vajra state: one memory, one mind. You have to attain a state of one mind before you do that. The baby has two minds, or three minds, in fact: mother, father, son.

Student: What happens when you see everything as just continuous events?
Trungpa Rinpoche: You begin to see it as continuity.
S: See what as continuity?
TR: What?
S: What's the continuity?
TR: Nothing.
S: What do you mean, nothing?
TR: Discontinuity.
S: Discontinuity?
TR: As continuity. You see, the whole point here seems to be to relate properly with egolessness. Before we embark upon our study of tantra, we have to realize a sense of egolessness—because of the ego. This is something that is continuous but is based on discontinuity. Thus the ego is subject to impermanence and the ego is also subject to pain, suffering. The three marks of existence—pain, egolessness, and impermanence— exist simultaneously.

Of course we should not forget the glorious bodhisattva path we have been discussing. People have tremendous insight connected with that, tremendous inspiration to dance on the bodhisattva path. Nevertheless they should be aware of the consequences of egolessness and pain and impermanence constantly happening at the same time, all the time. It's happening all the time. So some kind of awareness of the basic framework of Buddhism needs to be kept all the way through. This is necessary, extremely necessary.

Ego, self, is based on survival. And survival means being right on time, constantly on time. You live on time. Throughout death and rebirth, again and again, you survive with your time. And because time is such a prominent factor, it is a source of struggle and pain. The pain and time and survival are based on the same continuity. So life cannot exist without pain and impermanence and ego at the same time. It's extremely simple logic, kindergarten level.

Student: Is this pain based on the idea of securing something—because we have to secure some kind of permanent situation, we're in pain? But there's nothing to secure, and understanding that is the security. I mean, there just is no security, but realizing that is some kind of security.

Trungpa Rinpoche: And so forth. You begin to realize egolessness that way. But you have never stopped yourself or created a bank of memory or created anything basic and solid, because your ground is subject to continual change and pain. You have no ground *at all*. This seems to be very simple logic, which I hope everybody could understand.

Student: Rinpoche, isn't there an urge toward insecurity as well? Some sort of need to be insecure?

Trungpa Rinpoche: Yes. That's very simple. You use the same logic all over again. The logic is that death lives. It's the same thing. Death lives.

Student: How does this all tie in with the baby in the womb?

Trungpa Rinpoche: The baby in the womb has the same kind of insecurity. Insecurity constantly happening. Therefore processes happen at the same time, as you go along. Babies are regarded as innocent, but this is by no means the case. Things with the baby are already happening according to its karmic situation. There is a reason that it is *your* baby, the baby of certain parents, which is a condition, continuity.

Student: What you're saying is that pain and the knowledge of transitoriness depend on ego. You're saying that they exist along with the hollowness of ego. Is that right? Something is generated out of the sense of pain—

Trungpa Rinpoche: I don't follow your logic.

S: You're saying that there is pain and transitoriness and egolessness, and these are three facts. And I don't see whether there's any definite relationship between them. But I think the relationship between them is what you're trying to get across.

TR: The pain, impermanence, and suffering are linked. You have ego, but you don't have ego. That produces apprehension and pain. The reason why that apprehension developed altogether is that you didn't have a relationship with the time. The time was not sympathetic to you, toward your maintaining yourself anymore.

Student: Is that why paranoia seems to increase as—

Trungpa Rinpoche: Yes. To some extent you could say that you exist.

You think you exist. And your goal exists. But then you find that the existence of your goal needs maintenance, and that maintenance is a painful thing to do, to the point where *your* existence becomes questionable at the same time.

I mean, it's very simple logic, extremely simple, first-grade level. You distinguish between A and B and C. If you get beyond that, you relate with D, E, and F. It's that simple. The reason why A is A is because B is something else, and C is something else again, because the B is not the A, and the C is not the B. Then you go on experimenting until you get to the X. None of the letters are the same as the previous ones. They each have different characteristics. And so forth.

Well, perhaps we should stop at this point. Tomorrow, hopefully, we will discuss tantra. But I haven't asked my boss yet.

Thank you.

FIVE

Overcoming Moralism

WE HAVE DISCUSSED the hinayana level represented by the shra-vakayana and the pratyekabuddhayana and the mahayana level, represented by the practice ideal of the bodhisattva. Last, we discussed the shunyata principle. At this point, instead of discussing the first tantric yana, the kriyayoga tantra, it might be helpful to give an introduction to tantra as a whole. We could get into the details of the six tantric yanas later on.

As has been indicated, the impermanence, suffering, and egolessness that we discover on the hinayana level play an extremely important part, a crucial part, in tantra as well. We cannot deny this. It is important to understand and acknowledge that we are not just transcending hinayana and latching on to the higher hopes of tantra. Likewise, we cannot ignore the bodhisattva's path, involving the transplantation of bodhichitta into one's mind and the practice of the six paramitas.[1] Also the bodhisatt-va's understanding of nonduality is quite important.

If seems that we do need these technical understandings in order to understand the buddhadharma. The idea of the buddhadharma is not particularly to make you into professors or scholars as such. Neverthe-less, when we discuss big ideas, powerful ideas, those ideas have to have some specific elements to relate with. So tantra is desperately dependent on an understanding of the hinayana and mahayana, always. Some little technical knowledge of the hinayana principles concerning reality and the mahayana's principles of morality is a basic necessity, absolutely important. If you don't have any understanding of those, probably you will miss the whole point of vajrayana, or tantra.

People in the West usually think that tantra is concerned purely with pranayama, mudras, visualizations, and so on.[2] They think that's what tantra is all about, which is not quite true. There's something more than that.

To begin with, tantra is based on the understanding of who is practicing tantra. Who are we? Who am I? If you asked a tantric practitioner, "Who are you?" he would automatically say, using the same logic developed on the hinayana level, "I am a collection of stuff that actually doesn't exist, the five skandhas." This is also the hinayana answer and the mahayana answer. And if you asked the tantric practitioner, "Why are you practicing this path?" he would automatically say, "Because I have surrendered myself, and my work is dedicated to the benefit of all sentient beings." This is a pragmatic combination of both the hinayana ("I've surrendered") and the mahayana ("I've decided to dedicate my life to the benefit of all sentient beings").

The question might be asked? "What is the basic need to go beyond the hinayana and mahayana? Why don't we stay on in the hinayana and perfect the hinayana? Or why don't we stay on in the mahayana and perfect the mahayana? What's the point of going beyond those into another area?" The mahayana practitioner would say, "The perfection of the hinayana is the mahayana; I can't help it." And the tantric practitioner would say, "The perfection of the mahayana is the vajrayana; I can't help it."

One of the follies of the bodhisattva or mahayana path is that there is still a good intention involved. No matter how much we try to be detached from our good intention, we are still involved with it. There is some sense of a paramitas, of transcending, of reaching the other shore. There is an element of goodness that rejects the sense of energy. Bodhisattvas claim to be the bravest and most powerful warriors of all. But the bodhisattva's trying to live up to his virtue becomes a hang-up, a problem. Still searching for warriorhood rather than being a warrior becomes a problem. As bodhisattvas, when we sit down to meditate, we're trying to become good meditators rather than being in the meditation.

There is no pronounced good intention involved in tantra. Nor for that matter a bad intention either, if you're concerned about that.

We need to say a bit more about the mahayana notion of shunyata, which is discussed in the *Prajnaparamita Sutra,* for example. *Shunya* means "empty," and *ta* means "-ness." Shunyata is removing the barrier, the screen, between subject and object. Shunyata, the absence of the screen, is, for the time being, very important, very powerful.

A hinayana school of Buddhist philosophy says that everything is made out of atoms and everything is conditioned by time. Therefore it is impermanent. This atomist philosophy has been challenged by saying that such logic is not necessary. We don't need deductive logic to prove our point. In order to see the transparency of the world, we do not have to reduce everything to dust [atoms] or moments [atoms of time] necessarily. To do so is in some sense believing in nothingness. It's believing that things don't exist because they're made out of atoms. So what? Still there is some materialism left over [in the belief that the atoms and the moments exist].

Another philosophical school, referred to as pluralists, believes that a mass is a collection, which proves the nonexistence of the mass. All of the elements of the mass are conditioned by time and space. Things don't exist because the elements depend on a mutual space. And so forth and so on. It gets very complicated to discuss the pluralists' and atomists' view of reality.[3]

The notion of shunyata cuts through the position of the atomists and pluralists naturally by saying that we don't have to reduce everything into dust. In order to demonstrate the nonexistence of a table, we don't have to grind it to dust and then show it: "Look, this is the remains of the table." We don't have to do that. There's something else involved. If you are saying the table doesn't exist because it wasn't a table, it was a collection of dust, then you are creating the idea [that something does exist there that isn't a table]. Then you still have a pattern of fixed belief. The table consists of a pile of dust, garbage.

The shunyata principle in the bodhisattva's philosophy does not bother to say that. It does not matter whether the table is supposed to be solid or made out of a collection of atoms. That way, you still end up with a table in some form or other no matter what your belief is. But the bodhisattva would say that your belief itself doesn't exist. The reason your belief doesn't exist is that it is *you* who believe. Who are you, anyway? You don't exist in any case. That removes the barrier.

I'm afraid this is a very crude example. Very crude, kindergarten level. But in any case, since you as a fixed, ongoing entity do not exist, the so-called table, as you named it, as you believed it, as you used it, does not exist. Your version of the table does not exist.

So then the question is, what does exist? The barrier exists, the filter [between subject and object] exists. The optical illusion, the eyeglasses you use, do exist—rather than the projection or the projector.

What the shunyata teaching does is tell you that you do not need to have a barrier to name things. You do not need to have an interpreter to tell you what things are named. [The message here is] the nonexistence of the interpreter. Or the folly of the interpreter. [Without the interpreter, you have] no problem with language. You could have a relationship with language, in fact. Just kick out the interpreter—then you don't speak any language. That's fine. Then you are really relating with exploring things as they are. The interpreter doesn't tell you how things are.

So we come up with a very simple, simple-minded conclusion. Kick out the interpreter, then begin to explore. If nobody explains to you what a table is or what its function is, then you begin to explore its tableness—or potness or rockness or flowerness. You begin to explore, to work with things as they are.

That is what is being talked about in the *Heart Sutra* when it says "Emptiness is also form."[4] Form is no different from emptiness—things do exist in their own right without your judgments, preconceptions, and so forth. [When we drop those,] we begin to see in a very direct way, a straightforward, literal way. The colors are not called red, white, blue, but they are as they are. If we don't name them, conceptualize them, they become much redder, bluer, and whiter, and so forth. That seems to be the idea of the shunyata principle: seeing things as they are.

But there is the problem of the possibility that when you don't use preconceptions about things as they are, when you reject the whole language and begin to explore the true nature of things, somehow or other you might be reduced to infanthood. You might become like a deaf person who never heard the language, though you still have a relationship with the things you explore. There's that problem.

That is the problem of nihilism. If you cut down the preconceptions so that there are no ideas, no fantasies, no categorizing, no pigeonholing, there is the possibility that you might end up as a deaf person, a stupid person. (This is a danger from the tantric point of view, by the way.) And there is also the danger [that of eternalism] that you might end up in an absolute, completed, perfected, meditative state in which you don't care what things are called. You are only relating to what things *are*. Both those are possibilities of raising the ape instinct again. There is that problem.[5]

Of course the whole thing sounds good and beautiful: You become completely detached from the whole world of preconceptions—there are no concepts, no naming; things are constantly organic, relational. That's a very intelligent thing. But at the same time, there's something that does not quite click, shall we say. Things do not quite work ideally in terms of how we function in the world, in the world of human beings. There is that problem with the mahayana way. The whole thing is moralistic. You try to be good, noncategorizing, all perfect—good and great and kind to everybody. You don't listen to bad language. You do still acknowledge bad language, but you don't actually listen to it. That seems to be one of the biggest problems with the mahayana approach to reality. That is the biggest problem.

That is precisely the reason why tantra is necessary. As you can see, you have to cut down dualistic trips of all kinds, conceptualized notions of all kinds, all kinds of believing this and that. You have to cut down that whole thing. But then we are left with numbness. And the tantric approach to life from this point of view is to redefine, regenerate the whole thing again: reintroduce duality, reintroduce conceptualization— but at an entirely different level.

You can't just begin as a tantric practitioner. That is not possible at all. You have to cut down your things. Everything. You have to cut it all down. You have to reduce yourself to numbness. This is absolutely necessary. Having done that, then you regain your perception. Another evolution begins to happen. That is the evolution of what is called energy or power in tantric language.

In the tantric language, we have the idea of *chandali,* which means "ever-present force" or "ever-present energy." That energy comes in re-awakening from the sedations of the bodhisattva's trip. You awaken again, but still you have been cured of your dualistic problems. [You awaken to the notion that] duality is necessary. Samsara is necessary. In fact, tantric literature often talks about the sameness or indivisibility of samsara and nirvana. That means that some relationship is taking place that raises your intelligence after the devastating detachment, the devastating sweep, of mahayana. You have to regain energy from somewhere, which is from buddha nature.

So this reawakening fundamentally involves raising the principle of buddha nature, tathagatagarbha, as well as reintroducing the three marks of existence: suffering, impermanence, egolessness. But now they manifest in an entirely different light. Now suffering manifests as an adornment, energy; impermanence as a consort, to dance with; and egolessness as the basic strength to be. The whole thing is interpreted from an entirely different angle. But it is still in keeping with the understanding of life developed on the hinayana level.

Suffering is energy. Impermanence is a consort to dance with. And egolessness is a way to be. This becomes an extremely powerful tantric statement.

One of the founders of our lineage, Naropa, was a great student and scholar of the hinayana and mahayana. But he found that something was lacking in him. He had to give up his [monastic] robe and involve himself again with a teacher. He had to do all kinds of undesirable things that his teacher asked him to do. You can read about all that in Guenther's *Life and Teaching of Naropa*. You will find the details there. It's a very good book to read; worth reading if you are interested in tantra. You can find out more there about the outrageousness of the teaching—that nirvana is identical with samsara. That's one of the phrases that tantric teachers used: *khorde yerme* in Tibetan. That's a very powerful statement.

Similarly we could say that the teaching of the three marks of existence is a very samsaric statement. Life is pain, miserable. Impermanence—it's obvious: People are dying, we are all dying, constantly. Egolessness means that we have no substance whatsoever to hang on to. These are samsaric statements, obviously—the portrait of samsara. But embodying them in vajrayanic language makes them extremely powerful, tremendously powerful.

If you read Guenther's book on Naropa, you will probably find those three described as the three gates of liberation—in one of his footnotes, I think. That would be worth looking up.[6]

The whole point here is that tantric philosophy—we call it philosophy for lack of a better word—speaks the language of samsara. Tantra is the language of samsara—the redefined language of samsara. After one has gone through all the spiritual trips of the hinayana and the mahayana, tantra is coming to the world. But in a somewhat, we could say, reformed way. It is more intelligent than the samsara-samsara approach.

The tantric approach is samsara plus samsara rather than purely samsara-samsara. It is super-samsara, very intelligent samsara.

That is why tantra has been looked down upon by a lot of the hinayana schools and certain mahayana schools. And even in the twentieth century we have scholars who look down on tantra as being samsaric.

Dr. Edward Conze, a noted Buddhist scholar, is highly resentful of the existence of tantra. He would like to make the mahayana the glorious peak of Buddhism, make that the highest idea we could connect with. But then he finds there is another pyramid rising above that, and he says, "Oh, those tantric people are just freaks who just want to make love and drink. It's purely samsara, no good." Which is quite right from his point of view.

It is like Nagarjuna at an early age.[7] When he was a young man, he was an impressive, handsome logician of a mahayana school. At that stage, he would have defended Buddhism from tantra. But as he grew older and more experienced and began to think about himself twice, he became a tantric siddha. And that's the process Naropa went through as well. Why didn't he just stay at Nalanda University, remain a scholar? He couldn't do it. When people get older and more mature and begin to think twice about life, they always come back to tantra. That's true. It always happens that way. You may not call yourself a tantric practitioner as such, but you find yourself being one anyway.

The basic idea of tantra from this point of view is the sameness of samsara and nirvana. The samsaric experience with its chaos and problems is obviously neurosis. Neurotic problems should be related to with detachment and openness, from an entirely new angle.

Why should we be too polite to samsara or to nirvana? Why should we be to cultured, polite, and reasonable? Let us turn the world upside down! Let us! Let us see the spacious quality of the earth and the earthly quality of space. That's what we will see if we turn the world upside down. That is the tantric approach to life. Space is solid, earth is spacious. And by no means can you call this perverted, because there is no one to judge what is perverted and what is not. There's no reason. Who is the perverter? There's no one to watch. You just become either the earth or the space anyway. Nobody judges that. That is called crazy wisdom. There's no watcher to moderate, to gauge moral obligations of any kind. You are doing it yourself.

So I would like you to understand before we continue: The basic point in tantra at this point is a further approach to reality. Reality could be regarded as unreal, and unreality could be regarded as reality. That's the logic of tantra, fundamentally speaking. That's why samsara is regarded as nirvana and nirvana is regarded as samsara. And we do not have any obligation to stick to one doctrine or another. We are free from all dogma.

Student: Is the metaphor "stopping the world" [used by Carlos Castaneda] a tantric term from your point of view?

Trungpa Rinpoche: I don't think so. "Stopping the world" sounds too idealistic. Tantra creates more worlds. You have hundreds of millions of deities happening.

Student: Some time ago, when people used to ask you about LSD and other drugs, you described the drug experience as super-samsara. I feel confused, because at that time you used the term in a negative sense, and now you're using it in a positive sense.

Trungpa Rinpoche: That's very interesting. It is precisely a tantric statement in either case. When you think something is super-samsara, it is turned upside down and made super-nirvana. When you think of something as super-nirvana, it is turned upside down and made into super-samsara. LSD and other hallucinogenic drugs could be regarded as an adolescent level of nirvana. Therefore, it is super-samsara. I still maintain that. People speak about all kinds of inspirations they have gotten out of those experiences. They think it's nirvana, but it's still a little samsaric version of super-samsara.

Student: Could you describe how a student's relation to his teacher is affected by these various stages on the path. What is the importance of the teacher at different points?

Trungpa Rinpoche: That is very important at any point. You need someone who will perform operations on you and will guide you and challenge you—a physical guru who lives on this planet. And speaks your language, preferably. And behaves like you, preferably. Someone like that is necessary, absolutely necessary at all points. There's no doubt that you would try to get away into your imagination of a cosmic guru. You can't do that. You need guidance all the time. Even if you realize cosmic guruhood or achieve cosmic consciousness, you still need someone to bring those down to the level of "I do exist." The guru is absolutely necessary; there's no doubt about that.

Student: is the interpreter to be ignored or actively thrown out?
Trungpa Rinpoche: Actively thrown out. If necessary, call the police.
S: Who throws the interpreter out?
TR: You. Who else?

Student: Could you say something about children and shunyata?
Trungpa Rinpoche: Children and shunyata? Children and shunyata? I don't know. Well, they have a potential for shunyata, but they already have their karmic debts developed within themselves, which we really can't do very much about.

People have lots of trips, thinking their children can be scared or manipulated into a good psychological state of being. There are a lot of ideas about that. But it seems that you can't do that. When the children have developed to at least eighteen years of age, at which point the parents are able to see what the child's basic psychological functioning is like, then you can work with it. But I don't think you can regard children as fundamentally innocent persons. That ignores their whole karmic debt. If you think you are born pure and get fucked up by your life as you grow, that also suggests you could commit suicide to cut off karmic debts. Why don't you stop your life, kill yourself? Then you will be free. That seems to be one of the problems with that point of view.

In any case, children have their own hidden neuroses. At least as I watch my own children, I see it happens that way. Children have their own style of neurosis, and when they get to a certain age, like eighteen or maybe thirteen, they begin to speak out their demands, make their demands in their own style, which could be quite different from the style of the parents. And then, if the parents are well versed in working with people other than their children, then at that point they could work with them, relate with their style, and teach them.

S: But it seems that when children look at a table, they have a very simple version of it.

TR: Yes, naturally, they do, they do. But that doesn't necessarily mean a pure version. It's just that they haven't grown up, they haven't seen the viciousness of the world very much; therefore their ideas may be very innocent. But by no means are they particularly pure. [Thinking] that would be a big problem. In that case, there would be no reincarnation.

I suspect that all kinds of dangerous things may be coming up in my children. [Those things] haven't woken up, you know, but later they're going to come out. There may be Rudrahood of all kinds that hasn't come out so far. But we do not know.

Student: Rinpoche, you talked about the attitude toward suffering in the hinayana, and then that complete sort of flip that's done in tantra with regard to suffering—taking it as energy or food. But I'm not clear what the mahayana relationship to suffering is.

Trungpa Rinpoche: The mahayana relates to suffering just as a working base. It's a question of discipline. Whenever you feel pain, you are supposed to work harder. It's like when your tire gets a puncture, you have to work harder—fix the tire—to keep driving along.

Student: According to the theory of dependent origination, when there is cessation of desire and attachment, you also have cessation of karma, of the life-and-death cycle. How does that relate to tantric philosophy?

Trungpa Rinpoche: In think it's the same thing. If you transmute karmic relational action into energy rather than dualistic fixation, it becomes energy rather than karmic debts. It's a matter of attitude, a matter of having a sense of confidence that those neurotic hang-ups are meaningless and you have to transmute them.

Student: Are they still there, though?

Trungpa Rinpoche: The energy is there, but the neurosis is not there. That's the difference.

Student: Is it possible to deal with emotions using that principle? And if so, how do you develop enough detachment to do that?

Trungpa Rinpoche: Detachment, did you say? I don't see why you would become detached, particularly. In fact, you would be more loving toward your energy and emotions. They're a working situation, a workable situation, in any case. And if you begin to realize they are workable situations, then they begin to give *you* some kind of guidelines as well.

The whole thing becomes a mutual project, rather than you just trying to get something out of it, to win something else over [for yourself].

Student: Could you say something more about working with the neurosis in emotions?

Trungpa Rinpoche: Emotions *are* neurosis, as we said earlier, but they're not regarded as bad or good. You try to find the nature of the neurosis, of the emotions, rather than relate with the manifestations of them. Manifestations would be, say, killing somebody, making love to somebody, or throwing somebody out of your house.

S: You seem to say, follow it down to the root.

TR: The root, yes.

S: How do you do that?

TR: You just do it. When you ask how to do it, you are asking for sedatives or gloves or hammers or pliers. "How do I do that so that I don't have to get my hands greasy?" It's like you're saying, "I have to unscrew this thing on my car. Should I use gloves?" There's no how. You just do it. It's also a matter of trust in buddha nature, trust that you are going to pick up intelligent guidelines within yourself. If you have enough trust, you're going to do it. That's the whole point. Everybody is able to do anything. Everybody is able to act out of basic sanity, in an enlightened fashion, in any case. But nobody has trusted them to be able to do it. That's the problem. There's a lot of hypocrisy going on—self-destructive things happening—based on self-condemnation. People feel basically condemned. That's the problem. I'm sure we can do it. I've seen that people can do it. I did it myself.

Student: What does the ever-present energy or force you were talking about have to do with crazy wisdom?

Trungpa Rinpoche: Ever-present force is the basic field, the ground that crazy wisdom dances on. The wisdom is there, and crazy wisdom is the action of it. In tantric iconography we find pictures of the shakta and shakti, the principal figure and his consort. The consort activates the energy of the principal figure.

Student: You said that the three marks of existence are used for inspiration in tantra. I was wondering whether the six paramitas of the bodhisattva are used to do a similar thing.

Trungpa Rinpoche: Yes. We could discuss that as we discuss more about tantra. Yes, the virtuousness of the mahayana path, of the six paramitas, transforms into an entirely different area. They are no longer virtuous alone. They become crazy-wisdom expressions.

Student: Does Zen practice have anything to do with tantra?

Trungpa Rinpoche: Zen practice is a Yogachara meditative practice that developed in China and Japan. Beyond that, there is the Madhyamaka philosophy, which goes beyond the Zen tradition and Zen philosophy based on the Yogachara. But the craziness of the Zen tradition leads toward the Madhyamaka path. A lot of Zen masters have managed to get into that as well: for instance, when they did things like burning the image of the Buddha or tearing up their textbooks. Those actions are expressions of crazy wisdom. Strictly in the Madhyamaka style, however, rather than in the tantric style. So the Zen tradition brings crazy wisdom to the sutra teachings, the mahayana, rather than leading to tantra itself. You cannot say Zen is tantra. That's impossible. Zen is Zen, and tantra is tantra. You cannot say Zen is tantra, because there's never enough tantrum in it to begin with tantra.

Student: In hinayana and mahayana, they talk about the middle way. Is tantra also on the middle way, or does it turn that upside down?

Trungpa Rinpoche: Tantra is regarded as an extreme way rather than the middle way.

S: You talked about a kind of reverse.

TR: Yes, a reverse. Definitely so. In the Buddhist tradition, basically you have the sutra teaching, which consists of the hinayana and mahayana. And then there's the teaching of tantra in six yanas. Tantra is the reverse of everything that happened before, including the hinayana approach. Tantra believes in duality, whereas mahayana believes in nonduality, the middle way. Tantra believes in extreme paths. For instance, you have the four orders of tantra, which are the father tantra, the mother tantra, the neutral tantra, and the transcending tantra. Those are the aggression tantra, the passion tantra, the ignorance tantra, and the tantra transcending ignorance and aggression and putting all of them together. These are very gutsy, if I may say so. Very straight-forward.

S: I have one more question. Before his enlightenment, Buddha was practicing asceticism, and he almost destroyed himself fasting. In its reverse asceticism, its extremism, does tantra have the danger of being self-destructive?

TR: Yes. Unless you proceed according to the whole three-yana principle and have gone through hinayana and mahayana beforehand. I have been saying that constantly, again and again. You cannot practice tantra unless you start from hinayana and mahayana. Unless you have gone through hinayana and mahayana, you can't get into tantra at all. Without that, tantra becomes like a spiritual atomic bomb.

Student: How does tantra relate to the teachings of the Buddha as they've been passed down through sutras and so on? Can tantra actually be considered Buddhism? What is the connection between tantric philosophy and the teachings of the Buddha as they were presented?

Trungpa Rinpoche: I think they are the highlight of it. The tantra is Buddha's teaching. Buddha as Shakyamuni was purely a physical manifestation. His speech and mind are represented in the two stages of tantra. Any expressions of crazy wisdom or basic sanity can be related with the Buddha's teaching. To begin with, they are not deceptive; and moreover, they are workable. They are in accordance with all the yanas that Buddha presented. As I said, if you become a good hinayanist, you become a good mahayanist. If you become a good mahayanist, you become a tantric practitioner. Following along with that logic, Buddha himself is a heruka or the dharmakaya principle.[8] There is the story about Buddha being invited to teach by King Indrabhuti. King Indrabhuti was having his bath on the rooftop of his palace. He saw some orange birds flying in the sky, and he asked his minister what they were. The minister said, "Those are not birds; they are Buddha and his disciples flying by [wearing their saffron-colored monastic robes]." And the king asked, "How can I invite them to my palace to teach me the truth?" And the wise minister said, "Just invite them, prepare a seat and food, and they will come." The king did so, and the Buddha came. The first request for teaching King Indrabhuti made was: "I cannot give up sensory pleasures, because I cannot give up my kingdom. I want you to teach me something that will enable me to transmute my pleasures into wisdom." The Buddha responded, "That's fine. First I would like to kick out my orthodox disciples, the arhats." So they were kicked out of the place where the Buddha was teaching. Then Buddha transformed himself into a heruka. He created the Guhyasamaja mandala and gave instructions for seven days on how to transmute basic ordinary energy, confused energy, into wisdom energy.[9] That seems to be the basic story of tantra. Buddha was not interested in just banning the whole thing [the energy of confusion], but in relating with that as well as he went on with his teaching.

Student: Where does enlightenment come in? Is there a point at which it's said that you can't continue with such-and-such a yana unless you're enlightened? Is there a place for enlightenment in this?

Trungpa Rinpoche: It depends on what you mean by enlightenment. That changes as the yanas change.

S: Buddha speaks about the point at which the wick in the lamp burns out. That seems to be some kind of definition.

TR: If you think enlightenment is something secure, there's nothing. There's no wick, there's no burning, there's no lamp. If you think of enlightenment as something that continues like the flame in a lamp reestablishing its position again and again, constantly, as a spark of electricity, then there's always room for enlightenment. But it doesn't have to be nursed as too precious to let go. It comes and goes, comes and goes.

Student: What was that word you used that you equated with ever-present energy?

Trungpa Rinpoche: I don't remember.

Student: Chandali.

Trungpa Rinpoche: Chandali. Chandali is energy force. It literally means the consumer, that which consumes the universe.

S: It means the universe itself consuming itself?

TR: No. That which eats up the universe.

S: What does that?

TR: What doesn't?

S: Nothing. That's why I say it's the universe itself consuming itself.

TR: That's it, yeah. You got it. Gesundheit.

SIX

Introduction to Tantra

O NTO THE DISK the autumn moon, clear and pure, you transplant a seed syllable.[1] Cool blue rays of the seed syllable radiate immense, cooling compassion beyond the limits of space, which fulfill the needs and desires of sentient beings. They radiate basic warmth, so that the confusions of sentient beings may be clarified. Then, from the seed syllable you create a buddha, Mahavairochana, while in color, with the features of an aristocrat, with the appearance of an eight-year-old child: beautiful, innocent, and pure, with a powerful royal gaze. He is dressed in the royal robes of the Vedic age or the medieval Indian royal costume. He wears a golden crown inlaid with wish-fulfilling jewels. Half of his long dark hair is made into a topknot, and the other half floats over his shoulders and back. He is seated cross-legged on the lunar disk with his hands in the meditation mudra, holding a vajra in his hand that is carved from pure white crystal.

Now, what do we do with that?

The whole setting is uncomplicated, but at the same time immensely rich. There's a sense of dignity, and also a sense of infanthood, of purity. The whole image is irritatingly pure, irritatingly cool. At the same time, one feels good even to think about such a person. This is a symbolic image from the kriyayogayana, the first tantric yana.

As I described Mahavairochana, his presence seemed real in our minds. Such a situation could exist. There could be such a royal prince of eight years of age sitting in a dignified way on the lunar disk. He was born from the seed syllable.

The basic principle of the kriyayoga is purity, immaculateness. Now that the practitioner has discovered the transmutation of energy, has discovered all-pervading delight, the kriyayogayana prescribes that there is no room for impurity, no room for darkness. The reason is that there is no doubt. Finally, at last, we have managed to actualize tathagatagarbha, buddha nature. We have managed to visualize, to actualize, to formulate a most immaculate, pure, clean, beautiful white, spotless principle. This is absolutely necessary from the point of view of the kriyayoga tantra, because the rugged, confused, unclean, impure elements of the samsaric struggle have gone a long way from us. At last we are able to associate with that which is pure, clean, perfect, absolutely immaculate.

Interestingly, the effect of this is that we do not have a chance to turn our visualization into pop art. Such a visualization is quite different than, for example, if we confiscated a street sign in Paris and brought it back to America and pasted it on our wall. It might say "Rue Royale" or something like that. There is something quite crude about that.

Therefore the first tantric introduction to any practice is majestic and fantastically precise and pure, clean, and artful as well. In some sense we could say that the kriyayoga tantra is the tantric equivalent of the Yogachara approach of artfulness. There is that appreciation of purity and cleanliness.

One of the problems that comes out when we try to introduce tantra is that even if we do accept samsara as a working basis, we regard it as pop art. The crudeness is the fun. This is true with regard to sexuality, aggression, or whatever tantric element we might want to talk about. The general attitude we find is that the tantric view of sex, the tantric view of aggression, or the tantric view of ignorance is acceptance of the crudeness as a big joke, good fun.

This is one of the basic points we should understand through the example of kriyayoga tantra. Tantra does not begin with the idea that we have to live with death and make the best of it. Tantra is a self-secret teaching; therefore the teachers of tantra are not all that desperate to con us with the idea that we have to take the mess of our confusion as something livable and workable. Tantra is not telling us to cover up our pile of shit and think of it as nice fresh earthy soil that we're sitting on. There seems to be a misunderstanding about tantra that it came into being out of desperation: We can't handle our fucked-upness or the shit we are in, and tantra enters as the saving grace. Shit becomes pictorial, artistic, pop art, and tantra at last formally and legally acknowledges that we should put up with it.

Such an approach simply presents another problem. If tantra is simply willing to put up with these problems—without seeing their purity and cleanness—then tantra would just be another depression. It would also be uncompassionate. Still, a lot of people hold this view about tantra. They think its function is to accept the crudeness and clumsiness logically and legally into the spiritual picture. Because of tantra, we can be crude and dirty. In fact, we could jump into tantra by being crude and dirty and taking pride in it. Then we could freak out with crazy wisdom, and so forth.

However, just as bodhisattvas or those traveling on the bodhisattva path are good citizens, tantric yogis are also good citizens, equally good citizens, extremely good citizens. They are by no means to be regarded as the freaks or hippies of society, if I may use such terms.

We also have a problem about visualization practice and formless meditation in tantra, which it might be a good idea to bring out here at the beginning of our discussion. Visualization, in tantra is not a matter of fantasizing about a form, image, or object. Also, the students have to have a clear idea about which tantric yana they are involved in, whether it is the kriyayogayana, the upayogayana, the yogayana, the mahayogayana, or one of the others. There is a definite attitude and understanding appropriate to each one of these. The students' visualization practice has to undergo some growth, an evolutionary process [as they pass from one yana to the next].

Before we discuss the kriyayoga tantra approach to visualization, let me point out that the student of kriyayogayana, needless to say, has to have acquired the hinayana understanding of suffering, impermanence, and egolessness from the shravakayana level. Moreover, they must have some understanding of the structure of ego from the pratyekabuddhayana. The student of kriyayogayana should also have an understanding of the shunyata principle and its application in the six paramitas practices. By no means is the student expected to have reached perfection in any of those levels, but at least he should have had glimpses into all these things. He must have worked on those other stages of the path before he treads on the path of tantra. This is absolutely necessary.

One Nyingma teacher said that relating with tantric visualization practice is like going to bed with a pregnant tigress.[2] She might get

hungry in the middle of the night and decide to eat you up. Or she might
begin to nurse you and create a warm, furry space. The kriyayoga tantra
text, the *Vajramala,* speaks of those who have mistaken views about visualization. Instead of attaining Vajrasattvahood,[3] for example, they attain
Rudrahood, the highest attainment of egohood, they attain the level of
the cosmic ape, the cosmic monster.

A lot of tantric scriptures warn us about the difference between a
mistaken approach to visualization and complete, proper visualization.
In the case of the mistaken approach, the visualizations are related to
purely as mental objects—you create your own image out of wishful
thinking. In the middle of your ordinary meditation practice, you might
get sexual fantasies of all kinds and decide to go into all the details of
these fantasies: stage one, stage two, fourth stage, fifth stage, trying to
make the details as entertaining as possible. The same thing can happen
in tantric visualization. Even if you are visualizing a simple Mahavairochana, a child sitting on a lunar disk, you might have the same problem.
You simply re-create your own mental image, which results in the end
in the cosmic ape. You say, "I am Mahavairochana. I am one with him,
therefore I could become him." You take the [defiant] approach of "I am
what I am." There is a sense of the beast, of a powerful chest, the cosmic
gorilla.

Visualization practice has to be inspired by a sense of hopelessness,
or egolessness, which amounts to the same thing. You can't con yourself,
let alone your friends. There is a sense of desperation about losing your
territory. The carpet has been pulled out from under your feet. You are
suspended in nowhere. You have an understanding of egolessness, impermanence, and so forth, as well as a sense of nonduality—the barrier
between you and other doesn't exist. You need not have complete comprehension of this all the time, but if you have at least a glimpse of it,
then you can flash your nonexistence, shunyata, egolessness, and then
visualize. This is extremely important.

According to tradition, when the vajrayana teachings were brought
to Tibet, to begin with there was great emphasis on the teaching of surrendering. The teacher Atisha Dipankara,[4] an Indian master who established Buddhist practices in Tibet, was known as the refuge teacher
because he placed so much emphasis on surrendering, giving, opening,
giving up holding on to something.[5]

Taking this point of view of surrendering, before we start visualization, we have to use up all our mental gossip, or at least take out a corner of it. This doesn't mean that we have to achieve a state of mind in which there is no mental gossip at all, but at least we have to be approaching it. The starting point for achieving this is *anapanasati*, as it is called in Pali, *smriti-upasthana* in Sanskrit, which is mindfulness of breathing. The development of mindfulness and awareness, *shi-ne* and *lhakthong* in Tibetan [*shamatha* and *vipashyana* in Sanskrit], and *trenpa nyewar jokpa*, are important.[6] Without awareness of resting your heart, trenpa nyewar jokpa—*trenpa* literally means "recollection" or "reflection"; *nyewar jokpa* means "complete resting"—there's no way of beginning basic tantric visualization practice at all.

Having those basic foundations makes it possible for a person to realize why such emphasis is placed on purity and cleanness in the kriyayoga tantra. The immaculate quality of the visualization of Mahavairochana, born from a seed syllable and sitting on the lunar disk, becomes more impressive, highly impressive. That particular sambhogakaya buddha becomes so beautiful because you are unbiased to begin with.[7] If something comes out of unbiasedness, then the whole thing becomes so expressive, so fantastic. It's double purity, or 100 percent purity, shall we say. This is purity that never needed to be washed, bathed, cleaned. It never needed to go through a washing machine.

If you try to apply Ajax to clean up your dirty image to a state of purity, then you create a further mess. The purity of the tantric view is fantastically real. The visualizer does not have to question, "Am I imagining this, or is it really happening?" That question doesn't apply anymore at all.

People who live in New York City have a very vivid and definite recollection of yellow cabs or police cars. But it would be impossible to convey this to a Tibetan in Tibet who never had the experience of being in New York City. If you wanted a Tibetan to visualize New York City, you would have to say, "New York City goes like this. There are streets, there are skyscrapers, there are yellow cabs. Visualize them. Imagine you are in that scene." You could explain the minute details as much as you are able. You could expound New-York-Cityness to an infinite level. Still, Tibetans would have difficulty visualizing it, actually having the feeling of being in New York City. They would have tremendous difficulties. At the same time, they would also feel that New York City was some kind of mystery land. There would be a sense of novelty.

Teaching Americans to visualize Mahavairochana is like teaching Tibetans to visualize New York City, because they have never gone through that experience at all. So you might ask how we do that. We do it precisely by going through the three major stages of Buddhist practice: hinayana, mahayana, and vajrayana, or tantra. There is the hinayana practice of trenpa nyewar jokpa, the practice of recollection; and there is the bodhisattva sense of shunyata and of warmth and compassion. Those have to be gone through. Then you can begin to realize the quality of purity and cleanness and immaculateness of Mahavairochana Buddha.

Visualization is one of the basic points. The reason why it is a basic point is that through it you identify yourself with certain herukas or sambhoghakaya buddhas. This brings the reassurance of vajra pride. Vajra pride is not just stupid pride; it is enlightened pride. You do have the potential to be one of those figures; you are one already. It is not so much that there is magic in the visualization; there is magic in your pride, or inspiration, if you prefer to call it that. You *are* Mahavairochana, absolutely immaculate and clean and pure. Therefore you are able to identify with your own purity rather than that of an external god who is pure and who comes into you as a separate entity, as a foreign element. You are reawakening yourself as your basic purity is awakened.

A basic point about tantra is that it is not regarded as myth or magic. Tantra is the highest evolutionary process there is, and its whole logic applies to every step that you go through. That is extremely important.

There is tremendous emphasis on visualization in the kriyayoga tantra and also tremendous emphasis on mudras, hand gestures of all kinds. Executing mudras is trying to compete with the buddhas, trying to become one, trying to behave like them. Not in fact trying, but thinking you are one of them.

Vajra pride in Tibetan is *lha yi ngagyal*. *Lha* means "god," *ngagyal* means "pride." The idea is to develop the pride of being a buddha. You are one in fact; there's no doubt about that.

It is a very important point at the beginning that you *are* the gods, you *are* the deities, you *are* the buddhas. There's no question about that. But before you develop this pride, there might be a problem. If you don't think you are one of them, then you probably will think, "I am supposed to think that I am a god, that I'm Mahavairochana Buddha—I am supposed to think in that way. This is my goal. This is the message they're giving me. Therefore I should try to pull myself up." An approach like that is regarded as cowardly or stupid. It's quite flat.

In order to develop vajra pride, one also has to realize the pain—the vajra pain, so to speak—that is involved. Samsaric pains, indestructible pains, are also involved. So that pride has some valid point to be proud of.

In kriyayoga tantra, a lot of emphasis is made on a sense of purity. Things are fundamentally immaculately pure, because there's no room for doubt. At the same time, from mahamudra's point of view, the phenomenal world is seen as completely colorful, precisely beautiful *as it is,* without any problems. Things are seen that way because you have already cut through your conceptualized notion of self, the projector, and the conceptualized notion of other, the projection. Therefore there's no reason you can't handle the situation. It is precisely clear as much as it possibly could be—*as it is.*

I suppose one of the fundamental points that we have to understand is that tantra is by no means pop art. It's very clean-cut, clear-cut. Tantric practitioners are also good citizens rather than agitators or hippies. Tantric practitioners are real citizens who know [what is happening]. They are the good mechanics in the garage, who know the infinite details of how machines function. They have a clean mind, a precise mind. Tantric practitioners are good artists who paint good pictures—they don't try to con you. Tantric practitioners are good lovers who don't try to take advantage of their partner's energy, emotion, but make love precisely in a clean-cut way. Tantric practitioners are good musicians who do not fool around banging here and there; they make music precisely, as it should be made. Tantric practitioners are artistic poets.

Tantric practitioners are in the world, but in the world in a different way than just getting lots of help by being critical of others and being dirty oneself. That seems to be the problem with bohemian artists. They get away with their approach by criticizing other people's purity. They are dirty and rugged and they take pride in that. People have some kind of respect for them because their criticism of purity is so intense, people can't be bothered to challenge them. Or they leave no room for a challenge. So people [tend to be impressed] and they say, "What you say is good, okay. Come into our society. You seems to be a powerful guy. You are dirty enough, and we accept you. We take pride in your being dirty. Let's create a poster of you. Don't wash your face. Let's put it up with you 'as you are,' as they say. Let's put up that poster and take pride in it."

The approach to tantra seems to be entirely different from that. It's not sloppy, the way you might think. It is very pure, very clean, very definite, very precise, very well thought out.

And there's an introduction to tantra for you.

Student: You talked about a type of intensity and purity that emerges out of unbiasedness, but the visualization you described seemed to have something cultural about it. When I heard your description, it was really nice, but I got a sense of a Tibetan or Buddhist ritual. Would such an image be able to arise spontaneously in an unbiased fashion in me if I'd never heard you describe it?

Trungpa Rinpoche: You see, there is a tantric iconography that has already developed [so you don't have to generate it spontaneously]. And it should be easy for us to identify with the tantric figures, particularly the peaceful ones, because they originated in the Indo-European culture. They're neither particularly Indian nor particularly Western. They are in the classical style of the golden age of the Middle Eastern kingdoms, from which Western culture is also partly derived.

In any case, it is precisely the point that a pure and complete image is necessary. The idea is for you to visualize something that is pure and clean and complete to begin with, when you are introduced to tantra. Later on, you will encounter wrathful deities of all kinds, very gory things. But to begin with, you have to realize how pure you can be in your visualization, how complete, how absolutely complete—even if it means that the idea of purity has to be purified as well when you first begin to visualize. This purity is the ideal goal. The tantric tradition recommends the inspiration of ideal purity, clean and precise. Moreover, there should also be something like regal qualities. You're pure, clean, and majestic at the same time. That is why this is called vajrayana, the diamond vehicle, as opposed to the mahayana, which is just the big vehicle.

Student: Do you think that the visualization is implanted by particular conceptions of Buddhism, or is it something that emerges on its own?

Trungpa Rinpoche: I think it's cosmic. The features of the figure you visualize do not have to be Oriental; it does not have to have slitty eyes or anything like that, you know. There is just the idea of royalty. It is definitely necessary for you to associate yourself with a king. And in fact the vajrayana is sometimes known as the imperial yana.

Student: It seems kind of like the figure of the samurai the way it is portrayed in the movies. The samurai always seems to appear in immaculately clean dress and is immaculately together with his situation.

Trungpa Rinpoche: I think so, yes. It seems it's all right for him to be uncompassionate, but nevertheless he is clean and precise. The interesting thing about watching samurai films is the way they clean the blood from their swords. It's very beautiful. It is as though a work of art is being practiced rather than there is a bloody mess on the stairs that has to be gotten rid of.

Student: What is the difference between vajra pride and the pride of Rudra?

Trungpa Rinpoche: That seems to be quite basic. The pride of Rudra consists in trying to overpower the other. Vajra pride is identified with the pride of self rather than being worried about the consequences of the pride. There's no sense of conquest involved. Just being yourself is pride. In the case of Rudra, there is territory involved, as if you were a jealous king trying to conquer your territory. Whereas if you are a universal monarch already, you don't have to conquer your territory. Being yourself is being king, and you take pride in that.

S: Is vajra pride more than just an attitude, then?

TR: It's more than just an attitude, yes. It involves emotion and intuition as well. You feel you are the cosmic conqueror, and by logic you are, because there are no other worlds to compete with you. And by intuition, why not?

S: So it's something that will happen to us, rather than something we can create?

TR: Well, you can use the visualization as a means to feel that you are a king. All the sambhogakaya buddha visualizations are of kings. They always wear crowns and are dressed in royal costumes. You are trying to compete with a king. You *are* the king of the universe, in any case. There are no visualizations of subordinate figures; I can't imagine such a thing. All the visualizations of herukas are known as lords or kings.

Student: That sounds quite dangerous.

Trungpa Rinpoche: That's why it is said that wrong visualization will lead you to Rudrahood. Precisely. Yes, you could become an egomaniac. That's precisely why the whole thing is said to be very dangerous. If you do it wrong, you can become the cosmic ape king.

Student: If it's so dangerous, requiring that you work through hinayana and mahayana before getting into tantra, why are we talking about it like this? Even in the lecture about egolessness, suffering, and impermanence, I didn't feel like I understood anything you were talking about. And then you talk about tantra and refer to it as a spiritual atomic bomb. I really don't understand why this seminar is taking this direction.

Trungpa Rinpoche: That's a good question, an extremely good question. I'm glad you asked it. You see, it's like this: Suppose I was kidnapped in Tibet and blindfolded and put on an airplane. When my blindfold was taken off, I found myself in Berkeley, California. Then I was told, "This is your world. You have to stay here. Work with your world, work with the people here as your friends." I would have no working basis. I would have no idea what America is, what Americans are. I'd be bewildered. I'd be completely, totally freaked out. Whereas if somebody approached me in Tibet and said, "You're going to go to America. This is the map of America. These are the mountains, these are the rivers. These are the cities: There's New York City, there's Boston, there's Chicago, there's L.A. And there's San Francisco. You're going to San Francisco, which is here. The population is so-and-so." In that case, if I took a plane here and landed at this airport, I would feel more able to relate with my environment.

S: So these ideas that you're throwing out are not so much the real study—

TR: I think it's a matter of getting the perspective and seeing the consequences of the practices. Our goal is to work with tantra. Eventually you're going to do that. But as far as the individual meditation practice of the group here is concerned, everybody is working purely on the hinayana level to begin with. But there are possibilities beyond that, so let us not make a militant vow that what we are doing is good [and we're not going to do anything else]. That seems to be one of the problems the Zen tradition is faced with. You sit and meditate—this is the only thing, and everybody becomes highly militant and fierce and aggressive about it, saying that there are no other directions and this is the only thing you have. If I may say so.

Student: Rinpoche, don't we run the risk of not fully relating to any of the various stages? You know, we have one leg over here in hinayana and another leg over there in tantra—that sort of thing?

Trungpa Rinpoche: I don't think so. In any case, we can see what happens as we go along.

Student: It seems like this tantric approach is going to fill me with false pride and cause me to relate to something that's not real. How do I keep relating to the hinayana?

Trungpa Rinpoche: Your pain in your life is real enough, so that will take care of you. Maybe we could say that your pain is on the hinayana level, and that will take care of you. But when your pain has developed to the vajrayana level, that will be another matter. We can discuss that later.

Student: It's not clear to me how tantric visualization practice relates to the way you described tantra as coming back to the world, getting back into the energy of samsara.

Trungpa Rinpoche: It's relating to your ambition to become a powerful king, a cosmic ruler. That is possible. At least you can become the ruler of a household. And tantric visualization is visualizing yourself as the ruler, the exalted one, a sambhogakaya buddha, wearing a crown, being powerful, holding a scepter. Which is coming back to samsara, with the inspiration of nirvana. The original [hinayana] idea was to abandon everything, be a beggar, own nothing. Shouldn't we visualize ourselves as beggars, wearing ragged clothes, eating no food, being hungry? Shouldn't we try to accomplish beggarhood? No, in tantra, it's just the opposite. You're rich, you're the universal monarch. You wear a crown, jewelry, you hold a scepter, and are the conqueror of the whole universe. From that point of view, you have come back to samsara.

S: But the practice itself of visualizing seems very unworldly. There is a big difference between visualizing and actually being a king, an absolute monarch.

TR: Visualization is the middle part of a sandwich. To begin with, you have formless meditation, and you end with formless meditation.

In between the two, you have visualization happening. And this is also supposedly conditioned by the shunyata experience. So it is transformed samsara rather than samsara as neurosis.

Student: You have sometimes spoken of meditation as a process that grows on its own, starting with the initial form of shamatha meditation. Are these visualizations a continuation of that in the sense that they develop on their own, or are there points where there is outside instruction from a teacher?

Trungpa Rinpoche: As far as you basic formless meditation is concerned, that goes along through natural growth. Therefore you can afford to encompass visualization as well. But visualization is a new technique that is taught to you.

S: So it's something that comes from the outside, isn't it?

TR: Yes. It's similar to when your teacher says, "Go into retreat" or "Take a job" or "Get married."

Student: When you are this pride in visualization, is that like in the *Heart Sutra* where it says, "Emptiness is emptiness?"

Trungpa Rinpoche: Yes. Emptiness is emptiness, therefore it has form—in the image of the eight-year-old emperor.

Student: Are these symbols of royalty—the crown and the scepter and so on—symbolic of taking responsibility toward beings?

Trungpa Rinpoche: Yes. That is an extension of the bodhisattva's way. As a bodhisattva, you were going to take care of sentient beings. Now you are going to be the ruler of all sentient beings, because you are not discreet anymore. You know what you're doing. Now what you're doing is a greater responsibility—arranging a cosmic energy structure as though you are a king.

Student: There is something I don't understand. You just said that your desire is to be the king. Earlier you said that you considered it cowardly and stupid to try to pull yourself up to be the gods. I don't see how those two things reconcile.

Trungpa Rinpoche: That's the whole point. If you don't have the basic framework of shunyata and egoless practice of meditation, then it would be a pathetic gesture to try to appoint yourself king but not quite make it. Whereas if you have the basic training behind you connected with egolessness and awareness of suffering and impermanence, you don't even have to say it—you just become one.

Student: There seems to be a cultural situation involved here. Having been brought up to see everything in terms of democracy or anarchy or even communism, I can't imagine a king being anything other than a high-paid crook. Being that is desirable in some way, but—

Student: It strikes me that what we would like to be is president.

Student: We can't see a king as something positive.

Trungpa Rinpoche: That's a problem.

Student: I don't see the point of being king. Why take on that position?

Trungpa Rinpoche: What else would you suggest? Don't you want to have control of yourself, be king of yourself? That's it [that's what it amounts to]. You could visualize yourself as king of yourself. It doesn't have to be a king who is running a whole nation. You are the nation. You are the king. It's the same thing. Gesundheit.

Student: Along the same lines, do you see tantric visualizations in America taking a different form than they did in Tibet?

Trungpa Rinpoche: That has occurred to me, actually. But there is a big conflict about that among tantric masters. Very practically, should Americans be allowed to visualize seed syllables in Roman letters? Or should they memorize the Sanskrit or Tibetan? It is questionable, and I hope one day to sort that question out and put the whole thing on a real footing. That would seem to call for getting Shingon masters from Japan, Mongolian tantric masters, and Tibetans all to meet together. [They could discuss these questions and come to a definite conclusion.] Is there any magic in visualizing Sanskrit? The Tibetans didn't visualize in Sanskrit, but instead in Tibetan. At the time Buddhism was introduced into Tibet, Tibet was regarded as a land of savages. In fact it was called the land of the pretas, hungry ghosts, because Tibetans were so poor. They also were not as culturally rich as the Indians with their Brahmanistic culture. Still, they read the letters of the seed syllables in their Tibetan form. But certain practitioners would have a reaction against using Roman letters, because Tibetan calligraphy is more aesthetically appealing. They might think Roman letters look very flat, ordinary, silly. We have to work on those areas. I think that's our next project, to try and find a solution to these problems. Personally, I am more for nativizing—for making American tantra American tantra rather than imported tantra, as the Tibetans made tantra into Tibetan tantra. I'm all for it.

Student: The only thing I can think of that is like the tantric approach in the Western tradition is alchemy. The visualizations are not just the same, but in alchemy there's the visualization of a king. There are visualizations of a whole pantheon of aspects of the self—kings, queens, the coming together of the brother and the sister. I don't see these as too different from the symbolism presented in tantra.

Trungpa Rinpoche: Sure. Automatically the Western equivalent of tantra has been happening. There is another link of similarity: Christ is referred to as a king. The Christ principle is regarded as that of a conqueror or king. But what is the practical application for how Buddhist students should visualize and work with this symbolism? Should we visualize Mahavairochana in medieval Indian costume, or should we visualize him in medieval Western costume?

S: Alchemy would use a Roman king. You know, these are very powerful images. There is something in the West—

TR: I think there is. But you see the problem is that it gets more complicated when we begin to visualize wrathful deities with so many arms, so many eyes, so many heads. Western culture hasn't been outrageous enough to visualize a person with so many arms, so many eyes, who eats you up on the spot. The whole thing becomes so generous and kind, so cultured.

Student: There are deities like those in Bosch and Brueghel.
Trungpa Rinpoche: I hope so.

Student: Rinpoche, could you explain how this kind of practice involving the conception of oneself as king of oneself relates to the bodhisattva's aim of working for the benefit of all sentient beings?
Trungpa Rinpoche: It's going further with the same thing. The bodhisattva works for all sentient beings as a servant. Now that servant begins to take over and run the whole show as a revolutionary government, which is an entirely different twist. That's why there's a big gap between the bodhisattva path and tantra. A lot of people complain about that.

Practitioners of the bodhisattva path really do not understand the implications of the power, the vajra power. I think I already mentioned Dr. Conze, who is in fact terrified by the idea of tantra, because of such principles as the king principle. How could such a king principle be introduced as Buddhist idea, he wonders, because Buddhists are so kind and sociologically oriented. They are kind people who would never think of ruling a country. But that point of view is problematic.

Student: You mentioned the other day that at some point the guru is going to mess around with your life. Does that idea come from tantra?

Trungpa Rinpoche: No, that's a mahayana idea. That's the saving grace. In fact, if you were a tantric logician trying to refute the mahayanists, you could pick up that point. You could say that the mahayana teacher also minds the student's business. Then that approach could be elevated to that of a ruler rather than just a nosy friend. That is one of the links that exist between the mahayana and the vajrayana. We should tell Dr. Conze about that.

Student: Does one kill Rudra with a sword, or does one let him die a natural death?

Trungpa Rinpoche: Both. By the sword *is* a natural death.

Student: Do you see Castaneda's Don Juan as an expression of Western tantra?

Trungpa Rinpoche: I see Don Juan as Western tantra on the Yogachara level.

Student: Suzuki Roshi, who wrote *Zen Mind, Beginner's Mind,* says that any single method has its limitations, its techniques. He said if you do not realize the limitations of the particular method you are involved in, someday you're going to sink into a deep depression. The ground is going to fall out from underneath you. What do you see as the limitations of the tantric Buddhist viewpoint? And do you think there's another path that arrives at the same place as tantra?

Trungpa Rinpoche: The tantric viewpoint is not one solid thing. It has six steps, six levels, ending up at the maha ati level, which looks down on the whole thing as being confused. Maha ati cannot be attacked or challenged, because it doesn't advocate anything or criticize anything.

By being itself, it realizes that the lower yanas are simple-minded. After that, I think there's nothing. Tantra is not regarded as one block. There are several stages to tantra anyway.

Student: That stage that you call ati, at the point where you're looking at everything as confused—you have a particular term for that, and you call that ati. You call it something because of the perspective you're looking at. That's a space. Now, obviously that space doesn't have a name. Do you think that you have to go through a Buddhist perspective, where you call various spaces various yanas, to arrive at that stage?

Trungpa Rinpoche: Not necessarily. But if you transcend ati, then you are criticizing ati from a samsaric point of view, rather than seeing it with its own perspective of the highest enlightenment. You begin to regress. It is like you have climbed up to a ridge, and then you begin to slide down. That's for sure. Of course, there don't have to be doctrinal names or ideas.

SEVEN

The Five Buddha Families and Mahamudra

O N THE BASIS of our discussion of the kriyayogayana, we can say that basically what is happening in the tantric approach at this point is trying to build a relationship between yourself and your projection. We are still working with the projection and the projector. A relationship between those two can come about because of the tremendous emphasis on precision in kriyayoga. That precision relates to our working base, which is the basic tendency to reshape the world according to your particular nature. The purity of the kriyayogayana allows us a lot of space, a lot of room to explore the functioning of phenomena on the energy level.

The next yana is upayogayana, which means the yana of action or application. That has the sense of relating with our basic nature, our innate nature. The innate nature of different individuals can be described in terms of the five buddha families.

The kriyayoga is the first tantric yana, the introductory yogayana, which clears the air and also provides the ground. It can be compared, in setting up a room, to first sweeping the floors and cleaning the walls— clearing out all the garbage. That's the starting point. Through this, tantric practice becomes real practice rather than a game, in the sense that the tantric practitioner becomes a good citizen, as we have described already.

Kriyayoga puts tremendous emphasis on purification, purification and visualization. Upayoga, and particularly advanced upayoga, puts a lot of emphasis on actual practice [in life situations], actual practice that leads to living a pure life. Upayoga also brings in an element of crazy wisdom, which connects it with the next yana, yogayana. So upayoga-yana is referred to as the yana of transition [between kriya- and yoga-yanas]. It is also often referred to as the neutral yana, neither masculine nor feminine.

At this point it would be good to discuss mahamudra, which is also connected with relating with our innate nature the way we do in the yoga practices of vajrayana. *Maha* means "great," and *mudra* means "symbol." So *mahamudra* means "great symbol." This is the basic core, or backbone, of all the [lower] tantric yoga practices. Kriyayogayana, upayogayana, and yogayana all involve practices that relate with the basic origin, *shi* in Tibetan, which also means "background." So they are yogas of the basic origin or yogas of the background, or yogas of basic nature. There is a difference between the higher yogas that we haven't discussed yet and these lower yogas, which work with the basic ground. The three yogayanas of lower tantra still have some relationship with the mahayana practices, which also work with the basic potential. So there are a lot of references to relating with the origin, relating with the potential.

This is connected with mahayana's approach toward life, which em-phasizes the potential of tathagatagarbha, the basic nature. Therefore your situation is workable. And it has been said that mahamudra, the great symbol, is also working on the basic origin, the basic potential. Thus the yogas of the lower tantra are also connected with something you can work with. You have a potential already. There's a seed already.

Mahamudra is a way of bringing together the notion of the immense emptiness of space, shunyata, and manifestation within shunyata. The shunyata principle is associated with nirvana, and the manifestation of confusion that occurs around it is samsara. So mahamudra is concerned with how to bring about the indivisibility of samsara and nirvana. The samsaric messages of passion, aggression, and all kinds of things that we might experience in our life situation are not rejected but regarded as a workable part of our basic nature that we can relate with. Those are workable situations; but they are not just workable. They also contain messages that push us into situations in which we can work on our-selves. We are being pushed into that basic situation.

So mahamudra has to do with learning to work with the cosmic mes-sage, the basic message in our life situation, which is also teaching. We do not have to relate to teaching only in the religious context. We also have to read the symbolism connected with our life situation. What we live, where we live, how we live—all these living situations also have a basic message that we can read, that we can work with.

If you are speeding, you get a ticket. If you are driving too slow, you get a honk from behind. A red light means danger; a green light means go; an amber light means get ready to go or stop. If you try to cheat on your karmic debts, the tax authorities are going to get after you. There are numerous manifestations of all kinds. If you don't pay your telephone bill, the telephone will be disconnected. All those little things that you think are a hassle, that you think an organization or the authorities have created to belittle you, to make you public property—that's not true. There is always some kind of message constantly happening. In that sense, the existence of any regulations or rules or laws that exist in a country are manifestations of mahamudra. If you don't eat enough, you get hungry. If you don't eat enough because you don't have the money to pay for your food, because you didn't have the incentive to take a job, you are a reject of society. You can't be bothered with things; you can't get your trips together to go out and get a job so that you can have food and money to live.

We think all those little things are just a domestic hassle, but they also have tremendous messages behind them. Whether you are living in the twentieth-century automated world or living a rural, organic existence in Tibet, the hassles are the same thing. There is always something to hassle with, something to push you, pull you.

A lot of people leave this country because they can't be bothered with the taxation and money problems. They decide to go to India—that's the most obvious flow—because they think that in India nobody hassles you.[1] Nobody cares who is who and what is what, and there's no tax. At least, nobody talks about dollars. Instead, people talk about rupees, which is a refreshing name. Or they go to Europe, where people talk about pounds or francs, or whatever. But in vajrayana, you have to pay something. Even in an idealized vajrayana like vajrayana Disneyland, the vajrayana authorities still have to maintain that Disneyland. You have to pay something. You can't just get free hospitality. You can seek out hospitality, but still you have to be ingratiating to do that. Mutual hospitality is always important. When you begin to smile less, you have to pay more money. Even in vajrayana Disneyland, it depends on your reactions.

From this point of view, vajrayana means openness to the messages that are coming across to us. Acknowledging them, respecting them. Mahamudra also means that. There is a sense of appreciation of the basic buddha natures, that you are one of them, that you have a link to them.

Upayogayana relates enormously with both the practice and the inspiration coming to you from the situation at the same time. The practice is not as secure and clean and perfect as that of kriyayogayana. In kriya there is the sense that if you keep yourself clean and safe, you will be saved. But not anymore. Now you actually have to work harder, you have to relate with reality much more than just within the limits of keeping clean and pure.

At this point, it might be necessary to discuss the five buddha principles. They are important in relation to both upayogayana and the other tantric yanas we will discuss later on. The five principles of buddha nature refer to the buddha qualities in all of us. We are not, as we might imagine, expected to be uniform and regimented, to be ideally enlightened and absolutely cool and kind and wise. The five buddha principles are the different expressions of basic sanity. There are five different ways to be sane.

The first is the buddha principle of the buddha family, which is basically being even, not reacting. Being steady, not reacting to excitement, being basically solid yet open at the same time. Basically sound and earthy, steady, but somewhat dull. Not particularly enterprising.

Then you have the vajra buddha family, which is extremely sharp, intellectual, analytical. You can relate with things precisely, and you can also see the disadvantages of various involvements. You can see the holes in things or the challenges that might occur. Precisely open and clear, analytically cool, cold, possibly unfriendly, but always on the dot. Seeing all the highlights of things as they are. Very precise, very direct, very sharp. Reactivity is very high. You are ready to jump, ready to pursue and criticize. You are ready to analyze what's wrong with situations and what's wrong with ideas. *Vajra* means "adamantine," which is like diamond, or superdiamond.

The next family is *ratna,* which means "jewel," "gem," "precious stone." *Mani* [Skt., "jewel"], as in OM MANI PADME HUM. It sounds close to "money." You are always making yourself at home with collections of all kinds of richness and wealth. All kinds. The world of velvet and satin and jewels. Magnetizing all kinds of food and wealth. Swimming through food and wealth. Richness. A person with the ratna mentality could be in the middle of the Gobi Desert and still manage to make himself rich and fantastically homey. He could entertain himself—the richness makes it so that all kinds of things happen. There is a sense of constant magnetizing. Those magnetic qualities make the person a comfortable bed, a nest. He draws everything in, richness of all kinds. That's why ratna is represented by a gem, a jewel, a precious stone. It's self-existing richness.

The next one is *padma,* which literally means "lotus," or we could say "blossom." Padma has to do with seduction, which is also magnetizing, but not in the sense of making yourself at home and collecting lots of rich materials like ratna. Padma's seduction is magnetizing more in order to relate with itself, maintain itself, proves its own existence. It is constantly magnetizing, drawing in, and making use of what it draws in. The idea of copulation is a somewhat good symbol—magnetizing and then making use of what you magnetize. Things are collected and made love to. The object of seduction is not regarded as a nest, but it is used—perhaps as food or clothes. There is a supermagnetic quality that is so great that the projections cannot help being attracted by it. It is very passionate.

The next buddha family principle is karma. *Karma* literally means "action" or "activity." Karma in this case is the action of fulfillment. Situations have to be fulfilled, so everything around you has to be efficient, speedy, functional all the time. If anything does not fit your scheme, you destroy it. So everything has to become pragmatic, functional, efficient. Things are collected because you would like to relate with the functionality of everything. Speed and efficiency of all kinds.

Those five principles of buddha nature, traditionally known as the buddha families, are the basic working basis that tantra has to offer.

In the tantric tradition there are different deities, different approaches to your action, that are related with those five styles. One of the important implications of this is that in tantra, everybody does not have to be uniform as in the bodhisattva's approach, where everything has to be kept cool and skillful, steady all the time. There, all the paramitas are good as long as you keep up with a certain central logic: You realize that you have buddha nature in you, so you can be generous, patient, and so forth. But tantra does not have this kind of one-track mind that we find in the bodhisattva's approach. In tantra, there are all kinds of variations you can get into, based on the five different perspectives. There are five different kinds of relationships with things, and you can identify yourself with all or one of these, or partially with any of them. You could have one leading aspect and a suggestion of something else. You might have a vajra quality along with a padma quality and maybe a touch of karma as well, and so forth. Basically, psychologically, vajrayana permits the openness to work on all kinds of elements that you have in you. You don't have to tune yourself in to one particular basic thing. You can take pride in what you are, what you have, your basic nature. If your nature is made up of too much of the passionate element of padma, and too much of the efficiency of karma, those things are not regarded as hang-ups as such. Those things are regarded as basic qualities that you have.

I think that is the basic core understanding of tantra. Tantra permits different aspects of you to shine through, rather than your having to be channeled into one basic set of characteristics. It allows your basic nature to come through.

From upayogayana onward, into the other tantras we'll discuss later on, and in kriya as well, those buddha family principles allow you to work with mahamudra, the great symbol. They allow you to relate with the working basis of your lifestyle as such.

In the upayogayana, a framework of practice developed that is very much based on mudras and mantras. You visualize yourself as a Maha-vairochana, and then you visualize a Mahavairochana sitting on a lunar disk in front of you. Then you send rays of light out both from the Ma-havairochana visualized in front of you and from yourself and [with these light rays] invite the jnanakaya,[2] or wisdom body, of Mahavairo-chana—the true Mahavairochana as opposed to the visualized ones you have imagined. In fact you invite a host of Mahavairochanas sitting on lunar disks in clouds, along with all kinds of devas and devatas—goddesses, angels, cherubs—playing musical instruments. A rain of flow-ers falls toward you, music is playing, there are fluttering banners in the air, and songs of praise to Mahavairochana are heard. The wisdom body of Mahavairochana comes toward you; the little prince of eight years of age, the super eight-year-old, the higher wisdom body, descends and dis-solves into the Mahavairochana you visualized in front of you. In turn, you, as your imagination of Mahavairochana, however clumsy it might be, create out of your heart offering deities—goddesses, cherubs, angels—carrying food and musical instruments, who entertain the visualized Mahavairochana.

By this time the visualization in front of you has been united with the wisdom body. Now this becomes the authentic Mahavairochana in front of you. He is a real Mahavairochana principle, so you offer food, sing a song of praise, and so forth. All of this is accompanied by extremely complicated mudras, and mantras of all kinds. Then the Mahavairochana in front of you is satisfied with your entertainment and acknowledges the little attempts that you made with your visualizations, including the visualization of yourself as one of them, as a kind of immigrant to the Pure Land. You are accepted as a somewhat seemingly good citizen of Mahavairochana land. There is constant mantra practice and working on that situation. The visualized Mahavairochana in front of you comes toward you and dissolves into your body. That is the point where you develop your vajra pride. You identify with that Mahavairochana, you become one with it, completely one with it. Then you are crowned; there is a coronation ceremony in which all the buddhas of the universe come to you bringing jeweled crowns, which they place on your head. You are crowned as the Buddha, Mahavairochana himself—and so forth.

All those processes—acknowledgments of the higher imaginary buddha as yourself and the higher buddha who comes to you, and so forth—you could say are pure superstition. You have a higher god and that god is related with the imaginary god. You could also say that the imaginary god becomes god in you. Conventional mysticism would find that a highly workable description, extremely good, ideal. That is their idea of what you should try to work with: God is in you and you are the god, as Yogi Bhajan would say.[3]

But I'm afraid it's not as simple as that. You can't just say god is in you and you are the god, because god is not in you and you are not in the god. You have to make an effort. Those sambhogakaya buddha principles have to be invited, acknowledged, and then finally invited in to your whole being. That is an entirely different situation.

It is entirely different from the child in the home visualizing Santa Claus at Christmastime. The divine Santa Claus approaches you with his reindeer and so forth. Then he dissolves into your father. In turn your father becomes the true Santa Claus, brings presents, and puts them in your stocking. The father—the divine Santa Claus—then drinks the milk and eats the cookies. It's not as folksy as that, I'm afraid. One could create an American tantra purely by using those images, but that becomes too cheap, a plastic world. Transplanting Mahavairochana [into oneself] is more deadly, more powerful. It is not on the level of a Christmas celebration, as though in the name of a divine Mahavairochana we would put a neon light outside our door. Or maybe we could make a cartoon film of it, or hang out a gigantic balloon in the air, saying "Mahavairochana is coming to town." One could try all kinds of things, but I don't think Mahavairochana would quite be amused. Nor would the lineage of gurus of the tantric tradition quite be amused.

There seems to be a need for serious commitment to the whole thing. Maybe I should stop talking at this point and let people ask questions about the whole thing. That might be more helpful. Is there anybody who would like to ask questions about the whole thing?

Student: Are these visualizations actually things that come into you, or is it that you're visualizing in terms of art forms? In other words, is it just something you visualize, or are these situations that do happen because of that strategy?

Trungpa Rinpoche: I think you could say it's both. There is inspiration connected with these visualizations, but at the same time there is a format of visualization that has occurred culturally. They coincide, they come together.

S: As to the cultural aspect of these art forms: Are these the forms that the personages you visualize actually take? Do they take that cultural form, or are those just artistic expressions, drawings, representations, in which the colors and designs and textures just convey a taste of those personages?

TR: Yes, I think that's it. They are based on experience. Those figures have a crown, a skirt, a shawl, and ornaments, and that's all. They are not dressed in the [specific] imperial costume of China, nor in that of an Indian raja. They are very simple and straightforward. As far as Indo-European culture goes, they are very workable.

S: So they transcend culture in a sense, transcend Oriental culture.

TR: I think so, yes. The style is that of pre-Hindustan culture, before the Mongols invaded India. Those are just images that exist expressing the common idea of the Indo-European ideal of a king. So purely by chance, those visualizations are workable for us: a youthful king wearing a crown and a shawl, maybe a shirt with half sleeves—that's one of the inconographical forms—and lots of jewels, and a skirt. That's it. I don't think that this is particularly problematic. It's not particularly Oriental. In fact, it's highly Western. It is like Gandharan art, in which the Buddha's features are Western. Conveniently for us, this is Indo-European culture. I don't know what we'll do when Buddhism goes to Africa, which is maybe an entirely different area. But as far as Indian and European culture goes, there's no problem with that. There's no problem visualizing a king of this type. In fact, it's quite right.

Student: What's the relationship between mahamudra and the mandala of the five buddha families?

Trungpa Rinpoche: The five-buddha mandala is the expression of mahamudra. It is how mahamudra sees the world as the symbolic or real manifestation of sanity. It's the same thing, in fact. There's no difference at all. Mahamudra is the eye of wisdom that sees the five buddha principles as its vision.

Student: Is the god coming into you a confirmation of the fact that you already exist as a god?

Trungpa Rinpoche: Confirmation doesn't exist. You don't have to be confirmed. Because the confirmation "I'm the god and the god is me" doesn't exist, therefore the god doesn't exist, and the watcher, which is you, doesn't exist. So there's no god and there's no you. As far as Buddhism is concerned, there's no god at all. That's 200 percent sure. There's no god. God doesn't exist in Buddhism. And ego doesn't exist in Buddhism either.

Student: Who can be a guru?

Trungpa Rinpoche: Anyone who can reflect you as a mirror does and with whom, at the same time, you have a relationship as a personal friend. If a person is too formal, he cannot be a guru. A very formal person might be all right as the legalized head of your order, like the Pope for the Catholics or the Dalai Lama for the Tibetans. Someone might say, "I belong to this Tibetan sect, therefore the Dalai Lama is my guru." But basically a guru is someone who cares about you and minds your business, who relates with your basic being.

S: Would one of the qualities of a guru be that he is a realized being?

TR: Definitely, yes. And also a lot of it depends on you, on whether you think your guru is your friend. In that case, he could be called a spiritual friend. If you don't think your guru is your friend, but instead he is a spiritual cop [that is not so good].

Student: The tantric practice of visualization comes across as a kind of supertechnique as compared to hinayana and mahayana techniques.

Trungpa Rinpoche: Sure. The vajrayana mentality knows how to work with your basic being. The vajrayana approach is supposedly the highest way there is of relating with your psychology. It is more developed than the hinayana and mahayana. It is the highest, most refined and powerful technique that mankind, or even nonmankind, could ever think of. That's precisely the point: it's superfantastic. That's why it is called the vajrayana, the diamond vehicle, as opposed to just the small or big vehicle. It is a vehicle carved out of diamond.

Student: Is there any correlation between the five buddha families and the different yanas?

Trungpa Rinpoche: I don't think so. All the yanas have a connection with all the five buddha families. The five buddha principles are the inhabitants, and the yanas are different countries—more advanced and less advanced countries.

Student: I'm not sure how to relate to my basic nature in terms of the five buddha families. When I look at myself, I see not just one of them but parts of all of them. It's very confusing.

Trungpa Rinpoche: The important point is to have some kind of trust in your basic nature. Your style is not regarded as a mistake or derived from some original sin of some kind. Your style is pure and obvious. When you doubt your style, you begin to develop another style, which is called an exit. You begin to manifest yourself in a different fashion, to try to shield your own style to make sure it is not discovered by other people.

I think as far as basic nature is concerned, there is no mistake at all. That is where vajra pride comes in. In the vajrayana approach, you are what you are. If you're passionate, that's beautiful. If you're aggressive, that's beautiful. If you're ignorant, that's beautiful. And all the materials and manifestations in you are regarded as in the vajra realm, rather than your being condemned as a failure. The whole thing is really highly workable. That is why it is called the diamond vehicle. Because what goes on in your life is not rejected or selected.

Student: Is there one way we are, or are we all of those ways?
Trungpa Rinpoche: Well, one way is the convention. Vajra pride is the one way. Take pride in yourself.

Student: When you talk about not rejecting what goes on in your life, or when you talk about mahamudra as the world presenting messages or symbols—like when you're speeding, you get arrested—that just seems like common sense. It just seems like common sense that there are those kinds of messages. So it is not clear what the special quality is of working with those kinds of messages in the vajrayana.
Trungpa Rinpoche: I don't see any difference, actually. It's just pure common sense. But the message that comes out of that should be a firsthand account rather than a secondhand one.
S: Well, how do the practices you've described, such as visualization of Mahavairochana, connect to the common sense of responding to messages in our life?
TR: The visualization are also common sense. That is the whole point. You are not having a foreign culture imposed on you or awkward ideas presented to you. Even the visualizations themselves are common sense. Yes, that's true. Because the visualizations have something to do with you. That's why different aspects of the five buddha principles become your yidams.[4] *Yid* means "mind," and *dam* means "trust." Your mind can trust in certain particular aspects of the five buddha principles. You might be related with vajra Mahavairochana, ratna Mahavairochana, padma Mahavairochana, karma Mahavairochana, or buddha Mahavairochana. You can relate with certain particular principles and visualize them. It is like visualizing yourself. That's the whole point of the yidam—it means that you have a personal relationship with that principle. Those things are not given out haphazardly, like saying everybody should eat peanut butter and jelly because it's cheap and good for everybody.

Student: In your lineage, are those practices, those visualizations, considered transmissions from the teachers to students, or can one read about them in books and practice from that?
Trungpa Rinpoche: You can't get it from books. It might be written about in books, but books are just menus. You can't get a good meal just

by reading the menu. You have to relate with the chef. We are the chefs. You can't get a good [spiritual] meal out of a pamphlet.

S: So when you speak here about those visualizations, are you giving a transmission to the group about how to do it?

TR: I'm presenting my point of view. There are already things happening in America relating to this material. A lot of visualizations and ideas have already been shared and publicized. So I'm just presenting what I have to say as guidelines. We are all working toward the same goal. At the same time, however, I'm giving a warning. I'm saying that the food could be poisonous if you don't relate with it properly.

Also what I'm doing here is presenting these ideas as appetizers, not to convert you, so that you become Tibetan Buddhists, but there is that possibility if you would like to get into this thing. It is a highly beautiful, fantastic trip. Better than any other trip you have ever gone through. This is a triples trip, and a sensible and a good one as well.

Yes, I'm the chef.

Student: How do the visualizations relate to craziness?

Trungpa Rinpoche: They are related because the visualizations are crazy too. They are outrageous.

Student: Is a visualization a visual experience or a heart experience?

Trungpa Rinpoche: A heart experience. If you relate with visualizations as technicolor visual things, that's a problem. You might end up being Rudra. Or a superape, as we mentioned earlier. If you relate to the visualization as just a sense of inspiration that you have, that is when you are first getting a heart experience altogether.

Student: Are the buddha families complementary? Particularly, if you are thinking of connecting with someone as a marriage partner or a lover, should the partner be the same type or a different type?

Trungpa Rinpoche: It's like the four seasons. Summer does not get married to winter without going through autumn. The same thing applies here. Autumn would prefer to get married to winter, and winter would like to marry spring. And so forth. It's an organic situation.

Student: How do the five aspects of buddha nature relate to ego?

Trungpa Rinpoche: That's the whole point. Those buddha principles are ego's style as well as transcending ego. They are not just higher goals. They are something we can work with while we are here.

EIGHT

Anuttarayoga

THE NEXT YANA is the yogayana, which our time does not permit us to go into in great detail. The view of the yogayana is quite similar to that of the preceding yana, upayogayana. The sense of the practice is also fairly similar, but the relationship to the deity is more direct. There is more sense of union with the divine element—the meaning of *yoga* is "union."

At this point I would like primarily to discuss *anuttarayoga* [which emerges as the supreme level at this point]. It goes beyond the perspective on reality of the kriyayogayana—purity—and that of the upayogayana, which is a sense of bringing action and experience together, as well as beyond the sense of union with the deity of the yogayana. The Tibetan for *anuttara* is *la-me,* which literally means "none higher." *La* means "higher," and *me* means "not"; so there is nothing higher than this. Anuttara is the highest experience that one can ever relate with. There is a sense of personal involvement. The experience of tantra is extremely personal, rather than purely philosophical, spiritual, or religious. In general, there is really a definite sense of something personal. The reason that anuttarayoga is regarded as the highest of all is that the sense that everything is the mind's creation, a mental projection, is dropped. From the point of view of anuttara, everything is what is, rather than purely the consequence of certain causal characteristics based on purity or impurity. As far as anuttara is concerned, there is no notion of causal characteristics, or chain reactions, or ecological consequences. Things are based on *as-it-is.* The chain reactions have their own basic

289

nature; even the results of the chain reactions are as they are, and that is what you relate to, so you don't have origins or results or fruition of things at all. Things are cut-and-dried, so to speak. Things are straightforward, definitely straightforward—direct and precise.

There is something that we haven't yet discussed with regard to the tantric tradition, which applies to all levels of it: kriya, upa, yoga, anuttara, and so forth. That is the transmitter of the tantric strength or energy to the student—the importance of the vidyadhara. The vidyadhara is the holder of crazy wisdom, which in Tibetan is *yeshe chölwa*. *Yeshe* means "wisdom," and *chölwa* is "gone wild"; so it is the wisdom gone wild, crazy wisdom. The holder of crazy wisdom, yeshe chölwa, scientific knowledge, is the guru, the spiritual master. The tantric approach to the guru also applies to the kriyayogayana, the upayogayana, the yogayana—whatever tantric yana we talk about. The notion of the teacher is quite different from that of the bodhisattva level. On the bodhisattva level, the teacher is regarded as a ferryman. The idea of a ferryman is that he has to save his own life as well as care for his fellow passengers. Therefore there is a mutual understanding, a sympathetic approach, a sense of fighting a common enemy. The "spiritual friend," *kalyanamitra* in Sanskrit, from the mahayana point of view is the friend who saves you, the driver of the vehicle, the charioteer, or the pilot of the ship. Such a pilot is also in danger if he doesn't operate the ship properly. His life is equally at risk as those of the passengers. That is the mahayana tradition. But in tantra, we have the notion of the warrior we discussed earlier on. The guru, the spiritual master, has tremendous power and also possesses a lot of understanding regarding the situation he is dealing with. From the tantric point of view, the spiritual friend is no longer a spiritual friend. From the tantric point of view, the guru is a dictator—in the benevolent sense—who minds every step of your life experience and who also demands faith and trust in the context of the bondage of the samaya vow.

The Tibetan word for *samaya* is *tamtsik*, which literally means "sacred word." *Tam* means "sacred," and *tsik* means "word." A samaya vow is a sacred word. It has the significance of the student and the guru having a mutual experience. The guru's action is within the realm of sacredness, and the student's involvement in the tradition of the teaching is also sacred. Therefore there is mutual sacredness.

The guru is regarded as a buddha in the flesh, a buddha in a human body. The guru is the herukas; the guru is the definite manifestation of divine principles of all kinds. That is why when you are accepted into the tantric tradition you take certain abhishekas or empowerments from the guru. This is an important commitment that you make to the tantric tradition. It is in some sense comparable to confirmation in the Christian tradition, or anointment [in the biblical tradition]. Or maybe it is similar to the Jewish tradition of bar mitzvah. From that day onward, you are accepted into the circle of the grown-ups on the tantric level.

Abhishekas are popularly referred to as initiations. This is the wrong translation. The idea of initiation into a certain tribal status is not necessarily applicable. Translating *abhisheka* that way is not an accurate use of language. Nevertheless it gives some general idea. You are initiated into this particular creed, particular dogma, by the father or chief of the tribe, who executes the ceremony. In this case, the guru's role is that of a warrior chief who puts you through all kinds of trials. You can't just be initiated pleasantly, delightfully, smoothly. You have to be made to face certain challenges in which you are made aware of the phenomenal world.

Do you remember a movie called *A Man Called Horse*? The hero of that movie had to go through a whole process of acceptance into the tribal system. He had to go through all kinds of training, excruciating trials and challenges, until finally he saw himself in a vision. He saw himself in a vision seeing a vision of himself, and so forth. [In a similar way, when you are introduced to the tantric tradition,] you begin to realize who you are and what you are. It is an interesting analogy. The spiritual friend turns into a tribal chief, who begins to mind your business much more heavy-handedly than you expected on the bodhisattva level. It's extremely heavy-handed.

This applies to the tantric tradition generally. What we have been discussing is not a unique quality of anuttarayoga. We are discussing the general tantric approach to life, particularly as concerns the teacher or transmitter. We are discussing the need for devotion to the guru in the tantric tradition.

In Hinduism, which is a theistic tradition, devotion to the guru is very conveniently developed as devotion to God, or Brahman. The guru is the only link between you and God. God is that mysterious thing out there. He or she, or whatever, is there already, and in order for you to find out whether God is a he or a she, the guru has to tell you; only he can tell you what God is.

A similar approach developed in Christianity. Jehovah could be communicated with only through Christ, so one should worship the latter. Worship the spoon and fork and plate, which is related with the food. The link between you and the food is the spoon. You have to hold it in a certain meditative or contemplative way. You have to hold it with a certain discipline, represented by your hand. The hand of devotional practice relates with faith to the spoon, which is Christ. Christ, the spoon, relates with the food, which is Jehovah.

In the Buddhist approach, the idea of an external being is completely ignored. It is regarded as an extremely crude, primitive idea. You do not need an interpreter to translate the language of god into the language of human beings. The function of the guru, from the Buddhist point of view, is to communicate the sense of the mysteriousness of the world, to communicate to you the sense of reality from the Buddhist point of view. This is the nontheistic or atheistic approach of tantra. Your spiritual friend, who in this case is a benevolent dictator who minds your business, relates to you. The consequences of deception, passion, or ignorance are great, so you have to keep yourself within the bounds of law and order. You have to try to tune yourself in to the law and order of the cosmic kingdom. But there is no question of the guru functioning as a divine messenger. The guru is the sensible teacher, sensible scientist. He almost has the quality of a sensible attorney, your lawyer, who tells you how to handle your life. But in this case, we do not pay the attorney money; we pay our guru-attorney with faith and trust.

That seems to be a natural situation if we are in trouble. We are highly involved with our troubles. We are actually absolutely fucked up and helpless, desperate, so we begin to relate with the guru as our attorney. If we were not all that fucked up, we might think the attorney was rejectable, not indispensable; we might have a lighthearted relationship with our attorney. But spiritually, we are definitely completely fucked up in any case, in a complete mess, because we do not know who we are or what we are, let alone what we might be. We can't develop any argument, because we are uncertain who is arguing, who is putting our case; so we are absolutely fucked up. We do need our attorney very badly, extremely badly.

In the tantric tradition, the sense of guru plays an extremely important part. The reason why the guru plays an important part is that you are desperate. And when you commit yourself into a more involved situation like tantric discipline, the guru's word is regarded as absolute supertruth, not just ordinary old truth, but vajra truth, truth with power behind it.[1] If you reject such a truth, you can get hurt, you can be destroyed. So you commit yourself to the guru in a threefold way. The form of the guru is regarded as a self-existing manifestation of the truth in the search for the basic sanity of vajrayana. The speech of the guru is regarded as a mantra, a proclamation; anything from him on the sound or intellectual level is absolutely accurate. If you doubt that, you can get hurt, destroyed, your intuition can get cut down. And the mind of the guru is cosmic mind. If you doubt his mind, again you can get hurt, because you could end up suffering from insanity, a fundamental freakout of ego.

The tantric tradition places tremendous importance on the transmitter, the guru. He plays an extremely important part in all this. The form, speech, and mind of the guru have to be respected and surrendered to. You have to be willing to relate with that absolutely, one hundred percent. You are entering the fundamentally sane situation of a benevolent dictator. Once we tread on the path of tantric practice, we switch from the bodhisattva's world of kindness and gentleness and democracy to the realm of the benevolent dictator. The guru plays an extremely important part in this whole thing. If you disobey the guru's message on the level of form, speech, or mind, you are struck, you go straight to vajra hell.

Getting involved with the vajrayana without preparation seems to have extremely dangerous and powerful consequences. That is why I personally feel that introducing tantric practice to this country prematurely could be destructive for individuals and their development rather than a help. At this point, the practice of students studying with me is at the level of basic Buddhism: hinayana with an element of mahayana. We haven't gotten into the kill-or-cure level of tantra yet. Hopefully we will be able to get into that in the very near future.

I think there are something like seven hundred and fifty vows that have developed in the tantric discipline of samaya, samaya shila, and all of these are based on the guru.[2] If you mistreat the guru, if you have doubt about the guru, if you have a vengeful attitude toward the guru, you might be struck. Before you enter into samaya shila, the guru gives you the water of the samaya oath, and you drink it. Once you have drunk it, this water will either become a saving grace, helping toward the development of basic sanity, or it will turn into an absolute atomic bomb. You could be killed, destroyed in the direst manner one could ever imagine, in vajra hell.

Of course the idea of introducing tantra into this country is very exciting, but the consequences of the problems involved in tantra are very scary. People should be told the dangers of tantra rather than the advantages—that you could learn to walk in the air or fly, or develop inner heat, a central heating system—all those little things you think about. It's like thinking about what you will do when you become a millionaire. You can buy a Mercedes or a Jaguar and have all kinds of penthouses to live in. But that's not the point. Rather than thinking about how to become a millionaire, we should think about the dangers of becoming a millionaire. That is the problem we are facing.

At all levels of tantra, you need a transmitter to transmit this spiritual power. This power can be turned into something good or bad, powerful or destructive. An analogy that developed in Tibet is that entering tantric discipline is like putting a poisonous snake in a bamboo pipe. The snake might go either up or down. Once one has begun to relate with tantra, there is no compromise, no happy medium; there's no Madhyamaka, no middle way. There's no happy system of compromise anymore at all. Once you get into tantric discipline, you either go up or you go down. Either you become buddha or you become Rudra, a cosmic monster.

The basic point of anuttarayoga is trying to relate with the abhisheka principles that are found on all tantric levels. In this way, finally we begin to relate with the mahamudra principle we discussed earlier. We have a sense that it can be realized and worked with. There is no doubt about anything at all. The mahamudra principle can be seen and felt, and in consequence there's no doubt with regard to any of the tantric symbolism, the iconography of herukas and dakinis. Those symbols become very straight and direct—a real manifestation of your buddha nature can come through you. You are able to face it, to relate with it in the form of a heruka, a yidam. If your nature is vajra, you can relate with vajra nature; if you're padma, you can relate with padma nature. You have no doubt about the fact that that particular principle involved in life situations is workable, very powerful. You can relate with it and transcend [any doubts].

At this point the divine quality is no longer a foreign element. Your own existence also becomes a divine element. You begin to experience the highest point of vajra pride and the highest point of the mahamudra principle. All the mudras, or signs, that are seen in life situations also become something you can relate with, work with. Things become more vivid and more precise and extraordinarily powerful. At last we become able to solve the mystery of the cosmic games. Games are no longer games and jokes are no longer jokes. I think one of the basic points of anuttarayoga is that the world is seen as workable, no longer a mystery. Mysticism has profundities, as we know; but at the anuttarayoga level, those are no longer a mystery. They are something you can relate with and work with. The wetness of water is a direct message. The hotness of fire is a direct message. There is no longer any mystery involved.

Through understanding the whole thing, we begin to trust our world, to realize that there is no such thing as a cosmic conspiracy. The world is a rational world, a kind world, there's no joke involved. It is a workable situation. So we could say that the quality of the anuttarayoga level is the realization that the world is a safe world, a kind world, that the world is not trying to make a mockery of you—which is what we generally think until we reach this point.

Generally we think there is some trickery involved, that we should try to be smarter than what's happening. We should at least try to make sure that we are not conned by the situations of our life. We should be much smarter, more cunning. But at this point we realize that [counter-] conmanship is unnecessary, which is the highest discovery ever made by mankind. All sentient beings can realize that. If you realize that you don't have to con anybody, that is the ultimate anuttarayoga indeed. We don't have to con anybody, including ourselves.

Student: You say at a certain point the world is realized to be a benevolent, kind world. My immediate reaction to that is, how could that be? The forces of nature seem to be indifferent. If we have an earthquake right now, is that regarded as the manifestation of a kind and benevolent world?

Trungpa Rinpoche: Mm-hmmm.

S: That seems pretty far-fetched.

TR: At this point, your mind has not been trained to realize anuttarayoga, that's why.

S: I still don't see it. If there's an earthquake, who is the recipient of that kindness?

TR: Nobody.

S: Then who is it that calls it kind?

TR: You do.

S: As I'm swallowed up by a crack in the earth?

TR: That's your trip. You produce the teaching. You create Buddhism yourself. There's no Buddhism as such; you produce it by yourself. You want to relate with Buddhism rather than the samsaric world. You produce nirvana, because you experience samsara; it's your trip. The tantric tradition speaks in a much more powerful way than the hinayana or the mahayana when it says that it's your trip. The earthquake is a good message, saying that this is your world, which you produced, and it is highly energetic and powerful.

Student: You were talking about the relationship between teacher and student, which you said was based on trust. In your poetry, if I have understood it properly, you say emphatically, do not trust, do not trust. Is that trust that's necessary for the relationship between student and teacher the same thing as "do not trust"?

Trungpa Rinpoche: I think so; not trusting is the saving grace. When you do not trust, you're distrustful; then there is some continuity. It is precisely in that sense that the mahayanist talks about the emptiness of everything. Emptiness is the truth in reality; it is wisdom. If you trust in the emptiness, nonexistence, if you are distrustful in that way, that is continual trust. There's some kind of faith involved at the same time.

Student: You used the word *divine* a few times in this talk. At what point in the progression from hinayana to mahayana to vajrayana does that word start to become relevant?

Trungpa Rinpoche: The divine or divinity or benevolence can only be relevant if there is no perceiver of them. In other words, god can be a legitimate experience if there is no watcher of the god. The god can only be perceived if there is no worshiper of the god. In other words, Jehovah does exist as a workable experience if there are no Christians, no Jews, no Christ.

Student: It seems that we are practicing the hinayana and mahayana, but you are starting to teach us tantra in the middle of that.

Trungpa Rinpoche: A very important point is that we could relate with the vajrayana and mahayana levels in relation to how to handle our life situation. As far as practice itself is concerned, [at this point] we should relate purely with the hinayana with maybe just a little pinch of maha-yana. Our beliefs have to be destroyed through the rationale of hinayana Buddhism. But our relationship to our life activity could involve taking a chance. That has to be raised from the simple-minded level of hinayana to the mahayana and vajrayana levels if possible.

Student: Could you say something about what a karmic debt is?

Trungpa Rinpoche: That seems to be very simple. If we decide to re-create either good or bad activities, we are going to get involved with the results of that. Then, by getting involved with those results, we sow a further seed as well. It is like seeing a friend once; having lunch with your friend sows seeds for having another lunch with your friend. And so you go on and on and on and on.

Student: I'm a little mixed up about something. If you don't get to the tantric level before having gone through the hinayana and the maha-yana, after you've gone through the hinayana and mahayana, why should you still be so fucked up that you need the guru-dictator?

Trungpa Rinpoche: You do need that; that's precisely the point. You probably have accomplished and achieved a lot, but still you could be carrying the neurosis of the hinayana and the mahayana. You need someone to destroy those. They are very powerful, highly spiritually materialistic, extremely powerful—and you need to be cut down. You create wisdom by being involved with the hinayana, and you create the hang-ups that go along with it. Then when you get involved in the ma-hayana, you create further wisdom, greater wisdom, paramita wisdom, but you also create paramita hang-ups as well. Those things have to be cut down by the dictator, the guru, and the principle is much higher and more powerful still. There's no end. There's no end, my dear friend.

Student: With this feeling of commitment you were transmitting with regard to tantra, I got a feeling of desperation at the same time. That made me wonder: Is there also more of a feeling of egolessness at the tantric level, when it comes time to make that commitment? Does the student have less watcher at that point?

Trungpa Rinpoche: I think so. But at the same time, there will also be the problem of the hang-ups that this lady [the previous questioner] and I were just discussing. That happens as well. That goes on right up until maha ati yoga, which comes at the end of the seminar. You should hear that as well.

Student: You were saying that tantric practices have been prematurely introduced into this country and that they lead to a loss of individuality, or something like that, if they are introduced too early. Could you elaborate?

Trungpa Rinpoche: I think that tantra has been introduced too early in this country, definitely. Particularly, some of the Hinduism. Hinduism is tantra. There is no hinayana aspect to Hinduism as it has been presented in this country. In Hinduism as it exists in India, before you become a sannyasin, or renunciate, before you become a tantric practitioner involved with the religious tradition, you raise your children, you work on your farm, and you relate with your country. That is the equivalent of hinayana in Hinduism. That hasn't been introduced in this country. Only the glamorous part of Hinduism, the cream of it, which infants can't handle, has been introduced here. Students of Hinduism have not really been mature enough. Hinduism is a nationalistic religion. In order to become a Hindu, you have to become a good citizen of India, raise your children, cook good food, be a good father or mother—all those things. This is similar to what developed in Judaism. It seems that the problems we're facing is that without that basic grounding, highlights have been introduced that are extraordinarily electric and powerful. As a result, people have suffered a lot, because they are not even on the level of relating with their families, their parents. Many people have decided to regard their parents as enemies. There's no solid social structure. They decide they dislike their mother's cooking. They'd rather go to a restaurant than taste their mother's cooking. There's no sacredness in their relationship to their family. Maybe that's why there are so many restaurants around here.

That seems to be a problem, actually, sociologically or spiritually. The Hinduism that has been introduced in this country is highly powerful, extremely mystical. It is at the level of tantra. But there has been no hinayana introduced that relates with how to behave.

Student: I feel very much what you say about the danger of leaping over something that is supposed to be done first. I just wonder whether it has to do with the speedup of time that is going on. I feel right now that everything is happening with incredible speed. Everybody walks fast. And I wonder how that can be brought into connection with a tradition that has gone through centuries. It is dangerous to get into tantra without going through hinayana and mahayana, but everybody, particularly in America, wants instant nirvana.

Trungpa Rinpoche: I think that is because America has actually achieved a materialistic vajrayana, and Americans expect to get a spiritual equivalent. Because they're so spoiled. There's automation, and everything is materialistically highly developed. They have gone through the hinayana level of manual farming and so on, and the mahayana level of creating a republican, democratic society as the American world. They take pride in taking the pledge [of allegiance], worshiping the flag, and so forth, on a mahayana level of benevolence. Then beyond that, they have also achieved the vajrayana level of automation, and there are all kinds of power trips and all kinds of war materiel—missiles, bombs, airplanes—everything has been achieved on a vajrayana level. And now that they're so spoiled on that level, they are asking for the spiritual equivalent of that. They don't want to go back to the hinayana level. They have everything happening to their lives, so they are asking direct: "We have everything we want materially, therefore we want everything we want spiritually too." That is tantric materialism, spiritual tantric materialism. That seems to be the problem, and if there are any wise tantric teachers around, Americans won't get it.

Student: Would you say that most drug trips are tantric spiritual materialism?

Trungpa Rinpoche: No. The drug trips, LSD and so forth, are not as tantric as they think they are. It is purely on the level of mahayana materialism. The idea is that drugs are good for society, because they provide good vibrations, goodness and love, and realization leading to goodness. So the drug culture could be described as mahayana rather than tantric.

Student: Traditionally, surrender to the spiritual friend was enabled by the all-encompassing love the student had for the spiritual friend. That enabled the student to have faith and trust in him. Is there any room for that?

Trungpa Rinpoche: I think there's room for everything—your emotions and your trust and everything. That is what ideal devotion is: Your emotions and your trust and everything else is involved. It's a big deal, a hundred percent. That's why the samaya vow with the guru is the most important discipline in tantra. Without respecting your guru, you can't get tantric messages.

There's the story of Marpa visiting Naropa. Naropa had magically created a vision of the mandala of Hevajra, with the colors and everything, above the altar.[3] Then Naropa asked Marpa, "Would you like to prostrate to the mandala, or would you like to prostrate to the guru?" Marpa thought that the guru's magical creation was a fantastic discovery. He thought he would rather prostrate to the divine existence he could see, so he decided to prostrate to the magic show. He did that, and Naropa said, "You're out! You didn't place your trust in me, the creator of the whole show. You didn't prostrate to me, you prostrated to my manifestation. You still have to work harder."

So it's a question of whether to worship the magical achievement or the magician himself. The guru is, in fact, from the tantric point of view, the magician. Even in relation to our rational twentieth-century minds, the guru has all kinds of magic. Not that the guru produces elephants out of the air or turns the world upside down, but the guru has all kinds of ordinary magic. It is seemingly ordinary, but it is also irritating, unpleasant, surprising, entertaining, and so forth.

Student: What is the difference between the guru and the Christian godhead?

Trungpa Rinpoche: In the Christian approach, God is unreachable. The guru is immediate. For one thing, he is a human being like yourself. He has to eat food and wear clothes like you do, so it's a direct relationship. And the fact that the guru has basic human survival needs makes the situation more threatening. Do you see what I mean? It is more threatening because you can't dismiss the guru as being outside of our thing, someone who can survive without our human trips. The guru does thrive on human trips. If we need food, the guru also needs food. If we need a love affair, the guru also needs a love affair. A guru is an ordinary human being, but still powerful. We begin to feel personally undetermined, because the guru minds our trips too closely and too hard. That is why the guru is powerful: He asks you what food you eat and what clothes you wear. He minds your business on those levels as well as with regard to your relationships, your practice, your body, your job, your house. The guru involves himself with those things more and more. Whereas if he were God, he would just be hanging out somewhere. God doesn't make any personal comments, except in terms of your conscience—which is your fantasy anyway.

Student: Rinpoche, at one point when you were describing mahayana, you said that there's a role for doubt in mahayana. You said that there's a confluence of the river of the teaching and the river of doubt, and that by contrast, tantra was like a single thread. Does that mean that there's no role or function for doubt once you enter tantra? Is it completely eliminated?

Trungpa Rinpoche: That's precisely where the dictatorship comes in. You are not allowed to have any doubt. If you have doubts, they'll be cut. Doubt is not regarded as respectable in tantric society.

NINE

Mahamudra and Maha Ati

I T SEEMS NECESSARY at this point to clarify the classification of the tantric yanas. There is a gradual psychological evolution or development through the first three levels of kriya, upa, and yoga. Then there is a fourth stage of tantra in relation to that group known as anuttarayoga. This is the classification of the tantric yanas according to the New Translation school that existed in Tibet.

The New Translation school is particularly associated with the mahamudra teaching. The reason it is called the New Translation school is to distinguish it from the Old Translation school, the tradition associated with the maha ati teachings of tantra, which were introduced into Tibet earlier on, at the time of Padmasambhava. The maha ati teachings are connected with the mahayoga-, anuyoga-, and atiyogayanas, which we will be discussing.[1]

The New Translation school started with Marpa and other great translators who reintroduced tantra into Tibet later on. This later tantric school developed the teachings of Naropa and Virupa, two Indian siddhas. The teachings of Naropa particularly influenced the Geluk and Kagyü tantra traditions in Tibet, and the teachings of Virupa particularly influenced the tantric tradition of the Sakya order of Tibet.[2]

As I said, the mahamudra teaching is connected with the new tantric tradition, the New Translation school. The predominant meditation practice in the kriya-, upa-, yoga-, and anuttarayoga yanas is mahamudra. We discussed mahamudra earlier, but I think maybe we have to go over it more.

First we have to develop the clear perception that comes from re-moving the dualistic barrier in accordance with the notion of shunyata. This is the experience or insight of the bodhisattva. Having removed the obstacles or fog of that barrier, one begins to have a clear perception of the phenomenal world as it is. That is the mahamudra experience. It's not that mahayana only cuts through the dualistic barrier—it also re-creates our sense of richness; we have a sense of appreciating the world again, once more, without preconceptions, without any barrier.

In a sense the shunyata experience could be described as a totally negative experience, that of cutting down, cutting through. It is still in-volved with a sense of struggle. In some sense you could say that shun-yata needs a reference point. The reference point of the barrier between self and other creates the reference point of nonbarrier. The mahamudra principle does not even need the barrier to express itself or anything else at all to go against. It is just a pure, straightforward experience of the world of sight and smell and touchable objects as a self-existing mandala experience. There is no inhibition at all. Things are seen precisely, beau-tifully, without any fear of launching into them.

Within that experience of mahamudra is clear perception—we could use that expression: "clear perception." In this case, clear perception is the experience of the five wisdoms of the five buddha families. There is clear perception of the mirrorlike wisdom of the vajra family, seeing things precisely and sharp-edged. They appear methodical; everything's in order. There is also the wisdom of discriminating awareness of the padma family: You begin to relate with a sense of perspective and rela-tionship—in other words, there is a sense of sorting out. The vajra as-pect, the mirrorlike wisdom, is just precision, a vision; the discriminating awareness wisdom of padma is more discriminatory, more of a sorting-out process. Then the wisdom of equanimity of ratna provides a general background in relation to which everything is workable, everything is dealt with, nothing is missing. Then the wisdom of the fulfillment of all actions of the karma family is the driving force behind that makes it pos-sible for wisdom to be put into practice. And then there is the wisdom of dharmadhatu, of all-encompassing space, of the buddha family in which nothing is rejected. Absolutely everything is included in the experience, both samsara and nirvana, or anything that one can imagine at all.

The five wisdoms are somewhat connected with a sense of wildness, in the style of the crazy yogi. Fundamentally, in anuttarayoga's approach to life, there is no need for careful examination. Within those wisdoms, things are already sorted out. That is precisely what we mean by mandala: things are already sorted out. Things are seen as ordinary. Chaos is orderly chaos. Things might appear chaotic, but there is a pattern, there is an order. So, from that point of view, there is no reason for the crazy yogi to be careful—thing are already worked out.

This is not just purely blind faith, a matter of just jumping in. Rather it is a matter of seeing things in the right perspective so that you have no reason to be doubtful. Moreover, you have a relationship with a master or teacher, a person who pushes you if you are in doubt. So personal conviction in the teaching, in the wisdoms, and the close guidance of the teacher gives birth to the crazy yogi.

Crazy in this case means having no need to look twice. One flash of experience is enough, and it is a real flash of experience, of seeing the world in the light of wisdom, in the light of mahamudra. Everything happens in your life situation; even if you forget to acknowledge it, life come to you and acknowledges you. So it's a perpetual development: Practice goes on even in the absent-minded state. The teaching goes on; the learning process goes on.

We could say that that is the highest experience that anuttara can achieve. If you are studying a particular sadhana with a particular heruka, then in your life situation just as in the rest of your practice, the forms that you perceive are the images of the heruka, the sounds you hear are the voice of the heruka, and anything that occurs in the realm of the mind is the wisdom of the heruka.

Of course this does not necessarily mean that you start seeing pictures or that you re-create heaven. You see the traffic lights as traffic lights, and you see dollar bills as dollar bills. But they all have some vajrayana quality behind them, a vajra quality. A vajra quality in this case is the sense that things are very rich; even the function of just a grain of sand is a rich one. A broken bottle on the street, or some dog shit—whatever—is the vajra nature; the vajra quality is in them. I'd prefer not to use the word *divine* here, because when we use the word *divine* there is a sense of softness and a sense of a hierarchical setup. But when we use the word *vajra,* it does not have a hierarchical connotation. There's no feeling of saving grace or a higher or greater being; but it is a sharp and precise and highly profound experience. In that way, on the tantric level of practice, whatever happens in our life situation, the whole thing becomes the expression of the heruka or of mahamudra experience.

But still that is not the ultimate experience. There is more to go. We might wonder: If you have cut the dualistic barrier and you perceive the world as it is in the light of wisdom, and if, so to speak, you can dance with the gods and goddesses and converse with them in the most practical, simple way, what more could you want? It sounds great. But still there is something that doesn't click. There is still the sense of an experience. There's still a sense of a commuter, a back-and-forth journey, as all-pervasive as it might be, as serene and clear and tranquil as it may be, still it's experience. Still it's mudra, still it's message, still this is the truth, still this is the ultimate. All of those contain a reference point. Still this is regarded as the perfect one, and that seems to be the problem. We have three more yanas to go, and those three yanas, which are in the maha ati category, cut through those reference points.

Ati is called the end. It is called *dzokpa chenpo* in Tibetan, which means the "great ending." It is a gigantic full stop, rather than a beginning. The three yanas connected with the maha ati experience have to do with transcending reference point altogether. This means abandoning the idea of wisdom as opposed to confusion or being a fool. We cannot just cut on the level of language; we can't just start from the outside. Something has to happen right within.

As far as perceiving the herukas or relating with them is concerned, they have to be more terrifying or more peaceful. Even the reference point of logic cannot describe their extreme existence or the extreme experience of them. They are so extreme that even the word *extreme* does not apply anymore. It is a fathomless experience.

The first yana on the ati level is the mahayogayana. This is something beyond anuttara. When this yoga speaks of the ultimate power, it is in destroying the notion of power. When it speaks of the ultimate enlightenment, it is in beginning to destroy enlightenment, not just the enlightenment concept but enlightenment itself. What we have been doing so far is finding holes in some aspect of the teaching, then laying a heavy trip on that as being conceptual. We have been finding our scapegoat that way. So we have gotten rid of the concept, but we haven't gotten rid of the conceptualizer. Even on the level of subtlety we have reached by this yana, we still hang on to it. Even somebody who has achieved the highest form of mahamudra still hangs on to that logic, that style of dealing with oneself. So at this point we are destroying the destroyer and destroying the creator; or we could express it positively and talk about creating the creator and destroying the destroyer. That doesn't matter. That's not the point. There are no positive or negative things involved, no negation and no affirmation.

That seems to bring us to a glimpse of crazy wisdom as opposed to just the crazy yogi. There seems to be a difference between the two. The yogi is a practitioner and has the reference point of the spiritual journey. The yogi is still moving toward the goal, still walking on the path as a practitioner. He is still wise, but his wisdom is different from crazy wisdom. As we have already said, crazy wisdom in Tibetan is *yeshe chölwa*, wisdom run wild. That's the ultimate form of craziness, which is the highest form of sanity, needless to say. That is because it does not believe in any extremes at all, or rather doesn't dwell on them—because belief is very primitive, and after belief is destroyed, you dwell on that achievement.

The mahayogayana is the introduction to the maha ati principle, the starting point for crazy wisdom. The yana after that, anuyoga, is basically the experience that sifts out the hang-ups of all the previous yanas and provides the potential for the final yana, which is ati. In that sense anuyoga could be regarded as the tantric version of a sieve. It completely and thoroughly sifts out dualistic notions, beliefs in even the highest spiritual subtleties.

To reach that point, however, we have to relate with the energy level of the world more completely, the energy of appreciating sight, smell, feeling, and so forth on the level of the mahayogayana. The mahayogayana is one of the best ways of creating a complete mandala and relating completely with the various heruka principles. In the mahayogayana, there are what is known as the eight logos. *Logos* is the closest translation we can find for the Tibetan word *ka*, which also means "command" or "language." The eight logos can be laid out diagrammatically in a mandala. This involves a traditional way of relating with the directions, which is very similar to that found in the American Indian tradition. In this case, we start with the east and go clockwise.

Number one, then, in mahayogayana's expression of the heruka principle, is associated with the east. The symbol of this heruka is a skull cup filled with oil with nine wicks in it. This acknowledges the mirrorlike wisdom of the vajra family, which is also connected with the east. In this case the purity and cleanness of vajra is not manifested as a peaceful deity—by no means. He is a wrathful one. This heruka's scepter is a round dagger, like a big pin with a spearhead. An ordinary dagger is flat and has one edge, but this is like a big pin that pierces any conceptual beliefs. The Tibetan name for that heruka is Yangdak. *Yang* means "once more" or "again." *Dak* means pure. The meaning of the two together is "complete purity." Once more, having already been through the hang-ups of the previous yanas, you have now reached the first exit toward the real meaning of freedom, toward the open air, direct toward outer space.

The next development is that of the south, number two. Here we have Death, Yamantaka. This principle is associated with the owl, which has yellow eyes that see at night and has an acquaintance with darkness and death. This is quite different from the Westerner's idea of the owl as the bird of wisdom. Here the owl is associated with death because darkness is the owl's client. And death in this case is connected with the ratna family and considered an enrichment.

So the east is connected with vajra and one lamp with nine wicks, which is superluminous, like one torch with a hundred bulbs, each of a hundred watts. And then there is ratna as death, which is quite interesting. Usually we don't at all regard death as an enrichment. We regard death as a loss, a complete and tremendous loss. But here death is regarded as an enrichment—in the sense that the final cessation of existence could be regarded as the ultimate creativity. And the ultimate creativity or collecting process is also deathly at the same time. So there are those two polarities here. But by no means is relating with death, Yamantaka, regarded as something safe or something that will save you. Instead there is the interplay of those two polarities.

Then in the west, number three, there is the padma-family heruka, Hayagriva, who is related with passion. This is not passion in the sense of magnetizing alone, but also in the sense of proclaiming your passion. Hayagriva is associated with the horse, so Hayagriva's principle is referred to as the horse's neigh, the voice of the horse. The three neighs of that horse destroy the body, speech, and mind of Rudra. The symbol is a red lotus with flames as petals, a burning lotus, a burning heart, the proclamation of passion. But at the same time, this is a wrathful figure.

In the north, number four, is Vajrakilaya. *Kilaya* means "dagger." The kilaya is different from the dagger of the east, Yangdak's round dagger.

The kilaya has one point but three edges. It is like a three-sided pyramid with sharpened corners. This represents the karma buddha family. It has the sense of penetration. The traditional idea of the karma family is purely functionality, the fulfillment of ends, achieving things, but in this case the karma principle has to do purely with penetration. This should not be confused with the intellectual penetration of the vajra family. The karma family of Vajrakilaya has to do with precision. Whereas vajra is intellectual, still surveying the area, karma is penetrating and accepts no nonsense.

Then you have the fifth one, which is associated with Chemchok in the center. This principle is connected with amrita, the antideath potion. The symbol is a skull cup with liquor in it. Amrita, the best liquor, can only be brewed by the crazy-wisdom people. There is a sense of the transmutation of poison into medicine.

In the traditional sadhana practice connected with this principle, an accomplished guru and the sangha associated with him get together and brew a vajra liquor of eight main herbs and a thousand secondary ingredients. They ferment this mixture, which is called dharma medicine, in the presence of the shrine, and it is raised into liquor. Every process is a conscious one. When a person takes this alcoholic potion, the result is that hanging on to any of the yanas is freed.

I feel safe talking to this particular group about this, since they have some understanding of the hinayana, mahayana, and vajrayana principles. I think everybody here understands that they have to go through the whole training before they begin to "drop" amrita. So the transmutation of poison into medicine is connected with number five.

The next one, number six, is called "mother's curse," *Mamo Bötong* in Tibetan. Mother's curse in this case means that the phenomenal world begins to come into a closer relationship with you and your practice. You are in tune with the phenomenal world, and if you miss one second of relationship with the phenomenal world, you are cursed, bewitched. The symbol of the mother's curse is a bag full of liquid poison, with a snake as the rope fastening. This approach is so dangerous, extremely dangerous, and powerful at the same time. You can't miss an inch, a fraction of an inch, a fraction of a minute. If you are not in contact with anything, you can be destroyed instantaneously. Before you can think of being destroyed, it has already happened, and you go straight to vajra hell. The tantric approach, particularly the maha ati approach, is highly dictatorial. And it knows no limits. You are constantly under challenge.

The word *mother* is used here in the sense of the cosmic feminine principle, which is both seducer and destroyer. This is not on the messenger level, not just a warning. In actual solid situations, there is a difference between relating with the boss and relating with a messenger. Encountering the mother's curse is relating with the boss. If the boss dislikes you, dislikes your unskillful actions, he could really hurt you. There could be famine, war, madness, and all the rest of the worst consequences one could ever think of. But the mother's curse does not go too far. It is still at the facade level.

The next one, number seven, is *Jikten Chötö* in Tibetan. *Jikten* means "world," *chö* means "offer," and *tö* means "praise." We haven't practiced grounding ourselves in the world enough, so we have to praise our world, and also we have to offer our services to the world. This is a very interesting point, which seems to call for nationalism. A sense of nationalism is important. You don't regard your country as something to be abandoned or to be gotten rid of, as though you could step out of your country and enjoy another domain, another realm. So this seventh principle involves developing some basic nationalism. The place where you grew up, the place where you were raised and educated and where you are living, deserves some respect. Also, if you do not respect your country and take pride in your country, you might be struck, destroyed.

That is a very precise message, but we have little understanding of how to relate with our world, our nation. Americans have a problem relating with America. And national pride does not necessarily only mean worshiping the flag or the grand old presidents of the past, some of whom died peacefully and some of whom killed for the sake of the nation. That kind of nationalism is spiritual materialism. The kind of nationalism we are talking about is spiritual nationalism. Your country, where your belongings are and your life situation takes place, has spirituality, buddha nature in everything. This refers to the experience you have of your country, such as of the landscape—the beauty of America. Taking America as the basic image, let's suppose you went from California to Colorado to New York, and let's say you were walking instead of driving. You would begin to appreciate the beauty of your country enormously. It's almost fantastic: Who thought up these ideas, such as that such a beautiful rock could be there, that beautiful plants could be there, that beautiful cactus could grow, and there could be such beautiful rolling hills and such beautiful maple leaves—all these things that your country churns out and nobody else's? We are talking about the very physical existence of the American land, the United States of America, or North America as a whole, including Canada. It could also be South America. But this land that you're living in is an extraordinarily beautiful one. It has glamorous cities, beautiful landscapes, and everything is unique. It is a complete world, which brings pride on the individual level as well as having subtleties and spiritual implications. Your country is a really great country. There's very little need to take a trip to Tibet or visit Darjeeling to view the Himalayas. This is a tantric interpretation, a kind of vajra nationalism, which seems to be necessary at this point.

Then we have the last one, number eight, which is the principle of the ultimate spell, *Möpa Trak-ngak* in Tibetan. *Möpa* means "vicious," *trak* means "wrathful," and *ngak* means "mantra." This has the sense of "ultimate spell of wrathful action," which means that you are not afraid of striking anywhere, not afraid of challenging anything. If you have to sue somebody, you are willing to do it. You are not afraid of that. We have experienced the significance of that on the practical level. If you don't sue or take legal action against another party or an authority, you might end up economically as a zombie. So you have to take action.

This principle is a vajra curse or, better, a vajra incantation. We are not afraid to say that thus-and-such a person should be destroyed and thus-and-such a person should be developed. Which in fact is quite outrageous.

A lot of things that we encounter in these principles I feel the audience is trustworthy enough not to make into something else. This audience consists of good citizens rather than famous people, celebrities who might engage in wishful thinking about overpowering the nation. However, if someone did decide to make themselves important and try to rule the world or the nation, it's too late for them to do that. They could get struck.

Then we have anuyogayana, which is connected with bringing the head and heart together on a practical level. You may have read in the *Tibetan Book of the Dead* that the peaceful deities are stationed in the heart chakra and the wrathful deities are stationed in the brain chakra. On the anuyogayana level, a real relationship to the wrathful deities takes place, and they come alive. In the yanas associated with mahamudra, there is not enough emphasis on their wrathful aspect. Instead of being described as wrathful, they are described as threatening. The deities are described as threatening, passionate, and meditative in the mahamudra yanas. There are passionate ones with consorts or by themselves; the meditative ones are connected with ignorance; and the wrathful ones are described as threatening rather than wrathful. Threatening implies a certain objectivity—you can be threatening without losing your temper. Whereas in the case of the anuyogayana, you have to lose your temper. You have to be one hundred percent, if not two hundred percent, into the wisdom. It is real anger rather than trying to play games skillfully.

Another aspect of the wrathful deities is that they have adopted the raiment of the Rudra of ego. They subjugate the Rudra of ego and use his clothing. This means not abandoning the samsaric world as something bad, but rather wearing it as an ornament.

The wrathful principle is connected with the brain, intellect. The peaceful deities are connected with the heart, emotion. The intellect in this case is not necessarily the analytical, rational mind. The intellect here is something aggressive in the vajra sense, something extremely powerful. This is the reason for the timing in the *Tibetan Book of the Dead:* First you see peaceful deities, and if they are not able to help you, then those peaceful deities turn into angry ones; they lose their temper and strike you again. In relation to the wrathful deities, the ati tantric tradition speaks of immense anger, without hatred of course, the most immense anger that enlightened mind could ever produce, as the most intense form of compassion. There is so much kindness and compassion in it that it turns red.

That is the expression of crazy wisdom. At this point there is no problem of maintaining balance. Extremes are used as the reference point of balance rather than any kind of compromises.

The leading mandala in the anuyogayana is the one called the mandala of the hundred deities. It has forty-two peaceful divinities and fifty-eight wrathful deities related to the Vajrasattva principle, the principle of vajra nature. They all are manifestations of vajra nature—vajra passion and vajra anger.

It seems that we could discuss the iconographical symbolism connected with the growth in experience derived from the various yanas in great detail, but we don't have enough time. Also I feel responsible not to confuse you too much by introducing a lot of stuff—names and ideas.

That might cause you to fail to see the general pattern, and you might become fascinated by the details.

So that brings us to the final yana, maha ati. The spiritual discipline of maha ati falls into four categories. The first one is the revelation of dharmata, which means reality. Here everything is seen as real and direct. The next one is called *nyam kongphel* in Tibetan. *Nyam* means "temporary experience," *kongphel* means to acknowledge your temporary experiences but not hang on to them. The next one is called *rikpa tse-phep*. *Rikpa* means "intelligence," "intuition"; *tse* means "measure"; and *phep* means "in accordance with that." You have reached a point of real perspective in your practice. The last one is "wearing out dharmata." Dharmata is the isness of all the dharma constituted by both samsara and nirvana. So there is a wearing out of the whole thing; [you no longer prefer nirvana to samsara]. You are even giving up enlightenment.

One of the basic projects, if you can call it a project, on the maha ati level, and the point of all the practices that go on there, is to destroy the notion and the experience of enlightenment. So there's no goal, no search at all. That is what is called wearing out dharmata. And at that point there is a sense of being unleashed infinitely. There is a sense of craziness, the ultimate craziness, which does not believe in even trying to accomplish anything at all.

Usually when we feel crazy in the conventional, simple-minded way, it is because we have some political, spiritual, or domestic idea that we would like to communicate to the rest of the world. Therefore we feel crazy, dogmatic. In this case, there's a sense of being crazy and completely on the loose, but there's no game, no goal. That kind of crazy person doesn't have to say anything at all, or he could say a lot about the whole thing.

I feel that we cannot go too far with maha ati at this point. This is as far as we can go at the present time. I hope that you will all come back, so we can discuss the further development of the three stages of ati. That needs room and space. And at this point, we have been bombarded by all the yanas to the extent where we are uncertain who's who and what's what.

Student: You mentioned that in the anuyogayana, extremes could serve as a reference point for balance. Does this mean that there is still a reference point in the anuyogayana?

Trungpa Rinpoche: Yes, but it's a much better one. But we still haven't reached maha ati, so there's still a reference point. You see, finally, any technique, any method, any activity we might present becomes a reference point.

Student: I still don't understand how the practice of mahamudra is integrated with visualization practice.

Trungpa Rinpoche: The mahamudra practice is a highly visual thing. It is very much in tune with colors and sights and smells. It is so much in tune with any perceptions we might have, because there is no barrier anymore. So the visualization is not imagining something; you actually do feel whatever deity your practice is connected with. For instance, if you're doing a Kalachakra practice, you feel so overwhelmed by that that your life is completely bombarded by Kalachakra-ness.[3] Visualization comes to you and strikes you; therefore there's no problem with that. It's more a question of how far you're willing to go. It is a question of if you are willing to go too far or of the extent to which you are willing to go too far in opening, giving.

Student: It seems to me that visualization would be an unnecessary side trip that could distract you from the essence of the mahamudra experience.

Trungpa Rinpoche: That is possible. In fact the great Indian siddha Saraha attacked the idea of visualization, asking why there couldn't just be pure mahamudra without other trips. That is an expression of the mahamudra practice's yearning toward the maha ati level. It begins to break through, to become more revolutionary.

Student: Could you explain how extreme compassion turns into extreme wrath?

Trungpa Rinpoche: I don't know how to explain that. I mean, that's it. You have to experience it, I suppose. I could use all kinds of adjectives, but they would just be words.

Student: What should you do upon meeting a wrathful deity?

Trungpa Rinpoche: Meeting one? I don't think you meet them just like that. You become somewhat associated with that quality yourself. You are moving in that direction already, and so you're ready to see it, ready to experience that way.

S: So there would be some kind of identification with it?

TR: Yes, there would be some identification with it.

Student: This extreme anger of the maha ati yanas—is that something that is directed toward the self and relates purely to one's own growth, or can this extreme anger with compassion manifest in the world?

Trungpa Rinpoche: Manifest?

S: For someone who was at the level of the maha ati yanas, would this manifest in his teaching or purely in his practice, personally?

TR: I think it manifests in life experience altogether. There is a sense of crazy wisdom, of unreasonableness that is still being reasonable, a very dignified wildness that is very solid and very sharp at the same time. That manifests in relating to the lifestyles of individuals one is dealing with and in dealing with oneself. There are all kinds of possibilities. Wherever there is energy, there is that possibility.

S: It's a kind of fervor that that kind of energy produces?

TR: It's a product of long experience of dismantling yourself, starting from the hinayana level.

Student: Is there any relationship between the wrathful deities and vajra hell?

Trungpa Rinpoche: Yes. That's the jail of the wrathful deities, I suppose you could say. And no one can save you from that.

S: So the wrathful deities put you in vajra hell and keep you there?

TR: No, not necessarily. The wrathful deities are by no means jail wardens. They are more like a powerful friend who does not go along with you if you do not go along with him.

Student: Rinpoche, to what extent should these yanas and levels of awareness you're talking about be assimilated to Western forms, and to what extent do you think they need to be kept in their traditional Tibetan form?

Trungpa Rinpoche: I think people should have some understanding of the psychology of it, the whole idea of it, which is not a foreign idea, particularly. It's just general, universal logic, cosmic logic, that everybody could agree on. That is why the teaching is called the truth. Everybody can agree that fire is hot—it's that kind of thing. Once one has understood the basic principles of the tantric teaching and has had some experience of the practice of it, there should be no trouble in transplanting it. The images cease being seen as cultural expressions. They just become images on their own. So I think if people have a basic understanding of the psychology and philosophy, and especially if they have good background training in basic Buddhism—the hinayana and mahayana—tantra won't even need to be adopted. There's no need to try to cut it down or reduce it to make it presentable. If a person is able to feel it, see it, experience it, then it becomes almost too obvious. That's what seems to have happened in the past, in Tibet and also in Japan, when tantra was introduced. It was not adapted to anything. It was just transplanted—straight from the horse's mouth.

Student: Is there a merging of the wrathful and peaceful deities? Or do you experience them one after the other?

Trungpa Rinpoche: One after the other, yes. With either one of those, there's no choice. If there was a union, that would mean there would be some choice or compromise. But there's no compromise.

Student: In the mahamudra yanas, visualization was important. When you get to maha ati, is visualization still necessary, or is there a more direct method?

Trungpa Rinpoche: There is visualization up to a certain point. But it gets quite complicated here, because within maha ati itself, there are also three levels.

S: Well, let's say in the final stage of maha ati.

TR: No, there is no visualization.

S: But why is it necessary to have visualization to get to the great dzokpa chenpo?

TR: The basic purpose of visualization is to enable you to identify yourself with the principles of enlightenment and also to appreciate the colorfulness of the energy of the world around you at the same time. That way you can see your world as one of the deities. And, you know, it takes a lot of technique to enable you to do that, so that you begin to use head and heart together. Particularly the appreciation of energies in visual and auditory terms is very, very difficult. We probably feel that in listening to classical music or jazz, or some other kind of music, we are identifying with the sound, or going along with it or dancing with it; or when we watch a good movie, we might forget that we are sitting in a chair watching a movie. But in actual fact, we are fascinated rather than being one with the sound or the movie. So tuning in to the energy, cosmic energy, is very difficult. It's not a matter of just swinging with it. It needs a lot of techniques and manipulations, so to speak.

Student: Rinpoche, is there an equivalent in Western psychology for anything approaching mahamudra? Like in Jung, perhaps?

Trungpa Rinpoche: There is a touch of it in Jung, I suppose, but the problem is, it becomes so philosophical, rather than a matter of practice. It seems that he himself did not know how to handle the idea of practice. Anything on the mahamudra level could be a very profound and wild thing to talk about, but when it comes to how to practice it, people get very nervous—in case they might get sued.

Student: How does one destroy power?

Trungpa Rinpoche: By becoming completely one with the power. From the maha ati point of view.

Student: Rinpoche, it's not clear to me how these eight logos are related to by the practitioner.

Trungpa Rinpoche: I think it's very simple. Those practices are applicable if practitioners have difficulty relating with clarity or death or the proclamation of passion or the experience of penetration or the mother's curse. The whole thing is very practical. You might find to your surprise that you are challenged by all those elements already, but you are not conscious of those categories described in the texts.

S: Does the guru give the student practices that assist him in focusing on this or that particular matter? Does it go in a successive progression?

TR: It could go in progression or it could be training toward the development of your particular style as well.

S: So it must be very flexible.

TR: Yes, I think so. That's why, when you are working with tantric situations, you need a great deal of help from the guru, the benevolent dictator we discussed.

Student: Is there any parallel between number eight, the spell of wrathful action, and the idea of the warrior? Especially in terms of challenge?

Trungpa Rinpoche: I think so. If the warrior is training you in dealing with panic. Some people get completely paralyzed by a threat. They can't walk, they can't move, they become completely paralyzed. At that point the wise warrior would hit you very violently or decide to shoot you. Then you begin to pull yourself together by yourself and to carry out what you are doing properly. It is always possible that you might be too cowardly. You might see things so clearly that you become a coward. Then you have to be pushed, kicked, by the benevolent dictator.

Student: Does the history of Tibet show that this complicated theology has been successful in bringing forth numbers of enlightened people?

Trungpa Rinpoche: Yes. Right up to the present time. I experienced working with an enlightened teacher. There's no doubt about that. I'm a student of that enlightened person, and I am struggling as well to be a presumptuous person. So there's no doubt about that.

Student: Are the eight logos cross-cultural? Is the reason they're unfamiliar to us that we are unfamiliar with those elements in ourselves or because we happen to be Americans?

Trungpa Rinpoche: Tantra could be regarded as outlandish in any case. But it does have a transcultural element. It's like water. Anybody can drink water, including dogs and pigs. The Italians and the Jews and the Americans can also drink water. It's a transpersonal substance.

Student: When you were a student in Tibet, were you presented with this whole road map of the nine yanas before you started studying them?

Trungpa Rinpoche: No, I wasn't. I was highly confused. I wish they had done this. That's why I'm doing it. I wanted to look at it myself and share it with the rest of the people. The training program we had in Tibet was unorganized and chaotic. It was extremely rich, but, you know, all over the place.

Student: What is vajra hell like?

Trungpa Rinpoche: It's pretty hellish, so hellish you can't even think of getting out of it. But when you do think of getting out of it, you are punished even more. If you develop any notion of duality, you are pulled back. If you develop even the notion of "me" existing, you will be pulled back. Constantly sucked into the pain.

Student: Could becoming Rudra be similar to being in vajra hell?

Trungpa Rinpoche: Rudra is a candidate for vajra hell rather than a participant in it. Rudra has been enjoying himself too much, and he has to pay back for his enjoyment by going to vajra hell.

Student: Is the candidate for vajra hell a person who has worked through all the yanas and then suddenly freaks out?

Trungpa Rinpoche: I think until a person is caught up in the higher maha ati level of practice, he cannot be called a candidate for vajra hell. Up to the mahayana level, a person is immune to such consequences.

Student: Are these herukas of the eight logos related to as yidams?

Trungpa Rinpoche: Those are the yidams, yes. You could have one or another of them as a yidam.

Student: These techniques that you've been describing in the tantric yanas sound so similar to brainwashing. Aside from the fact, which you made very clear, that we have to go through hinayana and mahayana to prepare the ground for tantra, is there really any difference between these techniques and other techniques?

Trungpa Rinpoche: Definitely. These techniques are so daring, so personally challenging. Nothing else is that challenging. Other techniques provide confirmation, they create a nest, rather than exposing you to all kinds of cliffs where you could kill yourself or providing you with all kinds of instruments with which you could commit suicide. These techniques are so pointed, so crude and powerful, uncompassionate and wise, that you cannot really miss the point. Your fear is always there; that's the target they are getting to.

Student: You spoke about the student developing a state of mind that was solid, direct, and unwavering. If that is the case, where do the mother's curse and vajra hell come into the picture?

Trungpa Rinpoche: That's the whole point. As you get stronger and your state of mind gets more solid and unwavering, your strength has to be challenged. You can't just be born a solid person and go on solid without any reference point. So those provide the reference points or challenges. Until you get to maha ati, there are always challenges. There's always tickling and being pushed and pulled. That always happens.

Student: To what extent do individuals have a choice not to do any of this? Are these challenges inevitable for everybody?

Trungpa Rinpoche: Absolutely everybody. People are facing these things all the time in their everyday lives. But what we are doing is providing challenges that have a pattern and a workable orientation toward a path. That way the whole thing becomes more acute and precise.

I think we have to stop at this point. I would like to thank the audience for taking part in this. This seminar on the nine yanas has been one of the landmarks of my work in North America. I hope you will decide to stick with this, look through it some more, and study it. We could regard this particular situation, in May 1973 in San Francisco, as a historical occasion. True vajrayana and the true nine-yana principle have been introduced in America completely and thoroughly. I am glad there was no particular pride on the students' part, making a big point about having come here because of being confused or fucked up. The students here are serious in spite of some of them being dilettantes maybe. But at least you are serious dilettantes.

It is a very delightful thing that from today onward we will be approaching the point of working with American Buddhism in terms of the tantric teachings. You have taken part in the inauguration of it. Your being there made me say things, and I appreciate that very much. Your response has been fantastic, so kind and energetic at the same time. I am so pleased that you have witnessed this and participated in the bringing of tantra to America, properly, healthily, and officially—according to my boss. Thank you.

Notes

PART ONE

Chapter 1. The Journey

1. *Spiritual materialism* is a key term in the Vidyadhara's teaching. The first major book of his North American teachings was called *Cutting Through Spiritual Materialism* (Berkeley, Calif.: Shambhala Publications, 1973; reprinted 1987; see Volume Three of *The Collected Works*). Very simply, spiritual materialism means approaching spirituality with the intention of using it to achieve your preconceived ends rather than with an attitude of surrendering to reality.

Chapter 2. Hopelessness

1. The symbols for the twelve links (Skt. *nidana*) of the karmic chain of existence are a blind grandmother, the potter's wheel, a monkey, a person in a boat, a monkey in a six-windowed house, a married couple, an arrow through the eye, drinking milk and honey, gathering fruit, copulation, a woman in childbirth, a funeral procession.

2. The second and fourth of the great enlightened teachers of the Kagyü lineage of Tibetan Buddhism. Naropa (1016–1100 CE) was one of the best known of the Indian mahasiddhas, or possessors of spiritual powers, as was his teacher Tilopa. Naropa's student Marpa (1012–1097) was a farmer and the first Tibetan lineage holder of the Kagyü lineage. His student Milarepa (1052–1135 CE) is one of Tibet's most famous saints, known for spending many years in retreat in remote mountain caves, then having many enlightened students. Milarepa's main student, Gampopa (1079–1153 CE), founded the monastic order of the Kagyü.

3. Here and elsewhere in this book, "Don Juan" refers to the Yaqui Indian spiritual teacher depicted in the books of Carlos Castaneda.

4. Another way, besides the nine yanas, of delineating the Buddhist spiritual journey is in terms of the five paths. The five paths are the paths of accumulation, unification, seeing, meditation, and no more learning.

Chapter 3. The Preparation for Tantra

1. These two sentences ("First we prepare . . . Then we begin . . .") are a synopsis of the three main Buddhist yanas: hinayana, mahayana, and vajrayana.

2. The Vidyadhara is embarking on a description of five categories, sometimes known as the five powers (Skt. *bala*). The development of these five characterizes the path of unification. They are (with the Vidyadhara's eventual preferred English translations of them): faith (Skt. *shraddha;* Tib. *tepa*), exertion (Skt. *virya;* Tib. *tsöndrü*), mindfulness or recollection (Skt. *smriti;* Tib. *trenpa*), meditation (Skt. *dhyana;* Tib. *samten*), intellect (Skt. *prajna;* Tib. *sherap*). The fourth category is also often given as *samadhi* (Tib. *tingdzin*).

3. See *Shantideva* in Glossary.

4. According to the traditional cosmology of India, much of which became part of the Buddhist tradition, Mount Meru is the great cosmic mountain at the center of the universe.

5. The bodhisattva (Skt., "enlightenment being") is the ideal practitioner of the mahayana path. The bodhisattva's compassionate practice of virtues transcending ego is regarded as heroic and even warriorlike. The Vidyadhara discusses this in greater detail in part two, chapter 3, "The Dawn of Mysticism."

6. In Buddhism, the five skandhas (Tib. *phungpo,* meaning "heap" in both Sanskrit and Tibetan) are the five types of aggregates of psychophysical factors that, taken together, are associated with the sense of self or ego. Upon examination, no such self or ego is found, only these collections. They are form (Skt. *rupa*), feeling (Skt. *vedana*), perception (Skt. *samjna*), formation (Skt. *rupa*), feeling (Skt. *vedana*), perception (Skt. *samjna*), formation (Skt. *samskara*), and consciousness (Skt. *vijnana*). See part two, chapter 2, "Competing with Our Projections."

7. *Chutzpah* (*ch* as in Scottish *loch*) is a Yiddish word referring to boldness or audacity that proceeds vigorously rather than being cowed by obstacles.

Chapter 4. The Basic Body

1. The Vidyadhara describes the buddha families in more detail in part two, chapter 7, "The Five Buddha Families and Mahamudra." As stated, they are vajra, ratna, padma, karma, and buddha. Sometimes it is confusing when he refers to the last of these. Instead of spelling out the logically complete designation, "the buddha buddha family," he usually just calls it "the buddha family."

2. The five wisdoms are the enlightened expressions of the five buddha families. See part two, chapters 6, "Introduction to Tantra," and 7, "The Five Buddha Families and Mahamudra."

3. *Shunyata* (Skt., "emptiness") refers to the key mahayana notion that all dharmas (phenomena) are devoid of any autonomous essence. See part two, chapter 4, "The Juncture between Sutra and Tantra."

4. The Vidyadhara explains these points in the next chapter.

Chapter 5. The Crazy-Wisdom Holder and the Student

1. According to tradition, the Buddha, or enlightenment itself, has three modes of existence: dharmakaya, sambhogakaya, and nirmanakaya. These correspond to mind, speech, and body. The dharmakaya (Skt., "dharma body") is unoriginated, primordial mind, devoid of concept. The sambhogakaya ("enjoyment body") is its environment of compassion and communication. The nirmanakaya ("emanation body") is its physical form. The three kayas are also sometimes understood as existential levels, represented by buddhas. The dharmakaya buddha is supreme among these.

2. The Tibetan word *chö*, which literally means "cut off" or "cut through," designates a tantric practice the main part of which is cutting through the false concepts of ego by visualizing offering one's body to demons and requesting them to devour it.

Chapter 6. Alpha Pure

1. For more on vajra pride, see part two, chapter 6, "Introduction to Tantra."

2. *Satipatthana* is a Pali word (Skt. *smriti-upasthana*) meaning "four foundations of mindfulness." Working on the four foundations is one of the fundamental meditation practices of the hinayana. The four are mindfulness of body, mindfulness of life, mindfulness of effort, and mindfulness of mind. See

Chögyam Trungpa, *The Heart of the Buddha* (Boston & London: Shambhala Publications, 1991), pp. 21–58. (Also in Volume Three of *The Collected Works*.)

3. See note 6 for part two, chapter 6.

PART TWO

Chapter 1. Suffering, Impermanence, Egolessness

1. These three qualities are traditionally referred to as the three marks of existence. They are most often listed as suffering, impermanence, and egolessness. The Vidhadhara refers to them again in the next chapter as pain, transitoriness, and nonsubstantiality.

Chapter 2. Competing with Our Projections

1. See note 6 for part one, chapter 3.

2. The Vidyadhara later decided in favor of "concept" as the best translation for the name of this fourth skandha. Some years later he revised his translation once more and ended up with "formation." He felt that "concept" was quite close to the actual process of the skandha, but "formation" was also excellent in this respect and closer to the Sanskrit *samskara*.

3. Paramita practices are discussed in the next chapter.

Chapter 3. The Dawn of Mysticism

1. Padmasambhava (fl. eighth century CE) was a great Indian teacher and saint, one of the founders of Buddhism in Tibet. For the Vidyadhara's account of this major figure, see Chögyam Trungpa, *Crazy Wisdom* (Boston & London: Shambhala Publications, 1991. Also in Volume Five of *The Collected Works*). For Milarepa, see Glossary.

2. One of the key doctrines in Buddhism concerns not falling into the two extremes of eternalism and nihilism. Eternalism is the hope or belief that something solid and permanent exists that guarantees salvation or at least some good result if we can connect with it, or various levels of failure if we cannot. Nihilism is the conviction that, since there are no solid or permanent reference points, and even cause and effect is meaningless, human effort is futile. *Madhyamaka*, which means "middle way" in Sanskrit, has the sense of a way between eternalism and nihilism, existence and non-existence.

3. One of the landmarks of entering the mahayana is taking the bodhi-

sattva vow to renounce one's own liberation from samsara in order to continue working for the liberation of all sentient beings.

4. *Paramita* is a Sanskrit word literally meaning "that which has reached the other shore."

5. It was not long after this that the Vidyadhara came up with the translation "exertion" for *virya*, with which he remained quite satisfied.

Chapter 4. The Juncture between Sutra and Tantra

1. The sutra teachings are those related to the first three yanas, which are sometimes referred to collectively as the *sutrayana* in counterdistinction to the six tantric yanas, which are sometimes known as the *tantrayana*. The sutra teachings are based on the class of scriptures of the same name, and the tantra teachings are based on the class of scriptures known as the tantras.

Chapter 5. Overcoming Moralism

1. *Bodhichitta* is a compound Sanskrit word. *Bodhi* means "awakened," and *chitta* means "mind." The term is often simply translated "enlightenment" or the "mind of enlightenment." In spite of how it sounds, "transplantation of bodhichitta into one's mind" does not refer to bringing in a foreign element from outside. It means communicating the idea of enlightenment in such a way as to awaken the natural aspiration toward it that already exists within one.

2. These are meditative techniques used in the vajrayana, which Western students, in the period these talks were given, tended to seek out as picturesque and exotic esoterica. *Pranayama* refers to various kinds of special breathing techniques. Mudras here are various hand gestures that accompany liturgical practices, though the term has other meanings (cf. the discussions of mahayana in the later talks). Visualization of deities is also dealt with in the later talks.

3. The following passage from Gampopa's *Jewel Ornament of Liberation*, translated by Herbert V. Guenther (Boston: Shambhala Publications, 1986), p. 208, might help to situate and clarify these remarks:

> The Vaibhāṣika declares: Atoms by nature are spherical, undivided, singular and exist physically. A mass of them is an object (of perception) such as colour-form and so on. When massed together, there are intervals between each one. They appear to be in one place, like a yak's tail [made up of many shifting hairs] in the pasture. They remain in a mass because they are held together by the Karma of sentient beings.

The Sautrāntika claims that when atoms mass together there are no intervals between them, although they do not touch each other.

Although these people make such statements, no proof is forthcoming. Atoms must be singular or plural. If singular they must have spatial divisions or not. If so they must have an eastern, western, southern, northern, upper, and lower part. With these six parts their claim to singularity collapses. If they have no spatial divisions, all material things would have to be of the nature of a single atom. But this clearly is not so. As is stated in the . . . 'Viṃśatikākarikā' (12):

When one atom is joined with six others
It follows that it must have six parts;
If it is in the same place with six,
The mass must be the same as one atom.

If you assume that there are many, there must have been one which by accumulation formed the mass. But since you cannot find a single atom physically, neither many atoms nor a single physical object having the nature of one can be found.

4. The *Heart Sutra* says: "Form is emptiness, emptiness is itself form; emptiness is no other than form, form is no other than emptiness."

5. Cf. note 2 for chapter 3, page 324.

6. Herbert V. Guenther (trans.), *The Life and Teaching of Naropa* (Boston & London: Shambhala Publications, 1986). Cf. also *Naropa* in Glossary.

7. See *Nagarjuna* in Glossary.

8. Herukas are male, and dakinis female, deities visualized in tantric practice as embodiments of various aspects of awakened mind. On dharmakaya, see note 1 for part one, chapter 5.

9. Guhyasamaja is one of the principal herukas of the anuttarayoga tantra.

Chapter 6. Introduction to Tantra

1. "Seed syllable" is *bija mantrar* in Sanskrit: a single syllable, usually Sanskrit, that represents the essential reality of a particular deity.

2. The Nyingma is one of the four main orders of Buddhism in Tibet. It follows the earliest tradition of vajrayana Buddhism in Tibet, that of the Old Translation school. The other three orders are Kagyü, Sakya, and Geluk, which follow the New Translation school. See part two, chapter 9, "Mahamudra and Maha Ati."

3. See *Vajrasattva* in Glossary.

4. Atisha Dipankara (980/90–1055 CE), a Buddhist scholar of royal family, was a teacher at the great Indian monastic university of Vikramashila. He

spent the last twelve years of his life in Tibet and founded the Kadampa tradition of Tibetan Buddhism, which later merged with the Kagyü and Geluk traditions.

5. A person becoming a Buddhist takes refuge in the "three jewels," the Buddha, the dharma, and the sangha (the community of Buddhist practitioners). This means surrendering all other sources of refuge, such as prestige, wealth, or other doctrines.

6. Shamatha and vipashyana are the two main modes of meditation common to all forms of Buddhism. For shamatha (Tib. *shi-ne*), see part one, chapter 2, "Hopelessness." The Sanskrit term *vipashyana* (Pali *vipassana;* Tib. *lhakthong*) means "insight" or "clear seeing." Vipashyana meditation emphasizes broad or panoramic awareness rather than focused mindfulness as in shamatha. *Trempa nyewar jokpa* is a Tibetan phrase that literally means "mindfulness or awareness that is resting closely." It refers to ongoing bare attention to every detail of the mind's activity through resting undistractedly in awareness. While this is, properly speaking, an aspect of shi-ne, it is also indispensable for the development of lhakthong.

7. See note 1 for chapter 5, on page 323.

Chapter 7. The Five Buddha Families and Mahamudra

1. This comment sounds a bit odd nowadays, but it accurately reflects tendencies of the early seventies, primarily associated with hippies but also cropping up in people of other sociological descriptions.

2. The jnanakaya is more usually referred to in this context as the *jnanasattva*, a Sanskrit term meaning "wisdom being." In the early tantric yanas, a distinction is made between the practitioner's visualization of the deity, which is known as the *samayasattva* (Skt., "commitment being"), and the janaasattva. Whereas the samayasattva is regarded as the mere product of the practitioner's psychology, the jnanasattva, which descends upon the samayasattva and empowers it, is considered to be the very reality of the deity.

3. Yogi Bhajan is a Sikh spiritual teacher who has a large following in America.

4. A yidam is a deity that a practitioner especially practices visualizing and identifying with, one that corresponds to his or her psychological makeup or basic nature.

Chapter 8. Anuttarayoga

1. The word *vajra* has more than one meaning. Its principal sense is "indestructible" or "adamantine," as in the terms *vajrayana, vajra hell, vajra*

pride. It is also used in this sense as an adjective in terms that are not fixed, such as here, in "vajra truth." Something is indestructible in this sense because it is self-existing; that is, it exists (and nonexists) beyond the play of duality. In the next talk, the Vidyadhara contrasts this sense of the word with the notion of "divine." In another sense that we encounter in this book, the term is applied as the name of one of the five buddha families.

2. *Samaya shila* is a Sanskrit term. *Samaya* refers to a sworn bond of mutual commitment between guru and disciple. The disciple is solemnly committed to the discipline *(shila)* of maintaining and further cultivating this bond with the guru, who represents the principle of totally awakened mind, or enlightenment.

3. Hevajra is one of the major heruka principles in the anuttarayoga tantra.

Chapter 9. Mahamudra and Maha Ati

1. According to the later tradition of Buddhism in Tibet, the tradition of the New Translation school, only four yanas make up the vajrayana. According to the older tradition, that of the Old Translation school, there are six yanas making up the vajrayana.

In the latter view, the anuttarayogayana does not strictly count as a yana. The first three yanas are kriyayogayana, upayogayana, and yogayana. These are referred to as the lower tantras. The last three yanas are mahayogayana, anuyogayana, and atiyogayana (or maha ati, as Vidyadhara Trungpa Rinpoche preferred to call it). These are referred to as the higher tantras.

Sometimes also, in the older tradition, these last three higher tantras are collectively called the anuttarayogayana. This use of the same name does not, however, make the content of the higher tantras the same as that of the anuttarayogayana, according to the New Translation school. The anuttarayogayana in the tradition of the New Translation school contains, among others, the great tantras of *Kalachakra, Vajrayogini, Hevajra, Mahamaya, Chakrasamvara, Guhyasamaja.* It is most especially these that the Vidyadhara has in mind when he associates the tantras of the New Translation school with mahamudra.

The Vidyadhara's exposition, although favoring the total of nine yanas and laying great weight on the final three, approaches a fusion of the older and later traditions.

2. For Naropa and Marpa, see Glossary. Virupa was one of the eighty-four Indian mahasiddhas, "great possessors of powers," famous for his miracles, including consuming immense quantities of wine.

3. Kalachakra (Skt., "wheel of time") is one of the main herukas of the anuttarayogayana tantra.

THE DAWN OF TANTRA

HERBERT V. GUENTHER
and CHÖGYAM TRUNGPA

Edited by SHERAB CHÖDZIN KOHN

Illustrated by GLEN EDDY
and TERRIS TEMPLE

Introduction

WESTERNERS WANTING to know about tantra, particularly the Buddhist tantra of Tibet, have had to work with speculation and fancy. Tibet has been shrouded in mystery; "tantra" has been called upon to name every kind of esoteric fantasy; Buddhism has been left either vague or inaccessible. Academic treatments have been of little help, being in the main inaccurate or remote, failing either to comprehend or to convey.

In *The Dawn of Tantra* the reader meets a Tibetan and a Westerner whose grasp of Buddhist tantra is real and unquestionable. Dr. Guenther holds Ph.D. degrees from the Universities of Munich and Vienna. In 1950, he went to India to teach at Lucknow University and, in 1958, became Head of the Department of Comparative Philosophy and Buddhist Studies at the Sanskrit University in Varanasi. Since 1964, he has been Head of the Department of Far Eastern Studies at the University of Saskatchewan in Canada. Because of his tremendous intellectual energy and scholarly discipline, knowledge of Tibetan, Sanskrit, and Chinese, and his years of collaboration with native Tibetans, he has become one of the few Westerners to penetrate to a deeper understanding of Tibetan tantric texts. His books, such as *The Life and Teaching of Naropa* and the *Tantric View of Life,* bring us nearly the only accurate translations and commentaries from the Tibetan Buddhist tradition.

Chögyam Trungpa was born in the heart of the Buddhist tantra tradition. As the eleventh incarnation of the Trungpa line of spiritual teachers, he was enthroned at the age of eighteen months as abbot of a group of monasteries in eastern Tibet. Beginning at three, he underwent intensive training in the intellectual and meditative disciplines of Buddhism. He had completely assumed his responsibilities, both spiritual and temporal, by the age of fourteen and went on to become a master of tantric Buddhist meditation. His journey toward the West began in 1959 when he fled the Chinese Communist invasion of Tibet. He first experienced the modern world in India, where he spent four years studying English. Since then he has traversed the West. He studied comparative religion at Oxford and founded a meditation center in Scotland. He arrived in the United States in 1970, where he has published several books, among them *Cutting Through Spiritual Materialism,* founded a number of meditation centers, a community working in art and theater, and another for helping the mentally disturbed, based on tantric principles. He has not remained cloistered, but has fully and frankly encountered the Western mind on the learned and gut levels. He has mastered English to the level of poetry.

Having worked toward each other, so to speak, for years, Dr. Guenther and Chögyam Trungpa met in Berkeley, California, in 1972, where together they gave a public seminar on Buddhist tantra. *Dawn of Tantra* is the edited record of that seminar, including part of the general discussion. The "Visualization" chapter is from a seminar given by Trungpa in San Francisco in 1973. The "Empowerment and Initiation" chapter is from a talk given by Dr. Guenther when he visited Trungpa's meditation center in Boulder, Colorado, in 1973. Dr. Guenther has also since lectured at Naropa Institute, a university founded by Trungpa in Boulder, Colorado.

Guenther and Trungpa are an interface very much alive to the Tibetan tradition of Buddhist tantra and very much alive to the current everyday world of America. They communicate warmly and freely in both directions and give no quarter to wishful thinking.

SHERAB CHÖDZIN KOHN

ONE

Tantra

Its Origin and Presentation

THE TERM *TANTRA*, from the time of its first appearance in the West up to the present day, has been subject to serious misunderstandings. The term was introduced into the English language in 1799 when tantric works were discovered by missionaries in India. These were not Buddhist works. In fact at that time it was hardly known in the West that such a thing as Buddhism existed. The term *tantra* was then known only as the title of these works, the contents of which were quite different from what people expected in books dealing with philosophy and religion. The missionaries were for the most part quite shocked that other people had religious and philosophical ideas so different from their own. To them the word *tantra* meant no more than these expanded treatises; but since the subject matter dealt with in these treatises was so unusual from their point of view, the term began to acquire quite a peculiar connotation, a connotation which proper study of the texts has not borne out. Unfortunately, in this case as in so many others, once a false conception has been formed, a nearly superhuman effort is required to root out and set right all the wrong ideas and odd connotations that have grown up around it. I am going to try to tell you what the term *tantra* actually means in a technical sense.

First of all, one must distinguish between the tantra of the Hinduist tradition and the tantra of the Buddhist tradition. These two traditions, both indigenous to India, for a long period of time used the same

333

Padmasambhava (foreground) *and dGa'-Rab-rDorje* (background).
DRAWING BY GLEN EDDY.

language—Sanskrit. But each tradition stipulated particular uses for its terms. What one tradition understood by a specific term was not necessarily what the other tradition understood by it. When Buddhist studies originated in the West, which was only comparatively recently, it was assumed by the first investigators that since the Buddhists used the same Sanskrit terms as the Hindus, they would mean the same thing by them. This was the first of many wrong conclusions that they drew.

Let us apply ourselves to an understanding of tantra as it developed in the Buddhist tradition. A term that has been used from the beginning in close association with the term *tantra* is the Sanskrit *prabandha*. Prabandha means continuity. This is a continuity of being, which divides into two grounds: we have to start somewhere, and then go a certain way (and perhaps arrive at a goal). This is the way tantra was presented. It refers to an immediate human situation which arises out of the question of how we are going to *be*. Tantra also sees the question of how we are going to be in terms of relationship, realizing that man is always related to something or someone.

Tantra approaches the question of being in various ways; thus there is more than one presentation of it. The first approach is called *kriyatantra*. In the kriyatantra the emphasis is on how a person acts. *Kriya* means "action." Action is here seen symbolically and dealt with in terms of ritual. We need not be mystified by the idea of ritual. An example of ritual is the custom of a man's removing his hat when he meets a lady. It is a kind of formalized gesture. It is also a way of going about a human relationship. The emphasis in the kriyatantra is on relationship as expressed in this kind of formalized gesture. In this case the emphasis is far-reaching and covers many aspects of relationship. The kriyatantra is further particularized in its approach to human relationship in that it deals with the simplest and earliest stages of it.

The earliest form of relationship is that of a child with his parents. There is a kind of dominance involved here. Someone has to tell the child what and what not to do. When this relational situation is transferred into a religious context it becomes the idea that man is subject to a transcendental entity. This is perhaps the generally accepted idea and it is also the framework in the kriyatantra. Here the practitioner tries to gain favor with the one with whom he is interrelated. This and the strong ritualistic emphasis are two main characteristics of the kriyatantra. This tantra also stresses purification. The ritual includes various ablutions. Some of them are purely symbolic in importance, and perhaps the sense of cleanliness involved might seem somewhat exaggerated. We must realize, however, that the sense of being clean can become extremely important in an emotional context such as this one. It has a much more profound significance than in ordinary circumstances when someone says: "Now before you eat, wash your hands." So this emphasis on purity is another characteristic of kriyatantra.

But man is not content with merely being told what to do. He is also a thinking being and will ask questions. And here is where a further approach to tantra, known as the charyatantra comes in. Again here, tantra refers to a relational situation. But here the emphasis has shifted. We are no longer only concerned with following certain accepted rules of relationship, but also to a certain extent with understanding the implications of them. This marks the entry of a certain questioning of ourselves. Why are we doing these things? Why do we behave in such-and-such a way? Certainly we do not discard our behavior at this point, but we ask about its significance. And this we do by thinking more about it. We try to gain insight into it and this can be a kind of meditation.

Here there begins to be a balance between thought and action. This change from the previous mere acceptance of authority corresponds to a change in the character of our relationship with the one to whom we are relating. It is no longer a question of a master telling his servant or slave what to do. There is now more of a feeling of intimacy, of comradeship, more of an equal status. The one is still willing to learn, but the other now realizes that he is in the same situation as the first. It is a relationship of friendship and friendship can only be based on an acceptance of the other person in his or her own right. Servitude makes friendship impossible.

But friendship can be developed still further than this first intimacy. Friendship often entails our trying to find out more bout the relationship. What is valuable about this relationship that compels us to cultivate it? This questioning process leads to the further development of insight. The emphasis has shifted again. This new aspect of the total situation of how we are together brings us into the yogatantra.

The term *yoga* has many meanings. In the Buddhist context, it means "to harness." It is etymologically related to the English word yoke. It means to harness everything in us in order to gain more insight. Thus the situation, the tantra, in which this is the emphasis is called the yoga-tantra. Here there is a teamwork which is even better than that between two friends. But there is still room for further development because we still consider the other slightly different from ourselves. This is where the fourth division, the mahayogatantra, comes in.

Maha basically means "great," but here it is used not so much to mean great as opposed to small, but with the sense that there could be nothing greater. It is used in an absolute sense. The mahayogatantra partakes of this sense of absoluteness in its approach to the situation of relationship. We no longer make any distinctions; we just are, spontaneous, free. The question of whether or not the other is my friend no longer arises. There is a complete unity—we are just one.

So there is a progression in the tantras, beginning from the level of a child related to its parents and developing to the level of complete maturity. Thus when we use the term *tantra,* we not only refer to a particular situation, but we also describe a process of growth, a process of inner development which takes place when we try to understand what there is. This process goes on until we come to the proper assessment of experience, the proper way of seeing. There is a dialectical relationship between action, the way in which we behave, and the insight we have attained. The more we know, the more we learn about another person, the more responsive we become to that person. We begin to realize what he needs and stop imposing the idea of what we think he should need. We begin to be able to help that person find his own way.

This leads us to the practical significance of tantra. Tantra, as a way of inner growth, makes us see more, so that we really become individuals rather than mere entities in an amorphous context. But tantra goes still further. It goes beyond the idea of a growth or a progress. There are further stages and subdivisions within the tradition, which deal with the fact that even after we have learned to relate properly to our problems, life still goes on. The idea here is that spiritual practice is a continual movement. It is only from the point of view of discursive thought that we begin somewhere, progress or develop, and then reach a certain goal. It is not as though, having found enlightenment, the process is completed and everything comes to an end. Rather, the fact is that we continue to live, so we must continually start anew. Nevertheless, through the previous stages, we have found a way, a way of relating, a certain continuity. This continuity of a way of relating is the basic meaning of tantra. In a sense this is an extremely simple point. In general, however, we find that there is scarcely anything more difficult than this kind of simplicity.

TWO

Laying the Foundation

Professor Guenther and I decided that the best way for us to approach the subject of tantra together is for him to deal with the prajna or knowledge aspect of it and for me to deal with the upaya, the skillful means or actual application aspect of it.

From the practical side then, the basic idea of tantra is, like any other teaching of Buddhism, the attainment of enlightenment. But in tantra the approach to enlightenment is somewhat different. Rather than aiming at the attainment of the enlightened state, the tantric approach is to see the continuity of enlightened mind in all situations, as well as the constant discontinuity of it.

Experience on the tantric level corresponds to the utmost and most complete state of being that can be attained. On the other hand, tantra is not a question of attainment, but rather the actual work of relating to situations properly.

All kinds of emphasis have been laid on the various colorful attributes of tantra. One speaks of its ten special aspects. There is the sadhana, that is, the method or practice; there are the practices of meditation; there is the realization of one's innate nature through identifying with various deities; and so on. The basic nature of tantra can be defined in terms of ten such ways in which it differs from sutra teachings.

The tantric teaching is divided into the three categories of dharmakaya, sambhogakaya, and nirmanakaya. All tantric teachings have these three aspects. The teaching of tantra in terms of the three kayas can also be related to the three main vehicles of Buddhism. The nirmanakaya aspect of tantra is associated with the hinayana, the way of monastic discipline. The sambhogakaya aspect of tantra could be said to be its mahayana aspect; it is concerned with various yogic practices dealing with prana, bindu, nadis, and so on. The dharmakaya or vajrayana aspect of tantra is concerned with pure being or suchness. In Tibetan this is referred to as *de kho na nyid,* "that which is, that which just simply is." This is the ultimate aspect of the tantric teaching. Nevertheless, the basic quality of continuity continues even beyond this.

The Tibetan names for sutra and tantra give some insight into the difference between the two kinds of teaching. The Tibetan for "sutra" is *mdo,* which means "confluence" or "junction." It is a point where things can meet, coincide, conclude together. Most simply, it is the place where the teachings can come together with the problems of everyday life. Take the conclusions of the four noble truths: suffering, the origin of suffering, the cessation of suffering, and the path. These are conclusions that coincide with all kinds of human conflicts of mind. Tantra, as we know, means "continuity," which is something more than just junction. From the tantric viewpoint, the junction of the sutras is not important. Junction is just the sparkling experience of insight, a sudden glimpse of something that comes together because two aspects of all experience suddenly are in a chaotic relationship from the point of view of the ordinary ego-oriented setup. Hate and love, to take the example of emotions, come together. The solidity of hate, which depends on ego's setup, encounters the ego quality of love. Suddenly, both hate and love are there together and suddenly love does not exist and hate does not exist. The ego ground of the situation is exploded. So aspects of the situation come together and there is a flow. At the moment of coming together, there is an explosion, which is actually the discovery of truth.

Tantra does not lay strong emphasis on this moment of the discovery of truth, because it is not so interested in truth as opposed to confusion. Rather the principle of tantra is the continuity which runs through both truth and confusion. In Tibetan, tantra is called *rgyud,* which is like the thread which runs through beads. It continues from the beginning through the middle and the end. One speaks of the basic ground of tantra as continuity, the continuity as the path of tantra, and the continuity as the fruition of tantra. So tantra starts at the beginning, continues on the path, and ends at the goal or fruition. But it does not exactly end at that point. In terms of the practice, it ends; in terms of attainment, it does not end. There is still the play of what is called buddha activity. The general picture is that you attain the experiences first of nirmanakaya, then sambhogakaya, then dharmakaya. Then having mastered the ultimate experiences, buddha activity begins and you work back down from dharmakaya to sambhogakaya to nirmanakaya. Having achieved the peak experiences, you come back down in order to relate with sentient beings, people who are confused, relate with them through speech or through body or whatever may be appropriate. You speak the same language as they do. So tantra goes beyond the fruition level.

In the tantric tradition, ego or confusion or ignorance is personified as Rudra. All the tantric traditions of Buddhism are concerned with the taming of Rudra, the Rudra of ego. The Rudra principle is divided, especially in the atiyoga tradition, into the ego of the body, the ego of the speech, and the ego of the mind. This means the fixation or appropriation of the elements of body, speech, and mind by the ego in relation to its security or expansion. In speaking of the fixation of the body, we are not referring to purely physical attachment—lust, let's say—as a purely physical matter. We are talking about the mind-body situation, the body aspect of our mind, the solidity aspect of it which needs constant feeding, reinforcement. It needs continual reassurance that it is solid. That is the Rudra of the body.

The Rudra of speech is the fixation of the element which is related with both the body and the mind but at the same time is uncertain which. This is a fickleness or wavering quality, uncertain whether one's foundation is the fixed aspect of the body—the physical level of the textures and colors of life—or perhaps the emotional situation of whether to love or to hate. This uncertain wavering back and forth, this fickleness quality, is speech (or mantra, if you prefer), the voice. The fixation of this is the Rudra of speech.

The Rudra of mind is fundamentally believing that, if a higher state of spiritual development is to be attained, it has to be manufactured rather than uncovered. Rangjung Dorje, a great teacher of the Kagyü tradition, in his commentary on the *Hevajra Tantra,* says that the ultimate materialism is believing that buddha nature can be manufactured by mental effort, spiritual gymnastics. So that is psychological and spiritual materialism—the Rudra of the mind.

These three principles—the fixation and solidification of the security of the body; the fixation on the emotional level of being uncertain but still hanging on to something; the fixation on the mental level of believing in some ultimate savior principle, some principle outside one's own nature that, so to speak, can do the trick—these three principles of Rudra constitute one of the prime occupations of tantra, which is concerned with overcoming them.

The three Rudra principles also correspond to the threefold division of tantra. At the beginning, in order to relate to the Rudra of body, the student must begin tantric study on the hinayana level. This includes practices such as the satipatthana practices, which the hinayana developed for training the mind. These practices concentrate on breathing, walking, and other bodily movements. They simplify the basic nature of solidity. This can be understood if we realize that this kind of solidifying by the ego of its space is based on an attitude which trusts complexity. It places its trust on very complicated answers, complicated logic. Satipatthana is a way of simplifying the logical mind, which is body in this case, because it relates to something very solid and definite. The logical mind attempts to fixate, hold onto, grasp and thus is continually projecting something definite and solid. So the basic hinayana practice of simplifying every activity of the mind into just breathing or bodily movement reduces the intensity of the Rudra of body. It does not particularly transcend it or free one from it, but at least it reduces the intensity of it.

The next stage, dealing with the Rudra of speech, is on the sambhogakaya level. All kinds of practices have developed for this in the Tibetan tradition. Notably, there is what is known as the four foundation practices: one hundred thousand prostrations, one hundred thousand repetitions of the refuge formula, one hundred thousand repetitions of the hundred-syllable Vajrasattva mantra, and one hundred thousand offerings of one's body, speech, and mind as the whole universe. These preliminary tantric practices on the sambhogakaya level are related with prana, nadis, and bindu. They are based on making use of the speed, the movement, the rhythm of confused mind. At the same time, there is something very unconfused about these practices. One cannot go through them all without relating to the true nature of body, speech, and mind. They occupy a sort of intermediary place between confusion and clarity. And the basic continuity principle of tantra underlies the whole thing.

Having gone through the satipatthana of the hinayana or nirmanakaya level (which includes the samatha and vipassana practices), having completed the four foundation practices on the mahayana or sambhoga-kaya level, the student is now just ready to have a glimpse of the guru, of real relationship and practice with the guru, real commitment to the guru. This is where the guru yoga practice for attaining union with the guru comes in. When that has been completed, then comes what is called *abhisheka,* which could be translated as "initiation" or "confirmation." This is the entry to the dharmakaya level.

There are four levels of abhisheka and all take place within a realm of space in which the student and teacher meet in some basic understanding. This understanding is the result of the previous practices. The student has related to his body, learned to slow down the speed of muscles, veins, emotions, blood. Circulations of all kinds have been slowed down altogether. Now the student is finally able to relate to the ultimate space through his relationship and union with the teacher. In the Zen tradition this is known as transmission. It seems to be the same meeting of two minds as is found in tantra.

We can see from this brief look that the practice of tantra is not easy. The student has to begin at the beginning. He has to acquire an understanding of the principle of taming the mind. Understanding of the Rudra principle brings egolessness or Rudra-lessness. He has to get to know his own bodily situation through the preliminary tantric practices. Then he can achieve the final surrendering through abhisheka. Looked at as a whole, the practice of tantra is like building a house. First you put down the foundation, then you build the first story, then the second. Then you can put a gold roof on it if you like. We have looked at the sutra or hinayana aspect within tantra, the mahayana aspect within tantra, then the final subtleties of tantra within itself. Looked at in this way, the whole of the practice of Buddhism can be regarded as tantra, although all Buddhists outside the historical tradition of tantra might not agree with this.

THREE

Yogachara and the Primacy of Experience

THE IDEA OF TANTRA as continuity connects this inquiry with the philosophy of the Yogachara since this early Indian school of Buddhist philosophy was instrumental in developing the idea of tantra.

The Yogachara school was so named because its philosophy leads to application, working on oneself—yoga, harnessing. It has been called by various names in the West, one of the most common (also known in Japan) being *chittamatra,* which is usually translated "mind only." Now the word *mind* is very nebulous in meaning, different people understanding different things by it. Let us try to understand how the Yogachara school understood this term.

The Yogachara system is not, strictly speaking, a single system, but embraces a number of philosophical trends which are in certain ways quite distinct from one another. They are lumped together under this title in virtue of the main tenet which they hold in common: the idea that all the three worlds (the world of sensuousness, the world of form, the world of formlessness) are chittamatra, mind only.

The word *chitta* (mind), from early times was used to mean, not so much a container of thoughts, as perhaps we tend to understand it, but rather something like a clearinghouse that could both store and transmit impressions. It was thought of as something like a battery. It could be charged and then when it was charged it would do something. It had this double function which must be borne in mind if we wish to understand the idea of chittamatra. In the first place, since the concept of chitta revolves around the storing and transmission of experience, it would be more precise to translate the idea of chittamatra as "experience alone counts."

Buddhism has always placed great emphasis on experience. The four basic axioms of Buddhism are highly experiential in character. The first is that everything is transitory; the second that everything is frustrating; the third that everything is without essence; the fourth that nirvana is bliss. These first three axioms relate very much to our actual way of going through life. We observe life and see that nothing lasts; we feel that being faced with trying to build something on this basis is very frustrating. Then we think and we ask ourselves, "How is this? Why is this?" We get the answer that if everything is transitory it cannot have an essence; because an essence is by definition the principle by which something is what it is. If we started reasoning from the idea of an essence, we could not account for transitoriness, nor could we account for the constant frustration which we experience.

Now the continual frustration makes us feel that some other mode of being must be possible. This is where we come to the fourth basic axiom, which says that nirvana is bliss. Buddha's disciple Ananda asked him how he could make such a statement, having said that feelings and all such forms are transitory. The Buddha replied that he had qualified nirvana as bliss only by way of language, that he did not thereby mean a judgment of feeling, such as when we call something pleasant. The term he used for bliss was *sukha,* which is very close to what we have referred to as the peak experience. This seems to be an experience in which all conceptions and judgments, even the idea of oneself, completely pass away. So what is referred to as bliss can be understood to transcend transitoriness or permanence or any other form. In later Buddhist philosophical systems, especially the tantra, we find that further developments concerning this state have taken place to the point where even the last trace of experience as such has disappeared. Even the possibility of saying, "I had thus-and-such an experience" has evaporated. This view was developed directly from the idea of the Yogacharins that "experience alone counts."

But the question still remains of how it comes about that we are always in the realm of frustration. Also, how can we understand the fact that our sense of continual frustration leads us to feel that there is some other mode of experience which gets rid of this frustration? To see the answers to these questions, we must go still further in our understanding of the term *chitta*.

The Yogacharins developed an understanding of chitta involving eight aspects. What they were actually trying to do was to describe the process in which chitta emerges from its primordial, unqualified, and unconditioned state and glides into our ordinary way of thinking. If we understood this process thoroughly, we would be able to do away with it and let our minds remain in the primordial state. This would be the peak experience.

In describing this process, the Yogacharins used the concept of the alayavijnana, a concept which has been used differently by different Buddhist schools and which is very important in the tantric tradition. The alayavijnana is already different from the alaya or basic foundation. The latter we assume for the purposes of communication, without affirming that it is an ontological entity. The alayavijnana is already a trend developing into the split we usually describe as subject and object. We see here that the chitta is a dynamic factor rather than a static conception. In the function of the alayavijnana it is in constant transformation, developing into further dualistic forms.

Here we can see the influence of the old conception of chitta as something which stores something up and, once this storage has reached its high point, must be discharged. This idea of stored potentialities of experience that must at some point be actualized is constantly present in Buddhist philosophy. The precise forms which cause the alayavijnana to function in this way are called vasanas. These are deposits that are potentialities. They develop according to two principles, the one a principle of intrinsic similarity, the other a principle of taking on various specific forms in accordance with conditions. For instance, a scientist, by way of experience, might take some kidney cells and plant them on some other part of the body, say an arm. They will not develop as skin cells, but will continue to develop as kidney cells. This is the first principle. But the way in which these kidney cells develop as kidney cells will vary according to a multiplicity of conditions. Some people have kidney trouble and others do not. This illustrates the second principle.

As we have said, what develops in the course of the transformation of chitta is a split. As the initial step in the genesis of experience from the process known as the alayavijnana, there develops something else, which is known as *manas* in Sanskrit and *yid* in Tibetan. This aspect of chitta now looks back and takes the original unity out of which it developed as its real self. This original unity is what is taken as an ontologically real self by the Hindus.

The Hindus described the original unity as the transcendental ego and the manas as the empirical ego. The Buddhists rejected the reification of these aspects, having seen that they all belonged to the unity of a transformational process. According to the Yogachara, the split that occurs merely contrasts a limited form with a vital primordial form. The manas or yid then becomes the source of all subsequent mental functions in the way indicated by common speech when we say "I see" or "I think." But all these mental functions are part of the total process of transformation.

According to the Yogachara view, the original source (the alaya-vijnana) is undifferentiated and ethically or karmically neutral. When the split occurs it becomes tainted, but still the particular mental movement in question is not determined as ethically positive or negative. This determination takes place through elaborations of the movement which further specify it. This elaboration takes the form of our perceiving with the five senses, and also with the traditional Buddhist sixth sense, which we might loosely call consciousness; that is, the categorical perception which brings categories into sense data without abstracting them from it. Thus the alayavijnana, the manas, and the six senses are the eight aspects of chitta.

This process of transformation we have described is one of growing narrowness and frozenness. We are somehow tied down to our senses, to the ordinary mode of perception. We dimly feel that something else might have been possible. If we try to express this situation in traditional religious terms, we might say that man is a fallen being. But here he has not fallen because he has sinned or transgressed some commandment coming from outside him, but by the very fact that he has moved in a certain direction. This is technically known in Buddhism as *bhranti* in Sanskrit or *'khrul pa* in Tibetan, and is usually translated as "error." But error implies, in Western thinking, culpability; and there is absolutely no culpability involved. We might tend to feel that we could have done otherwise, but this attitude simply does not apply here. The process is a kind of going astray which just happens. The idea of sin is irrelevant.

Still we have the feeling of something gone wrong. If we accept our ordinary experience as error, then we ask the question "Is true knowledge possible?" Now the very question already implies that it is possible. That is to say, the sense of error implies the sense of truth. We could not know error without unerring knowledge. So there is this oscillation back and forth between error and knowledge; and this oscillation presents the possibility of returning to what we have referred to as the original or primordial state.

Here original does not have the sense of "beginning." We speak of it as the original state because we feel that our charge of creative power came from there. We experienced an energy which we felt to be of the highest value, quite distinct from the tone of our ordinary experience. The existential apprehension of this original state is technically known in the tantric tradition as the mahasukhakaya.

In the ordinary Buddhist tradition three is the nirmanakaya, sambhogakaya, and dharmakaya. Then if it is wished to emphasize the unity of the three and avoid any tendency to concretize them as separate, we speak of the whole as the svabhavikakaya. This is not a fourth kaya, but the unity of the three. The mahasukhakaya is a significant addition to this picture which came in with tantra. *Sukha* means "bliss"; *maha* means "than which there could be none greater." So we have the peak experience again; and this is always felt as being, which gives kaya.

Kaya is translated as "body," but not in the sense of the purely physical abstraction which is often made in defining "body," where we say that one thing is the mental aspect of us and the other thing is the physical aspect. This is a misconception. There is no such thing as a body without a mind. If we have a body without a mind, it is not a body, it is a corpse. It is a mere object to be disposed of. If we speak properly of a body, we mean something which is alive; and we cannot have a live body without a mind. So the two cannot be separated—they go together.

Thus the mahasukhakaya is an existential factor, which is of the highest value. This is not an arbitrary assignment of value that is made here. It is just felt that this is the only absolute value. This absolute value can be retrieved by reversing the process of error, of going astray; by reverting the energy that flows in one direction and becomes frozen, less active. It is this process of freezing which causes us to feel imprisoned and tied down. We are no longer free agents, as it were, but are in samsara.

So in answer to the question of whether or not there is some alternative to the continual frustration in which we live, the answer is yes. Let us find the initial, original, primordial, or whatever word you want to use—language is so limited—as a value. This is the mahasukhakaya.

The possibility of returning to the origin has been rendered manifest in the form of certain symbols of transformation, such as the mandala. Transformation from ordinary perception to primordial intrinsic awareness can take place when we try to see things differently, perhaps somewhat as an artist does. Every artist knows that he can see in two different ways. The ordinary way is characterized by the fact that perception is always related to accomplishing some end other than the perception itself. It is treated as a means rather than something in itself. But we can also look at things and enjoy their presence aesthetically.

If we look at a beautiful sunset, we can look at it as a physicist does and see it as a system of wavelengths. We lose the feeling of it completely. We can also look at it as a poignant symbol of the impermanence of all things and be moved to sadness. But this also is not just the sunset itself. There is a definite difference when we just look at it as it is and enjoy the vast play of colors that is there in tremendous vividness. When we look like this, we will immediately notice how free we become. The entire network of mental factors in which we usually labor just drops off. Everyone can do this but, of course, it requires work.

The art of the mandala has been developed to help us see things in their intrinsic vividness. Although all mandalas are fundamentally similar, each is also unique. The colors used in them, for instance, vary greatly according to the basic makeup of the practitioners. The character of a particular mandala is known as the dhatu-tathagatagarbha. *Dhatu* here refers to the factor of the particular individual makeup. *Tathagatagarbha* refers to the awakened state of mind or buddhahood. So a particular mandala could be seen as a specific index of the awakened state of mind. Care is taken to relate to individual characteristics because, although each person is capable of total buddhahood, he must start from the aspect of it that is most strongly present in him.

There is a Zen saying that even a blade of grass can become a Buddha. How are we to understand this? Usually we consider that a blade of grass simply belongs to the physical world; it is not even a sentient being, since it has no feelings, makes no judgments, has no perceptions. The explanation is that everything is of the nature of Buddha, so grass is also of this nature. It is not that it in some way contains buddha nature, that we can nibble away analytically at the various attributes of the blade of grass until there is nothing left but some vague leftover factor that we then pigeonhole as buddha nature. Rather, the blade of grass actually constitutes what we call buddhahood or an ultimate value.

It is in this sense that a blade of grass or any other object can be a symbol of transformation. The whole idea of symbols of transformation is made possible by the philosophical development of the Yogacharins, who saw that what comes to us in earthly vessels, as it were, the elements of our ordinary experience, *is* the fundamental mind, the ultimate value. The ultimate value comes in forms intelligible to us. Thus certain symbols such as mandalas, already partially intelligible to us, can be used as gateways to the peak experience.

So these symbols exist, differing according to the needs of individuals. We can slip into the world of running around in circles—that is what *samsara* literally means—or we can also, through such symbols, find our way out of it. But the way out is nowhere else but in the world where we are. There is no other world besides the world we live in. This is one of the main purports of Buddhist philosophy and one which Westerners often find hard to grasp. Buddhist philosophy does not make the distinction between the phenomenal and the noumenal. The phenomenon is the noumenon and the noumenon is the phenomenon; not in the sense of mathematical equation, but in the sense that you cannot have one without the other. The technical statement of this is that there is appearance and there is also shunyata; but shunyata is not somewhere else, it is in the appearance. It is its open dimension. The appearance never really implies any restriction or limitation. If there were such a limitation, we could never get out of it.

FOUR

The Mandala Principle and
the Meditative Process

TANTRA CANNOT BE understood apart from experience arising out
of the practice of meditation. Tantra, as we have said, can be regarded as the golden roof of the house. Before we can put on a roof, we
have first to have built a house, and before that even, to have laid a
foundation. I have already mentioned the four foundation practices. But
such practices by themselves are not enough; we have to do the basic
work of relating to ourselves. The work we must do to have a complete
understanding of the symbolism of tantra and of the mandala principle
begins at a very rudimentary level.

A mandala consists of a center and the fringe area of a circle. On
the basic level, it consists of the practitioner and his relationship to the
phenomenal world. The study of the mandala principle is that of the
student in his life situation.

In a sense spiritual practice in Buddhism in the beginning stages could
be said to be very intellectual. It is intellectual in the sense of being precise. It could also be seen as intellectual because of the nature of the
dialogue which has to take place between the student and the teacher,
the student and the teaching. A certain questioning process has to take
place. It is not a matter of memorizing texts or merely applying a variety
of techniques. Rather it is necessary that situations be created in which
the student can relate to himself as a potential Buddha, as a dharma-
body—he relates his whole psyche or whole makeup to the dharma. He
must begin with a precise study of himself and his situation.

Marpa (foreground) *and Two-Armed Hevajra* (background).
DRAWING BY TERRIS TEMPLE.

Traditionally there are twelve types of teaching styles proper to a Buddha. The sutras can be divided into twelve categories according to which of the twelve styles the Buddha has employed in it. One of the twelve styles is that of creating a situation in which the teaching can transpire. Take the example of the *Prajnaparamita-hridaya* or *Heart Sutra*. In the original Sanskrit version of this sutra, Buddha does not say a word; but it was Buddha who created the dialogue between Avalokiteshvara and Shariputra. Buddha created the situation in which Shariputra could act as the receiver or audience and Avalokiteshvara as the propounder of the analysis.

So creating the situation in which the student can relate to the teaching is the initial creation of the mandala principle. There is the hungry questioning, the thirsty mind which examines all possibilities. The questions are inspired by the basic suffering of the student's situation, the basic chaos of it. It is uncertainty, dissatisfaction, which brings out the questions.

Seen in the tantric perspective, the first stages of the creation of the mandala principle are the basic Buddhist practices on the hinayana level. The starting point is samatha practice, which is the development of peace or dwelling on peace. This practice does not, however, involve dwelling or fixing one's attention on a particular thing. Fixation or concentration tends to develop trancelike states. But from the Buddhist point of view, the point of meditation is not to develop trancelike states; rather it is to sharpen perceptions, to see things as they are. Meditation at this level is relating with the conflicts of our life situations, like using a stone to sharpen a knife, the situation being the stone. The samatha meditation, the beginning point of the practice, could be described as sharpening one's knife. It is a way of relating to bodily sensations and thought processes of all kinds; just relating with them rather than dwelling on them or fixing on them in any way.

Dwelling or fixing comes from an attitude of trying to prove something, trying to maintain the "me" and "my" of ego's territory. One needs to prove that ego's thesis is secure. This is an attempt to ignore the samsaric circle, the samsaric whirlpool. This vicious circle is too painful a truth to accept, so one is seeking something else to replace it with. One seeks to replace the basic irritation or pain with the pleasure of a fixed belief in oneself by dwelling on something, a certain spiritual effort or just worldly things. It seems that, as something to be dwelled on, conceptualized ideas of religion or spiritual teachings or the domestic situations of life are extensions of the ego. One does not simply see tables and chairs as they are; one sees my manifestation of table, my manifestation of chair. One sees constantly the "me" or "my" in these things; they are seen constantly in relationship to me and my security.

It is in relation to this world of my projections that the precision of samatha is extremely powerful. It is a kind of scientific research, relating to the experiences of life as substances and putting them under the microscope of meditative practice. One does not dwell on them, one examines them, works with them. Here the curiosity of one's mind acts as potential prajna, potential transcendental knowledge. The attitude of this practice is not one of seeking to attain nirvana, but rather of seeing the mechanism of samsara, how it works, how it relates to us. At the point of having seen the complete picture of samsara, of having completely understood its mechanism, nirvana becomes redundant. In what is called the enlightened state, both samsara and nirvana are freed.

In order to see thought processes (sensations and perceptions that occur during the practice of samatha) as they are, a certain sense of openness and precision has to be developed. This precise study of what we are, what our makeup is, is closely related with the practice of tantra. In the tantric tradition it is said that the discovery of the vajra body—that is, the innate nature of vajra (indestructible being)—within one's physical system and within one's psychological system is the ultimate experience. In the samatha practice of the hinayana tradition, there is also this element of looking for one's basic innate nature as it is, simply and precisely, without being concerned over the absence of "me" and "my."

From the basis of the samatha practice, the student next develops what is known as vipassana practice. This is the practice of insight, seeing clearly, seeing absolutely, precisely—transcendental insight. One begins to realize that spending one's whole time on the details of life, as in the samatha practice, does not work. It is still somehow an adolescent approach. It is necessary to begin to have a sense of the totality. This is an expansion process. It is parallel with the tantric practice of the mandala. Having started with what is called the bija mantra, the seed syllable in the middle of the mandala, there is then the expanding process of discovering the four quarters of the mandala. Working with the seed syllable has the samatha quality of precision, looking at the definite qualities of things as they are. Having established the seed syllable, one puts other symbols around it in the four quarters, one expands one's mandala. Similarly in the vipassana practice, having established the precision of details, one begins to experience the space around them. In other words, in making a pot, the importance is not so much on making the pot itself, but on shaping the space. Just so, in the vipassana practice the process is one of trying to feel the space around the pot. If one has a sense of the space one is going to create by producing a pot, one makes a good potter. But if one is purely concerned with making a shape out of clay without having a sense of the space, one does not make a good potter, or a good sculptor either, for that matter. In this way of beginning to relate with the space, vipassana is gradually letting go, a releasing and expanding.

From this point it is then possible to get a glimpse of the shunyata experience. The obstacle to the shunyata experience is the split between basic being and one's concept of it, between one's being and one's projections. All kinds of questions, problems, and obstacles arise in relation to this division. The reason that the first glimpse of shunyata becomes possible at this point is that, having seen the details of things as they are through samatha practice and experienced the space around them through vipassana, one begins to relax. One begins to experience the needlessness of defending or asserting oneself. At this point shunyata emerges as the simple absence of those walls and barricades of defense and assertion. One begins to develop the clear and precise experience of seeing a tree as just a tree, not one's version of a tree, not a tree called such-and-such, but a tree just as it is. The culmination of the experiential process of the development of intellect is the experience of shunyata, which is the experience of the nonexistence of duality. The research work is already accomplished; the process of searching for something has been laid to rest. This is the attainment of prajna.

From this point the intellect begins to turn toward jnana or intuition. Up until now the learning process has been regarded as receiving teaching; it has been an experimental course of study with the object of finding out who, what, and where we are. In that sense the practices of both the hinayana and mahayana levels are a step toward the understanding of the mandala within the body, the mandala within consciousness, and the mandala within the environmental situation of one's life. According to the tantric tradition, three levels of experience are always necessary— outer, inner, and secret. The outer experience is relating with form; the inner experience is relating with the subtleties of form. The subtleties of form *are* the space, in the sense we have referred to of a pot and the space around it. The secret experience is that the form and the space are the same, that there is no difference between form and space.

On the level of the secret experience the subtleties are no longer an object of concern. If one keeps attending to the subtleties, then that itself becomes a veil—one is still relating to the situation as a learning process, rather than the actual process of experience. But it is not possible to arrive at the level of direct experience without going through the learning process of understanding scientifically. The practice of meditation in Buddhism begins with scientific research in which one learns to make friends with oneself and learns what one is. Having completely and thoroughly understood that, then one can expand into the further dimension of understanding which is the level of direct experience without any props.

The Indivisibility of Openness and Compassion

I WOULD LIKE TO discuss the implications of the following Sanskrit verse:

śūnyatākaruṇābhinnaṃ bodhicittam iti smṛtaṃ

The indivisibility of *shunyata* and *karuna* is termed bodhichitta.

Here we have two terms which are of key significance in tantra, *shunyata* and *karuna*. The terms are not restricted to the tantric level, but appear fairly early on in the development of the Buddhist tradition. Shunyata was originally an elaboration of the concept of anatman. The meaning of anatman was that there is no abiding principle in things. Later on, shunyata became one of the central concepts of the mahayana. For the student of tantra, it remains a sort of objective reference of which he must be aware in order to pursue his practice onto further levels of subtlety.

Shunyata is usually translated "emptiness" or "void." These translations are thoroughly misleading, because *shunyata* is a highly positive term. Unfortunately, the early translators were not very sophisticated and allowed themselves to be misled by the sense of *shunya* in ordinary everyday language. In this popular language, if a glass had no water in it, it could be called *shunya*. But this is not at all the sense of *shunyata* in Buddhist philosophy.

Shunyata can be explained in a very simple way. When we perceive, we usually attend to the delimited forms of objects. But these objects are perceived within a field. Attention can be directed either to the concrete, limited forms or to the field in which these forms are situated. In the shunyata experience, the attention is on the field rather than on its contents. By "contents," we mean here those forms which are the outstanding features of the field itself. We also might notice that when we have an idea before our mind, the territory, as it were, delimited by the idea is blurred; it fades into something which is quite open. This open dimension is the basic meaning of shunyata.

This openness is present in and actually presupposed by every determinate form. Every determinate entity evolves out of something indeterminate and to a certain extent also maintains its connection with this indeterminacy; it is never completely isolated from it. Because the determinate entity is not isolated from the indeterminacy and because nevertheless there is no bridge between the two, our attention can shift back and forth between one and the other.

The perception of shunyata as openness is connected with the development of what is known as prajna. Because there are some very fantastic translations in vogue of this term *prajna*, it is worthwhile having a good look at what the term means. There are various words in Sanskrit which refer to the cognitive process. Two most frequently used ones are *prajna* and *jnana*. If we look at the words, we immediately notice that both contain the root *jña*, which signifies the cognitive potentiality. *Jnana* is the primary formation from this root in the Sanskrit language; in *prajna*, the same root *jña* is there with the prefix *pra*.

If we look at the Tibetan translations for these terms, we find that the very same root connection has been preserved. The Tibetan for *prajna* is *shes rab*, and for *jnana* it is *ye shes*. in both cases the *shes*, the cognitive potentiality, is there. *Ye* means "primordial" or "original." Thus *ye shes* refers to primordial awareness. The Sanskrit prefix *pra* and the Tibetan particle *rab* have the sense of "heightening" or "intensification." Therefore, *shes rab* or *prajna* refers to an intensification or heightening of the cognitive processes. The cognitive potentiality that is present in everyone is to be developed, intensified, and brought to its highest pitch. To bring this potentiality to its highest pitch means to release it, to free it from all the extraneous material that has accumulated.

What does it mean to free something? In the Western world, freedom has usually been used as a negative term: we speak of freedom from this, freedom from that. The logical conclusion from this usage, a conclusion which nobody likes to draw, is that we must also reach the point of getting rid of freedom from freedom. It does not help to have recourse to the construction of "freedom-to," freedom to do this, freedom to be that. Freedom-to implies subordination to some transcendental hocus-pocus and that makes freedom disappear as quickly as the negative proposition does. We see, then, that freedom cannot be considered as a separate thing relative to something else. It must be itself an existential fact. In this sense, freedom is not something that has to be achieved—it is basic to everything.

Freedom is inherent in all the cognitive processes. Here it helps to see that the opposite of freedom is not determination but compulsion. One is quite free to determine one's way of life, free to determine whether to look at things in a categorical way or an aesthetic way. That is, we can look at things relative to a set of goals to be achieved, or can simply appreciate them, and recognize their intrinsic value. So we must understand that freedom is a basic phenomenon and not some end-product of getting rid of something or subjecting oneself to some transcendental nebulosity, as it would seem that Western philosophy has generally approached it.

Prajna or shes rab as the heightening of the cognitive capacity, also means a weakening of the network of relative considerations in which, ordinarily, it is embedded. The weakening of this network permits the emergence of the cognitive capacity in its original freedom.

Prajna operates on different levels. It is operative when we listen to someone merely on a rudimentary level, when we merely hear something that the person we are listening to says. Just to hear what someone is saying, some understanding must be there. Prajna can be present on a more significant level. For instance, we can go beyond the mere momentary taking in of what someone says, to the point where we retain it and think about it. This may lead us to weigh seriously what we have heard and to try implementing our conclusions such that we embody them in our lives.

Prajna can operate on a still further level. Instead of attending to what we perceive, hear, or think about, in terms of categories related to the narrow limits of self-preservation or personal ends, we can come to appreciate things as values in themselves. When we come to this point there is a sort of a release, since there is no longer a need to manipulate our perceptions—we can let things be as they are. In speaking of arriving at this point it is possible to speak of freedom as an achievement, but we must see that this freedom has been there all the time. However, we have lost sight of this freedom through being involved with all sorts of unnecessary constructions—constantly seeing things as means in relation to our personal orientation. Having come to this basic appreciation and openness, we have the possibility of staying with it and seeing things as valuable, or we can fall back to seeing things as means for further means ad infinitum.

It is at this crucial point that shunyata comes in. Shunyata is the objective correlate of this heightened or opened state of awareness. In this state, we do not see different things but we do see things differently. When I meet someone, I can immediately snap into a state of mind where I am asking myself what I have to gain or lose from meeting this person and I can then involve myself in the appropriate strategy. Or, I can merely take in the impression of this person and relate to him without preconception. Very likely if I do the latter, a very satisfactory meeting will ensue. I have related to this open dimension of my impression. Now this is a very simple thing; there is nothing special about it and anybody can do it. But, as I have said, the simplest things are often the most difficult. Probably one of the most difficult things is for a person to do without his fixations and perceptions. They seem to provide so much security; yet a person who follows his fixations always suffers from a sense of lack or loss—as if something were missing.

When we speak of shunyata, we are speaking of the open dimension of being. We can be aware of this open dimension, but in order to perceive it our perceptive faculty must be open, without a bias of any kind. If our way of perceiving is tainted by any sort of predisposition or reservation, we are right then out of the openness. We have already narrowed our view, and this, in the end, will be quite unsatisfying.

We must be very careful not to regard openness as an entity. If we do that, we shall have made a concept of it, which automatically fixes it and makes it something definite. It is precisely this that we have had to break out of in order to perceive it. This is where past mistakes have been made in the history of Buddhism. Someone tried to say that prajna is shunyata. But prajna is not shunyata. Shunyata is the objective pole of prajna, the open quality of things which the cognitive process relates to when it reaches the level of true prajna.

We cannot predicate anything of prajna except to say that when it is properly prajna it must be as open as that which it perceives. In this sense we might say that subjective and objective poles (prajna and shunyata) coincide. With this understanding, rather than saying that prajna is shunyata, we can try to describe the experience by saying that it has gone beyond the dualism of subject and object. But we must not get too carried away by these descriptions and lose sight of the fact that they are only trying to bring home to us this simple experience that any of us can relate to directly if we so wish. We are free to do it. It is up to us.

We have now seen that shunyata is always a reference of perception. All action is based on perception, since, naturally, we always act in the light of our awareness. This is true on every level. The less I am aware of another person, the less able I am to act appropriately in my relationship with him. We have the example of certain types of people with so-called good intentions who do not take the trouble to become aware of what the people they are being "good to" really need. They are so involved in their preconceptions and biases that they think whatever they like must be good for everybody. Such a person might like milk and exert himself to get everybody to drink milk. But what about people who are allergic to milk? Such a thought would never make any impact on such a person's good intentions. The example may appear ridiculous, but it is precisely this sort of ridiculous action that we encounter constantly in life. We act on the basis of our understanding, our awareness, and if this is not open and alive, then our actions are necessarily clumsy and inappropriate.

This leads us to the subject of karuna. It seems that awareness is not just there for the fun of the thing, but it implies action. Action carried out in the light of the awareness of shunyata, that is, the action of prajna, is karuna. *Karuna* is usually translated as "compassion" and in many cases that may be correct. But the word itself derives from the Sanskrit root *kr*, which denote action. Just as with prajna, we can speak of karuna on many levels. On the highest level, on the level of the Buddha, we speak of mahakaruna, "the greatest karuna." Buddha's awareness was that of the awakened state of mind. He could not act otherwise than in the light of that complete awareness. This complete awareness is the fundamental example of the indivisibility of shunyata and karuna.

According to Buddhism there are three basic emotional complexes: passion-lust, aversion-hatred, and infatuation-bewilderment. These are named in terms of their ordinary or samsaric manifestations but they have latent possibilities of transformation. They are related to each other in a particular way. Bewilderment concerning the nature of what is going on can exist without entailing the extremes of passion or aversion. Passion or aversion, however, cannot come into play without the presence of basic bewilderment. Passion and aversion are emotional energies that have been distorted by an absence of precision which is this basic bewilderment.

Now in order to understand the nature of compassion, we can ask ourselves to which of these three basic emotional complexes compassion belongs. The usual response would be passion, since one ordinarily thinks that passion is related to love and love is not so different from compassion. But the Buddhist texts say the opposite: compassion belongs to hatred. The connection can be seen in the process that sometimes takes place when through enmity one person cuts another down and renders him helpless; then the one who has the power can aid the helpless one and feel himself a good person. This is the usual version of compassion and philanthropy.

But compassion is possible without aggression to create the original intimacy. On this level, the level of openness or shunyata, compassion is far more than the visceral emotion or sentimental urging that we ordinarily experience. On this level, we may speak of mahakaruna, which is based on the undistorted awareness of the awakened state of mind. There is a Sanskrit expression which runs as follows:

śūnyatākaruṇābhinnaṃ yatra cittam prabhāvyate
sā hi buddhasya dharmasya sanghasyāpi hi deśanā

Where an attitude in which shunyata and karuna are indivisible is developed, there is the message of the Buddha, the dharma, and the sangha.

Where the mind is such that it is able to perceive the openness in being, then its action is consonant with this openness because it takes into account what is real. If, on the other hand, awareness is tainted, the mind will manifest in all the emotional forms which are distortions of the real.

Ordinarily a distinction is made between jnana and klesha, primordial awareness and distorted emotional mind. We see here that they are not two different things—the one is a distortion of the other. Because klesha is a distortion of jnana it can be, so to say, rectified and returned to its source. This comes as a result of the development of prajna which, when heightened, can cut through the potentiality for distortion. This was the emphasis of the *Prajnaparamita* literature. Through prajna a person is led out of the narrow confines of his fictions, led not into some realm beyond, but into the actual world that is right here. Again, the awareness of the awakened mind is not of some new realm of objects; we do not see different things, we see things differently.

When, through prajna, the point is reached where shunyata and karuna are indivisible, there emerges bodhichitta (the bodhi-mind). Bodhichitta is that in which all that has been a limit has fallen away and all the positive qualities of mind have become active. This active aspect of the bodhichitta is what is meant by karuna. On this level, karuna is compassion in the true sense of that word—*con-passio,* "to feel with." This means to feel with what is real. It goes with the recognition of what is real and valuable in itself, not by virtue of some assigned or projected value which is basically subjective in character.

We have such a strong tendency to approach our experience only as a possible confirmation of the conceptions we already have. If we are able to be open, we grow. If we seek to relate everything to our preconceptions, then we are narrowing ourselves, narrowing being, and we become lifeless. If we fail to see the vividness of life and try to pigeonhole it, we ourselves become pigeonholed, trapped. We must attempt to relate to this innate capacity for openness that is there, this self-existing freedom. If we are aware in this way, we will act accordingly. If we see things as valuable in themselves, then we will act productively so that value is retained and augmented rather than destroyed and reduced.

If we constantly relate to and defend our preconceived ideas, everything is automatically reduced to what is known as vikalpa, concept, which means something that is cut off from the whole. Then we have just the fragmentary world in which we are usually involved.

The foundation of the creative approach is openness, shunyata. It is more than the "nothing," by which it is usually translated. According to Buddhist tradition, this openness is the basis on which we can enrich our lives. It is the basis of the various tantric practices.

SIX

The Development of Shunyata

W E HAVE DISCUSSED the meditation practices of samatha and vipassana. The union of the samatha experience with the vipassana experience leads to a further meditation practice, known as mahavipassana. The mahavipassana practice corresponds to the birth of the shunyata experience. The intensive experience of form of samatha and the intensive of totality, total environment, of vipassana combine to give birth to the experience of shunyata. This experience produces a new dimension—one finds one doesn't have to defend oneself any longer. The experience of shunyata brings a sense of independence, a sense of freedom.

This is not a matter only of sitting meditation practice; daily living situations are very much a part of these experiences. The six transcendental qualities of a bodhisattva—generosity, discipline, patience, exertion, meditation, and prajna or transcendental knowledge—all these together contribute to the development of the shunyata experience.

The experience of shunyata is a by-product of the process of letting go. This process consists in the application of the five transcendental qualities of a bodhisattva combined with the precision and clarity of prajna. The five qualities act as auxiliaries, which prajna directs. It is said that when the universal monarch goes to war he is accompanied by his army composed of five different kinds of forces—cavalry, elephant, chariots, and so on. So the birth of shunyata takes place through the application of the skillful action of these five qualities with the guidance of prajna providing the basic strength.

Being related with these active characteristics, shunyata is clearly not a state of trance or an absorption of some kind. It is a fearless state. Because of this fearlessness, one can afford to be generous. One can afford to acknowledge a space which does not contain any conflicts of that and this or how and why. No questions of any kind exist at this point. But within this state there is a tremendous sense of freedom. It is an experience, I suppose one could say, of having gone beyond. But this does not mean that one has gone beyond in the sense of having abandoned "here" and therefore having gotten beyond to "there." Rather it's that one is here, or one is there, *already.*

So a tremendous sense of conviction begins to develop with the shunyata experience. Shunyata provides the basic inspiration for developing the ideal, so to speak, of bodhisattva-like behavior.

But there is a further level of experience beyond that of bodhisattva, which is that of a yogi. It has been said that ordinary people should not try to act as bodhisattvas, bodhisattvas as yogis, yogis as siddhas, and that siddhas should not try to act as buddhas. There are these different levels of experience. The shunyata experience corresponds to the level of a bodhisattva. But the shunyata experience is in a sense incomplete from the point of view of the next stage, which is the experience of prabhasvara, luminosity. Prabhasvara is the ultimate positive experience. Shunyata is like the sky. That space of the sky being there, it becomes possible for cosmic functions to take place within it. It becomes possible for there to develop sunrise and sunset. In the same way, within the space of shunyata, of openness and freedom, it becomes possible for students to begin to deal with the actual experiences of nonduality, rather than celebrating the achievement of nonduality. This is the prabhasvara experience, which is a way of acknowledging the buddha nature that exists within one. One is now so positive and so definite that one no longer has the fear that dualistic notions and ego-clingings might reinstate themselves.

Prabhasvara is another kind of space within which all kinds of perspectives of the positive quality of spiritual development present themselves. Finally actually realizing that one is impregnated with buddha, one no longer has to look for external situations through which to create or build up enlightened experience. One acknowledges the enlightened being that is part of one's makeup, part of one's whole being.

From the prabhasvara experience, gradually a further development takes place, which leads to the mahamudra experience—still a further space. The space of mahamudra is even much more positive than that of prabhasvara. Frequently, explanations of mahamudra speak in terms of symbolism, since *mudra* means symbol. But on this level, symbols do not exist as such; the sense of experience ceases to exist. What one perceives is actual reality. That is why it is called *maha*mudra, the *great* symbol. It is the symbol born within, wisdom born within.

In Tibetan, this wisdom born within is referred to by the terms *ku* (sku) and *yeshe* (ye-shes). In this context *ku* means "body"—that aspect of the experience of the universe that is definite and solid, composed of forms. In the mahamudra experience forms become solid and definite forms, colors become bright and definite colors, sounds become definite sounds. Thought processes also become, in some sense, real, because at this point there is no longer any reason to condemn thoughts or try to mold them into a different pattern. It is just a spontaneous thinking of thoughts. Here spiritual development is not a matter of destroying anything but of rediscovering what is there through a process of unlearning preconceptions—constantly unlearning and unmasking. As a result of this constant unlearning, one begins to discover further details, further beauties in every area of one's being.

So ku, or body, is the direct experience of the living situation of the mandala spectrum, the whole range of life situations seen in terms of the mandala. And yeshe, or wisdom, has the same quality as ku—it is direct actual experience. It has nothing to do any longer with the spiritual learning process. It is complete and actual self-existing understanding.

The practice of mahamudra is to appreciate both positive and negative experiences as subtle symbolism, subtle expressions of basic being, to see the subtle basic situation, so to speak. The tantrism of mahamudra is very positive and spontaneous. Directly relating to the play of situations, energy develops through a movement of spontaneity that never becomes frivolous. The mahamudra experiences function naturally so that they lead us to destroy whatever needs to be destroyed and foster whatever needs to be fostered. The maturing process of mahamudra is one of extremely natural growth. One no longer has to try to struggle along the path. The notion of struggling along the path has dropped away at the level of shunyata.

Q: You say that having experienced shunyata, one no longer feels driven to struggle on the path?

R: Yes, that's right. You don't have to uncover any longer; you've uncovered already. At that point your innate nature begins to pick you up, and from then on spiritual development is a continually growing thing. It is as though you have reached the experience of the new moon; beyond that there is just a process of waxing. So the full moon begins to pick you up at the point of the shunyata experience.

Q: Could you say more about the difference between a yogi and a bodhisattva?

R: A yogi is one who has experienced the energy of the cosmos, the energy of the whole thing. He transmutes energies rather than trying to reform them, mold them into particular shapes. I wouldn't quite say the spirituality of the bodhisattva is molding energy into particular shapes, but still there is a constant note of gentleness in the bodhisattva practice, which suggests a subtle molding of some kind. The yogi's practice is more direct and rugged. Traditionally, the beginning of the yogi's practice is the understanding of symbolism, but not as symbolism. *Symbol* is really a rather inadequate word. The practice involves relating to the images that arise in living situations as decisive indications of one's psychological state. The bodhisattva experience has much less of this subtle moment-to-moment insight. It is much more of a general lifestyle, a question of general behavior, rather than a continual relating to vivid details.

Q: Somehow it seems that this distinction between bodhisattva and yogi is artificial, like an article of religious dogma.

R: It's a progress. You begin as a bodhisattva, then you become a yogi. The dogma of religion drops away right at the beginning when you become a bodhisattva. As a yogi you pick up further on the nondogmatic quality, but you also begin to enjoy the spiritual implication of things much more.

Q: Could you explain what you meant by the phrase "mandala spectrum"?

R: Actually, that's quite simple. At that stage you have developed very keen perception—sense of smell, of touch, of vision, of hearing—all these have developed to a very keen and acute level, a very precise level. We are speaking here of true perceptions, devoid of concepts. Nothing gets in the way. Having developed that ability, having entered this new dimension in which you are able to deal with situations directly, you see the world as it is; and this world-as-it-is becomes more and more complex. So many branches are branching out everywhere. At the same time, within this complex set-up of the world, simplicity presents itself as well: all these elements of the complexity branch out from one root, so to speak. The appreciation of this is the perception of the mandala spectrum. This appreciation, one might say, is curiosity in the fundamental sense—the actual, true curiosity; absolute curiosity. When you're absolutely curious about things, you lose yourself. You become completely part of the object. That's part of what is meant by letting go.

Naropa.
PAINTING BY GLEN EDDY.

SEVEN

The Guru-Disciple Relationship

O NE OF THE MOST important figures in the history of Indian and Tibetan Buddhism is Naropa. Unlike some mothers whose names figure in the lineages of Buddhist spiritual transmission, Naropa was certainly a historical figure. Naropa is part of the Kagyü lineage of Tibetan Buddhism, being with his teacher Tilopa and his disciple Marpa the spiritual founder of that order. He is also recognized and venerated by all the Tibetan schools as the exemplary disciple.

The relationship between guru and disciple is of tremendous importance in Buddhist spiritual transmission. The relationship is not merely a matter of historical interest; it continues as an important factor up to the present day. This relationship is based on trust. But before such trust can be developed, there must be a period during which the guru tests his disciple. This process of testing is seen in a very complete way in the trials and difficulties Naropa was put through by his teacher Tilopa. A long time passed before Tilopa was willing to impart his knowledge to his disciple.

The testing of a disciple by the guru is, in a way, quite simple. A student comes to a teacher and asks for instruction. The teacher might well say, "Well, I don't know very much. You'd better try some one else." This is an excellent way of beginning the testing. The student might well go away, which would be a sign that he is not really very serious.

Because of the intimacy of the relationship between teacher and disciple, whatever happens between the two is vital to the teacher as well as the disciple. If something goes wrong, it reflects on the teacher as well as the disciple. The teacher must know better than to accept a student who is not ready to receive the teaching he has to offer. That is why before giving instruction, he will test the readiness, willingness, and capacity of the student to receive it. This means the student must become, to use the traditional image, a worthy vessel. And because of the intimacy of the prospective relationship, the student must also in his way test the teacher. He must scrutinize him to see if he is really able to transmit the teaching, if his actions tally with his words. If the conditions are not fulfilled on both sides, the relationship is not worthy to be engaged.

The tradition of the guru-disciple relationship has been handed down from ancient times in India as we see from the texts. The Tibetans took over this practice from the Indians and to this very day they enact it in the traditional manner. This close relationship has not only the work of passing on the oral teachings, but also of preserving the continuity of personal example.

Naropa was a worthy vessel. He was willing to undergo every kind of hardship in order to receive teaching. His hardships began with his search for a teacher. Naropa spent years in his search. And this search was actually part of the teaching his teacher imparted to him. Before Naropa saw Tilopa in his own form, he encountered him in a succession of strange guises. He saw him as a leprous woman, a butcher, and in many other forms. All these forms were reflections of Naropa's own tendencies working within him, which prevented him from seeing Tilopa in this true nature, from seeing the true nature of the guru.

The term *guru* is an Indian word, which has now almost become part of the English language. Properly used, this term does not refer so much to a human person as to the object of a shift in attention which takes place from the human person who imparts the teaching to the teaching itself. The human person might more properly be called the *kalyanamitra,* or "spiritual friend." Guru has a more universal sense. The kalyanamitra is one who is able to impart spiritual guidance because he has been through the process himself. He understands the problem of the student, and why the student has come to him. He understands what guidance he needs and how to give it.

To begin with, spiritual guidance can only be imparted in the context of our physical existence by a person who shares with us the situation of physically existing in this world. So the teacher first appears in the form of the kalyanamitra. Then, gradually, as his teaching takes root within us and grows, its character changes and it comes to be reflected in the teacher himself. In this way an identification of the guru and the kalyanamitra takes place. But it is important that the guru be recognized and accepted as the guru and not confounded with the kalyanamitra in the manner of a mere personality cult. It is not a simple equation between the guru and the kalyanamitra. Still the kalyanamitra must be recognized as one able to give the knowledge which the student desires, which he needs, in fact, as a vital factor in his growth.

Here again we can refer to the example of Naropa. In the beginning, Naropa failed to understand the process in which he was involved. The inner growth that was already being prepared and taking root in him was still obscured by the many preconceptions he had. He continued to see the manifestations of his guru in the light of his ordinary conceptions, rather than understanding that they were symbols presenting the opportunity of breaking through preconceptions. These manifestations gave him the opportunity to be himself, rather than his idea of himself as a highly capable person.

We must remember that Naropa came from a royal family. His social prestige was great and he had become, in addition, a renowned pandit. And so in the process of trying to relate to his guru, his pride came into play. He felt that, as a person already renowned for his understanding, he should have all the answers already. But this was not the case. Only after the testing period did any real answers begin to emerge. This testing process actually effected the removal of his preconceptions. It was actually the teaching itself in the most concrete terms. No amount of words would have achieved the result that came about through his exposure to the rough treatment, the shock treatment, to which Tilopa subjected him. At the very moment in which he would think that at last he had understood, that at last these endless trials were over—at that very moment he would realize that he had again failed to see.

In the whole process of learning that is involved here, and one can say that the Buddhist way is a way of learning, there is a continual oscillation between success and failure. Sometimes things go smoothly. This is a fine thing; but it may also be a very great danger. We may become too self-sure, too confident that everything is going to come out as we would like it. Complacency builds up. So sometimes the failures that arise are very important in that they make us realize where we went wrong and give us a chance to start over again. Out of this experience of failure, we come to see things anew and afresh.

This oscillation between success and failure brings the sense of a way, a path; and here we touch upon the importance of the Buddhist tradition of the way. Buddhism has never claimed to be other than a way. The Buddha himself was only the teacher who showed other people the way which he himself had to travel, whatever the vicissitudes of success and failure. But it is always true that if a person fails, he can start again. If the person is intelligent, he will learn from the mistakes he has made. Then these mistakes will become ways of helping him along, as happened in the case of Naropa. Quite often Tilopa asked him to do things which were quite out of the question from Naropa's ordinary point of view, which quite went against the grain of his conventional frame of reference. But this was very much to the point. Conformity to the accepted way of looking at things would bring nothing. The point was to gain a new vision.

If we come to a new vision, a new way of looking at things, its mode of application may quite well be different from what is commonly accepted. This has always been the case with the great spiritual leaders of mankind, wherever we look. These people have broadened and widened our horizon. Through their action we have experienced the satisfaction of growing out of the narrowness of the ordinary world into which we happen to have been born.

When Naropa had shown that he was a person worthy of receiving instruction, the whole pattern we have been describing changed. Tilopa then showed himself the kindest person that could be imagined. He withheld nothing that Naropa wished of him. There is a Sanskrit expression, *acharya mushti,* which means the "closed fist." This is an expression that has often been applied to gurus who withhold the teaching. At a certain point, if the teacher withholds instruction, it is a sign that he is unsure of himself. But this was certainly not now the case with Tilopa. He gave everything that he had to his disciple.

This is the manner of continuing the teacher-disciple relationship. At a certain point the teacher transmits the entirety of his understanding to a disciple. But that the disciple must be worthy and brought to a state of complete receptivity is one of the messages of Naropa's life. And so, in his turn, Naropa led his disciple Marpa through the same preparatory process, and Marpa led his disciple Milarepa. Milarepa's biography tells us that Marpa had him build a house out of stone. He had hardly finished the house when Marpa told him to tear the house down and begin over again. This happened again and again. We need not ask ourselves whether this is a historical fact. The symbolic message is quite plain. Marpa asked him to do something and Milarepa reacted with pride, feeling that he could do it. Milarepa did it his way without waiting for the instruction. Naturally, the results were not satisfactory and there was no alternative but to have him tear it down and build again from the beginning.

Here we see another aspect of the guru-disciple relationship. The disciple must start at the beginning. And this comes almost inevitably as a blow to his pride, because he almost always feels that he understands something already. It is usually a very long time before this pride is broken down and real receptivity begins to develop.

Mahavairochana (foreground) *and Vajradhara* (background).
DRAWING BY TERRIS TEMPLE.

EIGHT

Visualization

O N THE DISK OF THE autumn moon, clear and pure, you place a seed syllable. The cool blue rays of the seed syllable emanate immense cooling compassion that radiates beyond the limits of sky or space. It fulfills the needs and desires of sentient beings, bringing basic warmth so that confusions may be clarified. Then from the seed syllable you create a Mahavairochana Buddha, white in color, with the features of an aristocrat—an eight-year-old child with a beautiful, innocent, pure, powerful, royal gaze. He is dressed in the costume of a medieval king of India. He wears a glittering gold crown inlaid with wish-fulfilling jewels. Part of his long black hair floats over his shoulders and back; the rest is made into a topknot surmounted by a glittering blue diamond. He is seated cross-legged on the lunar disk with his hands in the meditation mudra holding a vajra carved from pure white crystal.

Now what are we going to do with *that*?

The picture is uncomplicated; at the same time it is immensely rich. There is a sense of dignity and also a sense of infanthood. There is a purity that is irritatingly pure, irritatingly cool. As we follow the description of Mahavairochana, perhaps his presence seems real in our minds. Such a being could actually exist: a royal prince, eight years of age, who was born from a seed syllable. One feels good just to think about such a being.

Mahavairochana is the central symbol in the first tantric yana, the kriyayogayana. He evokes the basic principle of kriyayoga—immaculateness, purity. He is visualized by the practitioner as part of his meditation.

In the kriyayogayana, since one has already discovered the transmutation of energy, discovered all-pervading delight, there is no room for impurity, no room for darkness. The reason is that there is no doubt. The rugged, confused, unclean, impure elements of the struggle with samsara have been left far behind. Finally we are able to associate with that which is pure, clean, perfect, absolutely immaculate. At last we have managed to actualize tathagatagarbha, buddha nature. We have managed to visualize to actualize, to formulate a most immaculate, pure, clean, beautiful, white, spotless principle.

There is a widespread misunderstanding of tantra, which sees tantra as pop art. People have heard that the tantric approach is to accept samsara fully. The idea has developed that therefore we are declaring everything—sexuality, aggression, ignorance—as legitimate and pure, that we accept the crudeness as a big joke. "The crudeness is the fun." Therefore, the idea runs, we can jump into tantra by being crude and dirty: "Since we have to live with the crudeness, let's consider it beautiful." But visualizing Mahavairochana is far different from the gesture of stealing a "Rue Royale" street sign in Paris and sticking it up on our wall. The whole idea of tantra is very different from joining a club formed by tantric teachers in which it has been agreed to regard the mess of confusion as something livable and workable, to pretend that our pile of shit is nice, fresh, earthy soil that we are sitting on. This is a great misunderstanding.

The misunderstanding seems to be that tantra comes into being out of some kind of desperation, that since we cannot handle the confusion, we accept the convention of tantra as a saving grace. Then the shit of our confusion becomes pictorial, artistic—pop art. Supposedly tantra acknowledges this view eagerly and formally. But there is something very crude about this idea. If tantra merely acknowledged that samsara had to be put up with, without seeing the absolute purity and cleanness of it, tantra would be just another form of depression, and devoid of compassion.

Actually, far from beginning by exalting crudeness, the introduction to tantra is fantastically precise and pure, clean and artful. It could be said that the kriyayogayana is to the vajrayana what the Yogachara approach, which underlies Zen, is to the mahayana. There is a pronounced artful quality, a great appreciation of purity and cleanness.

Just as bodhisattvas embodying the magnificent vision of the mahayana are good citizens, tantric yogis are also extremely good citizens.

Tantric practitioners are the good mechanics in garages, who know the infinite details of the functioning of machines with clean and precise mind. Tantric practitioners are good artists, who paint good pictures that do not try to con one. Tantric practitioners are good lovers, who do not take advantage of their partners' energy and emotion, but make love precisely, accurately, purely. Tantric practitioners are good musicians, who do not fool around banging away at random, but play precisely, musically. Tantra is by no means to be associated with marginal life-styles, Bohemianism, where one is intensely critical of convention and takes pride in being rugged and dirty.

The right understanding of tantra is crucial for the practice of visualization. One Nyingma teacher said that undertaking the practice of visualization is like going to bed with a pregnant tigress. She might get hungry in the middle of the night and decide to eat you. On the other hand, she might begin to nurse you, creating the furry warmth and texture of basic space. Certainly practicing visualization without the proper understanding is extremely destructive. A kriyayoga text, the *Vajramala,* says that the practitioner of wrong visualization, instead of attaining the complete openness of Vajrasattva, attains the complete egohood of Rudra, the ultimate spiritual ape. The tantric scriptures abound with warnings about wrong visualization.

Generally, wrong visualization takes the form of intensifying ordinary mental objects. One creates an image out of wishful thinking. For example, in the middle of one's meditation practice a sexual fantasy arises and one decides to carry it out in complete detail—stage one, stage two, stage three, and so on. This same approach can apply to visualizations of tantric material. Even in visualizing Mahavairochana, a child sitting on a lunar disk, one might be re-creating one's ego projection. The result is the ultimate ape: "I am Mahavairochana, I am one with him; let no one challenge this." There is a sense of the beast, a great powerful chest, the cosmic gorilla.

There is a precise attitude and understanding of visualization corresponding to each level of tantra—kriyayoga, upayoga, yoga, mahayoga, anuyoga, and maha ati. The student's understanding evolves organically from one stage of tantra to the next. But for the student to arrive at any proper understanding of visualization at all, it is absolutely necessary to have gone through all the previous stages of the path. He had to have developed the hinayana understanding of suffering, impermanence, and egolessness and insight into the structure of ego. He must have attained the understanding on the mahayana level of the shuntata principle and its application in the paramitas, the six transcendental actions of the bo-dhisattva. It is not necessary to have completely mastered all of these experiences, but the student must have had some glimpse of their significance. He has to have used up his mental gossip or at least taken out a corner of it. Their must be some sense of having trod on the path of hinayana and mahayana before embarking on the tantrayana.

If one has done this, then rather than coming as a reinforcement of ego's deception, visualization will be inspired by a sense of hopelessness or, to say the same thing, egolessness. One can no longer deceive one-self. There is the despair of having lost one's territory; the carpet has been pulled out from under one's feet. One is suspended in nowhere or able at least to flash his nonexistence, his egolessness. Only then can one visualize. This is extremely important.

According to tradition, one of the principal masters who brought the vajrayana teachings to Tibet from India was Atisha Dipankara. Atisha prepared the ground for vajrayana by teaching surrendering. In fact he was known as the "refuge" teacher because of the extent to which he emphasized taking refuge in the Buddha, the dharma, and the sangha. Taking refuge in the Buddha, the dharma, and the sangha is a process of surrendering. Tremendous emphasis was laid by Atisha on surrendering, giving, opening, not holding on to something.

People who live in New York City have very vivid and definite impressions of that city—the yellow cabs, the police cars, the street scene. Imagine, for example, trying to convey this to a Tibetan living in Lhasa. If you wanted to teach him about America starting with New York, you could say: "New York City goes like this. There are streets, skyscrapers, yellow cabs. Visualize all that. Pretend you are in it." You could expound Newyorkcityness on and on and on, explain it in the minutest detail; but he would have tremendous difficulty visualizing it, actually having the feeling of being in New York City. He would relate to New York City as being some kind of mystery land. There would be a sense of novelty.

Teaching Americans to visualize Mahavairochana is like teaching Tibetans to visualize New York City. Americans simply have not had that kind of experience. So how is it possible to bridge such a gap? Precisely by going through the three levels of Buddhist practice. Without the basic mindfulness practices and the development of awareness, there is no way at all of beginning the visualization practice of tantra.

It is through these fundamental practices that one can begin to see why such emphasis is placed on purity and cleanness, on the immaculate quality of the Mahavairochana visualization. Because of those preparatory experiences, the infant born from a seed syllable, sitting on the lunar disk, becomes impressive, highly impressive. This sambhogakaya buddha becomes beautiful because one has developed the possibility of unbiased experience. One can relate directly, egolessly; then a principle arising out of this unbiased level of experience, Mahavairochana, for example, becomes fantastically expressive. This is complete purity, purity that never had to be washed. If one tried to produce this kind of purity by using Ajax to clean up one's dirty image, one would simply create a further mess. The purity of tantric experience is real beyond question. The practitioner does not have to think twice: "Is this really happening or am I imagining it?" The experience beggars uncertainty.

Visualization is a prominent part of tantric practice. One identifies with various iconographical figures—sambhogakaya buddhas, herukas, dakinis. This is done to develop vajra pride. Vajra pride is different from ordinary stupid pride. It is enlightened pride. You *do* have the potentialities of the deity; you are him already. The magic is not particularly in the visualization, but there is magic in your pride, your inspiration. You *are* Mahavairochana. You are absolutely clean, immaculate, and pure. Therefore you can identify with your *own* purity, *your* purity rather than that of an external god who is pure, rather than some kind of foreign element coming into you. You are awakening yourself.

So tantra is not magic in the sense of conjuring or involving oneself in a myth. Tantra is the highest level of a process of personal evolution. It is the ultimate development of the logic that runs through the entire Buddhist path.

Kriyayoga places particular emphasis on mudras, or hand gestures, as well as on visualization. In these practices you are, in a sense, competing with the buddhas and deities. You are making their hand gestures, behaving like them, trying to become one. But again, it is not really a question of trying, but of thinking that you *are* one. Vajra pride is the pride that you *are* Buddha.

That one *is* the deities, one *is* the buddhas is a big point for beginners in tantra. The problem may arise that one does not think one actually is.

So one thinks: "I am supposed to think that I am Samantabhadra Buddha, I am Mahavairochana. Therefore I had better crank myself into that role." This remote approach, instead of the directness of actually *being* that deity, is considered cowardice or stupidity. In order to develop vajra pride, one has to relate directly to the pain of situations, in this case the pain of actually being the deity, and see the value of it. Then that pride has something valid to be proud of.

It is in connection with the development of vajra pride that kriyayoga makes its strong emphasis on purity. You are spotlessly pure because there is no room for doubt. This is associated with the view of the phenomenal world in mahamudra. The phenomenal world is seen as completely colorful, precisely beautiful *as it is,* beyond acceptance and rejection, without any problems. You have seen things in this way because you have already cut through your conceptualized notion of a self and you have seen through its projections. Since that is the case, there is nothing that could come up that could be an obstacle in your handling the situation. It is totally precise and clear. *As it is.*

NINE

Empowerment and Initiations

I WOULD LIKE TO speak about the initiations or abhishekas, to put them in proper perspective in terms of how they apply, when they come, and what is meant by them. In order to understand this intricate pattern, we must have a picture of the whole gradual process of spiritual development in Buddhism.

The situation in which spiritual development takes place is represented visually in the tantrayana as a mandala. A mandala is understood as a center which is beautiful because of its surroundings which are present with it. It represents a whole situation in graphic form. There is the center which stands for the teacher, or more esoterically, for the guru. The guru is never alone, but exists in relation to his surroundings. The surroundings are seen as the expression of a new orientation in relation to this center. The mandala is set up in terms of the four cardinal points of the compass. These points symbolize an orientation in which all aspects (directions) of the situation are seen in relation to the guru and therefore have their message. The whole situation becomes, then, a communication on the part of the guru or teacher. It depends on our level of spiritual growth whether we see the guru only concretely as a person or can also see him symbolically.

The mandala has a certain specific quality in that each situation is unique and cannot be repeated. Only similarities can obtain. The mandala also has its own time factor which cannot be equated with the passage of time as we ordinarily understand it. It has a quality of simultaneity of all aspects which goes beyond our ordinary understanding of sequence. If properly understood, the mandala leads us back to seeing what the spiritual path is, back to the possibility of becoming more related to our own being without identifying it with this or that. Even the understanding embodied in the mandala is traditionally surrendered and offered up as a guard against reification.

The Buddhist path, which leads to seeing one's situation as a mandala, begins with taking refuge. We take refuge in the three jewels—the Buddha, the dharma, the sangha. This can happen on various levels. There is the ordinary physical level of just repeating the formula. But this also involves a process happening within us. Regarding this inner level, we have the instruction to take refuge in something which is abiding, something which can actually offer refuge. We can only take refuge in something certain; otherwise taking refuge would be a pure fiction and would not provide the security we want. So, on the inner level, taking refuge means surrendering to those forces of which we ourselves are, so to speak, the last transformation. These forces have, in a way, become frozen in us. Taking refuge thus means to commit ourselves to a process of unfreezing, so that life's energy, or whatever we want to call these forces that operate through us and somehow get blocked, can flow freely.

Beyond this, taking refuge can relate to still deeper layers, until we come to the point where the distinctions, differentiations, and separations that are introduced by our ordinary thinking no longer apply. At this level, when we speak of taking refuge in the three jewels, it means taking refuge in something which is unitary in character. We only speak in terms of three aspects in an effort to describe it.

So the first step in tantric discipline is to take refuge and understand it properly, not just as an outer performance which may in some way be beneficial, but as a ceremony that is meant to awaken the basic forces which are dormant within us. The ceremony can only be effective in this way if there is also present in us something known technically as an *attitude*. This means here an attitude we have developed which has as its aim to permit all that is within us to reach its fullest range of play.

There also comes into play something of a highly practical character which we might refer to as friendliness or compassion. This means taking account of the fact that the realm we are coming into contact with through taking refuge is a broader one than that in which we ordinarily operate. This automatically brings in a sense of openness.

The next step after taking refuge is training the mind. This does not mean intellectual training. It means seeing our very being in a different light. The movement has several stages. First, it is necessary to see our mental processes clearly. Then we will see that they must be cleansed of the presuppositions with which we ordinarily approach things. Then we must understand what the nature of this cleansing or purifying process is. The whole movement is one that goes deeper and deeper within, toward our hidden depths in which the energies are now being made to flow again.

The abhishekas in the tantrayana are the further developments of what was begun by taking refuge. This can be understood as a process of purification, which allows us more and more to see our situation as a mandala of the guru. Purification means overcoming what are technically known as the various maras. Maras are what we refer to in modern terminology as overevaluated ideas. They are a force of death that keeps us from growing. Overcoming them is part of the tantric discipline.

Of these maras one of the main ones is the ideas we have about our body. We unconsciously form and analyze it to the point where we no longer relate to it as a living structure. Our ideas about it have no use—they are only a limitation of the potentiality that is there. But even this limiting construct is never separated from its living source. Seeing this is a development which leads us more and more into the presence of the guru.

We may look at the relationship with the guru in terms of external and internal aspects. We may even see that the guru has appeared to us in various forms. Taking this broader view of the nature of the guru, we understand that there is always someone who points us toward or challenge us into spiritual growth. The relationship with the guru is always there—this is the point of view of tantra.

The process of seeing our life more and more directly also involves demolishing our fortress of conceptions about ourselves and the world. In this process there is a need for the so-called initiations or abhishekas. *Abhisheka* is derived from a Sanskrit root which means "to anoint." Its symbology is taken from the traditional Indian ceremony of the investiture of a ruler. Investiture takes place through the conferring of a certain power. This idea of power is taken up in the Tibetan translation of *abhisheka* as *wangkur* (dbang-skur). *Wang* means something like "power," but not in the sense of power politics or domination. Wangkur is an empowerment in the sense that henceforth the person so invested is enabled to give the greatest scope to the forces operating within him, forces which are of a fundamentally wholesome nature.

The first or jar empowerment is connected with the observable fact we have been discussing, namely, that we are attached to the conception we have of our body. In the Western world we are conditioned to think that the mind is superior to the body—we look down on the body. Now this is very naive. If the body were such a debased thing, then people should be only too happy to have it mutilated or weakened. But nobody would submit voluntarily to such a process, which in itself means that the body is very valuable. Our body is a most important orientation point. Everything we do is related to our body. You are situated in relation to me in terms of my body and in no other way. To realize the creative potential of this embodiment purification must take place.

The image of the first empowerment is purification. Essentially it is a symbolic bathing. A gesture is made of pouring water from a jar over the person receiving the empowerment. This is actually quite close to the normal Indian way of bathing, in the absence of modern plumbing facilities. It seems to mean just getting rid of dirt, in this case the conceptual structure we have with regard to our bodies. But this cleansing is also a confirmation of power, because it means that henceforth we will make better and more appropriate use of our being-a-body. It means we are on the way to realization of the nirmanakaya, realization of embodiment as ultimately valuable. This means being alive in certain measured-out and limited circumstances, to which we relate as the working basis of our creativity.

These empowerments or abhishekas are stages in a unitary process. Once what was implied by the first empowerment has come to its maturity in us, there is a second. In some way these stages are actually simultaneous, since all aspects of experience are interconnected. Nevertheless, we are obliged to take them one after another.

The second abhisheka, the *secret* or *mystery* empowerment, has to do with speech and language—our mode of communication. It has to do with communication not only externally (with others), but also with communication in our own inner world. We scarcely realize that mentally we are constantly acting out to ourselves our particular melodrama, our version of what is happening to us. And we actually talk to ourselves about it. So there are certain predispositions and neurotic patterns in our way of communicating. On the level of the second empowerment we work with this material. We have to come to another, a more whole-some level of communication. Talk can go on endlessly without commu-nicating anything. Many people talk and talk and talk and never have anything to say. In fact, the general run of our mental life is on this level of empty chatter. We use words as tacks to pin things down and lose the open dimension of communication. Our use of words in this way kills the very thing that makes life worthwhile. And it reflects back on the physical level and reinforces our limited way of being on that level.

But communication can go on in quite a different way. It need not take place even through the normal verbal forms. This is where mantra comes in. Mantra is communication on quite another level than the ordi-nary. It opens the way to the manifestation of our inner strengths, and at the same time it prevents our minds from going astray into the mode of empty talk. The second abhisheka is an empowerment to live on this superior level of communication.

Our presence involves not only our embodiment and an activity of communication, but also a pattern of thinking. Ordinarily we think in concepts, and certainly for the practical purposes of life we must use concepts. But, on the other hand, concepts are also images that we im-pose on things. Concepts are forms that we present to ourselves con-cerning the living forces that we are in order to give them a label. Our mental life then goes on in terms of these labels. Here we see that this way of limiting things in advance, so to speak, takes place on the think-ing level as well.

What we have been looking at on all three levels of body, speech, and thinking is an interlocking pattern of limitation. If we live, as we ordinarily do, in this pattern of limitation, we are stuck in a situation in which everything tends to get narrower and narrower. We are trapped in a web of decreasing possibilities. We are in a world where we can talk about less than we can think of, and do less than we can talk about.

The process of spiritual growth is about unfreezing this situation. And what a tremendous experience when life can flow freely again—when the buds bloom forth, when the rivers break up and the waters come flowing through in all their purity. The abhishekas are an opening into a new dimension, which one ordinarily never experiences. Suddenly one is introduced to something of which one has never been aware. In such a situation there is a great danger that the experience may be misunder-stood. There will be a strong tendency to reduce it to our habitual frame of reference. If this happens, the experience can be quite harmful, especially in the case of the third abhisheka, on the level of thought.

Whether the third abhisheka is properly understood or not depends very much on the accurate interpretation of the symbols that come into play at this point. These symbols are the karmamudra, jnanamudra, mahamudra, and samayamudra. The functioning of the process of spiritual growth depends on our seeing them in another mode than our ordinary one.

The term *mudra,* literally translated, means "seal." But what is a seal? It is something that makes a very deep impression on what it comes in contact with. So it might be better to understand mudra in this context as a tremendous encounter in which two forces come together and make a very deep impression.

Karma comes from the Sanskrit root meaning "action," what one does in encountering the world. Usually, our major encounters are with other people; and people are both male and female. Symbolically, the most potent form is our encounter with the opposite sex. Now we can look at this situation reductively and literally and think, in encountering a person of the opposite sex, of taking the other person as a kind of utensil. In that way we reduce the encounter to a very dead item. True, sex is fun, but if it continues very long we get bored with it. Here we have to understand the encounter on an entirely different level than the one usually seen. A characteristic of the sexual encounter is that we are never at rest; there is constant action and reaction. This by its very nature can create an opening of awareness beyond the normal level. An expanded awareness tinged with delight can arise.

If we have perceived the karmamudra in this constructive way, rather then reductively, there is automatically a tendency to go further in the direction of open awareness. This leads to the relationship with the jnanamudra. Suddenly the whole picture has changed. The relationship is no longer merely on the physical level, but there is an image involved here, a visualization which mediates a complete degree of appreciation and understanding. This opens up entirely new vistas.

The inspirational quality is much stronger and more far-reaching than with the karmamudra. We can reach a very profound level of awareness in which we become fused with the partner in a unitary experience. The distinction between oneself and the other simply no longer holds. There is a sense of tremendous immediacy, which also brings a sense of great power. Again there is a danger of taking the experience reductively and thinking that "Now I have achieved great power." But if we are able to relate to this moment as an open experience, we are then at the level of mahamudra or, in this context, the greatest encounter.

When we have had this peak experience, we wish to retain it or at least to make it manifest to ourselves again. This is done through the samayamudra. The samayamudra involves the various figures we see represented in the Tibetan thangkas or scroll paintings. These forms are expressions of the deep impressions that have come out of the encounters we have had with the forces working within us. It is not as though we were, so to speak, containers of these forces—rather, we are like partial manifestations of them. In these encounters our separateness and secludedness are momentarily abolished. At the same time, our deadening reductive tendencies are overcome. In the samayamudra we commit ourselves to the implications of this great experience of openness through the symbology of the tantric path.

After the abhishekas relevant to body, speech, and thought, there is still a fourth. As I have pointed out, these stages are part of a unitary situation which we approach sequentially only because of the limitations of our mode of experience. But it is much more sensible to see them as a part of a great tableau in which all the aspects are interrelated and fuse with one another. It is on the level of the fourth abhisheka that we see the previous experiences as aspects of a totality. These experiences fuse into an integrated pattern which cannot be destroyed. Through the empowerment their indivisibility is clearly established.

At this point we cannot quite say that we have become one, because even the idea of unity or oneness now no longer applies. The term one is only meaningful if we have a two or a three. Unity implies plurality as something else. But what we are dealing with here is a unity which includes plurality. Unity and plurality only seem contradictory when we conceive of them as isolated terms. There can never be isolation when everything is part of the whole pattern. Isolation is an abstraction, but plurality is whatever we happen to find in the world wherever we are. Not disrupting the unitary quality by isolating units is the basic meaning of unity. And this comes here as a deep inner experience.

This deep inner experience is the guru operating, and through such profound experiences he has his tremendous influence on the pattern of our spiritual growth. For in the ultimate sense, the guru is none other than the Buddha—not the historical Buddha but buddhahood itself. In this way all the empowerments are developments of the guru yoga. In the guru yoga we attempt to come closer to our basic nature through coming closer to the guru. In the empowerments we are actually in connection with him. We are also in connection with his lineage, those who have preceded him in the direct transmission of the teaching and in connection with whom he remains.

Like the refuge formula and the empowerment ceremonies, the guru yoga practice has an outward form betokening a deeper experience. In this case the outward form is a kind of litany. But if, in reciting this litany, there is awareness of where in us these words come from, they follow back to the person whom we have chosen as our spiritual guide. The litany itself is not the ultimate thing, but it involves us in the fact that throughout human history there have been persons who have awakened. The presence of their example challenges us to look into ourselves and awaken to our own being. And in the process of coming closer to what is meant by their example, the nature of the guru as we relate to him again changes and becomes deeper. It increasingly reveals itself as a principle which is much more attuned to the real than our habitual sham.

The various ceremonies—the refuge, the guru yoga, and the empowerments are all established in an outward form so as to be repeatable. But it is of the greatest importance to be aware of the highly symbolical character of tantra as expressed in these forms. We must distinguish between a symbol and a sign. A sign can be put on anything and acts as an identification tag. A symbol always points beyond itself. It is only a pointer to, in this case, what cannot be said.

A great deal of harm has been done by abusing the repeatable character of these rituals and using the texts indiscriminately, without being aware of the different levels of the symbology. Only when a person has grown up to the point where he no longer confuses a symbol with a sign does he begin to come into real contact with the guru. Only then does the pattern of development available in the tantric tradition, beginning with taking refuge and leading through the various traditional practices and the four empowerments, have the effect of awakening the power that is within us. It makes us more and more alive and brings us to a new perception of our situation in which we see that we are never alone, never isolated ends-in-ourselves.

We see that we are always in a force field, so to speak, in which every act of ours has its effect on others and the whole field constantly has its effect on us. The empowerments introduce us progressively into the dimension of this vision. Once we have glimpsed it, the guru is always present, although he may not be clearly perceived. When one's vision begins to mature, one perceives the guru as the great challenger in the quest to be true to oneself.

TEN

Questions and Answers: Guenther

Q: Can you say something about mantra?

G: The word *mantra* comes from the noun *manas* and the verbal root *tra* ("to protect"), according to the Indian explanation. The full explanation runs as follows:

manastrāṇabhūtatvād mantram ity ucyate

Since it has become a protection of mind, it is called mantra.

Mantra is usually associated with certain syllables or combinations of syllables. It is completely wrong to try to read a meaning into these syllables as with ordinary words. This goes exactly counter to the purpose of mantra, which is to protect the mind from straying away into habitual fictions. These fictions are very much tied up with words. The function of mantra is to preclude the tendency of the mind to, so to speak, flow downward. We are forced here to use this spatial metaphor; we might also speak of the tendency of the mind to glide off into something, or to fall.

We encounter this same metaphor in Western religious thought, where it is said that man is a fallen being. Our mental process tends always to run to the lowest level, just like water. With water rushing downward, once it has reached the bottom, it has lost its potential and there is practically nothing more that can be done. Well, it works the

392

same way with our minds, going off into this system of fictions we have developed.

To give an example of mantra, I might use the word *love*. This word can be used in an everyday way so that it is meaningless or in a way that renders it full of meaning. In the latter case, it keeps something alive; in the former it's just a piece of dead language. When a young man is courting a girl, he may say "I love you" or address her as "my love." So saying, he expresses something that no other word could better convey. Sometime later the couple goes to the divorce court, and he says, "Well, my love, let us separate." In one case, the word *love* is a mantra; in the other case, it's just an ordinary figure of speech. So there is nothing mysterious about mantras.

Q: Dr. Guenther, could you give an idea of the sense of the word *svabhava* in *svabhavikakaya;* it seems to be different than elsewhere.

G: In the term *svabhavikakaya, kaya* is derived from the other terms (dharmakaya, sambhogakaya, nirmanakaya). Then, in order to emphasize that existentially kaya is not dependent upon anything else, you say *svabhava.* Here *svabhava* has a sense something like "self-existing." The svabhavikakaya is not different therefore from the dharmakaya, being that which is not existentially dependent on anything else. The nirmanakaya and sambhogakaya are, however, dependent on the dharmakaya.

Q: So it could not be said that the svabhavikakaya is dependent on the dharmakaya.

G: That's right. The term *svabhavikakaya* obviously evolved in the clarification of what was meant by dharmakaya. Dharmakaya had two meanings. On the one hand, there is the usual sense in which it is associated with the very nature of buddhahood. On the other hand, it also meant the sum total of all the entities of reality. The latter sense is the early hinayana view of dharmakaya. This is still the meaning it has as late as in the Hua Yen or Avatamsaka school. In later mahayana Buddhism the two senses always go together. Even though they are both dharmakaya, there cannot be two dharmakayas. So we say that the absolute is dharmakaya, and that all things, seen as constituting and representing the absolute, are also dharmakaya. This insight presenting the rapprochement of these two senses of dharmakaya was a contribution of the *Avatamsaka Sutra*. This sutra, incidentally, has never been found in any Sanskrit version.

Q: Can you explain sambhogakaya?
G: *Kaya* refers to the existential fact of being and *sambhoga* to being in communication with dharmakaya. The sambhogakaya is between the dharmakaya and the nirmanakaya. It is dependent upon and in communion with the dharmakaya. It is the level on which, as it is said, the teaching of the Buddha goes on uninterruptedly in that the person tuned in to this level always hears the dharma taught. This is, of course, a figurative way of speaking.

Then from the sambhogakaya there is a further condensation which is the nirmanakaya, in which what was seen or felt on the sambhogakaya level is now made more concrete. *Nirmana* means "to measure out." On this level, the whole thing is put into a limited framework, which is understandable to us because, of course, our mind works within limitations.

Q: You've spoken quite a bit about the Yogachara. What about the role of the Madhyamaka in the development of tantra?
G: The philosophical systems that developed in Buddhist India, the Vaibhashikas, the Sautrantikas, and the Yogacharins (the mentalistic trends), were all lumped together in the traditional Tibetan surveys as reductive philosophies. They all try to subsume the whole of reality under particular existents, one under a particular existent of a physical kind, another under a particular existent called "mind." But in all cases they are reductive systems. Not to say that there wasn't a progress in the development of these systems.

The earliest, the Vaibhashikas, assumed mind and mental events, chitta and chaitta. Wherever there is mind there are also mental events. The Sautrantikas challenged this, showing that the mind *is* the mental events, so that there was no reason for this double principle. So they simplified it to saying a cognitive event was just mind. Still the Sautrantikas continued to speak of external objects corresponding to the objective pole of our cognitive experience, even though they regarded these external objects as only hypothetical causes of our cognitive experience. But further investigation showed that there was very little reason for assuming realities outside our experiencing of them. The realist formula would be $x = x + n$, where x is mind or experience and n is external realities. Now this is a nonsensical formula unless $n = 0$, which the realist will not accept. So if we analyze the situation in this mathematical form, the realist hasn't got a leg to stand on.

The uncertainty over the status of n (external reality) had already been initiated by the Sautrantikas. Then the Yogacharins drew the logical conclusion that there is only x, which *appears* as $x + n$. In reducing the whole epistemological formula to mind or experience alone, the Yogacharins still held on to this x. This is exactly what the Madhyamaka critique of the Yogacharins undermined, showing, in effect, that holding to the principle of mind was still reducing reality to some particular existent.

So, for the subsequent development of tantra, the Yogacharins and Madhyamikas were of equal importance. The Yogacharins with their principle of mind provided something to deal with. After all, you must have something in hand to deal with. The Madhyamikas contributed the insight that one cannot believe in this what-you-have-in-hand as an ultimate answer. This criticism of the reductionist tendency which had characterized all previous Buddhist philosophy was a very important one indeed.

Q: Is dharmadhatu in the vajrayana connected with the skandhas?

G: The skandhas are subdivisions of the dharmadhatu. This has always been accepted by all schools. Since the earliest times there has never been the slightest disagreement over the division that was made into the skandhas, the dhatus, and the ayatanas, all of which together compose the dharmadhatu. The schools differed only over the logical status of these elements.

The earliest classification was made by the Vaibhashikas in the *Abhidharmakosha*. All the following schools adopted this classification. Even the Yogacharins, who would accept only mind as ultimate took it up; in fact they divided it up even more intricately than their predecessors.

As the first to attempt a systematization of what had been given by Buddha in the sutras, the Vaibhashikas based themselves on the Abhidarma-pitaka, which itself originated from certain word lists. These word lists seem to have come about when, after the Buddha had died, his followers wanted to set up some kind of easy reference to the body of his teachings. It was to be something like an index. This began as word lists, almost like sets of synonyms and antonyms. In this way Buddha's followers began to organize the teaching. They would approach the whole of reality from the point of view of a single category they had under examination.

For instance, considering impermanence, they noted that there were certain things that were impermanent and other phenomena to which the term impermanence did not apply. Thus they came to make a great division between that which is impermanent and that which is permanent. Everything in the transitory category were particular existents, divided into physical, mental, and others which were neither physical nor mental. Particular existents which were neither physical nor mental were, for example, attainment, aging, or letters. Words are made up of letters—are these letters physical or mental? On the permanent side of this great division of reality was *akasha,* usually translated as space. We must be clear that in Buddhist philosophy the notion of space never indicates mathematical or locational space. It is more like life space or lived space. This space is irreducible and not transitory; it is there as long as one is alive (and after that, one can enunciate no philosophical theories).

This great division into permanent and impermanent was adopted by later schools, but the way of looking at it was subject to continual criticism and revision. Vasubandhu, for instance, criticized some of the earlier statements from the Sautrantika point of view. Some of the criticisms were quite simple and purely linguistic. The Vaibhashikas had said, "The eye sees." This seems legitimate; probably none of us can find any reason to object to such a formulation. But the Sautrantikas said, "No, *we* see *with* our eyes." The Sautrantikas began criticizing the Vaibhashikas in this manner.

Eventually they wanted to know exactly what was meant by what they themselves were saying. This led them into a thorough analysis of perception. They became quite involved in what differentiated veridical from delusive perceptual situations. What could the criteria be? They found that the inquiry can be shifted from one level of absoluteness-relativity to another and that what was veridical on one level might be delusive on another. In this way the epistemological inquiry was greatly expanded. The Sautrantikas tried to keep their criteria consonant with common sense; but in the analysis of perception, common sense is not a very reliable touchstone. Thus there was room for the Yogacharins to come in, make their critique, and draw their conclusions.

But the Yogacharins' view, for all its sophistication in relation to the earlier schools, remained naive. In dealing with mind, they concretized and affirmed it as a particular existent. The odd thing is that when we make positive statements, we exclude. If we want to be inclusive, we must make negative statements; we must continuously say "not this, not that." If I say "horse," I exclude everything that isn't a horse. But certainly there are also cows. So in affirming as ultimate a particular existent we fall into this trap. This is precisely the point at which the idea of shunyata as openness enters. Shunyata is an absolutely positive term in a negative form.

Q: Could you give an idea of the significance of *dakini?*

G: The Tibetan word is *khandroma (mkha' 'gro ma)*. Literally it means "walking over space." Again here, space, akasha, refers not to mathematical or locational space but to life space. "Walking over" signifies a kind of appreciation. This appreciation of space is inspiration, which is depicted symbolically in female form. This inspiration is the dakini; it is the inspiration of the openness of the space. The rich symbolism of the dance of the dakinis indicates that the inspiration of openness comes not in one form but many. This dance, a series of graceful movements, also expresses the fact that each moment is a new situation. The pattern changes constantly and each moment presents a new occasion for appreciation, a new sense of significance.

Q: What is *lalita?*

G: Lalita is the graceful movement of the dance. There is never a state of rest. *Lalita* also has a strong connotation of beauty. Beauty here is not different from the valuable; and the valuable is not different from what it is. When we try to catch it or grasp it, it is destroyed.

Q: It has been said that the Hindu and Buddhist tantras arose simultaneously, that one did not precede the other. Do you think that is accurate?

G: I think that is correct, yes. They are quite different and probably one could not be derived from the other. The emphasis in the Hindu tantra is on a way of doing, creating. The Buddhist tantra with its theory of prajna, appreciative discrimination, having equal status with upaya, action, has quite a different emphasis. For one thing, the Hindu term *shakti* never appears in Buddhist texts. Those who say it does can never have seen the actual texts. But the idea of shakti is of paramount importance in the Hindu tantra.

The Hindu tantra took over the Samkhhya system of philosophy, which is based on the dualism of purusha, the male factor, and prakriti, the female or shakti factor. *Purasha* is usually translated as "pure mind" and *prakriti* as "matter." This is not to be understood in terms of the Western division between mind and matter. Mind and matter as conceived of in the West are both in the prakriti. *Purusha* is a fairly useless term; the concept corresponding to it fits nicely into a male-dominance psychology. The purusha, according to the Samkhya system, throws its light on the prakriti, and this starts a process of evolution.

There are some definite difficulties in this conception. The purusha is defined as being ever-present. If this is the case, liberation can never take place—the ever-presence of the purusha means that he throws his light, irritates the prakriti, continuously. Since there is this dominance of the male over the female, and at the same time, everything takes place within the prakriti—all cognition, all action, everything—the system is logically untenable.

Still it has certain good points. The analysis of the prakriti into the three strands, or gunas—sattva, tamas, rajas—can account well for the psychological differences in individuals. Some people are more intelligent, lazy, temperamental than others. This is well accounted for. Metaphysically, however, the system is complete nonsense. It cannot do what it sets out to do, which is provide for the possibility of liberation. It says if a separation between purusha and prakriti takes place, there is liberation; but this is impossible if the purusha is ever-present. This was later understood by the followers of the yoga system of Patanjali. They tried to get out of the difficulty by postulating a super-purusha, an ishvara, a god. But this merely opens the way to an infinite regress. If one is not enough and a second is supposed to be, why not a third, a fourth, a fifth?

Such a set of improbable conceived principles was bound to present such difficulties. The prakriti is said to be unintelligent, but all intelligent processes occur in it. The purusha is said to be pure intelligence, but it doesn't cognize. This is like saying, "Look, I have a very special book; but this book has no pages, no print, no binding, no cover—but it is a book!"

Q: What is the movement of this relationship between purusha and prakriti supposed to be and how is it supposed to come to an end?

G: The prakriti or shakti is utilized by the purusha. The simile is that he asks her to dance and to perform various antics. Then he says, "Now I am fed up with this so stop it." Then he says, "Now we are free." This is a bit primitive.

Q: It is true that the Buddha's actual words were never recorded?
G: Yes.

Q: Would you be able to say anything, then, about how the sutras came about?

G: After the Buddha died, an effort was made to collect what the Buddha had said. But all the sutras begin with the form "Thus have I heard. . . ." Certainly there must be passages that were remembered correctly, but there are no means of verifying where the texts represent exact words, because none of the material was reported as direct quotation.

Q: It seems they could never have been the exact words, then.

G: The tremendous capacity for memory that existed in Eastern culture could counteract the likelihood that all the exact words were lost. The time when they codified and wrote down the Buddha's teaching was not necessarily the beginning of its preservation. It might have been decided at that point that it was a good idea to write it all down because the oral tradition *might* become disturbed. But up until that point the oral tradition can be said to have been highly exact. Since the words were rehearsed after the death of the Buddha, this is not very doubtful. The words were precious at that point since the Buddha himself was no longer there. It is true that, whereas in some passages the reciter might give the exact words, in other parts he might recite only as he had understood. But this became accepted.

Another point is that the Pali sutras do not contain everything that was preserved in the tradition. The Sanskrit version preserved in the agamas has sections that were left out in the Pali. The Theravada canon definitely reflects a vested interest.

Q: What would you say is the basic point in the Buddhist view?
G: One basic thing that must be learned is what is meant by the I or

the ego. We must understand this because the ego is the great stumbling block, a kind of frozenness in our being, which hinders us from any authentic being. Traditionally, the Buddhists ask what such an entity could consist of. Is it what we would call our physical aspect? Our feelings, motivations, our thought processes? These are the things we try to identify as ourselves, as "I." But there are many things that can be pointed out with regard to each one of these identifications to show that it is spurious.

The word "I" has very special peculiarities. We generally assume that this word is like any other; but actually it is unique in that the noise "I" can only issue in a way that makes sense from a person who uses it signifying himself. It has a peculiar groundless quality. "I" cannot apply to anything other than this act of signifying. There is no ontological object which corresponds to it. Nevertheless, philosophies, Oriental as well as Western, have continually fallen into the trap of assuming there is something corresponding to it, just as there is to the word "table." But the word "I" is quite different from other nouns and pronouns. It can never refer to anyone but the subject. It is actually a shortcut term which refers to a complicated system of interlocking forces, which can be identified and separated, but which we should not identify with.

To undermine the native persistence of the ego notion is one of the first steps in Buddhism, a prerequisite for all further study. Furthermore, we have to see that the various aspects of ourselves that we tend to identify with from moment to moment as "I"—the mind, the heart, the body—are only abstractions from a unitary process. Getting this back into perspective is also a basic step. Once these steps have been taken, a foundation is laid; although in fact for a very long time we must continue to fall back into spurious identification.

This identification also has its objective pole. When we perceive something, we automatically believe that there is something real corresponding to the perception. But if we analyze what is going on when we perceive something, we learn that the actual case is quite different. What is actually given in the perceptual situation are constitutive elements of an object. For example, we perceive a certain colored patch and we say we have a tablecloth. This tablecloth is what is called the epistemological object. But automatically we believe that we have not only an epistemological object, an object for our knowledge, but also an ontological object corresponding to it, which we believe to be an actual constitutive element of being.

But then, on the other hand, we have certain other perceptions, and we say, "Oh, well, there is certainly nothing like this." If someone has delirium tremens and he sees pink rats, we certainly say there are no pink rats. But here he goes ahead anyhow and tries to catch them—and he behaves toward them as we do toward ordinary objects. In a certain sense, from the Buddhist point of view, we are constantly chasing about trying to catch pink rats. So here the question arises: If one perception is adjudged delusive and the other veridical, what could be the criterion used to make the distinction? All that can be said is that any object before the mind is an object in the mind. Any belief in ontologically authentic objects is based on an assumption which cannot withstand critical analysis.

What we have, then, is a phenomenon which appears as having some reference beyond itself. But our analysis has shown us that this reference is only an apparent one in which we cannot rely as valid. Now this analysis is extremely valuable because it brings us back to our immediate experience, before it is split into subjective and objective poles. There is a strong tendency at this point to objectify this immediate experience and say that this fundamental and unassailable thing we have got back to is the mind. But there is absolutely no reason to posit such an entity as the mind; moreover, postulating this entity again shifts the attention out of the immediacy of experience back onto a hypothetical level. It puts us back into the same old concatenation of fictions that we were trying to get away from.

So there is a constant analysis, a constant observation that must go on, applied to all phases of our experience, to bring us back to this complete immediacy. This immediacy is the most potent creative field that can exist. The creative potential of this field is referred to in the tantric texts as bindu, or in Tibetan, thig-le.

Q: Is it possible, if one already has a certain experience of life, to start directly on the tantric path?

G: There's a certain danger involved in trying to do advanced practices without having the proper foundation. Unless one has actually gone through the preliminary experiences, conclusions may be drawn on the basis of insufficient information. And they may produce just the opposite effect of the one which is intended. Throughout Buddhist history there has been an emphasis placed on learning, learning more from the philosophical point of view. And this begins with seeing.

In traditional Buddhism what is usually learned at the beginning is the four noble truths. But even these basic truths are the product of a long, long process gone through by the Buddha. It was after Buddha had already gone through all the traditionally accepted practices that the moment came which made him the Enlightened One. It was only after this moment that he formulated these four truths.

The Buddha formulated these truths in the inverse order of cause and effect. Usually we think in terms of cause then effect, but these truths are presented here in the order of effect, then cause.

This order of presentation is educationally oriented. First we have to be brought face-to-face with what is there. Then, when we are willing to accept this, we can ask how it comes about. The third Dalai Lama wrote a very beautiful book on the stages of the spiritual path in which he uses an excellent simile to illustrate the nature of this learning process. A man is walking along, very contentedly, complacently, happily. He hasn't got a worry in the world. Suddenly there comes a great shock and he finds he has been hit by a torrent of cold water. This really gives him a jolt, and he looks right away to see what has happened. Having been brought face-to-face with a certain situation, his intelligence is entirely aroused. And he sees: "Oh yes, the waterpipe broke!" So he has seen the effect, determined the cause, and already he is at the point of the third truth—that there is a way to stop this. The third Dalai Lama goes on to apply this analogy on a much profounder level. First we must see what is there. In order to do this we need constant study. When we have really learned something about it, we automatically come to the point of beginning to practice in relation to what we have learned. There is a long process between my deciding I must be kind to others and the point where I actually am kind to others. Before such kindness becomes a part of us, we must learn a great deal about what there is.

In English there is the saying, "to see eye to eye." But perhaps more indicative of the actual attitude that exists in the West as the accumulated result of our tradition would be the saying, "to see I to I." Even if we had the tantric practices, they would be completely useless as long as we maintained this ego-oriented attitude.

In the tantric tradition we have the description of the experience of a brilliant light. It is a sort of formless energy which appears to us as a brilliant light. Now we cannot have this experience of light as long as we are involved with our ego's escaping the darkness. In fact it is this very ego involvement which blocks the light. So to begin with we must find out about this "I" which enters into and distorts our being. When we have understood what this is and how it has come about, then we can set those energies free which lead to transformation. The transformation to selflessness does not make us merely an amorphous entity, but leads directly to what the late Abraham Maslow called the "peak experience." Maslow also coined the term "plateau experience," which can be understood as the continuous extension of the peak experience. I think the plateau experience could be equated with buddhahood, while recurrent peak experiences could be associated with the bodhisattva or arhat.

But as Maslow also pointed out, before we reach these experiences, there is a lot of work to be done. A solid foundation must be laid; otherwise any extraordinary experience we have will be extremely precarious and without ground and the next blast of wind will simply blow it away. We will be right back where we were, except worse off because the rubble of this extraordinary experience will now be in the way. So although there is a great tendency to try some shortcut, unfortunately it simply does not work.

Q: Is the concept of the alayavijnana somewhat analogous to Jung's idea of archetypes as potential roots of death, decay, and rebirth?

G: It is close in some ways, but one should not directly equate the two. Jung comes quite close with certain of the archetypes, but being in the Western tradition, he falls into the idea that there is a someone, an entity, to whom the archetypes are related. This is where Jung was tied down by his Aristotelianism. I do not mean to demean Aristotelianism—after all, it is one of the finest systems produced by Western thought—but it definitely has its shortcomings.

To be more precise, Aristotle spoke of the psyche as an object of investigation. With this approach, we are already in a framework which presumes the division between subject and object. In this framework subject and object, rather than being complementary, different aspects of the same unity, are separate entities which are opposed to each other. The word "object" means "thrown against." The Indian terms do not have this dualistic character. The Indians spoke of the "apprehendable" and the "apprehender," which are very much on the same level, aspects of the same process. There cannot be one without the other.

Q: Is the process described through which the original split between the transcendental ego and the empirical ego takes place?

G: To try to put it on the level of ordinary experience, it seems to be similar to the process in which a person, feeling himself handicapped, frustrated, incomplete, projects the idea of what he would wish to be the case as his real self. This would be the projection of the transcendental ego. Strangely enough, in the Kantian tradition, this transcendental ego was viewed as something that the person never could reach; he was more or less condemned to the level of incomplete or inauthentic experience. It was only to the extent that he was able to submit himself to the dictates of the transcendental ego that he became a human being. Kant's very high conception of freedom, as modern philosophy developed, ceased to be attended to and developed, involving as it did this total submission to a fiction.

According to the Nyingmapa tradition of Tibetan Buddhism, when this split occurs, there is just the basic unknowing, avidya (*ma rig pa* in Tibetan) which is taken as the transcendental self by the empirical self. The empirical self, feeling incomplete or frustrated, mistakes the unknowing for its authentic self. The very clearly thought-out Nyingmapa analysis thus contains an implicit critique of the egoistic philosophy which actually glorifies this unknowing as the ultimate self. According to this analysis, once the positing of the transcendental self occurs, all the further processes of experience involving bodily awareness, etc., are related to this fictitious center.

Q: Can you relate tantra to advaitism?

G: The term *advaita,* as we use it, stems from Shankara's Vedanta. The Buddhists never used this term, but used rather the term *advaya.* *Advaya* means "not two"; *advaita* means "one without a second." The conception of "one without a second" puts us at once into the realm of dualistic fictions. Rather than remaining in immediate experience, with the idea of "one," we posit a definite object. This would then necessarily be over against a definite subject, which is the implication Shankara wanted to deny with the "without a second." By saying "not-two" you remain on solid ground, because "not-two" does not mean "one." That conclusion does not follow.

In the works of Saraha and other Buddhist teachers, it is said that it is impossible to say "one" without prejudgment of experience. But

Shankara and his followers were forced by the scriptural authority of the Vedas to posit this One and so were then forced to add the idea "without a second." What they wanted to say was that only atman is real. Now the logic of their position should force them to then say that everything else is unreal. But Shankara himself is not clear on this point. He reintroduced the idea of illusion which had previously been rejected by him. Now if only atman is real, then even illusion apart from it is impossible. But he was forced into a philosophical position which, if it were to be expressed in a mathematical formula, would make absolute nonsense. So intellectually, in this way, it could be said that the Vedanta is nonsense. But it had tremendous impact; and, as we know, the intellect is not everything. But as the Madhyamaka analysis showed, the Vedanta formula simply does not hold water. And Shankara himself, as I said, was not completely clear on this point.

In translating Buddhist texts, it is necessary to take great care with the word *illusion*. Sometimes it appears in what is almost an apodictic or judgmental sense. This happens especially in poetry, where one cannot destroy the pattern of the flow of words to make specific philosophical qualifications. But the basic Buddhist position concerning illusion, as prose works are careful to point out, is not the apodictic statement made by the followers of Shankara that the world *is* illusion. The Buddhist position is that the world may be *like* an illusion. There is a huge logical difference between saying the world *is* an illusion and saying the world may be *like* an illusion. The Buddhist position suspends judgment.

So while it has been suggested that Shankara was a crypto-Buddhist, because, in fact, he took over almost the entire epistemological and metaphysical conception of the Buddhists, there remains this very crucial difference.

ELEVEN

Questions and Answers: Rinpoche

Q: What is abhisheka?

R: The literal meaning of *abhisheka* is "anointment." Etymologically it means "sprinkle and pour." It is a sort of emergence into validity, the confirmation of your existence as a valid person as a result of having acknowledged your basic makeup as it is. But abhisheka cannot take place unless the student's training has brought him to a full understanding of the surrendering which is involved in it. He has related his body with the ground by prostrating. He has repeated over and over again the formula: "I take refuge in the Buddha; I take refuge in the dharma; I take refuge in the sangha." He has taken refuge in the Buddha as an example; taken refuge in the dharma as the path; taken refuge in the sangha as his companionship on the path. In that way he has accepted the whole universe as part of his security, warded off the paranoia that comes from the situation of maintaining the ego. In that way he has prepared the space of abhisheka. Having prepared the space, he can relax; he can afford to relax.

Then, the abhisheka takes place as the meeting of two minds. The guru identifies himself with the deity of a particular mandala and encourages the student to do the same. Then the student is crowned and enthroned with all the attributes of that particular symbolism. For instance, the particular deity in question might hold a bell and a vajra in his hands. The guru gives the student a bell and a vajra in order to help him identify himself with the deity. This is the development of what is known in tantric language as vajra pride, indestructible pride. You develop this because you *are* the deity. You have been acknowledged as such by your

406

colleague. He also has accepted you—you are sharing the same space together, so to speak.

Q: Do the various yanas and vehicles intermingle? Are they all part of the vajrayana?

R: It seems that basically the whole practice is part of the vajrayana, because you cannot have discontinuity in your practice. You start on the rudimentary level of samsaric ego and use that as the foundation of tantra; then you have the path, then the fruition. But unless you begin with some stuff, something, no matter how apparently crude it is, the process cannot take place. Because you begin with something, that starting point or stepping-stone is on the continuity of your path.

Still, however, as I see it, Westerners are largely unprepared for the practices of the vajrayana at this point, because they have not yet assimilated the basic understanding of Buddhism. In general they do not even have the beginning notions of suffering as explained by the four noble truths. So at this point, the introduction of Buddhism into the West has to be very much on the hinayana level. People have to relate with the pain of sitting down and meditating and churning out all kinds of material from their minds. This is the truth of suffering, that you are still questioning whether or not the world is the ultimate truth. If the world is the truth, then is pain the truth or is pleasure the truth? People first have to sort out these questions through the use of beginner's practices.

Hopefully, in the next twenty to thirty years vajrayana principles dealing with the creation of mandalas and identification with deities can be properly introduced. At this point it would be extremely premature. As Professor Guenther said, tantra has been misunderstood from the beginning. So this fundamental misunderstanding has to be corrected first. Having been corrected, then you begin to feel something, then you begin to chew it, swallow it; then you begin to digest it. This whole process will take quite a bit of time.

Q: Can you say something about experiencing deities?

R: Different types of mandalas with different types of deities exist in the iconographical symbolism of tantra. They are associated with all kinds of psychological states. When a person is involved with this symbolism, there is no problem in identifying himself with such deities. There are many different kinds. There is the father tantra, the mother tantra, and the nondual tantra. There is symbolism relating to the five buddha families: the family of anger, the family of pride, the family of passion, the family of envy, and the family of ignorance. When a person has prepared the ground and is able to relax, then he is able to see the highlights of his basic being in terms of these five energies. These energies are not regarded as bad, such that you have to abandon them. Rather, you begin to respect these seeds that you have in yourself. You begin to relate with them as all kinds of deities that are part of your nature. In other words they constitute a psychological picture of you. All this requires a long process.

Q: Could you explain the difference between vajra pride and spiritual pride based on ego? I see numbers of young people involved with spirituality who just seem to be swollen with self-righteousness.

R: Well that seems to be a crucial point. It is the difference, speaking in terms of tantric practice, between the actual faith of identifying with a certain aspect of oneself as a deity and just relating with those deities as one's dream of the future, what one would like to be. Actually, the two situations are very close in some sense because even in the first case one would like to attain enlightenment. Now here the possibility is presented of relating with an enlightened being, or better, of identifying with the enlightened attitude. This brings it home to one that there is such a thing as enlightenment and that, therefore, one can afford to give up one's clingings and graspings. There could quite easily be quite a thin line between this situation and just considering self-righteously that one is already there.

I think ego's version of spiritual pride is based on blind faith, or what is colloquially known as a "love and light trip." This is having blind faith that since one would like to be thus-and-such, one already is. In this way one could become Rudra, achieve Rudrahood. On the other hand, vajra pride comes from facing the reality of one's nature. It is not a question of becoming what one would like to be, but rather of bringing one's actual energies to full blossom. The confused ego pride is the indulgence of wishful thinking; it is trying to become something else, rather than being willing to be what one is.

Q: Can you relate the tendency to speed from one thing to the next to the fixity that is central to ego?

R: Fixation could be said to be self-consciousness, which is related with dwelling on something or, in other words, perching on something.

That is, you are afraid that you are not secure in your seat, therefore you have to grasp on to something, perch on something. It is something like a bird perching in a tree: the wind might blow the tree, so the bird has to hold on. This perching process, this holding-on-to-something process goes on all the time. It is not at all restricted to conscious action, but it goes on inadvertently as well. If the bird falls asleep in the tree, it still perches, still holds on. Like the bird, you develop that extraordinary talent to be able to perch in your sleep. The speed comes in when you are looking constantly for something to perch on, or you feel you have to keep up with something in order to maintain your perch. Speed is the same idea as samsara, going around and around chasing one's own tail. In order to grasp, in order to perch, in order to dwell on something, you need speed to catch up with yourself. So, strangely enough, in regard to ego's game, speed and fixity seem to be complementary.

Q: Is dwelling connected with the lack of perception of impermanence?

R: Yes, that could be said. In Buddhism there is tremendous stress laid on understanding the notion of impermanence. To realize impermanence is to realize that death is taking place constantly and birth is taking place constantly; so there really is nothing fixed. If one begins to realize this and does not push against the natural course of events, it is no longer necessary to re-create samsara at every moment. Samsara, or the samsaric mentality, is based on solidifying your existence, making yourself permanent, everlasting. In order to do that, since there actually is nothing to grasp on to or sit on, you have to re-create the grasping, the perching, the speeding constantly.

Q: What is the difference between prajna and jnana?

R: Prajna is precision. It is often symbolized as the sword of Manjushri, which severs the root of duality. It is the precision or sharpness of intelligence that cuts off the samsaric flow, severs the aorta of samsara. It is a process of creating chaos in the smooth circulation of maintaining the ego or samsaric mind. This is still a direction, an experience, a learning process, till trying to get at something.

Jnana transcends the learning process, transcends a struggle of any kind; it just is. Jnana is a kind of a self-satisfied samurai—it does not have to fight anymore. An analogy used to describe jnana by the Tibetan teacher Paltrül Rinpoche is that of an old cow grazing in the meadow quite happily—there is total involvement, total completion. There is no longer any need to sever anything. So jnana is a higher state. It is buddha-level, whereas prajna is bodhisattva-level.

Q: Does prajna include both intuitional insight and the knowledge that comes out of the rational mind?

R: You see, from the Buddhist point of view, intuition and rationality are something quite different from what is generally understood. Intuition and intellect can only come from the absence of ego. Here it is actually *the* intuition, *the* intellect. They do not relate with the back-and-forth of comparative thinking, which comes from the checking-up process of ego. While you are making the comparative journey, you get confused halfway through so that you lose track of whether you are coming or going. Real intellect skips this entire process. So the ultimate idea of intellect, from the Buddhist point of view, is the absence of ego, which is prajna. But here, in contrast to jnana, there is still a delight in understanding.

Q: Would visualization be on the sambhogakaya level of teaching, since it is based on the experience of shunyata?

R: The practice of visualization is on the dharmakaya level, because until you have reached that level you have not yet worked with the play of phenomena. You have not yet encountered the reality of phenomena as what it is. Up until the shunyata level, you are making a relationship with the phenomenal world; after that, you begin to see the colors, temperatures, textures within the shunyata experience. This is the first glimpse of the possible seed of visualization. Without this foundational development, the practice of visualization could lead to making use of the past and the future, fantasies and memories of shapes and colors. The romantic qualities and desirable aspects of the deities could be focused upon to the extent of losing contact with your basic being. Visualization then becomes a sort of re-creation of the ego.

Q: Is it good practice to meditate while listening to someone speak, you or someone else? Is meditating while listening a contradiction? How should one listen?

R: The traditional literature describes three types of listeners. In one case, one's mind is wandering so much that there's no room at all for anything that's being said. One is just there physically. This type is said to be like a pot turned upside down. In another case, one's mind is relating somewhat to what's being said, but basically it is still wandering. The analogy is a pot with a hole in the bottom. Whatever you pour in leaks out underneath. In the third case, the listener's mind contains aggression, jealousy, destruction of all kinds. One has mixed feelings about what is being said and cannot really understand it. The pot is not turned upside down, it doesn't have a hole in the bottom, but it has not been cleaned properly. It has poison in it.

The general recommendation for listening is to try to communicate with the intelligence of the speaker; you relate to the situation as the meeting of two minds. One doesn't particularly have to meditate at that point in the sense that meditation would become an extra occupation. But the speaker can become the meditation technique, taking the place of, let's say, identifying with the breath in sitting meditation. The voice of the speaker would be part of the identifying process, so one should be very close to it as a way of identifying with what the speaker is saying.

Q: Sometimes I have the strange experience in meeting someone, supposedly for the first time, that I've known that person before—a kind of déjà vu experience. And even, in some cases, that person will say that it seems to him the same way. It's as though, even though we've never seen each other in this particular life, that we've known each other somewhere before. How do you explain these phenomena?

R: It seems that successive incidents take place and that each incident in the process has a relationship with the past. The process just develops that way. It seems quite simple.

Q: Is it that you bring with you some sort of hangover from the past, some sort of preconception, and it's that that makes you think you've seen that person before?

R: You do that in any case. You bring some energy with you that makes you able to relate to situations as they are. Without that, you wouldn't be here anyway. But there doesn't seem to be anything the matter with that. That energy of being here in the way that we're here is something we have to accept. Partial realization of this might provide you some inspiration. But it doesn't exempt you from having to go through your situation.

Q: It seems very mysterious.

R: If you see the situation completely, somehow that mystery isn't a mystery anymore. It seems mysterious because we don't perceive all the subtleties of things as they are. If you accept the situation it ceases to be a mystery.

Q: You begin to cease in some way to see other people as being completely different people, separate from yourself. At times it seems almost like yourself looking at yourself. Almost, but not quite.

R: At that moment there seems to be a direct contradiction. You see people as separate, but at the same time you see them as part of your innate nature. Somehow the validity of the situation doesn't lie in the logic, but in the perceptions themselves. If there is an actual happening which goes directly against logic, there's nothing wrong with that.

Q: Can you give an example of things going against logic? I've never encountered that.

R: There are all kinds of things like that. You're trying to be an ideal person, trying to bring about ideal karma for yourself, to be good to everybody, etc. Suddenly, you're struck with a tremendous punishment. This kind of thing happens all the time. This is one of the problems unsolved by Christianity. "My people are good Christians; how come they were killed in the war? How does that fit with the divine law of justice?"

Q: I wouldn't say that's a question of logic. Logic doesn't reveal anything about what ought to happen in the world. It has nothing to do with that.

R: Logic comes from expectations. If I fall down I should hurt. We think we should feel pain because if we fall down we *expect* to hurt ourselves. We have set patterns of mind that we've followed all along. We've been conditioned by our culture, our traditions, whatever. This thing is regarded as bad; that thing is regarded as good. If you consider yourself good, then, by this logic, you consider yourself foolproof good. All kinds of good things should happen to you. But there is no fixed doctrine of anything, no kind of exemplary case history of what should be, no manual, no dictionary of what should take place in the universe. Things don't happen according to our conceptualized expectations. That is the very reason why we hasten to make rules for all kinds of things.

So if you have an accident, that might be good. It might bespeak something else besides disaster.

Q: You mean that if we have suffering in our lives, that can be a good thing because it provides us with the opportunity to meet the challenge of it and transcend it? That it could stand us in good stead in terms of rebirth?

R: I don't mean to say that things are always for the best. There could be eternally terrifying things. You could be endlessly condemned: Since you are suffering in this life, that could cause you to suffer in the next as well. The whole thing is not particularly geared toward goodness. All kinds of things might happen.

Q: When you have partial experiences of nonduality, do you think it's in any way harmful to talk about those experiences? Do you think labeling them can be destructive?

R: I don't think it's particularly destructive or unhealthy, but it might delay the process of development to some extent because it gives you something to keep up with. It makes you try to keep up all the corners and areas of your experiences. It makes you try to keep up with your analysis of the situation; without being poisonous, it is a delaying process. It sort of makes you numb toward relating directly with actual experiences. You don't relate directly because you're wearing a suit of armor. Then you act in accordance with the balance of comfort inherent in the suit of armor. "In accordance with my suit of armor, this experience has to be this way or this way."

Q: How do you take off your armor?

R: It's not exactly a question of taking it off. It is a question of seeing the possibility of nakedness, seeing that you can relate with things nakedly. That way the padding that you wear around your body becomes superfluous at some stage. It's not so much a question of giving up the mask; rather the mask begins to give you up because it has no function for you anymore.

Q: Is the urge to explain somehow a function of the ego's wanting to freeze the situation? Establishing where I'm now at rather than just going on and experiencing? What is that? Why is it happening?

R: Essentially because you're relating with some landmark. As long as you're relating to any landmark, any point of reference for comparative study, you're obviously going to be uncomfortable. Because either you're too far from it or you're not too close to it.

Q: A lot of problems in dealing with other people seem to be emotional. Sometimes feelings that are not appropriate to the immediate situation—that are appropriate to something else—just won't disappear. You can know intellectually that they are not appropriate to the situation, but still . . .

R: "Appropriate to the situation" is a questionable idea. To begin with you have to relate to the situation as you see it. You might see that you're surrounded by a hostile environment. The first thing necessary is to study the hostile environment; see how hostile, how intensive it is. Then you will be able to relate with things.

When you talk about situations, it's quite tricky. We have situations as we would like them to be, as they might be, as they seem to be. It's very up in the air. Situations are not really certain. So before you dance on the ground, you have to check to see if it's safe to dance on, whether it's better to wear shoes or whether you can dance barefoot.

Q: About speaking about one's experiences—if it were in any way harmful to you, would it also be harmful to the person you were talking to? In some circumstances, might it not be a generous thing? It might be useful to them even though it gets you unnecessarily into words. Or would it be harmful to them at the same time?

R: Basically the situation is that there are no separate realities, yours and his, for instance. There's only one reality. If you're able to deal with one end of reality, you're dealing with the whole thing. You don't have to strategize in terms of the two ends. It's one reality. That might make us very uncomfortable, because we would like to be in a position to manipulate and balance various factors so that everything is safe and stable, with things neatly territorialized—his end of the stick, my end of the stick. But basically it's necessary to give up the idea of territory. You are not really dealing with the whole territory anyway, but with one end, not with the peripheries but just with one spot in the middle. But with that one spot in the middle the whole territory *is* covered. So one doesn't have to try to maintain two sides all the time. Just work on the one thing. Reality becomes one reality. There's no such thing as separate realities.

Q: Would you say something about developing mandala in the living situation?

R: That's really what we've been discussing. The complexities of life situations are really not as complicated as we tend to experience them. The complexities and confusions all have their one root somewhere, some unifying factor. Situations couldn't happen without a medium, without space. Situations occur because there's fertile oxygen, so to speak, in the environment to make things happen. This is the unifying factor, the root perspective of the mandala; by virtue of this, chaos is methodically chaotic. For example, we are here and there are many people, a crowd. But each person is coming to some conclusion methodically in relation to the whole thing. That's why we are here. But if an outsider were to pass by and look at the spectacle, it would look like too many people, too complicated. He wouldn't see that there is one situation that we're all interested in, that we're all related to. This is the way it is with everything that happens in life situations. The chaos is methodically chaotic.

Q: You mean it's a matter of different perspectives? Each person has a different reason for being here; if a person looked at it from the outside, he'd see us all sitting here and maybe wouldn't know why. And then . . .

R: I mean we are trying to unify ourselves through confusion.

Q: The more confusion, the more unity?
R: That's what tantric people say.

Q: You mean the more confusion there is, the more difficult it is to stamp a system on reality?

R: You see, chaos has an order by virtue of which it isn't really chaos. But when there's no chaos, no confusion, there's luxury, comfort. Comfort and luxury lead you more into samsara because you are in a position to create more kinds of luxurious possibilities, psychologically, philosophically, physically. You can stretch your legs and invent more gadgets to entertain yourself with. But strangely enough, looking at it scientifically, at the chemistry of it, creating more luxurious situations adds further to your collection of chaos. That is, finally all these luxurious conclusions come back on you and you begin to question them. So you are not happy after all. Which leads you to the further understanding that, after all, this discomfort has order to it.

Q: Is this what you mean when you talk about working with negativity?

R: That's exactly what that is. The tantric tradition talks about transmutation—changing lead into gold.

Q: When you meditate, are you just supposed to space out as much as you can, or ought you to go over your past experiences? It seems more interesting in the direction of spacing out.

R: The basic chemistry of experience, the cosmic law (or whatever you'd like to call it), has its own natural balance to it. You space out, you dream extensively; but the dreaming on and on has no message in it. This is because you failed to relate to the actuality of dreaming, the actuality of spacing out. The point is that you can't reach any sort of infinite point by spacing out, unless you experience the space of earth, which accommodates the actual, solid earthy facts. So the basic chemistry of experience brings you back altogether, brings you down. Buddha's experience is an example of this. Having studied for a long time with mystical teachers, he came to the conclusion that there is no way out. He began to work his own way inward and found there was a way in. Enlightenment is more a way inward than a way out. I don't mean to suggest cultivating a sense of inwardness, but rather relating with the solid, earthy aspect of your experience.

Q: I used to think that there was a way out of conflict. But time went on and it was still there, so I figured there must be a way to live in the midst of conflict. But sometimes it's exhausting trying to keep up with it.

R: But what do you do if there's no conflict?

Q: I can't imagine what it would be like without it. I guess it might not be very alive.

R: It would be deadly. Working with conflict is precisely the idea of walking on the spiritual path. The path is a wild, winding mountain road with all kinds of curves; there are wild animals, attacks by bandits, all kinds of situations cropping up. As far as the occupation of our mind is concerned, the chaos of the path is the fun.

Q: Since Buddhism is starting to be taught here in America, and it's going to go through interpretations and changes, that being its nature, what pitfalls do you foresee for us in relation to it?

R: There's a danger that people might relate to various expressions about it they encounter rather than to their own experiences of the path. Commentaries and interpretations tend to be colored by sidetracks of all kinds. There is a tremendous danger of people relating to the views around the path rather than the path itself. This is because in the West the teaching is not seen as an understandable thing. It is seen as having some special mystery to it and people are frustrated feeling they're not able to understand it. That frustration looks in all directions trying to find interpretations. When we look somewhere else for a way of interpreting our frustration, when we try to look around it, then the view of the path becomes very much a matter of the roadside scenery rather than the road itself. In the tradition of Buddhism in the past, the path has not been regarded as a sociological or archaeological study of any kind. It has been very much a matter of one's own psychological portrait, one's own psychological geography. If the path is approached in this manner, then one can draw on one's own inspiration, even including the inspiration of one's own cultural background. This does not, however, mean that one should involve oneself with elaborate interpretations relating one's psychology to one's cultural background. This would be another sidetrip. One has to keep to the straight and narrow, keep to the path. Having done that, then one can interpret, because at this point the teaching is no longer a foreign language; it's a very familiar psychological portrait of oneself. The whole process becomes very obvious, very direct, very natural.

Q: Then once you know the strict rules and laws and have the experience, you can start to branch out a little?

R: You can start to branch out in terms of your experiences in daily living, rather than in terms of philosophy or other theoretical constructions. Philosophy or theoretical extrapolations of any kind have no personal relation with you at all. Dealing in terms of these is just collecting further fantasies.

Q: Would you speak about laziness?

R: Laziness is an extremely valuable stepping-stone. Laziness is not just lazy, it is extraordinarily intelligent. It can think up all kinds of excuses. It looks for all kinds of ways of manipulating the general situation, the domestic situation, the emotional situation; it invokes your health, your budget; it thinks around all kinds of corners just to justify itself.

At the same time there is a deep sense of self-deception. The application of the logic of laziness is constantly going on in one's own mind. One is constantly having a conversation with oneself, a conversation between one's basic being and one's sense of laziness, setting up the logic which make things seem complete, easy, and smooth. But there is a tacit understanding in yourself that, as a matter of fact, this logic is self-deception. This under-the-surface knowledge that it is self-deception, this guilt or discomfort, can be used as a stepping-stone to get beyond laziness. If one is willing to do this, what it requires is just acknowledgment of the self-deception. Such acknowledgment very easily becomes a stepping-stone.

Q: Do we know what we're doing most of the time?
R: We always know. When we say we don't know what we're doing, it's a big self-deception. We know. As I said earlier, a bird can perch on a tree while he's asleep. We know very well what we are doing, actually.

Q: Awareness is always there, no matter what?
R: There's always ego's awareness, yes. It's always there, a meditative state of its own.

Q: Why is it so hard to face up to that?
R: Because that is our inmost secret, our ultimate treasure. It is that which makes us feel comfortable and vindicated.

Q: Is what we need, then, to take responsibility?
R: Self-deception doesn't relate to the long-term scale on which responsibility is usually seen. It's very limited; it's related to current happenings, actual, small-scale situations. We still maintain our schoolboy qualities, even as grown-ups. There is that naughtiness in us always, a kind of shiftiness which is happening all the time, which completely pervades our experience.

Q: In meditation, can it be beneficial to try to relax?
R: From the Buddhist point of view, meditation is not intended to

create relaxation or any other pleasurable condition, for that matter. Meditation is meant to be provocative. You sit and let things come up through you—tension, passion, or aggression—all kinds of things come up. So Buddhist meditation is not the sort of mental gymnastic involved in getting yourself into a state of relaxation. It is quite a different attitude because there is no particular aim and object, no immediate demand to achieve something. It's more a question of being open.

Mgon-Po-Legs-Ldan (the "Grandfather" Mahakala).
DRAWING BY GLEN EDDY.

AN INTERVIEW WITH CHÖGYAM TRUNGPA

Things Get Very Clear
When You're Cornered

IN 1938 THE TENTH Trungpa Tulku, abbot of Tibet's Surmang monasteries, died. Shortly thereafter, the Gyalwa Karmapa was shown in a vision the circumstances of Trungpa's reincarnation. The child was discovered and tested. Offered various objects, he correctly chose those used by him in his previous life. At thirteen months, Chögyam Trungpa Rinpoche ("Precious One") was installed as the new Surmang supreme abbot.

After the Communist invasion of Tibet and his escape to India in 1959, Trungpa Rinpoche attended Oxford and founded a Buddhist center in Scotland. In 1970 he came to the United States and established Nalanda Foundation, which now consists of The Maitri Space Awareness Training Center in Connecticut, the Mudra Theatre Group and Naropa Institute in Colorado, and Vajradhatu, an association of Tibetan Buddhist meditation and retreat centers in nine states and Canada.

Trungpa Rinpoche is a very busy man. After waiting several months for an opportunity to interview him, I received a phone call from his secretary on December 8, 1975, indicating that I could interview him before he left for Vermont on the 12th. Two days later, I was in his office in Boulder setting up tape-recording equipment.

Trungpa Rinpoche entered the room so casually it seemed as though he were already in it. There was nothing contrived about him. He wore a Western business suit with a tie and greeted me openly, in a most ordinary and understated way. The only thing that belied his modest manner was a humorous, almost waggish smile. Speaking very softly, he seemed supremely relaxed. His face never showed a trace of concern. As I directed a series of often complex questions to him, Trungpa Rinpoche never became academic or theoretical. He responded directly to the point, and not from memory. His answers seemed to me to be a spontaneous expression of the centuries-old Tibetan wisdom he represents.

—CRANE MONTAÑO, *The Laughing Man* magazine

The Laughing Man: What liabilities do Americans, as typical spiritual materialists, face over against a Tibetan's more natural talent for practicing the Tantric path?

Chögyam Trungpa Rinpoche: All Buddhist countries are having political and spiritual difficulties, so practice becomes less important. Some corruptions are taking place. Despite the fact that our country has been completely desecrated, we Tibetans have been very fortunate. A few of us have survived with hot blood, a training and spiritual understanding which will allow Tibetan Buddhism to carry on. Otherwise the whole affair would become slow death.

Here in America we are not concerned with adapting across cultural barriers but with handling the teaching here in a skillful way. When Tibetans began to present Buddhism in this country, we did it in keeping with the people's mentality and language. As people understand it more and more, it begins to take a real traditional form. If we were to present all the heavy traditional stuff at the beginning, then all sorts of fascination with Tibetan culture and enlightenment would take place, and the basic message would be lost. So it is good to start with a somewhat free form and slowly tighten it up. This way people have a chance to absorb and understand.

LM: In your book *Born in Tibet,* you described how, when you made your own cultural adaptation, taking off the monastic robes and so forth, there were devastating karmic effects in your own life, represented particularly by your severe automobile accident. Do you see any such liability in your continuing work?

CTR: Tibetans generally have to break through the cultural fascinations and mechanized world of the twentieth century. Many Tibetans either hold back completely or try to be extraordinarily cautious, not communicating anything at all. Sometimes they just pay lip-service to the modern world, making an ingratiating diplomatic approach to the West. The other temptation is to regard the new culture as a big joke and to play the game in terms of a conception of Western eccentricities. So we have to break through all of that. I found within myself a need for more compassion for Western students. We don't need to create imposing images but to speak to them directly, to present the teachings in eye-level situations. I was doing the same kind of thing that I just described, and a very strong message got through to me: "You have to come down from your high horse and live with them as individuals!" So the first step is to talk with people. After we make friends with students, they can begin to appreciate our existence and the quality of the teachings. Later, we can raise the eye level of the teacher in relation to the students so that they may appreciate the teaching and the teacher as well.

LM: Your writings seem to provide a progressive description of the guru from a spiritual friend to a more and more intense confrontation with a very high form of function, the buddha-mind itself. What is that relationship to the guru?

CTR: There seem to be traditional approaches at three levels. At the beginning the guru is known simply as a wise man, a teacher. At that level the student regards the guru as a kind of parental figure. It is the toilet-training stage; the student is just learning to handle life. Then a relationship develops, and the guru becomes a spiritual friend. At this level he offers encouragement rather than criticism.

In the vajrayana relationship, the guru is more like a warrior who is trying to show you how to handle your problems, your life, your world, your self, all at the same time. This function of the guru is very powerful. He has the majestic quality of a king, but at the same time, the power he generates is shared with the student. It is not as if the king is looking down on his subjects as dirty and unworthy peasants. He raises the student's dignity to a level of healthy arrogance, so to speak. But the most important point is to develop an appreciation of the teachings and not to allow any kind of doubt or hesitation to prevent putting them into practice.

LM: You have indicated that it might take twenty to thirty years before the advanced vajrayana visualizations could be done in the West. In what practical ways are the foundations of tantric sadhana established in your present work with students?

CTR: Vajrayana is very easy to understand. It is very straightforward and direct, and it actually speaks to your heart. But just because of its simplicity and directness and power, it might be difficult for people to understand without some kind of preparation. Hinayana practice is valuable because it constantly raises people's sense of mindfulness. They become more aware and appreciative of the world around them. At the mahayana level, a sense of generosity and warmth is developed. People begin to relate to the world with openness rather than fear. This is necessary preparation for the vajrayana level. Even in Theravadin countries where vajrayana is not incorporated into Buddhist teachings, highly accomplished Theravadin students and teachers may also go through a similar kind of journey. We can say that the student of Buddhism is being led ultimately to vajrayana, whatever form of Buddhism he is practicing.

LM: Are any of your students involved in vajrayana practice at this time?

CTR: People have to pass through many hours of sitting practice before they are ready for that. But much more important is a sense of dedication and total development in their state of being. At the moment we have something like four hundred committed members here in Boulder, out of which there are about a hundred tantric students. Those hundred are still at the beginning of the beginnings, so you can't really call them tantra practitioners yet.

LM: Is it possible for an American student to pass through the various stages of spiritual development as quickly as someone who is born into the tradition?

CTR: Yes and no. Sometimes people born in native Buddhist countries encounter a different kind of cultural obstacle. Either they form a lot of preconceptions about spirituality as they grow up, or the language has become so technical that they have difficulty relating to it. So in some ways I think Americans are more fortunate. The language I use had to be created specifically to translate Buddhist ideas into English in a way that makes real sense to people. So Americans can be free of cultural preconceptions. On the other hand, it is much easier to be led astray if you have no idea where your practice is leading and you feel completely at the mercy of the teaching or the teacher. So it can be somewhat difficult and tricky.

LM: Apart from all the fascinating content, what is the real process that tantra represents?

CTR: The important thing is what's known as lineage, not so much the books or traditions handed down. There must be a transformation, some actual experience that people begin to feel. And that is happening all the time. Individuals begin to pick up new experiences from a teacher who has also experienced these things. So there is a meeting of the two minds. This makes the tantric tradition much more powerful, superior to any other tradition. Tantra doesn't depend upon any kind of external particularity. It is a very direct experience transmitted from person to person.

LM: A friend once told me about attending a session in which you ceremonially manifested the consciousness of your lineage. Some people had visions of Marpa and Milarepa, and he personally felt a rather extraordinary force being communicated. That transmission was obviously a real event in this guy's life. How is the transmission of the lineage communicated?

CTR: Well, I'm rather suspicious about visions of that nature. [*Laughs*] But in students who are committed, I think it is a matter of choicelessness. Choicelessness is having no room to turn around or retrieve anything from the past. Things get very clear when you are cornered but not held captive or imprisoned. When you don't have any choice you begin to give up. The student probably doesn't know that he or she is giving up, but something is let go. And when letting go begins to take place, there is some of that complete identification with the practice. It is not so much a matter of becoming certain of the truth of Buddhism or vajrayana as it is the awakening of your own understanding.

At this point, perhaps for the first time in the individual's life, he begins to realize immense new possibilities. But it is a matter of waking up. You cannot borrow it from somewhere. There is a tremendous sense of richness and power. So the individual becomes appreciative of the teachings and the teacher because they created that situation for him. Even so, it wasn't done deliberately. It was natural, and that particular event took place.

LM: What has to go on in a person's life in order for this letting go to be a real event instead of a contrived effort?

CTR: At the beginning of practice, even your sitting and meditation on your zafu is a pretense of meditation rather than the real thing. Whatever you do is artificial. There is no starting point except simply doing it. Then you begin to feel all kinds of restlessness. There is subconscious gossip, frustrations, and resentment. But at a certain point you find that you are no longer pretending. You are actually doing it. There is no particular moment in which this change occurs. It is just a process of growing up. You begin to realize that you are immersed in your own neurosis. You cannot really reject it. It is with you. At some point you give up hope of being able to get rid of that. You begin to accept it rather than trying to dispel it. Then something begins to happen. You just have to let go. You give in.

LM: In order for that to take place, doesn't there have to be a certain persistence in the ongoing basic practice?

CTR: Definitely. At this point we aren't talking about intellectual speculation. It has to be a real thing. [*Laughs*] I don't speak to people about themselves analytically. I don't suggest what things should happen to particular people or what is wrong with them personally. In our community we make it very direct: "Get a job." I ask people, "How much are you sitting? What are you studying? Where are you working?" I conduct occasional seminars, but they do not involve much interpretation or analysis. I try to highlight what students can relate to their own experiences.

LM: I have read about the practice of tummo, which evidently involves higher forms of realization than simply melting snow through the generation of extraordinary body heat. Is this kind of technical, intricate, advanced, and characteristically Tibetan form of yoga something that you see taking place in the West?

CTR: I think so. There is no particular limitation as long as the endurance and devotion of the student continues. There is no reason for the teaching to stop halfway through.

LM: Your writings indicate that the mahamudra is not the highest form of Buddhist realization. Is this because it tends to lock into shunyata as a final experience?

CTR: Intuitive realization is the backbone of the whole thing. But intuitive realization of shunyata without any application to the world is helpless. There is no way to grow without it. So those two go hand in hand. Mahamudra is one of the first levels of tantric spiritual understanding. It was known as the new school of tantric tradition. We also have an old school, in which there is a further understanding, which is called ati, maha ati. In maha ati, that shunyata experience is brought directly to the manifest world. So that also needs to be applied practically. Tantra is basically defined as continuity, the continuity of play within this world, the dance within this world. So those two, intuitive realization of shunyata and skillful means of application in the world are like the two wings of a bird. You cannot separate them.

LM: The maha ati realization is the return to ordinary life in the world rather than relying on that intuitive realization exclusively?

CTR: Suppose you have a glimpse of the space inside a cup, and you build larger and larger cups in order to appreciate more spaciousness. Finally you break the last cup. You know the outside completely. You don't have to build a cup to understand what space is like. Space is everywhere.

LM: Is this kind of breaking of the cup brought about through any specific visualization?

CTR: The breaking through takes place all the time. There is no particular time or situation. It is like learning how to balance on a bicycle. Nobody can actually tell you how to do it. But you keep on doing it and you keep falling off. And finally you can do it. It is a stroke of genius of some kind. [*Laughs*]

GLOSSARY

THE DEFINITIONS given in this glossary are particular to their usage in this book and should not be construed as the single or even most common meaning of a specific term.

abhisheka (Skt., "anointment"): A ceremony in which a student is ritually introduced into a mandala of a particular tantric deity by a tantric master and is thus empowered to visualize and invoke that particular deity. The essential element of abhisheka is a meeting of minds between master and student.

amrita (Skt., "deathless"): Consecrated liquor used in vajrayana meditation practices.

arhat (Skt.): A "worthy one" who has attained the highest level of hinayana.

bardo (Tib., "in-between state"): A state between a previous state of experience and a subsequent one in which experience is not bound by either. There are six bardos, but the term is most commonly used to designate the state between death and rebirth.

bodhichitta (Skt.): "Awakened mind" or "enlightened mind."

bodhisattva (Skt.): One who has committed himself or herself to the mahayana path of compassion and the practice of the six paramitas. The bodhisattva vow is one of relinquishing one's personal enlightenment to work for all sentient beings.

buddhadharma (Skt.): The Buddha's teaching; Buddhism.

chakra (Skt.): One of the primary centers of the illusory body. Most often, five are distinguished: head, throat, heart, navel, and secret centers.

chandali (Skt.; Tib. *tummo*): A vajrayana term for a kind of psychic heat generated and experienced through certain meditative practices. This heat serves to burn up all types of obstacles and confusion.

dakini (Skt.): A wrathful or semiwrathful female deity signifying compassion, emptiness, and transcendental knowledge. The dakinis are tricky and playful, representing the basic space of fertility out of which the play of samsara and nirvana arises. More generally, a dakini can be a type of messenger or protector.

dharma (Skt.): The Buddha's teaching, or Buddhism; buddhadharma. Sometimes *dharma* is also used to mean "phenomenon."

dharmadhatu (Skt.): The "space of things" or "space of phenomena." The all-encompassing, unoriginated, and unchanging space or totality of all phenomena.

dharmakaya (Skt.): One of the three bodies of enlightenment. See note 1 for part one, chapter 5, of *The Lion's Roar*, on page 323.

dharmata (Skt.): The ultimate nature of reality; suchness.

dhyana (Skt.): Meditation, one of the six paramitas.

duhkha (Skt.): "Suffering." Duhkha satya, "the truth of suffering," is the first of Buddha's four noble truths. The term refers to physical and psychological suffering of all kinds, including the subtle but all-pervading frustration we experience with regard to the impermanence and insubstantiality of all things.

five buddha families: A tantric term referring to the mandala of the five sambhogakaya buddhas and the five fundamental principles of enlightenment they represent. In the mandala of enlightenment, these are five wisdom energies, but in the confused world of samsara, these energies arise as five confused emotions. Everything in the world is said to be predominantly characterized by one of these five. The following list gives the name of each family, its buddha, its wisdom, its confused emotion, and its direction and color in the mandala: (1) buddha, Vairochana, all-pervading wisdom, ignorance, center, white; (2) vajra, Akshobhya, mirrorlike wisdom, aggression, east, blue; (3) ratna (jewel), Ratnasambhava, wisdom of equanimity, pride, south, yellow; (4) padma (lotus), Amitabha, discriminating-awareness wisdom, passion, west, red; (5) karma (action), Amoghasiddhi, all-accomplishing wisdom, north, green. Some of these qualities differ slightly in different tantras.

four noble truths: The basis of the Buddhist teaching. The four noble truths are (1) the truth of suffering, (2) the truth of the origin of suffering, (3) the truth of the cessation of suffering, (4) the truth of the path that leads to the cessation of suffering.

guru yoga (Skt.): A devotional practice in which one identifies with and surrenders to the teacher (guru) in his or her vajrayana form as a vajra master and representative of the lineage of ultimate sanity.

heruka (Skt.): A wrathful male deity.

hinayana (Skt.): The "lesser" vehicle, in which the practitioner concentrates on basic meditation practice and an understanding of basic Buddhist doctrines such as the four noble truths.

jnana (Skt.; Tib. *yeshe*): The wisdom-activity of enlightenment, transcending all dualistic conceptualization.

kalyanamitra (Skt.): The spiritual friend or the manifestation of the teacher in the mahayana.

karma (Skt.): Literally, "action." In a general sense, the law of cause and effect: positive actions bring happiness; negative actions bring suffering.

kilaya (Skt.): A three-edged ritual dagger.

mahamudra (Skt.): The "great seal," one of the highest teachings in the vajrayana. See part one, chapter 4, "The Basic Body," and part two, chapter 7, "The Five Buddha Families and Mahamudra," in *The Lion's Roar*.

mahayana (Skt.): The "great vehicle," which emphasizes the emptiness (shunyata) of all phenomena, compassion, and the acknowledgment of universal buddha nature. The ideal figure of the mahayana is the bodhisattva; hence it is often referred to as the bodhisattva path.

mandala (Skt.): A total vision that unifies the seeming complexity and chaos of experience into a simple pattern and natural hierarchy. The Tibetan word *khyilkhor* used to translate the Sanskrit term literally means "center and surroundings." A mandala is usually represented two-dimensionally as a four-sided diagram with a central deity, a personification of the basic sanity of buddha nature. Three-dimensionally, it is a palace with a center and four gates in the cardinal directions.

mantra (Skt.): A combination of words (usually Sanskrit) or syllables that expresses the quintessence of a tantric deity. A mantra may or may not have conceptual content. Recitation of mantra is a vajrayana practice that is always done in conjunction with visualization.

Marpa (1012–1097 CE): Marpa Lotsawa (Marpa the Translator) was the third of the great enlightened teachers of the Kagyü lineage of Tibet and the first Tibetan of that lineage. He was an unruly farmer's son who made three epic journeys to India in search of the dharma. There he became the student of Naropa and other gurus, which enabled him to bring the tantric Buddhist teachings back to Tibet. His most famous student was Milarepa. See *The Life of Marpa the Translator*, translated by the Nālandā Translation Committee under the direction of Chögyam Trungpa (Boston & London: Shambhala Publications, 1986).

Milarepa (1052–1135 CE): "Mila the Cotton-Clad" was the fourth great enlightened teacher in the Kagyü lineage of Tibetan Buddhism. A black magician in his youth, he underwent a period of extreme hardship and trial at the hands of his guru Marpa. He then spent many years in solitary meditation in caves in the high mountains of Tibet before attaining enlightenment and attracting many students. His chief student was Gampopa (1079–1153 CE). See *The Life of Milarepa*, translated by Lobsang P. Lhalungpa (Boston & London: Shambhala Publications, 1985).

mudra (Skt.): Most often the term is used to refer to symbolic hand gestures that accompany the vajrayana practices of visualization and mantra recitation. More generally, *mudra* refers to the provocative highlights of phenomena.

Nagarjuna (second/third century): A great Indian teacher of Buddhism, the founder of the Madhyamaka school of Buddhist philosophy. He contributed greatly to the logical development of the doctrine of shunyata and was the author of many key texts as well as, in legend, the guru of various important Buddhist teachers who lived centuries apart.

Naropa (1016–1100 CE): A great Indian siddha, second of the great enlightened teachers of the Kagyü lineage of Tibetan Buddhism. See *The Life and Teaching of Naropa*, translated by Herbert V. Guenther (Boston & London: Shambhala Publications, 1986).

nidanas (Skt.): The twelve "links" of the karmic chain of existence. See note 1 for part one, chapter 2, of *The Lion's Roar*, on page 321.

nirvana (Skt.): The idea of enlightenment according to the hinayana. It is the cessation of ignorance and conflicting emotions and therefore freedom from compulsive rebirth in samsara.

Padmasambhava: Also referred to as Guru Rinpoche, or "Precious Teacher." Padmasambhava introduced vajrayana Buddhism to Tibet in the eighth century CE. See note 1 for part two, chapter 3, of *The Lion's Roar*, on page 324.

paramita ("that which has reached the other shore"): The six paramitas, or "perfections," are generosity, discipline, patience, exertion, meditation, and knowledge.

prajna (Skt.; Tib. *sherab*): Literally, "transcendental knowledge." Prajna, the sixth paramita, is called transcendental because it sees through the veils of dualistic confusion.

pratyekabuddha (Skt.): One who concentrates on his or her own liberation without being concerned about helping others, The pratyekabuddha's approach characterizes the second of the nine yanas.

preta (Skt.): A hungry ghost, one of the six kinds of beings in the samsaric realms. The other five are gods, jealous gods, humans, animals, and hell beings.

Rudra (Skt.): Originally a Hindu deity, an emanation of Shiva. In the vajra-yana, Rudra is the personification of the destructive principle of ultimate ego. According to tradition, Rudra was originally a tantric student who perverted the teachings and killed his guru. He was thus transformed into Rudra, the embodiment of egohood, the complete opposite of buddhahood.

samaya (Skt.): The vajrayana principle of commitment, whereby the student's total experience is bound to the path.

sambhogakaya (Skt.): One of the three bodies of enlightenment. See note 1 for part one, chapter 5, of *The Lion's Roar*, on page 323.

samsara (Skt.): The vicious cycle of transmigratory existence. It arises out of ignorance and is characterized by suffering.

sangha (Skt.): The community of people devoted to the three jewels of Buddha, dharma, and sangha: the Buddha, his teaching, and this community itself. The term preeminently refers to the Buddhist monastic community.

shamatha (Skt.): A basic meditation practice common to most schools of Buddhism, the aim of which is developing tranquillity through mindfulness.

Shantideva (fl. seventh/eighth century CE): A prince who became a Buddhist monk and a teacher of the Madhyamaka school of mahayana Buddhism. He was the author of the *Bodhicharyavatara*, a classic text of the mahayana, written in a beautiful poetic style. One English translation is *Entering the Path of Enlightenment*, translated by M. L. Matics (New York: Macmillan Company, 1970). Another is *A Guide to the Bodhisattva's Way of Life* (Dharamsala, India: Library of Tibetan Works and Archives, 1979).

shila (Skt.): Discipline, the second paramita.

shravaka (Skt.): Shravaka was a disciple who actually heard the teachings of the Buddha directly. With a small *s*, the term is also the name of the first of the nine yanas, in which the practitioner concentrates on basic meditation practice and an understanding of basic Buddhist doctrines such as the four noble truths.

shunyata (Skt., "emptiness"): A completely open and unbounded clarity of mind.

siddha (Skt.): One who possesses siddhis, or "perfect abilities." There are eight ordinary siddhis: indomitability, the ability to see the gods, fleetness of foot, invisibility, longevity, the ability to fly, the ability to make certain medicines, and power over the world of spirits and demons. The single "supreme" siddhi is enlightenment.

skandha (Skt., "heap"): One of the five types of aggregates of psychophysical factors that are associated with the sense of self or ego. See note 6 for part one, chapter 3, of *The Lion's Roar*, on page 322.

sutra (Skt.): One of the hinayana and mahayana texts attributed to Shakyamuni Buddha. A sutra is usually a dialogue between the Buddha and one or more of his disciples, elaborating on a particular topic of dharma.

tantra (Skt.; Tib. *rgyud*): A synonym for vajrayana, the third of the three main yanas of the buddhadharma. The vajrayana teachings are said to have been taught by the Buddha in his sambhogakaya form. They are recorded in scriptures known as tantras. *See also* vajrayana.

tathagatagarbha (Skt.): A term of primary importance for the mahayana. *Tathagatha* literally means "thus-gone" and is an epithet a for a fully realized buddha. *Garbha* means "embryo" or "egg." The term refers to buddha nature, the enlightened basic nature of all beings, which the mahayana regards as being temporarily covered over by dualistic confusions. It is compared to the sun behind clouds or a jewel in a dung heap.

three marks of existence: A basic Buddhist doctrine. Existence is characterized by suffering, impermanence, and egolessness. See part two, chapter 1, of *The Lion's Roar*, "Suffering, Impermanence, Egolessness."

Tibetan Book of the Dead (Tib., *Bardo Thödol*, "Book of Liberation in the Bardo through Hearing"): This famous text sets forth the process of death and rebirth and how to become liberated from it. Its origin can be traced to Padmasambhava.

vajra (Skt.; Tib. *dorje*): A vajra is a tantric ritual implement or scepter representing a thunderbolt, the scepter of the king of the gods, Indra. This thunderbolt is said to be made of adamantine or diamond, and this is connected with its basic symbolism: the indestructibility of awakened mind. When used with the ritual bell, or ghanta, the vajra symbolizes skillful means, and the bell, transcendental knowledge. Vajra is also the name of one of the five buddha families, whose enlightened quality is pristine clarity and whose confused or neurotic quality is aggression.

Vajrasattva (Skt.): One of the deities visualized at various levels of tantric practice. He is associated with primordial purity.

vajrayana (Skt., "diamond vehicle"): The third of the three main yanas of the buddhadharma, synonymous with *tantra*. It is divided into six, or sometimes four, subsidiary vehicles.

vidyadhara (Skt.): "Knowledge-holder, " "crazy-wisdom holder."

vipashyana (Skt.): "Insight" or "clear seeing." With shamatha, one of the two main modes of meditation common to all forms of Buddhism. See note 6 for part two, chapter 6, of *The Lion's Roar*, on page 327.

virya (Skt.): Exertion, one of the six paramitas.

yana (Skt., "vehicle"): A coherent body of intellectual teachings and practical meditative methods related to a particular stage of a student's progress on the path of buddhadharma. The three main vehicles are the hinayana, mahayana, and vajrayana. These can also be subdivided to make nine yanas.

yidam (Tib.) The vajrayana practitioner's personal deity, who embodies the practitioner's awakened nature. Yidams are usually sambhogakaya buddhas.

SOURCES

The Dawn of Tantra, by Herbert V. Guenther and Chögyam Trungpa. Edited by Sherab Chödzin Kohn (Michael H. Kohn). Illustrated by Glen Eddy and Terris Temple. Berkeley & London: Shambhala Publications, 1975. The Clear Light Series. © 1975 by Herbert V. Guenther and Diana J. Mukpo. Reissued 2001, Shambhala Publications.

Journey without Goal: The Tantric Wisdom of the Buddha. Boulder & London: Shambhala Publications, Inc., 1981. © 1981 by Chögyam Trungpa.

The Lion's Roar: An Introduction to Tantra. Edited by Sherab Chödzin Kohn. Boston & London: Shambhala Publications, Inc., 1992. © 1992 by Diana J. Mukpo.

"Things Get Very Clear When You're Cornered," an interview with Chögyam Trungpa in *The Laughing Man*, volume 1, no. 2 (1976): 55–60. Reprinted by permission of the copyright owner, The Da-Ananda Samrajya Pty Ltd, as trustee for the Da Love-Ananda Samrajya.

ACKNOWLEDGMENTS

JAMES MINKIN, former editor of *The Laughing Man* magazine, provided me with a copy of "Things Get Very Clear When You're Cornered" and helped me negotiate the permission to use this material. A copy of this article was also given to me by Malcolm Moore, who responded to an e-mail appeal. Thanks to both of them. To all the editors who worked on the books that appear in Volume Four, thanks from all of the readers for the excellent editorial efforts. Thanks to L. S. Summer for the index. Thanks also to Shambhala Publications for support of this series and of the publication of works by Chögyam Trungpa in general; to Diana Mukpo and the Mukpo family for their ongoing vision and for making the works of Chögyam Trungpa available in so many ways; and finally the deepest thanks to this great master of dharma himself, for these lucid and profound teachings. May they wake us from the slumber of samsaric ignorance!

A BIOGRAPHY OF
CHÖGYAM TRUNGPA

THE VENERABLE CHÖGYAM TRUNGPA was born in the province of Kham in eastern Tibet in 1939. When he was just thirteen months old, Chögyam Trungpa was recognized as a major tulku, or incarnate teacher. According to Tibetan tradition, an enlightened teacher is capable, based on his or her vow of compassion, of reincarnating in human form over a succession of generations. Before dying, such a teacher may leave a letter or other clues to the whereabouts of the next incarnation. Later, students and other realized teachers look through these clues and, based on those plus a careful examination of dreams and visions, conduct searches to discover and recognize the successor. Thus, particular lines of teaching are formed, in some cases extending over many centuries. Chögyam Trungpa was the eleventh in the teaching lineage known as the Trungpa tulkus.

Once young tulkus are recognized, they enter a period of intensive training in the theory and practice of the Buddhist teachings. Trungpa Rinpoche, after being enthroned as supreme abbot of Surmang Monastery and governor of Surmang District, began a period of training that would last eighteen years, until his departure from Tibet in 1959. As a Kagyü tulku, his training was based on the systematic practice of meditation and on refined theoretical understanding of Buddhist philosophy. One of the four great lineages of Tibet, the Kagyü is known as the practicing (or practice) lineage.

At the age of eight, Trungpa Rinpoche received ordination as a novice monk. Following this, he engaged in intensive study and practice of the traditional monastic disciplines, including traditional Tibetan poetry and monastic dance. His primary teachers were Jamgön Kongtrül of Sechen and Khenpo Gangshar—leading teachers in the Nyingma and Kagyü lineages. In 1958, at the age of eighteen, Trungpa Rinpoche completed his studies, receiving the degrees of kyorpön (doctor of divinity) and khenpo (master of studies). He also received full monastic ordination.

The late 1950s were a time of great upheaval in Tibet. As it became clear that the Chinese communists intended to take over the country by force, many people, both monastic and lay, fled the country. Trungpa Rinpoche spent many harrowing months trekking over the Himalayas (described later in his book *Born in Tibet*). After narrowly escaping capture by the Chinese, he at last reached India in 1959. While in India, Trungpa Rinpoche was appointed to serve as spiritual adviser to the Young Lamas Home School in Delhi, India. He served in this capacity from 1959 to 1963.

Trungpa Rinpoche's opportunity to emigrate to the West came when he received a Spaulding sponsorship to attend Oxford University. At Oxford he studied comparative religion, philosophy, history, and fine arts. He also studied Japanese flower arranging, receiving a degree from the Sogetsu School. While in England, Trungpa Rinpoche began to instruct Western students in the dharma, and in 1967 he founded the Samye Ling Meditation Center in Dumfriesshire, Scotland. During this period, he also published his first two books, both in English: *Born in Tibet* (1966) and *Meditation in Action* (1969).

In 1968 Trungpa Rinpoche traveled to Bhutan, where he entered into a solitary meditation retreat. While on retreat, Rinpoche received[1] a pivotal text for all of his teaching in the West, "The Sadhana of Mahamudra," a text that documents the spiritual degeneration of modern times and its antidote, genuine spirituality that leads to the experience of naked and luminous mind. This retreat marked a pivotal change in his approach to teaching. Soon after returning to England, he became a layper-

---

1. In Tibet, there is a well-documented tradition of teachers discovering or "receiving" texts that are believed to have been buried, some of them in the realm of space, by Padmasambhava, who is regarded as the father of Buddhism in Tibet. Teachers who find what Padmasambhava left hidden for the beings of future ages, which may be objects or physical texts hidden in rocks, lakes, and other locations, are referred to as tertöns, and the materials they find are known as terma. Chgyam Trungpa was already known as a tertön in Tibet.

son, putting aside his monastic robes and dressing in ordinary Western attire. In 1970 he married a young Englishwoman, Diana Pybus, and together they left Scotland and moved to North America. Many of his early students and his Tibetan colleagues found these changes shocking and upsetting. However, he expressed a conviction that in order for the dharma to take root in the West, it needed to be taught free from cultural trappings and religious fascination.

During the seventies, America was in a period of political and cultural ferment. It was a time of fascination with the East. Nevertheless, almost from the moment he arrived in America, Trungpa Rinpoche drew many students to him who were seriously interested in the Buddhist teachings and the practice of meditation. However, he severely criticized the materialistic approach to spirituality that was also quite prevalent, describing it as a "spiritual supermarket." In his lectures, and in his books *Cutting Through Spiritual Materialism* (1973) and *The Myth of Freedom* (1976), he pointed to the simplicity and directness of the practice of sitting meditation as the way to cut through such distortions of the spiritual journey.

During his seventeen years of teaching in North America, Trungpa Rinpoche developed a reputation as a dynamic and controversial teacher. He was a pioneer, one of the first Tibetan Buddhist teachers in North America, preceding by some years and indeed facilitating the later visits by His Holiness the Karmapa, His Holiness Khyentse Rinpoche, His Holiness the Dalai Lama, and many others. In the United States, he found a spiritual kinship with many Zen masters who were already presenting Buddhist meditation. In the very early days, he particularly connected with Suzuki Roshi, the founder of Zen Center in San Francisco. In later years he was close with Kobun Chino Roshi and Bill Kwong Roshi in Northern California; with Maezumi Roshi, the founder of the Los Angeles Zen Center; and with Eido Roshi, abbot of the New York Zendo Shobo-ji.

Fluent in the English language, Chögyam Trungpa was one of the first Tibetan Buddhist teachers who could speak to Western students directly, without the aid of a translator. Traveling extensively throughout North America and Europe, he gave thousands of talks and hundreds of seminars. He established major centers in Vermont, Colorado, and Nova Scotia, as well as many smaller meditation and study centers in cities throughout North America and Europe. Vajradhatu was formed in 1973 as the central administrative body of this network.

In 1974 Trungpa Rinpoche founded the Naropa Institute (now Naropa University), which became the first and only accredited Buddhist-inspired university in North America. He lectured extensively at the institute, and his book *Journey without Goal* (1981) is based on a course he taught there. In 1976 he established the Shambhala Training program, a series of seminars that present a nonsectarian path of spiritual warrior-ship grounded in the practice of sitting meditation. His book *Shambhala: The Sacred Path of the Warrior* (1984) gives an overview of the Shambhala teachings.

In 1976 Trungpa Rinpoche appointed Ösel Tendzin (Thomas F. Rich) as his Vajra Regent, or dharma heir. Ösel Tendzin worked closely with Trungpa Rinpoche in the administration of Vajradhatu and Shambhala Training. He taught extensively from 1976 until his death in 1990 and is the author of *Buddha in the Palm of Your Hand*.

Trungpa Rinpoche was also active in the field of translation. Working with Francesca Fremantle, he rendered a new translation of *The Tibetan Book of the Dead*, which was published in 1975. Later he formed the Nā-landā Translation Committee in order to translate texts and liturgies for his own students as well as to make important texts available publicly.

In 1979 Trungpa Rinpoche conducted a ceremony empowering his eldest son, Ösel Rangdröl Mukpo, as his successor in the Shambhala lineage. At that time he gave him the title of Sawang ("Earth Lord").

Trungpa Rinpoche was also known for his interest in the arts and particularly for his insights into the relationship between contemplative discipline and the artistic process. Two books published since his death—*The Art of Calligraphy* (1994) and *Dharma Art* (1996)—present this aspect of his work. His own artwork included calligraphy, painting, flower ar-ranging, poetry, playwriting, and environmental installations. In addi-tion, at the Naropa Institute he created an educational atmosphere that attracted many leading artists and poets. The exploration of the creative process in light of contemplative training continues there as a provoca-tive dialogue. Trungpa Rinpoche also published two books of poetry: *Mudra* (1972) and *First Thought Best Thought* (1983). In 1998 a retrospective compilation of his poetry, *Timely Rain*, was published.

Shortly before his death, in a meeting with Samuel Bercholz, the pub-lisher of Shambhala Publications, Chögyam Trungpa expressed his inter-est in publishing 108 volumes of his teachings, to be called the Dharma Ocean Series. "Dharma Ocean" is the translation of Chögyam Trungpa's

Tibetan teaching name, Chökyi Gyatso. The Dharma Ocean Series was to consist primarily of material edited to allow readers to encounter this rich array of teachings simply and directly rather than in an overly systematized or condensed form. In 1991 the first posthumous volume in the series, *Crazy Wisdom*, was published, and since then another seven volumes have appeared.

Trungpa Rinpoche's published books represent only a fraction of the rich legacy of his teachings. During his seventeen years of teaching in North America, he crafted the structures necessary to provide his students with thorough, systematic training in the dharma. From introductory talks and courses to advanced group retreat practices, these programs emphasized a balance of study and practice, of intellect and intuition. *Trungpa* by Fabrice Midal, a French biography (forthcoming in English translation under the title *Chögyam Trungpa*), details the many forms of training that Chögyam Trungpa developed. Since Trungpa Rinpoche's death, there have been significant changes in the training offered by the organizations he founded. However, many of the original structures remain in place, and students can pursue their interest in meditation and the Buddhist path through these many forms of training. Senior students of Trungpa Rinpoche continue to be involved in both teaching and meditation instruction in such programs.

In addition to his extensive teachings in the Buddhist tradition, Trungpa Rinpoche also placed great emphasis on the Shambhala teachings, which stress the importance of meditation in action, synchronizing mind and body, and training oneself to approach obstacles or challenges in everyday life with the courageous attitude of a warrior, without anger. The goal of creating an enlightened society is fundamental to the Shambhala teachings. According to the Shambhala approach, the realization of an enlightened society comes not purely through outer activity, such as community or political involvement, but from appreciation of the senses and the sacred dimension of day-to-day life. A second volume of these teachings, entitled *Great Eastern Sun*, was published in 1999.

Chögyam Trungpa died in 1987, at the age of forty-seven. By the time of his death, he was known not only as Rinpoche ("Precious Jewel") but also as Vajracharya ("Vajra Holder") and as Vidyadhara ("Wisdom Holder") for his role as a master of the vajrayana, or tantric teachings of Buddhism. As a holder of the Shambhala teachings, he had also received the titles of Dorje Dradül ("Indestructible Warrior") and Sakyong

("Earth Protector"). He is survived by his wife, Diana Judith Mukpo, and five sons. His eldest son, the Sawang Ösel Rangdröl Mukpo, succeeds him as the spiritual head of Vajradhatu. Acknowledging the importance of the Shambhala teachings to his father's work, the Sawang changed the name of the umbrella organization to Shambhala, with Vajradhatu remaining one of its major divisions. In 1995 the Sawang received the Shambhala title of Sakyong like his father before him and was also confirmed as an incarnation of the great ecumenical teacher Mipham Rinpoche.

Trungpa Rinpoche is widely acknowledged as a pivotal figure in introducing the buddhadharma to the Western world. He joined his great appreciation for Western culture with his deep understanding of his own tradition. This led to a revolutionary approach to teaching the dharma, in which the most ancient and profound teachings were presented in a thoroughly contemporary way. Trungpa Rinpoche was known for his fearless proclamation of the dharma: free from hesitation, true to the purity of the tradition, and utterly fresh. May these teachings take root and flourish for the benefit of all sentient beings.

BOOKS BY CHÖGYAM TRUNGPA

Born in Tibet (George Allen & Unwin, 1966; Shambhala Publications, 1977)
Chögyam Trungpa's account of his upbringing and education as an incarnate lama in Tibet and the powerful story of his escape to India. An epilogue added in 1976 details Trungpa Rinpoche's time in England in the 1960s and his early years in North America.

Meditation in Action (Shambhala Publications, 1969)
Using the life of the Buddha as a starting point, this classic on meditation and the practice of compassion explores the six paramitas, or enlightened actions on the Buddhist path. Its simplicity and directness make this an appealing book for beginners and seasoned meditators alike.

Mudra (Shambhala Publications, 1972)
This collection of poems mostly written in the 1960s in England also includes two short translations of Buddhist texts and a commentary on the ox-herding pictures, well-known metaphors for the journey on the Buddhist path.

Cutting Through Spiritual Materialism (Shambhala Publications, 1973)
The first volume of Chögyam Trungpa's teaching in America is still fresh, outrageous, and up to date. It describes landmarks on the Buddhist path and focuses on the pitfalls of materialism that plague the modern age.

The Dawn of Tantra, by Herbert V. Guenther and Chögyam Trungpa (Shambhala Publications, 1975)

Jointly authored by Chögyam Trungpa and Buddhist scholar Herbert V. Guenther, this volume presents an introduction to the Buddhist teachings of tantra.

Glimpses of Abhidharma (Shambhala Publications, 1975)

An exploration of the five skandhas, or stages in the development of ego, based on an early seminar given by Chögyam Trungpa. The final chapter on auspicious coincidence is a penetrating explanation of karma and the true experience of spiritual freedom.

The Tibetan Book of the Dead: The Great Liberation through Hearing in the Bardo, translated with commentary by Francesca Fremantle and Chögyam Trungpa (Shambhala Publications, 1975)

Chögyam Trungpa and Francesca Fremantle collaborated on the translation of this important text by Guru Rinpoche, as discovered by Karma Lingpa, and are coauthors of this title. Trungpa Rinpoche provides a powerful commentary on death and dying and on the text itself, which allows modern readers to find the relevance of this ancient guide to the passage from life to death and back to life again.

The Myth of Freedom and the Way of Meditation (Shambhala Publications, 1976)

In short, pithy chapters that exemplify Chögyam Trungpa's hard-hitting and compelling teaching style, this book explores the meaning of freedom and genuine spirituality in the context of traveling the Buddhist path.

The Rain of Wisdom (Shambhala Publications, 1980)

An extraordinary collection of the poetry or songs of the teachers of the Kagyü lineage of Tibetan Buddhism, to which Chögyam Trungpa belonged. The text was translated by the Nālandā Translation Committee under the direction of Chögyam Trungpa. The volume includes an extensive glossary of Buddhist terms.

Journey without Goal: The Tantric Wisdom of the Buddha (Shambhala Publications, 1981)

Based on an early seminar at the Naropa Institute, this guide to the tantric teachings of Buddhism is provocative and profound, emphasizing both the dangers and the wisdom of the vajrayana, the diamond path of Buddhism.

The Life of Marpa the Translator (Shambhala Publications, 1982)
A renowned teacher of the Tibetan Buddhist tradition who combined scholarship and meditative realization, Marpa made three arduous journeys to India to collect the teachings of the Kagyü lineage and bring them to Tibet. Chögyam Trungpa and the Nālandā Translation Committee have produced an inspiring translation of his life's story.

First Thought Best Thought: 108 Poems (Shambhala Publications, 1983)
This collection consists mainly of poetry written during Chögyam Trungpa's first ten years in North America, showing his command of the American idiom, his understanding of American culture, as well as his playfulness and his passion. Some poems from earlier years were also included. Many of the poems from *First Thought Best Thought* were later reprinted in *Timely Rain*.

Shambhala: The Sacred Path of the Warrior (Shambhala Publications, 1984)
Chögyam Trungpa's classic work on the path of warriorship still offers timely advice. This book shows how an attitude of fearlessness and open heart provides the courage to meet the challenges of modern life.

Crazy Wisdom (Shambhala Publications, 1991)
Two seminars from the 1970s were edited for this volume on the life and teachings of Guru Rinpoche, or Padmasambhava, the founder of Buddhism in Tibet.

The Heart of the Buddha (Shambhala Publications, 1991)
A collection of essays, talks, and seminars present the teachings of Budddhism as they relate to everyday life.

Orderly Chaos: The Mandala Principle (Shambhala Publications, 1991)
The mandala is often thought of as a Buddhist drawing representing tantric iconography. However, Chögyam Trungpa explores how both confusion and enlightenment are made up of patterns of orderly chaos that are the basis for the principle of mandala. A difficult but rewarding discussion of the topic of chaos and its underlying structure.

Secret Beyond Thought: The Five Chakras and the Four Karmas (Vajradhatu Publications, 1991)

Two talks from an early seminar on the principles of the chakras and the karmas, teachings from the Buddhist tantric tradition.

The Lion's Roar: An Introduction to Tantra (Shambhala Publications, 1992)

An in-depth presentation of the nine yanas, or stages, of the path in the Tibetan Buddhist tradition. Particularly interesting are the chapters on visualization and the five buddha families.

Transcending Madness: The Experience of the Six Bardos (Shambhala Publications, 1992)

The editor of this volume, Judith L. Lief, calls it "a practical guide to Buddhist psychology." The book is based on two early seminars on the intertwined ideas of bardo (or the gap in experience and the gap between death and birth) and the six realms of being.

Training the Mind and Cultivating Loving-Kindness (Shambhala Publications, 1993)

This volume presents fifty-nine slogans, or aphorisms related to meditation practice, which show a practical path to making friends with oneself and developing compassion for others, through the practice of sacrificing self-centeredness for the welfare of others.

Glimpses of Shunyata (Vajradhatu Publications, 1993)

These four lectures on the principle of shunyata, or emptiness, are an experiential exploration of the ground, path, and fruition of realizing this basic principle of mahayana Buddhism.

The Art of Calligraphy: Joining Heaven and Earth (Shambhala Publications, 1994)

Chögyam Trungpa's extensive love affair with brush and ink is showcased in this book, which also includes an introduction to dharma art and a discussion of the Eastern principles of heaven, earth, and man as applied to the creative process. The beautiful reproductions of fifty-four calligraphies are accompanied by inspirational quotations from the author's works.

Illusion's Game: The Life and Teaching of Naropa (Shambhala Publications, 1994)

The great Indian teacher Naropa was a renowned master of the teachings of mahamudra, an advanced stage of realization in Tibetan Buddhism. This book presents Chögyam Trungpa's teachings on Naropa's life and arduous search for enlightenment.

The Path Is the Goal: A Basic Handbook of Buddhist Meditation (Shambhala Publications, 1995)

A simple and practical manual for the practice of meditation that evokes the author's penetrating insight and colorful language.

Dharma Art (Shambhala Publications, 1996)

Chögyam Trungpa was a calligrapher, painter, poet, designer, and photographer as well as a master of Buddhist meditation. Drawn from his many seminars and talks on the artistic process, this work presents his insights into art and the artist.

Timely Rain: Selected Poetry of Chögyam Trungpa (Shambhala Publications, 1998)

With a foreword by Allen Ginsberg, this collection of poems was organized thematically by editor David I. Rome to show the breadth of the poet's work. Core poems from *Mudra* and *First Thought Best Thought* are reprinted here, along with many poems and "sacred songs" published here for the first time.

Great Eastern Sun: The Wisdom of Shambhala (Shambhala Publications, 1999)

This sequel and complement to *Shambhala: The Sacred Path of the Warrior* offers more heartfelt wisdom on Shambhala warriorship.

Glimpses of Space: The Feminine Principle and Evam (Vajradhatu Publications, 1999)

Two seminars on the tantric understanding of the feminine and masculine principles, what they are and how they work together in vajrayana Buddhist practice as the nondual experience of wisdom and skillful means.

The Essential Chögyam Trungpa (Shambhala Publications, 2000)

This concise overview of Trungpa Rinpoche's teachings consists of forty selections from fourteen different books, articulating the secular path of the Shambhala warrior as well as the Buddhist path of meditation and awakening.

Glimpses of Mahayana (Vajradhatu Publications, 2001)

This little volume focuses on the attributes of buddha nature, the development of compassion, and the experience of being a practitioner on the bodhisattva path of selfless action to benefit others.

RESOURCES

FOR INFORMATION regarding meditation instruction or inquiries about a practice center near you, please contact one of the following:

SHAMBHALA INTERNATIONAL
1084 Tower Road
Halifax, NS
B3H 2Y5 Canada
Telephone: (902) 425-4275, ext. 10
Fax: (902) 423-2750
Website: www.shambhala.org (This website contains information about the more than 100 meditation centers affiliated with Shambhala, the international network of Buddhist practice centers established by Chögyam Trungpa.)

SHAMBHALA EUROPE
Annostrasse 27
50678 Cologne, Germany
Telephone: 49-0-700-108-000-00
E-mail: europe@shambhala.org
Website: www.shambhala-europe.org

DORJE DENMA LING
2280 Balmoral Road
Tatamagouche, NS
B0K 1V0 Canada
Telephone: (902) 657-9085
Fax: (902) 657-0462
E-mail: info@dorjedenmaling.com
Website: www.dorjedenmaling.com

KARMÊ CHÖLING
369 Patneaude Lane
Barnet, VT 05821
Telephone: (802) 633-2384
Fax: (802) 633-3012
E-mail: karmecholing@shambhala.org

SHAMBHALA MOUNTAIN CENTER
4921 Country Road 68C
Red Feather Lakes, CO 80545
Telephone: (970) 881-2184
Fax: (970) 881-2909
E-mail: shambhalamountain@shambhala.org

SKY LAKE LODGE
P.O. Box 408
Rosendale, NY 12472
Telephone: (845) 658-8556
E-mail: skylake@shambhala.org
Website: http://ny.shambhala.org/skylake

DECHEN CHÖLING
Mas Marvent
87700 St Yrieix sous Aixe
France
Telephone: 33 (0)5-55-03-55-52
Fax: 33 (0)5-55-03-91-74
E-mail: dechencholing@dechencholing.org

Audio- and videotape recordings of talks and seminars by Chögyam Trungpa are available from:

KALAPA RECORDINGS
1678 Barrington Street, 2nd Floor
Halifax, NS
B3J 2A2 Canada
Telephone: (902) 421-1550
Fax: (902) 423-2750
E-mail: shop@shambhala.org
Website: www.shambhalashop.com

For publications from Shambhala International, please contact:

VAJRADHATU PUBLICATIONS
1678 Barrington Street, 2nd Floor
Halifax, NS
B3J 2A2 Canada
Telephone: (902) 421-1550
E-mail shop@shambhala.org
Website: www.shambhalashop.com

For information about the archive of the author's work—which includes more than 5,000 audio recordings, 1,000 video recordings, original Tibetan manuscripts, correspondence, and more than 30,000 photographs—please contact:

THE SHAMBHALA ARCHIVES
1084 Tower Road
Halifax, NS
B3H 3S3 Canada
Telephone: (902) 421-1550
Website: www.shambhalashop.com/archives

The *Shambhala Sun* is a bimonthly Buddhist magazine founded by Chögyam Trungpa. For a subscription or sample copy, contact:

SHAMBHALA SUN
P. O. Box 3377
Champlain, NY 12919-9871
Telephone: (877) 786-1950
Website: www.shambhalasun.com

Buddhadharma: The Practitioner's Quarterly is an in-depth, practice-oriented journal offering teachings from all Buddhist traditions. For a subscription or sample copy, contact:

BUDDHADHARMA
P. O. Box 3377
Champlain, NY 12919-9871
Telephone: (877) 786-1950
Website: www.thebuddhadharma.com

Naropa University is the only accredited, Buddhist-inspired university in North America. For more information, contact:

NAROPA UNIVERSITY
2130 Arapahoe Avenue
Boulder, CO 80302
Telephone: (303) 444-0202
Website: www.naropa.edu

INDEX

All books, articles, and seminars are attributed to Chögyam Trungpa unless otherwise cited. Illustrations are indicated by italics and follow text entries. Books contained within this volume are indicated by initial page number and "ff."

Empowerment (Tib. *wangkur*). *See*
  Abhisheka
Energy
  centralizing, 50
  conventional understanding of, 45
  self-existing, 45–47, 120
  in tantric language, 251–252
  types of, 120–122
  working with, 50, 106
Enlightenment, 213, 260
  attainment in one lifetime, 187
  hopelessness and, 158–160
  mahayana and vajrayana views of, 191
  number of people who attain, 197
  styles of, 79
  tantric understanding of, 339
Error (Skt. *bhranti*, Tib. *'khrul pa*), 347–348
Eternalism, 250–251, 324n.2
Ethics and energy, 46
EVAM, 122–123; *118*
Evans-Wentz, W. Y., x, 243
Exchange of self for others, 8
Existence, 73–74, 112–113
Existentialism, 74
Experience
  "echo" of, 123
  importance of, 34, 345, 427
  openness and, 363–364
  three levels of, 355–356

Faith, 166–167
Fearlessness
  crazy wisdom and, 131–132
  in mahayogayana, 189–190
  in upayoga, 179–180
Feeling, skandha of, 216
Feminine principle, 309
First Thought Best Thought, 446
Five buddha families, 77–79, 104, 280–282, 288, 432
  basic nature and, 286–287
  mahamudra and, 285
  mandala of, 84–85
  See also Five wisdoms; Under individual family
Five buddha principles. *See* Five buddha families
Five paths, 322n.4
Five powers, 166–172, 322n.2, 365
Five skandhas, 174, 215–218, 322n.6, 395
Five wisdoms, 182–183, 197, 303–304

Form
  emptiness and, 250
  formlessness and, 50
  skandha of, 215–216
Four foundation practices (*ngöndro*), xiii, 342
Four foundations of mindfulness (Skt. *smriti-upasthana*), 323n.2
  See also Satipatthana
Four noble truths, 151, 156–158, 205, 345, 402
Freedom, 359–360
Fremantle, Francesca, x

Gampopa, 321n.2
Garab Dorje (dGa'-Rab-rDorje), *334*
Gates of liberation, three, 252
Geluk tradition, 302
Generosity, paramita of, 229–230, 235
Ghanta (bell), 92–93; *78*
God, 29, 285, 300–301
Groundlessness, 58, 152
Guenther, Herbert, x, xv–xvi, 160, 252, 331, 332
Guhyasamaja, 259, 326n.9
Guhyasamaja Tantra, 94, 119
Guru
  Christian god, differentiated from, 300–301
  devotion to, 10, 166–167, 291–293
  inner, 389–391
  mahayana link, 275
  mandala of, 383
  qualities of, 285–286
  role in transmission, 58, 185–186
  tantric approach to, 290–294
  See also Teacher(s)
Guru-disciple relationship, 371–375, 385
Guru yoga, 343, 390, 432

Hatha yoga, 122
Hayagriva, 307
Heart Sutra, 249–250, 353
Helplessness, 161
Heruka, heruka principle, 306–310, 326n.8, 433
Hevajra, *352*
Hevajra Tantra, 341
Hinayana
  atomist philosophy in, 249
  emphasis of, 214–215

misconceptions about, 59–60, 248,
  262–263, 333–335
necessity of, 251
presentation of, 27, 32–33, 94–95, 270,
  298–299, 331
qualities of, 27–28
relationship to hinayana/mahayana,
  181, 236, 258–260, 296, 297, 426
sutra, differentiated from, 339–341, 343
See also Continuity; Vajrayana
Tantric name, 93
Tantric practitioner (tantrika)
  advice to, 132–133
  qualities of, 28–29, 267–268
  in the West, 425, 426–427
Tantric View of Life (Guenther), 331
Tantric world, 61–62, 94
Taranatha, 121
Tathagatagarbha, 278, 436
  See also Buddha nature
Teacher(s)
  attitudes toward Western students, 55,
  425
  necessity of, 254–255
  responsibilities of, 60, 371–372
  roles in the three yanas, 63, 195–196,
  425
  trust in, 86–87
  See also Guru; Spiritual friend; Vajra
  master
Tendzin, Vajra Regent Ösel, 4, 446
Theism
  devotion in, 291–292
  nontheism and, 47–50, 65, 113
Theravada tradition, 196, 399
"Thingness," 156–158
Three kayas, 103, 104, 323n.1, 339–340, 341,
  348, 393–394
Three marks of existence, 217–218, 244–
  246, 324n.1
  in tantra, 247, 252
Three yanas, 7–9, 28, 94, 115, 127, 183,
  339–340
Tibet
  modern attitudes and, 424–425
  spiritual materialism in, 89
  tantra in, 302
Tibetan Book of the Dead, x, 35, 108, 190,
  199, 243, 310, 311
Tibetan Buddhism
  introduction in America, 424–425

introduction in Tibet, 273
misconceptions about, x
reformation of, 88–89
Tilopa, 371, 372, 374
Time, as understood in mandala, 383–384
Timely Rain, 446
Transmission
  emotions in, 56–57
  levels of, 87
  preparation for, 53–54, 86–87
  role of guru in, 58
  students, attitudes of, 55–56, 58
  of visualizations, 287–288
  See also Abhisheka
"Treasury of Oral Instructions," 89
Trungpa (Midal), 447
Trungpa XI (Chögyam, Chökyi Gyatso)
  arrival in North America, 445
  biographical information, 331–332, 423,
  443–448
  monasticism of, 443–444
  names and titles, 447–448
  on origins of tantra, 95
  personal seal of, 118
  presentation of vajrayana in the West,
  ix–xi, xv–xvi, 188
  recognition of, 423
  training of, 95–96
Trust
  in buddha nature, 257, 286
  ego and, 185
  faith and, 166–167
  in the student-teacher relationship,
  86–87, 296
Tummo, 428
Twelve links (nidanas), 157–158, 321n.1

Upayoga yana, 179–180, 272–278
  mantra and mudra in, 282–284
  relationship to kriyayogayana, 280

Vaibhashika school, 394–396
Vajra (Tib. dorje), 78
  definitions, 34–35, 79, 176, 327–328n.1,
  436
  quality of, 304–305
  scepter, 79, 92
  usage of, 80
Vajra (buddha family), 79–80, 84, 91, 280,
  306–307, 308